# Easy Cooking
# for
# Special Diets

How to Cook for Weight Loss/Blood Sugar Control,
Food Allergy, Heart Healthy, Diabetic and "Just Healthy"
Diets – Even if You've Never Cooked Before

Nicolette M. Dumke

ii

# Easy Cooking for Special Diets:

## How to Cook for Weight Loss/Blood Sugar Control, Food Allergy, Heart Healthy, Diabetic and "Just Healthy" Diets – Even if You've Never Cooked Before

Published by

Adapt Books
Allergy Adapt, Inc.
1877 Polk Avenue
Louisville, CO 80027
(303) 666-8253

© 2006 by Nicolette M. Dumke
First Printing, January, 2007
Printed in the United States of America

Cover design and typesetting by Ed Nies, Mel Typesetting,
1523 S. Pearl Street, Denver, CO 80210

Editing by Joan Hinkemeyer, Editorial Services,
2465 S. Humboldt Street, Denver, CO 80210

**Publisher's Cataloging in Publication**
*(Provided by Quality Books)*

Dumke, Nicolette M.
    Easy cooking for special diets : how to cook for weight loss/blood sugar control, food allergy, heart healthy, diabetic and "just healthy" diets, even if you've never cooked before / Nicolette M. Dumke.
356 p. 23.4 cm.
Includes bibliographical references and index.
LCCN 2006900079
ISBN-13: 978-1-887624-09-1
ISBN-10: 1-887624-09-0

1. Cookery, American.  2. Dietetic foods.  3. Diet therapy.    I. Title.

TX715.D866 2007                    641.5'63
                                   QBI06-600027

# Dedication

*To my mother, Mary Jiannetti,*
*who loved cooking for her family,*

*and to my sons, Joel and John,*
*who were the lights of her life,*
*and who will, in the same way,*
*always be my greatest joys.*

*Cooking reflects the bonds of love*
*from generation to generation.*

*Whenever you cook with this book*
*written for you,*
*I hope you will remember*
*how much I love you.*

*Love,*
*Mom*

# Disclaimer

The information contained in this book is merely intended to communicate food preparation material and information which is helpful and educational to the reader. It is not intended to replace medical diagnosis or treatment, but rather to provide organizational information and recipes which may be helpful in implementing a diet and program prescribed by your doctor. Please consult your physician for medical advice before changing your diet.

The author and publisher declare that to the best of their knowledge all material in this book is accurate; however, although unknown to the author and publisher, some recipes may contain ingredients which may be harmful to some people.

There are no warranties which extend beyond the educational nature of this book. Therefore, we shall have neither liability nor responsibility to any person with respect to any loss or damage alleged to be caused, directly or indirectly, by the information contained in this book.

If you do not wish to be bound by the above, you may return this book to the publisher for a full refund.

# Table of Contents

# Foreword

This project is a wonderful idea! Over 29 years of medical practice, I have dealt with many patients with food allergies and intolerances. It has been readily apparent that the majority of individuals with these sensitivities have no idea how to prepare a "real and healthy" meal. As one patient told me, "I don't really cook. I thaw!"

Even the experienced cook can benefit from the various topics covered in *Easy Cooking for Special Diets*. The primer on nutrition is not only helpful to the novice, but also to the seasoned food preparer who might not have a solid foundation on nutrition in healthy cooking. All of the topics covered in the book have information that adds to the enjoyment of cooking.

Certainly the book is a must for cooks at any level to develop both the art and the chemistry of healthy food preparation. A healthy lifestyle requires a healthy, nourishing diet. The variety of wonderfully organized recipes and menus displayed in the book counters the "monotony" of the average American diet.

My compliments go to Nickie on a job well done. As a finishing touch, a final upper level course could now be added – Enjoyment 409!

– Nicholas G. Nonas, M.D.
Allergy and Environmental Medicine, Littleton, Colorado

This book will put you at "the head of the class" in safe and healthy food preparation. We would have a healthier world if *Easy Cooking for Special Diets* were a required course for high school seniors or college freshmen – or maybe even for graduate students and young professionals who need ideas that can be incorporated into their time-pressured lives!

You will enjoy the glimpses into Nickie's family and will sense her love of wholesome food that nourishes body and soul. Be sure to read about Nickie's husband and sugar on page 18 – a life enhancing gem of a lesson!

"Nutrition 105" is quite detailed and you might be tempted to skip over it, but this chapter will motivate you to eat a wide variety of foods and to cook as much from scratch as possible so you can load up on health-providing nutrients, assuring you the energy to pursue your active life.

If you've been cooking for years, you will still find new knowledge and recipes in this book and will enjoy the challenge of using alternative grains such as spelt and sweeteners other than sugar. Start your new cooking adventure with the easy recipes which will simplify your life in the first several recipe chapters. Then after you have had some practice, enjoy making the fun recipes in "Recipes to Impress" for guests.

Do you need help cooking for a special diet? Would you like to be more alert and full of vibrant energy? To avoid "flu" symptoms by using better food handling practices and making wise choices when eating out? To entertain with ease? Then don't underestimate the messages in this book. This book belongs in the hands of as many graduates, brides, friends, and family members as possible. Give it to your friends and then get together with them and motivate each other to make improvements in your and your family's health.

– Ann Fisk, B.S., R.N.
Founder of "An Ounce of Prevention" and mother of two young adults

# Cooking 101

In years gone by, learning to cook was as natural as learning to walk. Mothers spent much of their time in the kitchen, and children "helped" them cook from an early age. It was fun to sprinkle flour into the mixing bowl as a cake was made, watch the frosting grow fluffy under the spell of the mixer, and then lick the beaters. As the children grew older, their help became real and they began to take over some of the cooking chores.

Now our lives are much busier and parents do not spend as much time cooking. Take-out is what's for dinner, or frozen entrees heated in the microwave make lunch. When adults do cook, it is often in such a rush that "help" from the children cannot be permitted to slow them down. Busy families barely have time for dinner, let alone for cooking lessons before dinner! Learning to cook nowadays often means learning to microwave foods prepared by other people.

However, in the interests of maximum health and saving money, homemade food is still best. It also tastes better than most things you can buy pre-made! Many a desperate allergy patient has called me and said, "I just found out I'm allergic to several foods. My doctor told me there are substitute foods I can use, but I have no idea of how to cook anything from scratch!"

Older people develop high blood pressure or heart problems and have to follow a special diet, and find themselves in a similar predicament. Everyone should know how to cook! However, a Gallup Poll showed that by the year 2005, one-third of the U.S. population will know nothing about cooking.

My children grew up helping in the kitchen but gradually outgrew the "fun" of it. The need for cooking education in our family became obvious when my older son Joel attended an engineering institute at a nearby college during the summer before his senior year in high school. The first evening he called home to tell us that he was O.K. and about what they had done. He said that for dinner the students had been served, "something they called spaghetti, but I don't see how anyone could think it was really spaghetti." I reminded him that he is half Italian and therefore has higher standards for pasta than most of his fellow students. However, I could tell that dormitory food might be his least favorite part of the college experience, so that very evening I began writing this book.

Most young people today enter college well educated in mathematics and science, history and language, computers and the arts, but knowing little or nothing about cooking. In college they eat dorm food, fast food, and junk food. Those who have microwave ovens and small refrigerators in their dormitory rooms use them for popcorn and sodas. By eating this way, they deprive their bodies of much-needed nutrients and starve their spirits of the pleasures of good food. This physical and psychological deprivation may lead them to eat more food than they need. The high-fat foods they consume also contribute to the notorious "freshman fifteen" – the fifteen pounds which most students gain during their first year of college.

Some students have health challenges such as food allergies or diabetes. For them, control of their diets is more than just a way to stay slim, trim, and energetic; it is absolutely essential medically. If they are to survive college in good health, they will have to eat the dormitory cafeteria offerings very selectively and supplement them with good food from their rooms, or they may need to live in an apartment where they can do their own cooking.

My desire is that this book will help people of every age learn to cook so that they will be able to feed themselves healthily and easily. I hope it will help those on special diets stay on those diets for good health, help all college students get the real nutrition they need to keep up their active lives while retaining their trim high school figures, and help young adults (or anyone on their own for the first time) easily and healthily use the kitchens in their first apartments. Also, the old adage "The way to a man's" – or woman's – "heart is through his stomach" is still true. Now, more than ever, cooking for someone is a good way to show your love. And good cooking and good nutrition are the best ways to be kind to yourself. Learning to cook is an investment in your health that will pay off for the rest of your life.

# First Things First

Let's face it, when you're hungry you may not want to take time to read the first ten chapters of this book in their entirety before you start cooking! But please read this chapter. Many of the subjects addressed briefly here are covered in more detail in other chapters, but if you read just these few pages, you'll learn enough of the cooking basics to get started safely and successfully. Read and always do the things below.

## Health and Safety:

**Wash your hands** before you start cooking. This does not mean a quick rinse – scrub them with soap for 20 seconds. For more about food safety, see "Microbiology 103" on pages 8 to 16.

Do not burn yourself! **Use potholders** to remove dishes from the microwave oven as well as the conventional oven. When cooking in a microwave, dishes may remain cool, but often the hot food can heat up the dish.

When you cover a dish to be microwaved with plastic wrap, make sure the cover is not air-tight. There should be a vent hole or loose edge to **allow steam to escape.** When your food is hot, **remove the plastic carefully** starting with the edge away from you so the steam doesn't burn you.

**Before reheating leftovers** stored in a container such as a casserole dish with a plastic lid or a plastic tub with a lid using a microwave oven, be sure to **loosen or remove the lid.** If you don't, the buildup of steam inside the container may cause it to explode in the microwave oven. I often completely loosen the lid but leave it resting loosely on top of the food to retain moisture.

When stirring a pot of a thick heavy liquid on the stove, such as chili or sauce for spaghetti or lasagne, **move the pot off the hot burner before lifting the lid to stir it.** Otherwise, the hot sauce may boil and splash you on the arm, hand, or face which can cause a serious burn. If you do get splashed, immediately rinse off the food with very cold water.

Be careful with knives and peelers. When you peel vegetables and fruits, **peel away from yourself.** Use a cutting board to protect your counter tops. **Keep your fingers well away from the knife** when chopping.

**Always use cool water** when you are making the recipes in this book. Yes, I know, if you start with the hottest possible tap water your cocoa will be ready 20 seconds sooner! But hot water picks up dissolved, and in some cases less-than-friendly, minerals from hot water tanks and the pipes to your room or apartment. For more about this see page 51.

**Cook all meats, poultry, and fish thoroughly.** If you're going to invest in a turkey, also invest in a meat thermometer. Microwave ovens have hot spots and cool spots, so I would advise that you **not use a microwave oven to cook any meat you cannot stir.** That means that I personally recommend that you don't use your microwave for any animal products except ground meats! This is a very busy time of your life; you don't need an intestinal upset or worse. Don't eat sushi! If you want to be safe, eat your fish cooked until it is opaque throughout. Again, this is what I personally advise my own children. Fish that is so slightly infested with parasites that the chef can't detect it will make you just as sick as obviously tainted fish. You're an adult now – you can make your own decisions. Decide for yourself whether you will listen to an overconfident sushi chef or a mom with a degree in microbiology.

**Never put anything metal in a microwave oven.** This includes decorative metal trim on dishes. Also, **don't use anything that can melt**, such as Styrofoam and some soft plastics, in a microwave oven or as a container for very hot food.

## Measuring Is Critical To your Success!

You've seen experienced cooks throw in a little of this and a little of that and never measure anything, it seems. This is fine if you're seasoning a roast or pot of chili; season and then taste. But don't try this as a beginner to baking. When your mom doesn't measure the flour accurately as she bakes yeast bread, she gets away with it because she knows by feel what the consistency of the finished dough should be and she will add enough flour to reach that point. When you've learned what that consistency should be, then you can be creative about measuring when you are making yeast breads. For cakes, quick breads, and most other baked goods, even your mom probably needs to measure accurately, and so should you.

**Measure dry ingredients with the right measuring cups.** These are nested cups, sold in sets, and are usually metal or opaque plastic. To measure flour, **stir the flour** to loosen it. Using a large spoon, **lightly spoon it into the cup. Level it off** with a straight edged knife or spatula. To measure flour, cornstarch, salt, baking powder, spices, and other dry ingredients with measuring spoons, **dip the spoon into the container**, stir up the ingredient to loosen it, and fill the spoon generously. Pull it out and **level it off** with a straight edged knife or spatula, or level spices using the straight edge of the hole in the spice container.

To measure white sugar, just spoon it into the cup and level it off. **To measure brown sugar, press it into the cup firmly** until it is level with the top edge of the cup.

Nut butter and shortening are also measured with the cups used for dry ingredients. Press these ingredients into the cup with a spatula, pressing out all the air. Level them off with a straight edged knife or spatula. Then use a spatula to thoroughly remove them from the cup.

Measure liquids using the right measuring cups. These will be glass, pyrex, or clear plastic cups with markings on them. Pyrex or glass are especially nice because you can also cook in them in your microwave oven. To measure, fill the cup with liquid until the meniscus (the bottom of the curve of the liquid) lines up with the line on the cup. Get down on your knees so you can read the cup at eye level as it sits on your counter.

You can measure more than one liquid ingredient in the same cup by adding them sequentially to the cup. This will save you washing extra dishes. For instance, if you are baking and need ½ cup water, ¼ cup thawed apple juice concentrate, and ⅛ cup (same as 2 tablespoons) of oil, try this: Add water to the ½ cup line, add apple juice to the ¾ cup line, and then add oil to the ⅞ cup line. Stir them together right there in the cup and add them to the dry ingredients. That saves you washing an extra bowl.

To measure small amounts of liquids in measuring spoons, fill them until the surface is level. If you let the liquid bead up over the top of the spoon, you'll get more of the liquid than is intended in your recipe.

A measurement chart is found on page 318. If you need to halve a recipe, it will be useful to know things from this chart, such as that half of ¼ cup is ⅛ cup which is the same as 2 tablespoons.

# Don't Cook Without Thinking, "Recipe Book Style," Especially with a Microwave Oven:

Cooking is a science and an art. Use your brain and common sense when you do it! The cooking times given in the recipes in this book are given as approximate times rather than as absolute times. This is because stoves and ovens, and especially microwave ovens, vary in how they cook. Microwaving is also affected by the altitude, initial temperature of the food, water content of the food, etc. When using these recipes, check your food as the time for it to be done approaches. Look at it and, unless it contains eggs or meat that may be undercooked, taste it to see if it is done.

One exception to the cooking times being approximate is when ground meat is cooked in the microwave. Microwave the meat until it is no longer pink. Then, in all of the meat-containing recipes in this book, the meat is also cooked in liquid for at least ten minutes. This ten minutes IS absolute! Do not skimp on this time.

## How To Use Your Oven:

To judge whether foods such as muffins, cookies, or bread baked in a conventional oven are done, first **look at the color of the food.** Usually it should be light brown when it is time to remove the food from the oven. If the recipe directs, test the baked item with a toothpick inserted in the center of one of the items. If the toothpick comes out wet, continue baking for another few minutes and test again. When the toothpick comes out dry, your goodies are done and ready for you to devour.

**Know when to preheat your oven.** When you make baked goods, you need to turn your oven on in time to be at the correct temperature before you put the food in. If you put muffins into a cold oven, the heat for the first few minutes will be so intense that the outside of the muffins will be brown long before the inside is cooked. You do not need to preheat the oven when roasting meats or cooking casseroles or vegetables.

## Stirring Skill Is Essential:

To make the quick breads, muffins, cakes, and cookies in this book successfully, there are a few things you have to do correctly. **Preheat your oven and get your pans greased or lined FIRST**. Mix the dry ingredients in a large bowl. Mix the liquids in a small bowl or measuring cup. Stir the liquid ingredients into the dry ingredients using folding as well as stirring motions to reach all parts of the bowl, but **don't overmix.** It is perfectly all right to have a few small dry spots in your batter; stop while you're ahead. If you overmix, the chemical reaction that makes gas to make the dough rise will happen in the bowl instead of happening in the oven, and you'll end up with very dense baked goods. After mixing, quickly put the batter into the pans and pop them into the oven.

## For Making Bread:

When you make yeast bread, either by hand or using a bread machine, **have your ingredients at room temperature.** Warm milk in a saucepan or your microwave oven. Take the chill off eggs by placing them in a cup or bowl of warm water for a few minutes. **Accurate measuring is especially important when using a bread machine.**

# Take Care of Yourself:

**Be kind to your body.** It is the only one you will ever have. If you abuse it as a young adult, you may live with the consequences for the rest of your life. Some things, such as taking illicit drugs, are obviously dangerous. Others, such as missing meals regularly, staying up all night often, and eating foods that might expose you to parasites or other infections, are not illegal nor immoral, but can have long-lasting effects. Be wise in all that you do. Take care of yourself, and **cook with love** for both yourself and others.

# Microbiology 103:
## Food Safety

In the Disney movie, "The Sword and the Stone," Merlin and Madame Mim have a wizard's duel in which they change themselves into other creatures in an attempt to destroy each other. One of the rules of the game is, "No turning invisible." As the game nears its end, Merlin seems to vanish. Madame Mim protests, and Merlin explains that he has turned himself into a germ and is about to make her very sick. Of course, Merlin wins the duel.

This chapter is not meant to scare you or gross you out. However, you are adults who are responsible for taking care of yourselves now. As such, you should know that the world is not always a safe place to be. There are lots of "critters" that we cannot see lurking all around us. They can make us as sick or sicker than Madame Mim was, sometimes for years. Many of them enter our bodies on the food which we eat. Therefore, when you learn to cook, you should also learn some microbiology so you know how to handle food safely and can protect yourself from the bacteria, viruses, and parasites which often contaminate our food.

Even if you don't end up doing much cooking for yourself, a basic understanding of the principles of microbiology and food safety will be useful to you. If you're not cooking for yourself, you may be eating out much of the time. You need to know how to beat the odds of getting bacterial food poisoning, a parasite, or a food-borne virus even more when you are eating someone else's cooking than if you cook for yourself. Therefore, this chapter will address safe eating as well as safe cooking.

The germs that make people sick are usually those that are best suited to live inside us. They like to live at about 98.6°F, or human body temperature. They need moisture and food such as they find in our bodies. Some of them are quite fragile and are easily destroyed by heat, cold, drying, high concentrations of sugars or salts, or an acidic environment. Many germs which will make you sick if you eat them with your food are human organisms which are spread from person to person with food being a passive carrier rather than being organisms that like to live in the food as well as they would like to live in a person.

A historical example of a human pathogen being spread by food is the story of Typhoid Mary. Mary Mallon was a kitchen worker who lived in the early 1900's. Wherever she worked, people got sick with typhoid fever. She was not sick herself, but carried *Salmonella typhi* (the bacteria that causes typhoid fever) in her intestine. She was taken into custody in 1907 and forced to live in a cottage on North Brother Island near New York City. Between 1910 and 1915 she was released "under strict conditions," which she ignored, and cases of typhoid fever again followed in her wake. She was then again isolated on the island until her death in 1938. Personal liberty was secondary to the public good in those days. Perhaps if she had followed good hygiene, she would not have been re-isolated in 1915.

Amoebas and some worms are strictly human parasites. As in the case of Typhoid Mary, they are spread only by substandard bathroom habits. If a person who is infected with one of these parasites uses the bathroom, doesn't wash his hands, and then touches something that will end up in your mouth, you get the parasite. Like Mom said, you should always wash your hands after using the bathroom! (If only everyone listened to their mom and every mom said this!) In a public restroom, you may want to use the paper towel with which you dry your hands to open the door when you leave. We have no control over other people's hand washing habits! Who knows if the people ahead of you didn't wash their hands and left their parasites on the door handle, which you will then touch right before picking up the sandwich you will eat for lunch? We should take precautions to make up for the substandard hygiene that might be practiced by other people.

Never eat sushi or other foods containing raw fish! Raw fish can be contaminated with a variety of worms. Sushi chefs are trained to recognize diseased fish flesh. However, very slightly diseased fish can look fine to them and still make you sick. When you eat fish, be sure it is cooked thoroughly until it is opaque throughout.

*Trichinella spiralis* is a parasitic worm that is not fussy about its host. It most commonly lives in pigs but can infect many mammals. In the 1930's, about 16 percent of the American population was infected with it due to the practice of feeding garbage containing uncooked pork to hogs. This infection can be prevented by always cooking pork thoroughly so any parasites present in the meat are dead before you eat it. Today, the pork industry tells us that the incidence of *Trichinella* in hogs is very low, so you don't have to cook your pork as thoroughly. Yet, why gamble with your health by eating undercooked pork? If you cook your pork chops right, you can cook them thoroughly and still have them be moist. See page 159 for the recipe.

Hepatitis A is a virus that you can get from food. It is a human pathogen that is excreted in feces. If oysters grow in water that is contaminated with human sewage, they may pick up the hepatitis A virus. Since oysters may be eaten raw, if you eat a contaminated oyster, you could end up very sick for months and possibly even have permanent liver damage. Is it really worth it to eat any animal food raw or undercooked? Hepatitis A, or "infectious hepatitis," can also be transmitted from person to person by substandard bathroom habits. Hepatitis B, or "serum hepatitis," is caused by a different virus which is transmitted sexually, by contaminated needles, and by infected blood products.

Raw eggs can transmit food poisoning caused by the bacteria *Salmonella enteriditis.* Years ago the health "rule" for eggs was to avoid using eggs with cracked shells. However, in recent years we have learned that some strains of this bacteria can infect the ovaries of seemingly healthy hens. Thus the bacteria may enter the eggs while they are being formed and will be present inside the shells of intact eggs. Ordinary eggs should never be eaten raw or undercooked. If you like Caesar salads, soft cooked eggs with runny yolks, or raw homemade cookie dough, you should use pasteurized eggs to make these foods. Pasteurized eggs are available in grocery stores in certain areas of the country at the time of this writing and should be available nationwide soon. (See "Sources," page 321). If you wish to make mayonnaise and can't find pasteurized eggs in your area yet, use a commercial egg substitute such as EggBeaters™. Due to improvements in the practices used to raise hens for egg-laying, the incidence of *Salmonella enteriditis* is decreasing. The USDA now says that unless you have compromised health, an occasional raw egg won't hurt you. However, this microbiologist mom says, "Why gamble with your health?" Just use EggBeaters™ or wait patiently for those Caesar salads. Pasteurized eggs will reach your neighborhood soon!

*Giardia lamblia* is a parasite that is transmitted by water rather than by food. Its natural host is the beaver. If you are camping, especially in the Rocky Mountain states, be sure to bring your own water. If you must drink stream water, boil it for at least 10 minutes to kill this parasite. If beavers have been in the stream from which you take your water, no matter how pristine it looks, the water could be contaminated with *Giardia*. *Giardia*, amoebas, and other intestinal protozoan parasites can be very difficult to get rid of once you have them, and prolonged infestation with them can lead to massive food and environmental allergies which can literally rule the rest of your life. Don't take the risk of drinking untreated water from a mountain stream!

When we think of food-borne illnesses, we tend to think of animal foods. We remember the outbreak of enteropathogenic *E. coli* that was spread by undercooked hamburgers a few years ago. Indeed, meat, fish, and eggs should always be cooked throughly before you eat them. However, fruits and vegetables can also carry disease. The same type of *E. coli* that came from the hamburgers has been found on lettuce and in unpasteurized apple juice and has made some strict vegetarians very sick after being transmitted by plant foods. An outbreak of the parasite *Cyclospora* was recently traced to imported raspberries which were contaminated with this organism. If you are very healthy, as described at the end of this chapter, don't be paranoid. But keep in mind that any human bacteria or parasite can be transferred from a carrier to raw fruits and vegetables by substandard sanitary habits. You don't know the bathroom habits of the people who grew, picked, or handled your fruits and vegetables unless you grow them yourselves. It's better to be safe than sorry. Either cook fruits and vegetables thoroughly before you eat them or disinfect them as described on page 13.

# Safe Cooking, Food Storage, and Kitchen Practices

The principles of keeping your food safe are simple. Just remember what bacteria, viruses, and parasites like and don't like. Don't give them what they like, and do plenty of what they don't like.

**Temperature:** Bacteria like a nice, cozy, warm environment. Therefore, your food will be safe as long as it is very cold or very hot. The temperature in your refrigerator should be 41°F or less. Check it with a thermometer occasionally and adjust the temperature control dial until it maintains a temperature of about 40°F. At this temperature, bacteria will not be killed but neither will they multiply rapidly. Keep all animal foods and most plant foods, with the exception of ripening fruit, in the refrigerator or freezer at all times. Freezer temperatures will kill some parasites and bacteria. If you are not planning to eat the meat you bought on your weekly shopping trip in a couple of days, freeze it until you're ready to eat it. Put all of your groceries away promptly when you get home from the grocery store, giving meats, dairy products, and other refrigerated and frozen foods the highest priority.

Don't let leftovers sit at room temperature after dinner until you happen to get around to storing them in the refrigerator. Refrigerate them as soon as possible, and never permit them to sit at room temperature for more than two hours from when you took them from the stove.

When refrigerators were the newest appliance on the block, people were advised to let hot foods cool to room temperature before putting them into the refrigerator. It's true that this saves your refrigerator some work, but it is not a safe practice from the standpoint of bacteria. The safest and most efficient way to handle hot leftovers is to divide them into small portions for storage, which allows the heat to dissipate more quickly, cool them by external means, such as adding ice cubes to hot soups, and then refrigerate or freeze them promptly.

Cook foods thoroughly. Dr. Leo Galland recommends cooking meats and vegetables conventionally because microwave ovens often have hot spots and cold spots, and certain areas of the food may not reach a high enough temperature to kill bacteria and parasites which may be present.[1]

If you have a kitchen, I would recommend cooking your meals conventionally and using the microwave oven for reheating leftovers. If you live in a dorm room and a microwave oven is your only means of cooking, be sure to stir your foods during the cooking process to insure sufficient heating of all parts of the food.

When cooking meat and poultry, use a meat thermometer to determine when large cuts of meat, such as roasts and turkeys, are done. Turkeys should be cooked until the temperature in the deepest part of the breast is 185°F. Roasts can be cooked to a range of thermometer temperatures depending on how well done you like your meat. Beef roasts and steaks are safe when cooked rare because they are cuts of muscle meat that are sterile on the inside. Only the cut surfaces will be contaminated with bacteria. Therefore, the entire inside of the roast does not need to reach a temperature high enough to kill bacteria. Ground meat, however, is another story. It is basically all cut surfaces which are subject to bacterial contamination. Therefore, cook your ground meat until the pink is all gone, and then cook it a little longer. Pork should always be cooked thoroughly. Test pork roasts with a meat thermometer and don't remove them from the oven until the temperature registers at least 170°F in the deepest part of the meat.

Frozen meat or poultry should be thawed by placing it in the refrigerator, never by allowing it to stand out at room temperature. If you can't wait as longs as it will take to thaw your turkey this way (and in the case of a large bird, it may be several days), you can thaw it in a sink of cool water. Check the bird and replace the water with fresh cool water regularly. As soon as the turkey feels spongy, remove it from the water and refrigerate it or cook it immediately. Small cuts of meat may also be defrosted in your microwave oven, but only do this if you are going to cook them immediately after thawing them this way.

Fish is highly perishable and should be kept cold from the minute it is taken from the water until it is cooked. Never buy fish from a fisherman's truck; only buy it from reputable markets which get their fish from FDA-inspected fisheries. After you purchase fresh fish, get it home and into the refrigerator quickly. If you are a fisherman, be sure you take plenty of ice along on your trip to ice your catch and keep it cold until you reach a refrigerator or freezer. Cook fresh fish within one or two days of purchase. Keep frozen fish frozen until you plan to eat it. Then thaw it in the refrigerator. If it is not thawed in time for dinner, don't worry. You can cook small pieces of fish starting from frozen, although it will take them a few minutes longer to be done.

Always cook fish thoroughly. Test it for doneness by piercing it with a fork. If it flakes easily and is opaque throughout, it has been cooked enough. If you poach fish, it is impossible to dry it out and you can err on the side of overcooking without any consequences.

Ordinary eggs should be cooked until both the white and yolk are set. Cook scrambled eggs until there is no liquid egg remaining. If you like your eggs soft-cooked or prefer fried eggs with soft yolks, use pasteurized eggs. Get eggs into the refrigerator as soon as you get them home from the store. If there happens to be a contaminated egg in your carton and you leave it at room temperature, the bacteria will multiply to a number that is much more likely to make you sick if the eggs are undercooked.

**Chemical environment:** Bacteria, parasites, and viruses are affected by the chemical environment in which they find themselves as well as by temperature. Before the days of refrigeration, foods were preserved using salt, vinegar, and spices. We can use the sensitivity of germs to chemicals to help make our food safer to eat.

When you plan to eat fresh fruits or vegetables raw, for maximum safety you should disinfect them as well as washing them. *In Guess What Came to Dinner*, Ann Louise Gittleman suggests that raw fruits and vegetables be disinfected by soaking them in a solution of ½ teaspoon of Clorox™ for each gallon of water. Thin skinned fruits and leafy vegetables should be soaked for 15 minutes and thick skinned produce should be soaked for 30 minutes.[2] Dr. Leo Galland recommends soaking fruits and vegetables in a solution of 2 teaspoons of 3% hydrogen peroxide to each gallon of water.[3] Nutribiotic™, a grapefruit seed extract, can also be used for disinfecting foods. In laboratory testing, this non-toxic food-based extract has been shown to be effective against a wide range of bacteria, yeast, fungi, and parasites. At our house, as soon as we get home from the grocery store, any produce we plan to eat raw is soaked for 30 minutes in a sink full of cool water with about 30 drops of Nutribiotic™ added. If you purchase fragile produce, such as berries, you may wish to hold off on soaking them until right before you plan to eat them. Nutribiotic™ can be purchased at most health food stores, or for a mail-order source, see page 325.

You can also use the sensitivity of germs to chemicals to keep from spreading them in your own home and kitchen. Dr. Leo Galland says that hand washing is a very effective way to remove pathogens and prevent the transmission of disease of all kinds.[4] As soon as you come home, wash your hands to keep from bringing bacteria, viruses, or parasites into your environment. Wash your hands thoroughly with warm water and soap, sudsing for a few minutes, before you begin cooking every time you cook. If you handle raw meat or poultry while cooking, wash your hands thoroughly again. Any time you think you may have touched something that could possibly be contaminated while cooking, re-wash your hands.

Cutting boards can also spread infection. Do not use wooden cutting boards because they can harbor bacteria in grooves or cracks in the wood and are nearly impossible to clean thoroughly. Glass or plastic cutting boards can be washed in soap and hot water or put in your dishwasher to clean and disinfect them. If you use a cutting board for raw meat, poultry, or fish, wash it thoroughly before using it for anything else. Food poisoning bacteria can be easily transmitted by cutting raw meat on a cutting board and then using the same cutting board to cut vegetables that will be eaten raw.

Your kitchen counters should be kept thoroughly clean and disinfected regularly. Wash your counters with hot soapy water and/or with a disinfectant on a regular or daily basis. Also wash and disinfect them whenever they are dirty or especially when they may have become contaminated with juice from raw meat or poultry. I like to disinfect our kitchen counters routinely every day as I am cleaning up the kitchen after dinner. For maximum safety, first wash your counters with hot soapy water to remove food and grease. (Disinfectants will only work if they can get to the germs. Grease and dirt are germ protectors). Then disinfect the counters by moistening a piece of paper towel with hot water and a teaspoon of Clorox™ or a good squirt of Nutribiotic™ and wiping the counters down with the disinfectant-soaked paper towel.

Apply your knowledge of microbiology when washing dishes. Don't leave your dishes and dishwater at a nice, cozy, lukewarm temperature that bacteria will love for hours and then rinse the dishes and call them clean! The food that is left on the dishes will dissolve in the water, making a nice soup for bacteria to enjoy. Keep your dishwater hot and soapy. If you must leave the dishes half-done and the water cools, replace it with hot soapy water before you finish washing your dishes. Whether you wash the dishes by hand or in a dishwasher, it is most hygienic let them air dry if possible. That way you won't add bacteria to them with your hands or a dishtowel.

Dishwashers are very good for killing bacteria. However, the hot water and detergent must be able to get to the plates, glasses, and silverware. If you put your dishes into the dishwasher with dried food on them and they don't get clean, bacteria can be lurking under the food that remains on them when you take them out of the dishwasher.

Throw away your dishrags and sponges. This is one area where health issues should take precedence over environment concerns. Dr. Leo Galland recommends that we use paper towels to wipe counters and other kitchen surfaces, not a sponge or dishrag. For washing dishes, use disposable dishrags and replace them often rather than using a sponge or cloth dishrag. Bacteria love to grow in wet sponges and dishrags. The kitchen sponge is usually the germiest object in the house! Save sponges for washing cars and windows.

# Safe Eating

As Americans, we are used to thinking that our food, water, and environment are pure and healthy. However, Dr. Leo Galland says that in some areas of the country, especially costal areas, the food and water may be as unsafe as in underdeveloped areas of the world. He gives several recommendations for avoiding food-borne disease when eating out or traveling. They are:

1. Never eat food purchased from or prepared by a street vendor.

2. Avoid salad bars. Sure, they are loaded with healthy fruits and vegetables, but who has been touching these foods that you intend to eat raw? If you eat a dinner salad served by a waitress, it has only been handled by the kitchen staff, and hopefully they did so in a hygienic manner. However, food in salad bars may have been handled by many customers who came before you. Handles of serving utensils often fall into the food, causing contamination with whatever was on the customers' hands. Personally, I avoid all raw fruits and vegetables when eating out. However, if you are strong and healthy and the restaurant is hygienic in its practices, you need not be this paranoid.

3. In a restaurant, order only foods that are cooked right before serving and served hot. In many restaurants, soups and sauces are prepared ahead of time and then reheated, possibly inadequately, in a microwave oven before being served.

4. Avoid restaurants where there are lots of flies. Flies can spread bacteria and parasitic cysts.

5. In foreign countries or parts of our country where the water supply may not be safe, drink only bottled water. Boiling or reverse osmosis filtration are the only means of assuring the safety of the water you drink. Do not take ice in your drinks because it may have been made with contaminated tap water. Use bottled water to brush your teeth. If you are traveling in areas of the world where parasites are endemic, you may wish to take herbs such as berberine and artemisia with every meal.[5]

# *A Final Word*

Now that you've been thoroughly scared by this brief microbiology course, please don't be paranoid. You have survived to adulthood, which indicates that you are not totally defenseless against germs! Normal, healthy people have natural defenses against bacteria in the foods they eat, such as the hydrochloric acid produced by their stomachs. Most of the bacteria ingested by a normal, healthy person will be killed by this acid, so if you are a healthy person and consume just a few unfriendly bacteria, you will probably be O.K. Also, the intestine of a normal person is populated with good bacteria, such as *Lactobacillus* and *Bifidobacterium,* which can keep bad bacteria from gaining a foothold.

However, there are some situations in which your stomach acid will not protect you. Some types of food poisoning are caused by bacterial toxins in foods rather than by the bacteria themselves; in these cases your stomach acid does you no good. Most parasites are transmitted encapsulated in a protective cyst that can withstand stomach acid and which only opens and liberates the parasite when it reaches the intestine.

Also, many people are deficient in stomach acid. If you take antacids or acid-reducing drugs such as Zantac™ or Tagamet™, you could be setting yourself up for food poisoning, intestinal infections, or food allergies brought on by inadequate digestion of your food. People become less efficient at making stomach acid as they age, so older people are more susceptible to intestinal infections. About 40% of people with food allergies make too little or no stomach acid at all, and so have either no defense or a compromised defense against food poisoning, parasites, and other intestinal infections.

However, if you are young and healthy, you don't need to be as paranoid as I am. Just cook for yourself as much as you can, follow the kitchen and food safety advice in this chapter, and when you eat out, do so carefully.

## Footnotes

1. Galland, Leo, M.D., *The Four Pillars of Healing,* Random House, New York, 1997, p. 215.
2. Gittleman, Ann Louise, *Guess What Came to Dinner: Parasites and Your Health,* Avery Publishing Group, Inc., Garden Park, NY, 1993, p. 128.
3. Galland, p. 215.
4. Galland, p. 214.
5. Galland, pp. 214-216.

# Nutrition 105

This chapter is the heart of this book because good nutrition is the basis of good health. If you develop nutritious eating and cooking habits now, as you are learning to cook, they will serve you well for the rest of your life.

In this country and at this time, one's nutritional status is judged by many medical professionals with only a glance at the scale. They assume that if you are of normal weight, you are adequately nourished. If you are overweight, they think you need to be on a low calorie, low fat, and probably high carbohydrate diet; this judgement is made without any assessment of whether you might be deficient in essential fatty acids or what your blood sugar status is. (If you do have an essential fatty acid deficiency, a diet that is indiscriminately very low in all fats could be detrimental to your health. If you have a blood sugar problem, a high carbohydrate diet may lead to weight gain). If you are underweight, you will probably be advised to consume as much as you can of "fattening" foods such as sugar-laden nutritional milk shakes. (If your low weight is due to intestinal problems causing sub-optimal absorption, these sugary foods may worsen the problem).

Weight is not what counts! Good health is what you should be concerned about. If you pay attention to your nutritional status and achieve good health, you will probably lose or gain weight as needed, or stay at an optimal normal weight throughout your adult life. Concern yourself with how you eat rather than with what the scale says. Good nutrition will lead to the correct body weight for YOU! If you eat nutritiously and in a way that helps your appetite to be a good indicator of how much food you need, your figure will become what is right for you. Keep in mind that we are all individuals with different body builds. Good health does not include obesity, but we weren't all meant to look like Twiggy either! (For those of you who are too young to remember people from the 1970's, Twiggy was an English model who weighed about 95 pounds and was actually too thin to be attractive).

An estimated 80% of overweight people have an underlying blood sugar or blood glucose imbalance.[1] The swings in blood sugar level and the periodic low blood sugar they experience drive their appetite to a high level that they cannot resist. When such a person's brain is deprived of glucose, it will scream out until they give in and eat that chocolate cake! Their blood sugar will rise; but because of the type of food they ate, the rise will not be sustained, and an hour or two later they will be starved and looking for something sweet to eat again. Their appetite will be totally out-of-pace with their actual need for food. Low blood sugar will lead them to eat sugary foods which will rapidly raise their blood glucose, which will then fall with equal rapidity. However, eating proteins and complex carbohydrates will promote a sustained normal blood glucose level.

Another factor that can lead to obesity is food allergy. A detailed discussion of food allergy and its diagnosis and treatment is beyond the scope of this book. (If you need more information on this subject, see *The Food Allergy Survival Guide*, which is described on the last page of this book). However, if a person has a "masked" allergy to a commonly eaten food, such as wheat, they will crave that food. Eating it "ties up" some of the antibodies they have in their system to wheat and reduces their symptoms temporarily. Because of allergic cravings, their appetite will lead them to eat more food than their bodies really need and will also lead them to eat the foods that are the most detrimental to them.

Don't fall into the fallacy of thinking that calories taken in versus calories expended is all that counts as far as weight is concerned. If you've tried to diet by counting calories, you know that it's very difficult to eat a lot less than your body is begging you to eat. The level of willpower needed for such a diet cannot be sustained indefinitely. The way to control your weight is to reprogram your appetite to be a good indicator of what you need. This can be done by avoiding foods to which you are allergic, getting any blood sugar imbalance from which you may suffer under control, and engaging in moderate exercise. The appetite-controlling effects of a diet that is right for you should cause you to lose weight without tremendous strain and without counting calories even if you do not exercise a lot. However, moderate exercise can contribute to your weight control program and is good for your health in a multitude of ways. For more about exercise, see page 45.

To give a personal example concerning weight control, about 16 years ago my husband gave up eating sugar. He didn't give up desserts; he ate many of the fruit-sweetened desserts in this book. He changed just one small thing about his diet, his sugar consumption, and he lost 35 pounds in a 6-month period without any strain. Even better is the fact that he has maintained his weight loss. Refined table sugar (sucrose) is, in my opinion, the major cause of obesity. Not only does it add a large number of calories that are totally devoid of nutrition to our diets, it makes us hungry for more, more and MORE! If my husband eats sugar, he then wants to eat everything in sight! Sure, maybe that piece of cake that is calling to you contains only 200 calories. But what about the 1000 calories you eat from being excessively hungry after eating the cake? For many people, blood sugar control is the key to weight loss. For more about the type of diet that will control blood sugar, see pages 43 to 45.

Another commonly-held fallacy in the area of nutrition is that we all have the same, or very similar, nutritional needs. However, more "aware" doctors are coming to realize that we are all individuals nutritionally as well as in other ways. This principle of "biochemical individuality" was first proposed by Dr. Roger Williams in 1956 in his book of the same name. His clinical studies revealed that a ten-fold difference in the requirement for vitamins from one person to another is not at all uncommon. When he compared vitamin levels in the blood of 92 people who were on the same diet, he found as much as a 31-fold difference in the levels of some vitamins.[2]

"Conventional medicine" teaches that the recommended daily intake of most vitamins and minerals is the same for all adults. These standards are set by governments and vary from country to country. For example, in the United States we are ALL supposed to need just 5000 International Units per day of vitamin A. I know from personal experience that this is not true. A doctor (an M.D.) recommended that when I began to catch a cold, I take a nutritional protocol of vitamin C, zinc, and three days of vitamin A. A few years ago when I had a bad chest cold, I began his protocol. It helped for the first three days of the cold, but then my cough began to get worse. I had continued taking vitamin C and zinc; the only thing that had changed was that I had discontinued taking vitamin A. So I decided to repeat the three days of vitamin A, and again my cold got better. After I again stopped taking the vitamin A, my cough again became worse. I had heard warnings against taking too much vitamin A because it is fat-soluble and is stored by the body. So before again repeating the three days of vitamin A, I talked to a friend who is a nutritionist. She said that, in spite of the warnings, I should take the extra vitamin A for two weeks, and then, if my cold worsened when I stopped taking it, to take it for another two weeks. She said that the Crohn's disease which I have probably makes my need for vitamin A much higher than that of most other people.

The recommended daily intake of calories given by the government tables does vary from person to person, but it varies with sex and age only. For instance, by the official tables, men ages 19 to 24 are said to need 3000 calories a day; women that age need only 2100. Men ages 25 to 49 are said to need 2700 calories a day; women that age need 1900. On your 25th birthday, does your caloric need suddenly drop? And do not both 45-year-old men and women notice that they don't need as much food as they did when they were 25? According to the tables, their needs should be the same as a 25-year-old's until their 50th birthdays! And who doesn't know a family where one person eats constantly and is thin, while another person eats very carefully and frugally of the same diet and is heavy? It will be obvious to any thinking person that our individual nutritional needs must be more complex than government-set tables of recommended daily intakes.

My mother and mother-in-law, who are in their late 70's and 80's, tell me that people of their generation were, in middle age, "tougher" and healthier than people in my generation are. What has happened to our health and nutrition over the last few decades? One change is that agricultural methods have been "improved." No longer do farmers fertilize their fields with manure; no longer are they powerless against insects. Chemically defined fertilizers and insecticides are sprayed on almost all of our produce. Most chickens no longer eat table scraps. They are kept with thousands of other birds in chicken "factories" and fed chemically defined feed. Most animal feed contains antibiotics, and some animals are given hormones. My mother-in-law thinks that the "free range" chicken she can buy at health food stores tastes like chicken used to when she was a girl. Perhaps the reason is that these chickens are raised more like chickens were half a century ago.

Food processing has also been "improved." Refining flours and hydrogenating fats makes them less susceptible to spoilage. Our food lasts a long time, but this longevity is at the expense of the removal of essential nutrients. The food industry has also appealed to the natural human sweet tooth. Sugar sells, and the more of it we eat, the less appetite we have for complex carbohydrates, good proteins, fruits, and vegetables. As our lives get busier and busier, the food industry comes to our rescue by selling more and more ready-made foods and meals. These convenience foods are usually high in sugar and less-healthy fats, and are always much more expensive than their homemade counterparts. We have spent less and less time over the last half century preparing our own food, and we have paid the price not only in increased cost but also in sub-optimal nutrition.

It is time for us to take charge of our own health. One way to do this is to take charge of our nutrition. Learn to cook. Spend some time in the kitchen. As you gain experience, you will find cooking relaxing, creative, and enjoyable. You will save money on food and hopefully also on current and future medical expenses. You will enjoy an improved energy level as your nutrition improves, and your body will thank you for taking good care of it.

# What Are Our Nutritional Needs?
## How Can We Meet Them?

It is commonly believed that anyone who is not living in a third-world country and who eats a "normal" diet will get all of the nutrients that he or she needs. The fact is that the "standard American diet" (SAD for short, and it really can be sad!) is lacking in adequate levels of many essential nutrients. Surveys show that even people who think they are eating nutritiously fail to achieve an ideal intake of vitamins, minerals, essential fatty acids, and fiber.[3]

Our nutritional needs and biochemical makeup are as individual as the color of our eyes, our height, and the shapes of our noses and ears. No table can tell you exactly what YOU need to eat. If you are very healthy and eat very nutritiously, you might be able to get all of the nutrients you need from your foods. You must also be very careful about how your food is handled and cooked to minimize vitamin losses caused by air, heat, light, water, and acid or alkaline pH.[4] Because of these limitations on getting all of your nutrients from foods, many people prefer or need to supplement their diets with vitamins, minerals, and/or other nutrients. (See Appendix C for more information on determining your individual nutritional needs). It is beyond the scope of this book to give a full treatise on vitamins, minerals, and macronutrients, but I hope the next several pages of this book will to help you make your diet as nutritious as possible. Therefore, these pages list the currently-known nutrients which are essential to our health, what they do for us, and the common food sources of these nutrients.

## Macronutrients

Macronutrients are nutrients which we need in large amounts. They include proteins, carbohydrates, and fats.

**PROTEINS:** Proteins are the building blocks from which our bodies are made. They are essential for growth, repair, and immunity. *Protos* is the Greek word for "first," and proteins are the first and most basic materials that make up all of our cells. Proteins are composed of nitrogen-containing subunits called amino acids. We can make some amino acids from other amino acids or from simple sugars. The ones we cannot make from something else are called "essential" amino acids and must be supplied in our daily diets. The nine essential amino acids are leucine, lysine, isoleucine, threonine, tryptophan, methionine, valine, phenylalanine, and histidine. Taurine and glutamine are sometimes considered semi-essential amino acids; under certain conditions we cannot make enough of them to meet our needs, and then they also must be supplied in our diets.[5]

A deficiency of any essential or semi-essential amino acid can "put the brakes on" the process of protein synthesis by our bodies. The balance of essential amino acids in any protein food determines how usable it is for protein synthesis by our bodies, or the quality of the protein. Foods that are low in one or more of the essential amino acids are less useable than foods that contain all of them in the right balance. Protein from animal sources is balanced in its amino acid make up. Protein from plants can still be used to build our bodies, but the least plentiful amino acid in the protein might limit how much of the protein we can use for the synthesis of new protein. However, spare amino acids can still be used for energy. Eating a plant protein with animal protein or with another plant protein that has plenty of the amino acid the first plant protein is low in is a way to overcome this problem. Plant protein foods are usually low in fat and economical, so don't let anyone tell you that you should not eat them because of an imbalance in their amino acid make up. Animal protein sources such as fish, meat, and poultry may have drawbacks of their own, such as a higher fat content (which may be "good" or "bad" fat depending on the animal) and traces of hormones and antibiotics.[6]

**CARBOHYDRATES:** Carbohydrates are the main source of "fuel" in our diets. The carbohydrates in highly refined foods are quickly absorbed and the energy in them is just as quickly released. This, unfortunately, may lead to wide swings in blood sugar levels. However, unrefined carbohydrate foods are digested and absorbed more slowly, and the energy in them is released slowly and in a more sustained fashion. This is the kind of carbohydrate we should eat! Unrefined carbohydrate foods also are plentiful in fiber and nutrients such as B vitamins that our bodies need to process these foods.

Eating concentrated sources of sugar, which is the most refined carbohydrate, is, in my opinion, a major cause of weight gain. The sugar is quickly absorbed and blood sugar levels rise rapidly. This causes insulin to be released (often more than we need), which drives the sugar into our cells. If we don't need all that energy right then, the excess is stored as fat. If too much insulin is released in response to the sugary food, our blood sugar level then plummets, making us very hungry, so we eat again.

White table sugar, or sucrose, has about 90% of its vitamins and minerals removed. In order to metabolize white sugar, we must "borrow" vitamins and minerals from other foods. In essence then, white sugar is an anti-nutrient.

Fructose, or fruit sugar, is also quickly absorbed when eaten in pure form. When eaten in fruit, which contains fiber, it is absorbed more slowly. However, after it is absorbed, it is slow to release its energy because the body cannot use fructose as it is but must convert it to glucose. This slows down its effect on our blood sugar levels. Some fruits, such as apples, contain mostly fructose and are good foods to eat for stable blood sugar. Others, such as dates, grapes, and bananas, contain a fair amount of glucose. These fruits have a more pronounced immediate effect on blood sugar levels. However, ANY fruit is better for you than sugar! Fruits contain all the vitamins and minerals that are required to utilize sugars, so they are very nutritious carbohydrate foods.

Honey contains about half slow-releasing sugars and half fast-releasing sugars. Less refined honey is slower releasing than highly refined honey. Although honey has not been stripped of its vitamin and mineral content as has sugar, the levels of these nutrients in honey are low. Thus honey may be a better sweetener for us than white sugar, but fruit sweeteners are the best to use in cooking. Most of the dessert recipes in this book give you a choice between using a fruit sweetener or honey just because honey is readily available in grocery stores, and you might have to visit a health food store or place a mail order to get fruit sweeteners such as Fruit Sweet™, Grape Sweet™, or Pear Sweet™. Grape Sweet™ is likely to be faster releasing and have a more profound immediate effect on blood sugar levels than Fruit Sweet™ or Pear Sweet™. However, in baked goods, the fiber in the other ingredients should slow down the absorption of the fruit sugar.

Complex carbohydrates, or starches, are the best carbohydrates for us to eat. Because they must be digested into simple sugars before they can be absorbed, they are slowly absorbed and the sugars in them are slowly released, making them ideal foods for promoting stable blood sugar levels. Starchy foods, such as whole grains, potatoes, and other starchy vegetables, contain fiber as well as carbohydrate. Fiber is essential for good digestive function and elimination. Dried legumes are also a very good source of fiber, complex carbohydrates, and protein.[7]

FATS: Not all fats are the "bad guys" they often are made out to be. Some fats are truly very detrimental to our health while others are not only good for us but are absolutely essential to good health. The trick is to know which fats are bad and which are good and then eat the right kind.

Saturated fats are hard at room temperature. Naturally saturated fats, such as those in beef, pork, butter, and whole-fat dairy products are not something that we need, but eaten in moderation (meaning they make up less than one-third of our fat intake), they are not harmful. Unnaturally saturated fats, like those in margarine and shortening, are deadly. These "trans fats" are produced from good polyunsaturated oils by partial hydrogenation, the process of adding hydrogen atoms to some of the double bonds in the fat. These bonds have a "trans" configuration rather than the "cis" configuration that occurs naturally. Hydrogenation makes fats very stable and unlikely to go rancid, so food manufacturers love these unnatural fats because they have a very long shelf life. However, trans fats are like keys that fit the body's chemical locks but cannot open the doors. They block our ability to use the good fats we eat. They take the place of essential fatty acids (that have a normal cis configuration) in our cell membranes. This makes the cell membranes less flexible and less able to do their job of selectively letting things in and out of our cells. Trans fats can raise the level of LDL cholesterol, or "bad" cholesterol, in the blood while lowering the level of HDL cholesterol, or "good"cholesterol.

Heating polyunsaturated oils to a high temperature also creates damaged fats. If you must fry or pan fry foods, do not use polyunsaturated oils. High heat changes the configuration of the double bonds in polyunsaturated oils so that they become unhealthy trans bonds instead of retaining their original cis configuration. Olive oil, which is monounsaturated and therefore less prone to damage, is good for pan frying, as is butter, which is a naturally saturated fat. Saturated fats are actually the most stable fats for frying because they do not contain double bonds which can be affected by heat. However, if you wish to eat for optimal health, it is best to completely avoid fried foods.

Monounsaturated fats, like those in olive oil, are not "essential" in our diets but may be beneficial. There is speculation that Italians have less cardiac disease because their diets are high in olive oil. However, their diets are also high in fruits, vegetables, and fiber, so the jury is still out on this issue.

Polyunsaturated oils are the best fats for us to eat because they contain essential fatty acids. There are two fatty acids which are called "essential" because our bodies cannot make them and which we must ingest daily in our diets. These essential fatty acids are linoleic acid and linolenic acid. Each of them is processed into a "family" of fatty acids in our bodies. Linoleic acid and the fatty acids we can make from it, such as gammalinoleic acid (GLA) and di-homo gamma-linoleic acid (DGLA), are referred to as omega-6 fatty acids because the first double bond in them is six carbons from the methyl end of the molecule. Omega-6 fatty acids are made into series-1 prostaglandins which prevent blood clots, relax blood vessels, lower blood pressure, help maintain water balance in the body, decrease inflammation, improve nerve and immune function, and help insulin do its job properly.

The second essential fatty acid is linolenic acid. Linolenic acid and the fatty acids we make from it, such as alpha-linolenic acid, eicosapentaenoic acid (EPA), and docosahexaenoic acid (DHA), are referred to as omega-3 fatty acids because the first double bond in them is three carbons from the methyl end of the molecule. Omega-3 fatty acids are made into series-3 prostaglandins which are essential for proper brain function, vision, learning ability, coordination, blood cholesterol levels, immunity, and water balance. They also reduce inflammation.

Prostaglandins are very short-lived so they cannot be supplemented. Instead, we need an adequate daily intake of omega-3 and omega-6 fatty acids so we can make enough prostaglandins for ourselves. Because of the importance of prostaglandins, a very low fat diet can be detrimental to your health since it probably does not contain enough essential fatty acids. The average American diet is deficient in both omega-3 and omega-6 fatty acids. However, we tend to get more omega-6 fatty acids from sources such as corn oil, safflower oil, and sunflower oil than we get of omega-3 fatty acids. In order to get both omega-6 and omega-3 fatty acids, the best food oils to use are canola*, walnut, flax, hemp, and pumpkin. Evening primrose oil and borage oil (usually available as supplements in capsules rather than for use in foods) are good sources of omega-6 fatty acids. Some people cannot process linoleic acid (such as from corn oil) into GLA and DGLA and must "overcome" that metabolic block by taking evening primrose, borage, or other omega-6 oils. Flax oil and fish oil, which are available as supplements in capsules, are the best sources of omega-3 fatty acids. Nuts and seeds and their oils, game meats, dark green leafy vegetables, and high-fat fish such as salmon are excellent dietary sources of essential fatty acids. Salmon is an especially rich food source of omega-3 fatty acids.[8]

So in light of all this, what should a person spread on toast? NOT the average margarine! Butter is a much healthier spread and is all right to use in moderation. The best option, and the spread we use at our house, is EFA-butter. (See the recipe on page 142). This is a mixture of half walnut or canola oil (good sources of essential fatty acids) and half butter, which will give it good flavor and spreadability. If you are allergic to butter, there is one brand of margarine on the market that does not contain hydrogenated trans fats. It is Earth Balance™ margarine, and it contains some palm oil, which is a naturally saturated fat, to make it spreadable. It does not work well in baking, however. If you cannot find this margarine in your grocery store or health food store, see "Sources," page 322.

---

*Note on canola oil: Canola oil comes from the seeds of the rapeseed plant. "Natural" rapeseed contains toxins. The recently developed strain of rapeseed used for canola oil production has been bred to be low in toxins. However, some experts feel that canola oil should be used in moderation or not at all due to the possibility of toxins. Nevertheless, the plant used to produce canola oil was developed by breeding for oil production because its oil contains one of the most healthy fatty acid profiles.

# Micronutrients

Micronutrients are those nutrients that we need in only small quantities, such as in gram, milligram or microgram amounts. This category includes vitamins, minerals, and antioxidants. Most antioxidants are also vitamins or minerals. In order to function optimally, vitamins and minerals have to be present in the body in the proper balance. This is because they work together synergistically. "Synergy" is a phenomenon in which two nutrients work together to do a job better than would be achieved by the added effects of both of them without the other. For instance, vitamin C and bioflavonoids are more effective at healing bruises and bleeding gums if they are taken together than they would be if you added effects of either of them taken alone. Fortunately, both are found together in citrus fruits!

Taking megadoses of one vitamin or mineral can upset the balance of other vitamins and minerals. For instance, taking high doses of one B vitamin alone can deplete the other B vitamins. High doses of zinc interfere with the absorption of iron. However, you are unlikely to upset the balance if you get your vitamins and minerals from foods and low-dose supplements, such as multiple vitamin-mineral preparations. On the other hand, some "less healthy" people need more of certain nutrients. See Appendix C on page 328 for information on how to determine what your individual proper balance of supplements may be.

**VITAMINS:** Vitamins are molecules that are essential to life. They function in the biochemical processes that release energy from food and in the regulation of metabolism. Vitamins often function as coenzymes, or factors that work with enzymes to allow the necessary chemical reactions of our body to proceed.

**Vitamin A** can be found in foods in two forms. The first is preformed vitamin A, which is ready for our bodies to use. Retinol is the natural form of preformed vitamin A and is found in animal foods. There are two other kinds of preformed vitamin A that are made synthetically, vitamin A palmitate and vitamin A acetate. These are in vitamin pills and foods that have been fortified with synthetic vitamins.

The second form of vitamin A is not preformed and must be processed by the body before it can be used. Beta-carotene and other carotenoids are precursors of vitamin A and can be converted to vitamin A in our bodies with varying degrees of efficiency.

Vitamin A is essential for night vision, general eye and corneal health, bone health, immunity, reproduction, the maintenance of epithelial tissue found in the skin, lungs, gastrointestinal tract, and reproductive organs, and for cancer prevention. Good food sources of vitamin A include liver of all kinds, dark green and orange vegetables, and orange fruits. Specific fruits and vegetables that are good sources of vitamin A include carrots, sweet potatoes, winter squash, spinach, romaine lettuce, tomatoes, cantaloupe, broccoli, turnip and mustard greens, apricots, papayas, and mangos.

The most common food supplement source of retinol is cod liver oil or other fish liver oils. Because vitamin A is fat soluble, excess amounts are stored in the body. Overdosing with cod liver oil or synthetic forms of pre-formed vitamin A can lead to a vitamin A excess and symptoms such as loss of appetite, fatigue, peeling skin, hair loss, headaches, vomiting, liver problems, bone problems, excessive pressure in the cranium which causes a bulge on the head in infants, or birth defects in the baby when the vitamin is taken by pregnant women. Beta-carotene supplements are normally safe because if you take too much, your body just doesn't convert the excess amount into active vitamin A. The unneeded beta-carotene may be deposited in your skin, however, turning your skin yellow. Unconverted carotenes may have a protective effect against cancer.[9]

**Vitamin B1, or thiamine**, is a water-soluble vitamin which is essential to the production of energy in the body. It is part of a coenzyme that catalyzes the citric acid, or Kreb's cycle, by which the body obtains energy from all foods. (This tidbit of information is included for those of you taking a biochemistry class!) A deficiency of thiamine causes the disease beriberi, which means "I can't, I can't" in Sinhalese. This is a very descriptive name for a disease characterized by debilitating weakness, loss of appetite, irritability, depression, tingling, lack of coordination, muscle pain, and eventually edema (swelling and water retention) and an enlarged heart.

Since thiamine is water soluble, excess amounts are promptly excreted. Therefore, there is little risk of toxicity, and conversely, we need to take in adequate amounts of thiamine in our diet every day. A diet consisting of mostly white rice, with the thiamine refined out of it, is the main cause of beriberi in Third World countries. The best food source of thiamine in the American diet is pork. Other good food sources of thiamine include sunflower seeds, whole grains, wheat germ, enriched grains, green beans, dried beans, peanuts, and organ meats. Thiamine is easily destroyed in cooking and by alkaline solutions, such as water with baking soda in it. This is a good reason to avoid the practice of adding baking soda to the water in which you cook your vegetables to retain their bright green color. Alcoholics and others with chronic diseases may have difficulty absorbing the thiamine in their diets.[10]

A useful "side effect" of vitamin B1 is that it will render you unattractive to mosquitoes. Taking a supplement of 100 mg. of vitamin B1 for two days before an outdoor excursion and every day you are gone will pre-

vent mosquito bites. However, do not continue taking this amount of vitamin B1 for long periods of time without balancing it with supplements of
other B vitamins.

**Vitamin B2, or riboflavin,** is another water soluble vitamin which is
also active in the citric acid cycle and helps us derive energy from our food.
In addition, it functions in the breakdown of fatty acids. It is water soluble, so toxicity is rare, and we need to consume it in our diets every day.
It is likely to be needed in larger quantities by people who exercise heavi-
ly. A deficiency is characterized by inflammation of the mouth and tongue,
skin problems, and confusion. Riboflavin is needed for the formation of
red blood cells, growth, maintenance of the mucus membranes in the
digestive tract, and for eye health.

The best sources of riboflavin in the American diet are milk products
of all kinds, including low-fat milk products. Other good food sources of
riboflavin include liver, mushrooms, spinach, other dark green leafy vegetables, and enriched grains. Riboflavin is easily destroyed by light, so milk
should be stored in opaque containers.[11]

**Vitamin B3, or niacin,** is another water soluble vitamin that is
involved in the processes of deriving energy from our foods and in fatty
acid metabolism. A niacin deficiency causes widespread changes in many
parts of our body. Pellagra, which means "rough," is a disease that is caused
by a deficiency of niacin. The most obvious sign of pellagra is rough and
painful skin. The disease is characterized by four problems that begin with
the letter "d" – dementia (extreme mental confusion), diarrhea, dermati-
tis (skin inflammation), and eventually death. Early symptoms of niacin
deficiency include weakness, poor appetite, and weight loss. Niacin is
needed for the proper functioning of the nervous system and the synthesis of sex hormones.

Good food sources of niacin include tuna, salmon, and other fish,
chicken, beef, lamb, turkey, mushrooms, wheat bran, asparagus, peanuts,
and enriched grains. Corn is also a source of niacin if it is soaked in an
alkaline solution to release the niacin from the protein to which it is tightly bound. Because people from Hispanic cultures soak their corn in lime
water before making tortillas, they are not prone to niacin deficiencies.

The effects of large amounts of niacin, which you can get only from
supplements, can include flushing, itching, headaches, worsening blood
sugar levels in diabetics, liver problems, and gastrointestinal problems.
High dose niacin supplements may be prescribed by doctors to help
lower blood cholesterol levels. Niacin is water soluble, so we need to get
it in our diets every day. Alcoholics and people with chronic malabsorption diseases and cancer may become deficient in niacin more easily than
the general population.[12]

**Vitamin B5, or pantothenic acid**, forms a part of coenzyme-A, which is an essential player in the citric acid cycle, and thus is vital to our ability to derive energy from our foods. It is also involved in fatty acid metabolism and the synthesis of adrenal hormones. Pantothenic acid is essential to the synthesis of acetylcholine, a molecule involved in the transmission of impulses by the nervous system. Thus, low pantothenic acid has been suspected of contributing to memory loss and senile dementia, or the extreme mental confusion of the elderly.

Pantothenic acid is a vital nutrient for people who are under stress or have allergies. This is because allergies and stress both overwork the adrenal glands, and pantothenic acid helps them keep up with their job of making adrenal hormones.

*Pantothen* means "from every side" in Greek, and pantothenic acid is widespread in many foods. Especially good food sources of pantothenic acid include liver, peanuts, eggs, beef, pork, milk, mushrooms, broccoli, legumes, dates, pecans, and salmon.[13]

**Vitamin B6, or pyridoxine**, is necessary for the function of more than 50 enzymes involved in carbohydrate, protein, and fat metabolism. It is also needed for the synthesis of DNA, RNA, and the non-essential amino acids. Without vitamin B6, we would have to take in all amino acids in our diet in the proper ratios for protein synthesis. Vitamin B6 is needed to make hemoglobin, the oxygen-carrying compound in red blood cells, and for the formation of white blood cells, which are essential to immunity. It is also used in the synthesis of neurotransmitters. Without sufficient levels of neurotransmitters, headaches, depression, confusion, and seizures occur. Vitamin B6 may also help with premenstrual syndrome by increasing the synthesis of the neurotransmitter serotonin.

The symptoms of a deficiency of vitamin B6 include anemia, digestive problems, depression, confusion, irritability, skin irritation, and weight loss. Although it is a water soluble vitamin and must be consumed every day, vitamin B6 is potentially toxic in large doses, causing nerve damage which may result in the loss of the ability to feel normal sensations such as touch and loss of coordination. Some of these effects may continue even after one stops taking vitamin B6. In *The Right Dose*, nutritionist Patricia Hausman, M.S., recommends not taking more than 50 milligrams per day of vitamin B6 in supplements.

Good sources of vitamin B6 include chicken, turkey, salmon, tuna, eggs, carrots, spinach, sunflower seeds, and wheat germ. Vitamin B6 is more easily absorbed from animal foods than from plant foods.[14]

**Vitamin B12, or cyanocobalamin**, is needed for healthy red blood cells, for the metabolism of folic acid, and to maintain the myelin sheath that protects our nerves. Because B12 is necessary for folic acid to be useable, it is essential to all cell division. The major symptom of a deficiency of vitamin B12 is pernicious anemia which eventually progresses to nerve damage. Vitamin B12 deficiency is common in elderly people because with age, our stomachs lose the ability to secrete a protein called intrinsic factor which binds vitamin B12 in the stomach and enables it to be absorbed in the final few inches of the small intestine. Pernicious anemia is best treated with injections of B12 which bypass the absorption problem. Unlike most B vitamins, vitamin B12 is stored in the body, so a deficiency may take years to develop. Most deficiencies are due to impaired absorption rather than low dietary intake.

Vitamin B12 is found in animal foods, with liver, oysters, clams, eggs, and beef being the best sources. Strict vegetarians should take B12 supplements or drink soy milk that is fortified with B12, or they will be at risk for vitamin B12 deficiency, although it may take years to develop.[15]

**Folic acid,** also a B vitamin, is needed for the synthesis of DNA and RNA, and thus it is essential to all cell division. The most clinically diagnostic symptom of a folic acid deficiency is anemia characterized by large red blood cells. This type of anemia also occurs with a vitamin B12 deficiency because B12 is necessary for folic acid to do its job. Other symptoms of folic acid deficiency include inflammation of the tongue, diarrhea, confusion, impaired immunity, and poor growth. If an expectant mother is low in folic acid in early pregnancy, there is an increased risk of neural tube birth defects such as spina bifida.

Folic acid is water soluble and generally non-toxic, but large doses can impair our ability to absorb and use zinc and cause gastrointestinal symptoms. Also, taking large doses of folic acid can mask a vitamin B12 deficiency until it is too late to prevent nerve damage.

Folic acid is found in green leafy vegetables, organ meats (especially liver), brewer's yeast, legumes, whole grains, and oranges. It is easily destroyed by heat so vegetables and fruits should be served raw or lightly cooked to preserve their folic acid content. Orange juice is one of the best sources of folic acid, as well as being high in vitamin C.[16]

**Biotin** is essential to the citric acid cycle and fatty acid metabolism. It helps us metabolize all three of our fuel sources – proteins, carbohydrates, and fats. Altered serum fatty acid profiles occur with a biotin deficiency. Good food sources of biotin include cauliflower, egg yolks, yeast, liver, peanuts, and cheese. In addition to being found in foods, biotin is made by our intestinal bacteria. Raw egg whites contain a protein which binds biotin. Eating lots of raw egg whites can cause a biotin deficiency, but cooked eggs do not pose this problem. There are no known symptoms caused by having too much biotin.[17]

**Vitamin C, or ascorbic acid,** is a water soluble vitamin that is required for tissue growth and repair, adrenal gland function, control of bruising, as well as for immunity, collagen formation, wound healing, and healthy gums. Vitamin C is the most important water soluble antioxidant and thus helps prevent free radicals from causing damage. It aids in the absorption of iron and the synthesis of the neurotransmitter serotonin and of many hormones, including thyroxin, epinephrine, norepinephrine, and steroid hormones. It is also needed for the metabolism of folic acid and protein.

Most animals make their own vitamin C from glucose in relatively large amounts. For instance, pigs make about 8 grams per day. The recommended daily allowance for human beings is 60 milligrams per day, but supplement doses of 500 milligrams or one to two grams are commonly suggested for treatment of the common cold. The main side effect of large doses of vitamin C is diarrhea because we absorb only as much as we need, and the unabsorbed vitamin C draws water into the intestine. It is sometimes claimed that the right dose of vitamin C for an individual is the amount just under what causes diarrhea. If you routinely take large doses of vitamin C, you should not quit "cold turkey" or you may develop symptoms of deficiency. Rather, you should gradually taper your supplement intake. Vitamin C supplements should be avoided by people who have an iron overload because vitamin C enhances the absorption of iron. An added precautionary fact is that chewable vitamin C can be hard on the enamel of your teeth.

Vitamin C is a good general anti-allergy supplement. Allergy symptoms result when an allergen-antibody complex causes mast cells to release histamine and other substances which produce allergic symptoms. Vitamin C helps stabilize mast cells so they are less likely to release these substances.[18]

**Vitamin D** is called the sunshine vitamin because we make it in our skin when we expose ourselves to sunlight. It is a fat soluble vitamin and is required for the absorption of calcium and phosphorus and thus for the building of strong bones. It is also essential for normal immunity, blood clotting, and thyroid function.

Fifteen minutes of outdoor sunlight three times a week is enough exposure for adequate vitamin D status in light-skinned people. Deficiency of vitamin D is rare. The main symptom of deficiency is weak bones, or rickets in children and osteomalacia in adults. Intestinal, liver, and gallbladder disorders and cystic fibrosis can interfere with the absorption of vitamin D. Since vitamin D is fat soluble, it is stored in the body. Toxicity can result if it is supplemented in doses just slightly above the recommended daily allowance. The symptoms of vitamin D toxicity include elevated blood calcium levels, muscle weakness, vomiting, diarrhea, and confusion.

The best food sources of vitamin D are fortified milk and dairy products and fatty fish.[19]

**Vitamin E,** which is actually a family of compounds called tocopherols, is the most important fat soluble antioxidant. As such, it helps protect our cells from damage caused by free radicals. It also protects red blood cells from breakdown, aids in the absorption of vitamin A, and protects unsaturated fatty acids from oxidation. Vitamin E may be good for the treatment of premenstrual syndrome and the prevention of cancer and heart disease. Vitamin E supplements should not be taken by people taking anti-clotting drugs because vitamin E can further prolong their clotting time. Good food sources include avocados, peaches, and asparagus.[20]

**Vitamin K,** which is a family of compounds, is vital to the process of blood clotting. It functions in the formation of various clotting factors including prothrombin. Anti-clotting drugs antagonize the action of vitamin K. Since vitamin K is made by intestinal bacteria, a deficiency is most likely to be found in people who take antibiotics (thus destroying their intestinal bacteria) or who have severe malabsorption problems. Newborn babies are often given a shot of vitamin K to insure good blood coagulation while they are in the process of building up normal intestinal bacteria.

Although vitamin K is fat soluble, it is poorly stored in the body so a daily supply is needed. Fortunately, this supply is made by our intestinal bacteria. Good food sources of vitamin K include green leafy vegetables, peas, beans, and liver.[21]

**MINERALS:** Minerals are elements that are essential to life. They are needed for the proper balance of body fluids, the formation of blood and bones, good nerve function and muscle regulation, and the proper function of many enzymes. The minerals needed for life fall into two classes, macrominerals which are needed in large amounts, and trace minerals which are needed in very small amounts. The macrominerals include calcium, magnesium, sodium, potassium, and phosphorus. Trace minerals include boron, chromium, copper, iodine, iron, manganese, selenium, and zinc. Minerals interact with each other and with other components in our foods, such as fiber, during the process of their absorption. Phytates in grains and oxalic acid in some vegetables bind minerals, making them hard to absorb. Thus, grains are more nutritious as far as available mineral content when they are made into breads, and the iron in spinach is less well absorbed than the iron in meat. Except for magnesium, minerals are found in higher concentrations in and are best absorbed from animal foods. Minerals are needed in the proper balance to each other. Because minerals can be toxic, they should be supplemented in small amounts as in a multiple vitamin-mineral formula, or if supplemented individually, should be taken in accordance with your personal need for them. See Appendix C for more information about determining your individual need for mineral supplements.

## MACROMINERALS:

**Calcium** is the first thing we think of when we think about minerals. Calcium is the most prevalent mineral in our body, making up about two percent of our body weight. 99% of this amount is in our bones and teeth. Calcium is vital for strong bones and healthy teeth, the transmission of nerve impulses, blood clotting, the regulation of blood pressure, and muscle contraction. Adequate calcium intake may also help prevent colon cancer. However, with all the recent publicity for calcium as a way to prevent osteoporosis, it is well to remember that it must be taken in balance with magnesium and other minerals.

Many factors affect our calcium status. Vitamin D enhances the absorption of calcium, and too much vitamin D combined with excess calcium intake can increase your risk of forming kidney stones. A high protein or high sugar diet can deplete calcium reserves in the body.

The best dietary sources of calcium are dairy products and green leafy vegetables. However, the calcium in vegetables may be poorly absorbed due to being bound to oxalic acid. Some calcium supplements, such as calcium carbonate, may be poorly absorbed by people who are low in stomach acid. Also, calcium supplements can interfere with the absorption of iron and zinc.[22]

**Phosphorus** is the second most common mineral in our bodies, making up about one percent of our body weight. It combines with calcium to form the mineral complex deposited in a protein matrix which makes up our bones. In addition to being needed for strong bones and teeth, phosphorus is vital for cell growth, energy production, kidney function, and contraction of muscles, especially heart muscle.

Since phosphorus is present in many foods, deficiency is rare. The best dietary sources of phosphorus are meats, dairy products, eggs, fish, poultry, legumes, nuts, grains, and seeds. Soft drinks are also very high in phosphorus and may cause depletion of calcium and magnesium as a result.[23]

**Magnesium** is the mineral that makes plants green; it is at the vital center of the chlorophyll molecule. Over 300 enzymes in our body use magnesium as a cofactor. Magnesium functions in the production of energy, transmission of nerve and muscle impulses, cardiac regulation, and blood pressure control. Magnesium works with calcium to maintain bone density. A lack of magnesium is associated with cardiovascular disease. Low levels of magnesium in heart muscles may cause them to go into spasms and ultimately lead to heart attacks.

Dark green leafy vegetables are the best dietary sources of magnesium. This mineral is also found in broccoli, whole grains, squash, nuts, seeds, dairy products, meats, chocolate, and hard water. Milk and dairy products, which are good sources of calcium, are very poor sources of magnesium.[24]

**Sodium** has received a lot of bad press, in my opinion. It is one of the most important macrominerals and contributes to the function of our bodies in a myriad of ways. It is necessary for maintaining proper water balance and blood pH, stomach function, and the transmission of nerve and muscle impulses. A sodium deficiency, which can be caused by heat and excessive perspiration, diarrhea, or diuretic use, can cause muscle cramps, headache, heart palpitations, nausea, vomiting, low blood pressure, shock, and coma. A high level of sodium, which is usually associated with impaired kidney function, can result in swelling, high blood pressure, and potassium deficiency.

Almost all foods contain some sodium. The major source in our diets is table salt. Some people with high blood pressure are sodium sensitive and can lower their blood pressure by following a low sodium diet. A high sodium diet may be recommended for chronic fatigue syndrome since sodium is necessary for the function of the adrenal glands and maintenance of blood pressure at a normal level.[25] While we should not eat highly salted snacks, for most people, stringent restriction of sodium intake is not necessary and may be counterproductive. Instead, we should try to increase our intake of potassium so the two minerals are in proper balance. Dr. Paul Eck suggests that the adverse effect of sodium on some people with high blood pressure may be due to deficiencies of other minerals, such as calcium, magnesium, potassium, and zinc, rather than an excess of sodium. People with allergies often have "overworked" adrenal glands which cannot make enough of the hormone aldosterone. The judicious addition of salt to their diets can help compensate for this problem.[26]

**Potassium** is the partner of sodium in the maintenance of fluid balance in our bodies and the transmission of nerve and muscle impulses. Sodium is the main ion in the fluids outside of our cells and potassium maintains fluid balance inside our cells. Potassium will lower blood pressure. It is essential for the optimal functioning of many enzymes, for the proper transmission of nerve and muscle impulses, for the regulation of heart rhythm, and for the transfer of nutrients through cell membranes. Potassium deficiency, which may occur in alcoholics, in people who take certain diuretic medications, or after prolonged diarrhea or vomiting, can be life threatening. Symptoms include weakness, muscle cramps, confusion, apathy, and irregular heartbeat. A relative deficiency of potassium in relation to sodium can also occur if you eat a lot of high-sodium foods.

The best dietary sources of potassium are leafy vegetables, fruits, dairy products, meats, legumes, whole grains, potatoes, coffee, and tea.[27]

## TRACE MINERALS:

**Boron** is a trace mineral needed by the body in very small amounts for the formation of bone, brain function, and the metabolism of calcium, magnesium, and phosphorus. Boron may help prevent postmenopausal osteoporosis. Good dietary sources of boron are fruits, vegetables, nuts, and unrefined sea salt. Apples are the best source of boron in our diets.[28]

**Chromium** is involved in the metabolism of glucose and the synthesis of cholesterol, fats, and proteins. It is essential to the normal uptake of glucose by cells and therefore helps with the regulation of blood sugar levels in both diabetes and hypoglycemia. A deficiency of chromium leads to impaired glucose tolerance, high blood cholesterol and triglyceride levels, and possibly to coronary artery disease. The best dietary sources of chromium are whole grains, brewer's yeast, egg yolks, cheese, and meat. Chromium is removed in the refining of grains and is not replaced by the enrichment process even though carbohydrate foods such as grains require chromium to be used. High sugar consumption and continued stress deplete the body of chromium.[29]

**Copper** is important for the formation of red blood cells, hemoglobin, collagen, and bone, and for iron absorption, the healing process, and the maintenance of the myelin sheath around nerves. Copper and iron compete with zinc for absorption. Thus a very high zinc intake can produce a copper deficiency. Copper is widely available in foods, including meats, shellfish, nuts, avocados, cocoa, legumes, fresh fruits and vegetables, and whole grains. It is also in most tap water because of copper pipes used in plumbing. Copper excess is more common than copper deficiency because it is present in our drinking water and so many foods.[30]

**Iodine** is essential for the production of thyroid hormones, the metabolism of fat, and the normal mental development of unborn babies. Before the advent of iodized salt, goiter was a common problem among people who did not live near the ocean and could not consume seafood and those who lived in areas with iodine-poor soils. A goiter is a swelling on the neck due to the thyroid gland becoming enlarged in an attempt to produce hormones without enough iodine. Today, consumption of an adequate amount of iodized salt protects us from this problem. In addition to iodized salt, you can get iodine in your diet from saltwater fish, molasses, and sea vegetables such as kelp. People on low-salt diets are more prone to iodine deficiencies.[31]

**Iron** is the heart of the hemoglobin molecule and is responsible for our blood's capability to transport oxygen to our cells. It is also an essential part of many enzymes, functions in the energy production systems of our cells, and is needed for the synthesis of collagen, as well as being important for immunity and growth. Women need more iron than men to compensate for their monthly loss of blood. The most common symptom of iron deficiency is anemia. Iron excess can also cause problems such as liver and heart damage.

Iron absorption from foods varies from 3% to 10%. This mineral is best absorbed from animal foods. Phytic acid in grains and oxalic acid in vegetables bind the iron in these foods making the iron more difficult to absorb. However combining plants high in iron with animal foods in a meal will result in better absorption of the iron in the plant foods. The best food sources of iron are red meats, the dark meat of poultry, eggs, and enriched grain products. Green leafy vegetables are also high in iron, but in a form which cannot be easily absorbed. Vitamin C enhances the absorption of iron, so if you are iron-deficient, eat vitamin C containing foods or take a vitamin C supplement with your iron-containing meals to enhance absorption. Since coffee and tea interfere with the absorption of iron, so you should avoid these beverages with your high-iron meals if you are iron-deficient.

Anemia is not always due to iron deficiency, but can also occur when there is a deficiency of folic acid, vitamin B12, or other trace minerals.[32]

**Manganese** is an essential component of twenty enzyme systems in our bodies, including enzymes involved in carbohydrate metabolism and antioxidant enzymes. It is also needed in small amounts for protein and fat metabolism, the production of insulin, blood sugar regulation, immunity, reproduction, the formation of bone and cartilage, and healthy nerves. Good food sources of manganese include avocados, tropical fruits, nuts, seeds, and whole grains.[33]

**Molybdenum** is required in extremely small amounts as a component of some enzymes and for nitrogen metabolism. Molybdenum inhibits the absorption of copper. Good food sources of molybdenum include legumes, nuts, and whole grains.[34]

**Selenium** is a cofactor in enzymes that participates in detoxification. It works with vitamin E to protect us from free radicals and other harmful substances. Selenium has made headlines in recent years as a nutrient that possibly offers protection from cancer. Surveys have shown that cancer rates are lower in areas where the soil, and therefore food grown in that soil, is richer in selenium. Deficiency of this mineral is also associated with "Keshan disease," a type of heart disease. However, because there is little regulation in our bodies of the absorption of selenium, this mineral has potential for toxicity even from dietary sources. The symptoms of excess selenium are weakness, garlicky breath, nausea, vomiting, and liver damage. The best food sources of selenium are seafood and sesame seeds. Selenium, and all minerals, are best absorbed from sesame seeds if the sesame seeds are ground, as in tahini.[35] (Tahini is ground sesame seed butter and can be purchased at health food stores).

Zinc is a very important trace mineral in many ways. It is a part of several vital enzymes and is required for protein and nucleic acid synthesis, growth, immunity, wound healing, the production and proper function of the hormone insulin, the production of prostaglandins from essential fatty acids, the production and repair of DNA, the senses of taste and smell, bone formation, red blood cell health, fertility, and prostate health. Very slowly sucking on a zinc lozenge may help shorten the duration of and decrease the severity of the common cold. Zinc competes with copper and iron for absorption, so a very high zinc intake can contribute to a copper or iron deficiency. Very high zinc intake may also lead to impaired immunity and the lowering of "good" HDL cholesterol. Although there are many foods high in zinc in most of our diets, alcoholics, smokers, strict vegetarians, and people with chronic infections or inflammatory diseases can easily become deficient in zinc. Good food sources of zinc include meats, shellfish, poultry, eggs, legumes, and greens. Zinc is more plentiful in and more easily absorbed from animal foods than from plant foods.[36]

# The Bottom Line – Your Diet

Now that you've learned everything you ever wanted to know about the nutrients your body needs, the question is what should you do nutritionally to insure good health? According to Dr. Leo Galland, a pioneer in combining conventional medicine with the best insights of alternative medicine, we all should eat a nutrient-dense diet for optimal health. This means when you are choosing what to eat, pick those foods that have the greatest number of nutrients for the number of calories you will be getting from them. Eat unprocessed or minimally processed foods whenever possible. If you have food allergies, you should avoid your allergenic foods when you choose what to eat. If you are overweight or have blood sugar problems, choose your foods to minimize large swings in your blood sugar level. There is more specific information about these and other special diets below.

Practically speaking, how do you go about getting a nutrient-dense diet? By making the right choices every time you eat. When you want a snack, skip that sugary doughnut made from highly refined flour and fried in hydrogenated fat and instead choose a piece of fresh fruit, some nuts, or a whole grain cracker with a little natural nut butter or cheese. Learn to cook for yourself and then do it most of the time. It takes a little effort to learn but will soon become easy. Home cooking is the best thing you can do for both your health and your wallet.

Plan your meals in advance to include nutritious whole foods. When you grocery shop, fill your basket with fruits and vegetables, nuts and seeds, fatty fish that are rich in essential fatty acids, lean meats and poultry, low-fat dairy products, and whole grain cereal products. Well, all right, if you are like many young people and hate whole wheat, at least avoid processed grain products which contain hydrogenated fats. Maybe a little oatmeal or brown rice, which are also whole grains, can go into your grocery basket instead of whole wheat.

The foods we eat come from several groups. The United States Department of Agriculture has developed a food pyramid which is designed to tell us how much to eat from each of these groups in order to be well nourished. Some of their guidelines, in my personal opinion, should not be applied to everyone. Others, like limiting the amount of fat and sugar you eat, are good advice for most of us. Excessive fat intake increases your need for essential fatty acids. If you are underweight and trying to gain weight by increasing your fat intake, make sure the fat you eat is mostly "good" fat such as polyunsaturated oil. Too much sugar is not good for anyone because it stresses our blood sugar control mechanisms and leads to weight gain and tooth decay.

The base of the food pyramid is the grain group. The USDA recommends that we eat six to eleven servings of grains per day. One serving is one piece of bread, a roll, biscuit, or muffin, a half of a hamburger bun, or ½ cup cooked cereal, rice, or pasta. In my opinion, eleven servings can excessive for many people. I know several people who decided to eat more healthily, began eating lots of whole grains, and developed grain allergies. Loading up on any one food can trigger latent allergies to that food. In addition, too much carbohydrate, even complex carbohydrate, can overload some people's blood sugar control mechanisms unless the carbohydrates are "balanced" with protein. So let your own body be your guide as to how many servings of grains you eat per day. If you are allergic to wheat, substitute other grains such as barley, oats, rye, spelt, kamut, rice, millet, milo, or teff, or non-grain alternatives such as amaranth, quinoa, and buckwheat. Dr. Galland feels that white potatoes are not nutrient-dense enough to "count" as a vegetable serving; however, they are healthy whole complex carbohydrate foods. I recommend "counting" them as a complex carbohydrate in this food group instead of counting them as a serving in the vegetable group.

The second level of the food pyramid contains the vegetable group and the fruit group. The USDA recommends that we eat three to five servings of vegetables and two to four servings of fruit per day. One serving is ½ cup cooked or raw vegetables or canned, cooked, or chopped fruit, 1 cup of leafy raw vegetables such as lettuce or spinach, ¾ cup fruit or vegetable juice, a whole fruit such as an apple, banana, or orange, ½ cup of berries, or ¼ cup of dried fruit. Eating five to nine servings of fruits and vegetables daily is a worthy nutritional goal because fruits and vegetables are our best sources of vitamins. However, I feel that the USDA recommendations could be more specific. There is a lot of difference nutritionally between 1 cup of raw spinach and 1 cup of iceberg lettuce! Dr. Leo Galland recommends that iceberg lettuce, cucumbers, and white potatoes not be counted as vegetable servings, or you will be shortchanging yourself on essential vitamins.[37]

When you choose fruits and vegetables, try to pick the ones whose names appeared in the last several pages of this book as good sources of specific vitamins and minerals. Be sure to eat dark green leafy vegetables, orange vegetables or fruits, and vitamin C-rich fruits or vegetables every day. Orange vegetables and fruits, such as carrots, squash, and cantaloupe, are excellent sources of vitamin A. Dark green vegetables contain vitamin A, magnesium, and many B vitamins. Citrus fruits, strawberries, and tomatoes are good sources of vitamin C. When choosing fruits and vegetables, go for color! Since red leaf lettuce and other dark colored lettuces are very nutritious, choose them over iceberg lettuce. People eating hash browns for breakfast and an iceberg lettuce salad and french fries with their lunch and dinner might think they have met their need for fruits and vegetables if the diet is judged only by USDA standards. But the person who has orange juice with breakfast, a romaine lettuce salad and strawberries with lunch, and a spinach salad and cantaloupe with dinner will have taken in much larger quantities of vitamins and minerals in his or her five servings of fruits and vegetables.

The third level on the food pyramid contains both the milk, yogurt, and cheese group and the meat, poultry, fish, dry beans, eggs, and nuts group. The USDA recommends that we eat two to three servings of dairy foods and two to three servings of protein foods per day. One serving from the dairy group is 1 cup of milk or yogurt, 1½ ounces of natural cheese, or 2 ounces of processed cheese. These foods are the most common sources of calcium in the American diet. The calcium from yogurt is more easily absorbed than that in milk and cheese. Dairy products in general are excellent sources of protein, vitamins, and minerals.

One serving from the protein foods group is one egg, one ounce of meat, poultry, or fish, ½ cup cooked beans, or 2 tablespoons of nut butter. The USDA's recommended two to three servings of protein foods per day should total five to seven ounces of protein foods. Our need for protein for healing, repairs, and synthesis of new body tissues can usually be satisfied by this amount of protein foods. However, for people who have difficulty controlling their blood sugar levels, protein foods offer an advantage over most other foods in that they do not set off an insulin response. Any excess protein we consume is slowly metabolized for energy, and may be one of the best sources of energy for people with severe blood sugar imbalance. (See pages 43 to 45 for more about diets for blood sugar control). It is important to make wise choices from this group. Women especially may need some red meat for iron. But ideally your food choices from this group should include more foods that are low in saturated fat such as fish, poultry, and beans.

At the top of the food pyramid is the group containing fats, oils, and sweets. The USDA advises that these foods be used sparingly. Although refined sugar is not essential to our diets in any way, fats are essential. Most people need at least three teaspoons of oil of a type which richly provides essential fatty acids every day or a good intake of nuts and seeds such as walnuts and sesame, sunflower, pumpkin, and flax seeds. Dr. Leo Galland recommends using one tablespoon of flax oil as a dressing for salads or on cooked vegetables every day to meet this nutritional requirement. If you are not able to meet this requirement through diet, you might consider supplementing your diet with capsules of essential fatty acids.[38]

Perhaps the best approach to choosing the foods that make up your diet is not the strict counting of servings, but simply using common sense. Eat whole, minimally processed foods and avoid junk foods. Choose only nutrient dense foods and avoid foods that are anti-nutrients such as refined sugar and trans fats. Refined sugar contributes only calories to our diets; the vitamins and minerals that are required to metabolize sugar have been refined out of it. So sugar is essentially a nutrient robber because it uses the vitamins and minerals from other foods to be metabolized. Excessive sugar consumption can lead to adult-onset diabetes. Trans fats, such as the partially hydrogenated fats in margarine, shortening, and many processed foods, are also anti-nutrients. They increase your need for essential fatty acids and replace the correct fats in your cell membranes, making them stiff and abnormal in their responsive abilities.[39] High consumption of trans fats raises cholesterol levels and increases the risk of heart attacks.[40]

Use the same common sense when you use the nutritional analyses* of the recipes in this book. Calorie counting is generally a much better way to drive yourself crazy than it is to lose weight. (See pages 42 to 43 for more about weight loss). Use the nutritional analyses of the recipes to compare recipes and make the choices that are best for you. Diabetics are an exception to the "don't count" rule because they must strictly balance their food consumption with their insulin intake. The diabetic exchanges given with each recipe will enable them to do this. See pages 104 to 106 for more about how to use the nutritional analyses in this book.

*Note: The nutritional analyses of the recipes in this book were calculated using Food Processor for Windows, Version 7.7, by ESHA Research, Inc., P.O. Box 13028, Salem, OR 97309.

# Special Diets

Hippocrates said, "Let your food be your medicine and your medicine your food." Many medical conditions can be treated effectively with special diets. It helps tremendously to be able to cook for yourself if you need to be on a special diet! I hope that the special diet section of this chapter, the general cooking instruction given in other chapters, and the recipes in this book will help many readers to improve their health in a way that no doctor can. Diet can be a permanent solution to some health problems without the risk of side effects inherent in many drugs.

**Allergy diets:** Food allergies are commonly treated by avoiding the foods to which you are allergic. The most common food allergens are wheat, milk, eggs, corn, soy, and yeast, which are ubiquitous in processed and convenience foods. This book contains some recipes that are free of these common allergens. Most of these recipes are "near-normal" and are made with the tastiest and easiest to handle of the alternative grains, etc. This level of restriction may not be enough for those with more complex food allergies. For a complete discussion of food allergy, its diagnosis and treatment, the use of rotation diets for allergies, and recipes which are beyond the scope of this book, see *The Ultimate Food Allergy Cookbook and Survival Guide* as described on the last page of this book.

**Diabetic diets:** Diabetics must strictly control their intake of calories and macronutrients and balance their food consumption and exercise against their insulin intake or their body's production of insulin. This is usually accomplished by using a system of "exchanges" to budget food intake. If you are a diabetic, your doctor or nutritionist will work out a diet for you which tells you how many of which food exchanges to eat for each meal and snack. The nutritional analyses of the recipes in this book include diabetic exchanges. You can use these to determine how much of each recipe will fit into your allotted exchanges for each meal.

**Heart-healthy low-fat diets:** People on heart-healthy diets are usually advised to control the amount of saturated fat and cholesterol they consume. Actually, consuming trans fats, such as those in margarine, shortening, and processed foods, is more likely to lead to cardiac disease than consuming cholesterol, a normal component of our cell membranes and the compound from which our bodies make many hormones. Almost all the recipes in this book use healthy fats, such as vegetable oils. A few recipes use a little butter. None of the recipes, if eaten in the quantities your doctor recommends, is unsuitable for a heart-healthy diet except for the butter pie crust recipe on page 275. If you are on a heart healthy diet, just make your pie crusts with oil (recipe on page 274) and keep your portions small.

If you wish to omit eggs from your diet because of their cholesterol content, many of the baking recipes in this book are egg-free. Others include an egg-free option in the ingredient list, such as using ¼ cup more water in place of an egg. As an alternative, you can use an egg substitute such as Egg Beaters™ in place of the eggs in the recipes in this book. The nutritional analyses of the recipes indicate how much fat each recipe contains and if it is saturated or unsaturated. Let these numbers guide your choices of foods. Most of the cholesterol in your blood has been made by your own body. Studies have shown that dietary cholesterol has very little effect on blood cholesterol levels.[41]

**Low sodium diets** may be recommended for the treatment of high blood pressure, heart disease, or kidney disease. While the recipes in this book have not been designed for low sodium diets, they are lower in salt than standard restaurant food or processed foods from your grocery store. With the exception of the yeast bread recipes, the salt can be omitted from any recipe in this book, thus making the recipe usable on your diet. The nutritional analyses of the recipes in this book will tell you how much sodium the recipes contain and help you to limit your intake of sodium. If you are on a low sodium diet because of high blood pressure, it may also be advisable to supplement your diet with calcium and magnesium and to increase your intake of potassium from foods such as fruits to help bring your blood pressure down.[42]

**Weight loss diets** usually involve counting calories and limiting fat so that the amount of energy you expend each day is more than the amount of energy you are taking in from your food. Exercise is usually added to the program to increase energy expenditures. (See page 45 for more about exercise). In the wisdom of conventional weight loss diets, every 3500 calories which you expend but do not consume as food is a pound of weight lost. However, our bodies were designed to cope with adverse circumstances such as starvation. When we cut down our food intake, our metabolism slows down to compensate for it. Off-and-on dieting can lead to a spiral of decreasing metabolism that will make you fatter rather than thinner in the long run. Also, it is very difficult to resist hunger. A much better approach to weight loss is to "reprogram" your appetite to reflect what your body really needs in food intake. This can be achieved by not eating foods to which you are allergic, since these foods may cause you to overeat due to allergic cravings. Controlling your blood sugar is also essential for weight control. In *The Optimum Nutrition Bible,* nutritionist Patrick Holford says, "Keeping your blood sugar balanced is probably the most important factor in maintaining even energy levels and weight."[43] See the next section for the detail of blood sugar control diets.

**Blood sugar control diets:** An estimated three in ten people have an impaired ability to keep their blood sugar level on an even keel. Some of these people are diabetics, who cannot make sufficient insulin to get the sugar from the foods they eat into their cells. Therefore, their blood sugar soars high. But most of these people have "functional hypoglycemia," or low blood sugar not due to organic causes such as a pancreatic tumor. Many of them don't realize they even have a physical problem that is causing weight gain, lack of energy, impaired concentration, dizziness, headaches, irritability, nervousness, depression, and a host of other symptoms.

The level of glucose in your blood is the major factor that determines your hunger level and appetite. When it drops, you get hungry. A normal person eats when hungry, and his blood sugar rises to a normal level which is sustained for several hours. A person with functional hypoglycemia eats and his pancreas secretes too much insulin for the amount of food he ate. His blood sugar then rises temporarily but often not as much as a normal person's would. It then falls to a very low level, making the person hungry again even though it may have been less than a hour since the last food intake. This leads to a vicious cycle of overeating and weight gain.

Sugar promotes a larger release of insulin than other foods. In order to control your blood sugar, and thus your weight, you need to completely give up eating sugar. You should also avoid caffeine, nicotine, and if possible, excessive stress. These cause your liver to release sugar just as if you had eaten a candy bar, and the same up-and-down reaction in your blood sugar levels occurs.

Your diet should contain slow-releasing carbohydrate foods instead of fast-releasing carbohydrates such as sugar. Whole grains, starchy vegetables such as potatoes, and beans are good sources of complex carbohydrates. The mainstay of a blood sugar control diet is protein. Protein foods must be metabolized into glucose by your body before they can be used as energy, so they do not provoke a large insulin response. Contrary to popular "food combining" protocols, research has found that eating some protein with your carbohydrates is the best way to achieve good blood sugar control. A cracker with natural nut butter is a great blood-sugar-control snack, as is an apple with a slice of cheese or a few nuts. Beans, lentils, and other legumes are good blood sugar control foods because they contain protein, complex carbohydrate, and lots of fiber which slows their absorption.

Fruit sugar, or fructose, is "slower releasing" than sucrose, or table sugar. It is also found with fiber in fruits, which slow its absorption, and with the minerals and vitamins that are needed to metabolize it. So fruit, in moderation, has a place in a blood sugar control diet. You don't have to give up all desserts. Just make them with fruit sweeteners and eat them in small quantities with a meal containing protein.

In order to control your blood sugar, you should eat frequently. In *Low Blood Sugar and You*, nutritionist Carlton Fredericks and Herman Goodman, M.D. recommend eating a small snack every two hours between meals. This snack should be protein or protein plus complex carbohydrate or fruit. Dr. Goodman believes that there should be no quantity limits on the diet. Mr. Fredericks proposes a slightly different diet for weight loss which spells out meals and quantities. His diet consists of six meals (or three meals and three snacks) per day with protein foods of animal origin (eggs, meat, fish, poultry, or cheese, one to three ounces) in each meal or snack. The total amount of protein you should eat per day is 13 ounces cooked weight, with one egg per day counting as two ounces of protein. Five teaspoons of vegetable oil are allowed for salad dressings, cooking, and to put on vegetables. Two cups of skim milk and two pieces of fresh fruit are permitted each day. You should consume between two and four cups of low-starch vegetables each day. Intake of starchy foods is limited to four servings of a half-slice of bread per day.

People with hypoglycemia crave sugar, and as you begin a blood sugar control diet, your body will cry out for sweets! Yet if you resist, your blood sugar level will even out and you will find it easier and easier to stick with the diet. The amount of food you are hungry for will decrease, and gradual sustained weight loss should follow naturally. Good energy levels and overall improved health should also be your rewards for perseverance.

As you implement a blood sugar control diet, exercise common sense and listen to your body. Eat when you get hungry because hunger can cause the release of stress hormones, which may raise your blood sugar so high that it provokes insulin release. The release of too much insulin causes your blood sugar to plummet, starting up the vicious cycle again. Mr. Frederick's weight loss diet, above, does not allow for eating every two hours unless there are only twelve waking hours in your day! (Perhaps this is why the two co-authors of the book proposed two different diets). Add another snack or two if you decide to try this diet and become hungry more often than six times per day.[44]

Some nutrients are helpful to people attempting to control their blood sugar. Chromium is often recommended, as are B vitamins. Many people with hypoglycemia benefit from a personalized supplement program. See Appendix C for more about determining your personal supplement needs.

**The role of exercise in weight loss and general health:** Moderate exercise is good for you! It contributes to cardiac health, good digestion, and your ability to cope with stress.[45] If you get in the habit of exercising twenty to thirty minutes three times a week while you are young, your health will benefit greatly for the rest of your life. The type of exercise you chose to do should be something you enjoy. Taking a brisk walk or bike ride in a park or along a scenic path will refresh both body and soul while conferring health benefits.

Hours of highly strenuous exercise done in an attempt to burn calories and lose weight are likely to be hours wasted. Get your blood sugar under control to lose weight instead.

## A Final Word

Your health is possibly the most crucial circumstance of your life which will determine what you can or cannot do. Since it is vital to have good nutrition to have good health, improving your nutritional status is one of the most important things you can do for yourself. But don't forget that food fills needs in our lives other than just nutritional needs. Let it be fun! Don't become so legalistic about your diet that you miss out on the social aspects of food. Unless you have serious health problems, you can probably get away with choosing the right foods most of the time and just forgetting "the rules" and having fun eating with your friends occasionally. If you want to have the best of both worlds, nutritional and social, you might even cook for your friends! This book contains many fruit sweetened dessert recipes and other good recipes for entertaining your friends. See pages 264 to 289 and 297 to 313 for these recipes. Eat well, improve or maintain your health, and enjoy life!

Footnotes

1. Holford, Patrick. *The Optimum Nutrition Bible.* Judy Piakus Publishers Ltd., London, 1997, p. 184.

2. Holford, p. 15.

3. Holford, p. 27.

4. Hausman, Patricia, M.S. *The Right Dose: How to Take Vitamins and Minerals Safely.* Ballantine Books, New York, 1987, pp. 9-10.

5. Holford, p. 34.

6. Holford, pp. 34-44.

7. Holford, pp. 51-59.

8. Galland, Leo, M.D., *The Four Pillars of Healing,* Random House, New York, 1997, pp. 142-147; Buttar, Rashid and Andrew Halpner, Ph.D., "The Impact of Essential Fatty Acids on the Aging Process," *Nutri-News,* November-December 2000, pp. 1-12; and Holford, pp. 24 and 45-52.

9. Hausman, pp. 21-28; Holford, p. 63; Wardlaw, Gordon M., Ph.D., R.D., L.D. and Paul M. Insel, Ph.D., *Perspectives in Nutrition,* Mosby College Publishing, St. Louis, 1990, pp. 310-318.

10. Hausman, pp. 54-56; Wardlaw et al, pp. 336-339.

11. Hausman, pp. 72-75; Holford, p. 64; Wardlaw et al, pp. 339-341.

12. Hausman, pp. 87-106; Holford, p. 64; Wardlaw et al, pp. 341-343.

13. Hausman, pp. 157-158; Holford, p. 150; Wardlaw et al, pp. 343-345.

14. Hausman, pp. 113-123; Wardlaw et al, pp. 347-349.

15. Hausman, pp. 144-150; Wardlaw et al, pp. 354-357.
16. Hausman, pp. 158-159; Wardlaw et al, pp. 349-354.
17. Hausman, pp. 158-159; Wardlaw et al, pp. 345-346.
18. Hausman, pp. 176-198; Wardlaw et al, pp. 357-361.
19. Hausman, pp. 206-222; Wardlaw et al, pp. 318-322.
20. Hausman, pp. 228-239; Wardlaw et al, pp. 322-325.
21. Wardlaw et al, pp. 325-327.
22. Hausman, pp. 266-306; Holford, pp. 71-72; Wardlaw et al, pp. 389-398.
23. Hausman, pp. 398-400.
24. Hausman, pp. 249-262; Holford, p. 73; Wardlaw et al, pp. 400-401.
25. Galland, p. 142.
26. Eck, Paul, Ph.D., "Common Misconceptions Associated With Salt," Eck Institute Articles, Eck Institute of Applied Nutrition, Ltd., pp. 1-2; Wardlaw et al, pp. 383-385.
27. Hausman, pp. 309-332; Holford, p. 74; Wardlaw et al, pp. 387-388.
28. Galland, p.; Wardlaw et al, pp. 436.
29. Hausman, pp. 431-434; Holford, p. 74; Wardlaw et al, pp. 434-435.
30. Hausman, pp. 343-346; Holford, pp. 76-77; Wardlaw et al, pp. 428-429.
31. Wardlaw et al, pp. 431-433.
32. Hausman, pp. 336-362; Holford, pp. 74-75; Wardlaw et al, pp. 416-422.
33. Hausman, pp. 436-437; Holford, p. 76; Wardlaw et al, pp. 434-436.
34. Wardlaw et al, pp. 436.
35. Hausman, pp. 401-426; Holford, p. 76; Wardlaw et al, pp. 429-431.
36. Hausman, pp. 367-398; Holford, pp. 75-76; Wardlaw et al, pp. 422-427.
37. Galland, p. 135.
38. Galland pp. 142-147; Holford pp. 45-51.
39. Galland pp. 141-144.
40. Katan, M. B., "Exit Trans Fatty Acids," *Lancet,* Vol. 346, 1995, pp. 1245-1246.
41. Holford, p. 115.
42. Holford pp. 113.
43. Holford, p. 55.
44. Fredericks, Carlton, Ph.D. and Herman Goodman, M.D., *Low Blood Sugar and You,* Grosset & Dunlap, New York, 1969, pp. 133-146; Holford, pp. 53-58, 156.
45. Murray, Michael, N.D. and Joseph Pizzorno, N.D. *Encyclopedia of Natural Medicine,* Prima Publishers, Rocklin, CA, 1991, p. 94

# Chemistry Lab, Section A

Cooking is a science as well as an art. A lot of chemistry goes on in the cooking process! Just remember what you did in chemistry lab and you'll have a head start on cooking. If you learn the basic principles of cooking chemistry, you will understand the "why's" of cooking rather than just cooking "recipe book" style.

The first principle for success in the chemistry lab is to weigh and measure accurately. When you are learning to cook, this is also good advice. As you become experienced, you will know which recipes permit some flexibility in measuring and you will soon develop a sense of when a recipe is "right" so you won't need to measure accurately all the time. But for beginners, measuring accurately is the key to success. Even experienced cooks need to measure accurately when making most baked goods. Refer to Appendix A on page 318 for a table of measurement conversions and a review of how to measure both liquid and dry ingredients.

You will remember from your chemistry lab that heat speeds up chemical reactions. This is also true in cooking. In cooking we often quantify the amount of heat we add to our "reaction" by baking a recipe at a certain temperature for a specified length of time. For baking breads, cakes, cookies, and similar foods, it is important that the "reaction" is at a constant temperature the whole time. Therefore, for these foods you should pre-heat your oven. Turn it on to the temperature your recipe specifies a few minutes before you will be ready to put your baked goods into the oven. For roasting meats or baking casseroles, having a constant temperature the first few minutes of the baking time is not critical. Therefore, you can turn the oven on at the same time you put in your meat or casserole.

The most important chemical reaction you should know about when you cook is the acid-base reaction involved in leavening (or causing to rise) non-yeasted baked goods such as quick breads, muffins, biscuits, cookies, and cakes. As a kid, and maybe also in chemistry lab, you may have combined baking soda with an acid, such as vinegar, and watched it foam. This is what happens in the leavening process in baking. All non-yeast leavening uses baking soda plus an acid. When these ingredients are combined in a solution (liquid condition), a reaction occurs that produces water and carbon dioxide gas.* This gas makes bubbles in your quick bread or cake, and these bubbles cause it to rise. For good texture you have to produce just enough carbon dioxide. If you produce too much, the batter will foam

*Note: My chemistry expert son tells me that the production of carbon dioxide occurs only with bases containing carbonate, such as sodium or potassium bicarbonate.

excessively and then deflate. You also have to produce the carbon dioxide gas at the right time, which is immediately before you put the bread, cake, or muffins into the oven. If you make up your cake batter and leave it on the kitchen counter while you grease the pan and preheat the oven, the chemical reaction is happening on the kitchen counter instead of in the oven where the bubbles will be "set" by the heat. Therefore, when making non-yeast baked goods, always prepare your pans before you do anything else for the recipe and preheat your oven in time to be hot before you mix the dry and liquid ingredients together.

The most common mistake beginning cooks make when preparing non-yeast baked goods is to overmix when stirring the dry and liquid ingredients together. Just think about it; if you keep stirring and stirring as the chemical reaction that makes carbon dioxide is going on, you will break up the bubbles and release the gas into the air rather than keeping those bubbles trapped in your batter. So the procedure for making non-yeast baked goods is this: First, stir the dry ingredients together in a large bowl. Mix the liquid ingredients in another bowl or in the cup you used to measure them. Before the oil and water or other liquids can separate, quickly stir them into the dry ingredients until they are just mixed. It is better to undermix than overmix. If you undermix, the floury spots will usually moisten up in baking. If you overmix, you will "use up" the chemical reaction of the baking soda and acid ingredient during mixing, rather than having this reaction occur in the oven where the leavening should cause your bread to rise. It is especially important not to ovemix when you are making non-wheat baked goods because alternative flours do not have as much "strength" for holding the carbon dioxide bubbles created by the leavening process.

A variety of acidic and basic ingredients can be used to make non-yeasted baked goods rise. The most common base is baking soda, or sodium bicarbonate. Some "health food" baking powders are made with potassium bicarbonate for people on low sodium diets. There are many acid ingredients that can be used for leavening. Buttermilk is often used. Lemon juice or lime juice can be the acid component of the leavening process. Fruit juice concentrates and fruit sweeteners may contribute acid to the leavening process in some recipes. People with food allergies may use rhubarb concentrate or unbuffered vitamin C crystals or powder for the acid component of the leavening because they may need to avoid citrus, buttermilk, and the cornstarch in most baking powders. For vitamin C leavened recipes, see *The Ultimate Food Allergy Cookbook and Survival Guide* as described on the last page of this book. When you leaven with vitamin C, be sure to get *unbuffered* vitamin C. Buffered vitamin C has had mineral salts added to make it non-acidic. Buffered vitamin C is much easier on a sensitive stomach, but you need acid for leavening.

Baking powder is a combination of sodium or potassium bicarbonate as the basic ingredient, monocalcium phosphate (most commonly) as the acid ingredient, and stabilizers to keep the acid and base from reacting until you want them to, such as when they are wet in a recipe. These stabilizers can be wholesome food ingredients, such as cornstarch or potato starch, or they can be chemicals. Avoid baking powders that contain aluminum which may be detrimental to your health. (See page 51 for more about aluminum). Rumford™ brand baking powder is commonly available in supermarkets and does not contain aluminum. Featherweight™ baking powder is a "health food" brand that contains only potassium bicarbonate, monocalcium phosphate, and potato starch. (See "Sources," page 320).

Altitude affects the leavening process. (For purposes of baking, "high altitude" is anything over 3000 feet. However, the recipes in this book are not for fragile baked items such as angel food cake and should work well at any altitude). The air pressure in the room where you are baking is less at high altitude than at sea level. Therefore, when the bubbles of carbon dioxide are formed in your batter, they will expand more and may tend to burst. To compensate for this in non-yeast baking, you may need to decrease the amount of leavening ingredients you use and/or increase the "strength" your batter has to hold the bubbles. Try one or more of the following suggestions to help your low-altitude recipe work at high altitude:

1. Increase the baking temperature by 15 to 25°F. This will cause the walls of the bubbles to "set" more quickly. Watch how fast your cake, quick bread, or whatever you are making is browning as it bakes and be prepared to take it from the oven early.
2. Decrease the sweetener by 1 to 3 tablespoons for a batch using 3 to 4 cups of flour. This makes the leavening bubbles "stronger." If you are using a liquid sweetener, replace it with the same amount of water.
3. Increase the liquid in the recipe. For each cup of liquid in the recipe, increase it 1 to 2 tablespoons at 3000 feet, 2 to 4 tablespoons at 5000 feet, and 3 to 4 tablespoons at 7000 feet.
4. Decrease the leavening ingredients. How much you should decrease them varies with the altitude. At 3000 feet, decrease the baking powder by ⅛ teaspoon and the baking soda by a "smidge." At 5000 feet, decrease the baking powder by ⅛ to ¼ teaspoon and the baking soda by ⅛ teaspoon or less. At 7000 feet, decrease the baking powder by ¼ teaspoon and the baking soda by ⅛ teaspoon.

Recipes that work at high altitude can almost always be used at sea level. However, there are some sea-level recipes which are impossible to make successfully at high altitudes even using the "tricks" above.

For yeast breads, two adjustments may be needed at high altitudes. The first is that you may need to add slightly more liquid or slightly less flour to the dough to reach the right consistency. (See the "Breads" chapter for more about how to judge the right consistency of yeast dough). This is because flour tends to contain less moisture at high altitudes. The second adjustment that might be necessary with hand-made yeast breads is to realize that the rising times will be shorter. Watch your bread carefully and bake it when it is doubled, even if that is a shorter time than the recipe specifies. Regular active dry yeast may be a better choice than bread machine or instant yeast for bread machine baking at high altitudes. When making yeast breads in a bread machine, if your breads are over-rising and collapsing, you may decrease the yeast by ⅓ of the amount called for per loaf or increase the salt by 25 percent to "slow down" the yeast. The altitude is likely to cause your bread to over-rise and collapse only at altitudes of 7000 feet or over.

For more about other situations you might encounter in baking yeast breads, see *Easy Breadmaking for Special Diets* as described on the last page of this book.

Remember the lecture on freezing point depression and boiling point elevation from chemistry class? This information applies to making candy and ice cream. The reason ice cream is not rock hard at freezer temperatures is because the sugar in it causes freezing point depression. Ice cream made with artificial sweeteners or the herb stevia will be like a brick after being frozen overnight because these substances are not present in high enough amounts to depress the freezing point of the ice cream. Ice cream made with fruit sweeteners in place of the sugar are much creamier. Furthemore, the fat in the cream and egg yolks helps stabilize homemade ice cream and gives it a good texture.

When you make candy, you boil a solution (usually a sugar solution) until the boiling point is very elevated. The recipe will specify a certain temperature at which you are to stop cooking the solution and throw it on a marble slab or heavy ceramic platter to cool it quickly and arrest further cooking. This temperature is really a measure of the super-concentration level of the sugar in the solution. Candy making can be "tricky" if you do not stop the cooking at exactly the right point. In addition, altitude affects candy making because the boiling point of water is lower at high altitudes than it is at sea level, and recipes are geared to sea level. If you wish to make candy at a high altitude, use your candy thermometer to measure the boiling point of water before you start. Then subtract the number of degrees the boiling point is under 212°F from the "end point" temperature given in your recipe. For example, if water boils at 208°F and you are supposed to cook your taffy to 270°F, stop cooking it at 4°F less than the recipe specifies because at the altitude where you are, water boils at 4°F less than what the cookbook assumes. Cook your taffy to 266°F instead.

Caramelization is a chemical change that heat produces in sugars. When making caramel candies or syrups, it is important to stop cooking the sugar at the "caramelized" stage rather than to proceed to the "burnt" stage. The time between caramelized and burnt can seem like a split second! Again, watch your thermometer closely while you are cooking the sugar solution and make adjustments for the altitude if you are not near sea level. Candies are beyond the scope of the recipes in this book, but the book does contain oven vegetable recipes in which the vegetables brown and taste sweeter. This is because long, lower moisture oven cooking caramelizes some of the natural sugars in the vegetables. Try "Oven Carrots," page 209. Even people who hate vegetables will like them!

There are also health aspects of cooking chemistry. Our bodies contain many minerals, but not all minerals are good for us. If you are low in "good" minerals, the less friendly ones may replace the good ones in crucial enzyme systems in your body. Some minerals, like arsenic, mercury, and lead, are extremely toxic even to people who have plenty of "good" minerals. Copper at levels that are too high, aluminum, and other less-friendly minerals are very common in our environments and should not be in our bodies. (However, we do need a low level of copper). There are several "rules" to follow to avoid consuming unfriendly minerals with your food. The first is always to use cool tap water when you are cooking. Yes, I know that if you start with the hottest possible tap water, your cocoa will be ready 30 seconds sooner! But hot water picks up dissolved less-than-friendly minerals from hot water tanks and the pipes to your room or apartment. Most plumbing systems contain some copper pipes. Copper is a necessary nutrient, but because of our plumbing systems Americans tend to have too much rather than too little copper in their bodies. Lead also can be present in plumbing pipes and solder.

Never cook acid foods in aluminum pans. The acid will dissolve (ionize) some of the aluminum and it will end up in your food and then in you! Personally, I would recommend not owning aluminum pans at all. Aluminum has been implicated in Alzheimer's disease, although the connection has not been proven. When you choose baking powder, read the label and get one that does not contain aluminum, such as Rumford™ brand baking powder. This type of baking powder will work just as well as the brands that do contain aluminum. For best health, also avoid aluminum-containing antacids and deodorants and brands of table salt that use aluminum compounds as anti-caking agents. If you also need to avoid salt that contains dextrose as an anti-caking agent due to corn allergy, use Baliene™ Iodized Sea Salt. (See "Sources, page 324).

Remember the chemistry lecture on soap? Soap is a compound in which the molecules have one side that is attracted to water and another side that is attracted to fat. This is why soap works to remove fat from our dishes. The fat-loving end of the molecule is attracted to the bacon grease and helps you pull it off of the dish and into the water, which you then wash down the drain. So if you want your dishes to end up really clean rather than greasy, use enough soap and keep the water hot. (There is more about dishwashing in the chapter on microbiology; don't miss it!) Also, wash the least greasy dishes, such as glasses and silverware, first. Then do the plates you ate from. Wash the cooking pans last because they are the most greasy and will "use up" the soap. If you want to wash your dishes in a different order, that's fine. Just drain and replace the water after washing the greasy dishes and use new soap and hot water for the glasses and less greasy items.

You may remember from your chemistry class that water expands when it freezes. This means that if you fill a glass (or even plastic) container to the top and put it in the freezer, the expansion that occurs during freezing can crack the container. Always leave one-half to one inch of air space at the top of containers of food which you plan to freeze.

Cooking chemistry will help you understand why things happen when you cook. For example, if you decide to change the sweetener in a recipe to a more acidic fruit sweetener, you will be aware of the possibility of changes in the leavening process. If the recipe doesn't come out as well as you expected, you can reduce other acid leavening ingredients the next time. Cooking is not difficult to do or to understand; and if you understand it, you will enjoy it and do it well. You science majors, who are so dear to my heart, know half of what you need to know already! You can do it! Go for it!

# Terminology 107

When you begin learning to cook, it may seem as if cooks speak a different language. The purpose of this chapter is to help you learn that language. Not all of the terms listed here are used in this book, but my hope is that this book will lead you into the exciting world of cooking, and that after reading this chapter you will be prepared to understand any cookbook.

## The Cook's Dictionary

*Al dente:* Italian for "to the tooth." Pasta that is cooked *al dente* offers some resistance to the tooth when you bite it.

**Bake:** To cook with dry heat in an oven. Cakes, cookies, pies, muffins, and other baked goods are baked uncovered. Casseroles are often baked covered.

**Baste:** To brush, drizzle, or spoon pan drippings over meat or vegetables as they cook. Basting keeps the surface of the food from drying out and adds flavor. The only food basted in this book is roast turkey. A bulb baster is a nice item to have for drizzling the pan drippings over the bird.

**Beat:** To stir rapidly in a circular motion. 100 strokes by hand is the equivalent of one minute of beating at medium speed with an electric mixer.

**Blanch:** To immerse food briefly in boiling water and then in cold water. Blanching is just enough cooking to stop the enzymatic breakdown that occurs in fresh fruits and vegetables and to set their color. Fruits and vegetables are commonly blanched to prepare them for freezing. You may also blanch some fruits and vegetables, such as peaches and tomatoes, to make them easy to peel; after blanching you can just slip the skins off. This is one way to lighten your workload if you are peeling peaches for canning or for a pie.

**Boil:** To cook food in liquid that is heated to the boiling point. To bring food to a boil means to heat it (in liquid, if it is not a liquid) until it bubbles. A full boil is a boil that cannot be eliminated by stirring the liquid.

**Braise:** To cook food slowly in a covered pan over low heat in a small amount of liquid. The liquid may be almost completely evaporated by the end of the cooking time.

**Bread:** To coat food, usually with a flour or crumb mixture, before cooking it. This book contains recipes for chicken and fish which are dipped in oil and flour or crumbs before baking. If you wish to bread meats before frying, a more substantial and "sticky" breading process is required. Usually the food is dipped in a beaten egg-and-milk mixture and then into flour or crumbs for frying.

**Broil:** To cook food a few inches from a heat source. Electric ovens have a top element under which you place the food you wish to broil. Gas stoves have a separate broiling drawer under the gas burner for the oven. Cooking food on an outdoor barbecue is also broiling.

**Bruise:** To partially crush a food to release its flavor. Garlic is commonly bruised by pounding it with the side of a knife before adding it to foods.

**Butterfly:** To cut a food down the center without cutting all the way through to the other side. The food is then spread open so the two sides resemble the two wings of a butterfly.

**Caramelize:** To caramelize is to break down the sugars in a food, producing a brown substance. When you caramelize vegetables such as onions or carrots, you cook them in just a little oil until they are browned and sweet. Cooking them this way actually changes the flavor of these vegetables. ("Oven Carrots," page 209, are caramelized carrots and are very easy to make. Even people who don't normally like cooked carrots will like these). When you caramelize sugar, you heat it to about 320 to 350°F until it just begins to brown but does not turn black. Watch carefully – the time between brown and black can seem like a split second! In candy making, you will usually add milk or cream to the sugar at the crucial moment to stop the heating process between "beautifully browned" and "scorched."

**Cheesecloth:** A cloth with open holes in it that is used to strain the curds from the whey in cheesemaking. It is also used for straining in other cooking or for enclosing spices and seasonings in a packet that can be cooked with a food and then retrieved at the end of the cooking time. You can usually purchase cheesecloth in a grocery store or a gourmet cooking store.

**Chiffonade:** To cut vegetables into thin strips or shreds. Salad greens are often cut in this way to make a bed for other foods.

**Chop:** To cut foods with a knife into cubes or pieces that are a little smaller than bite-sized. If foods are cut more finely, they are referred to as diced or minced.

**Clarify:** To make foods clear. In soup making, broth may be clarified with egg whites, which remove the particulate substances from the soup. Clarified butter, also called **ghee**, is butter which has been melted, skimmed of foam from the top, and poured off from the milk solids which settle to the bottom. Clarified butter is less allergenic than "regular" butter because the milk solids have been removed. Therefore, clarified butter can sometimes be tolerated by people who are allergic to milk. Then too, with the milk solids removed, clarified butter is very stable and can be stored at room temperature (as in a dorm-room pantry). Ghee can be purchased in health food stores.

**Coat:** To cover a food with another ingredient. When you bread meat (see "bread," above) you coat it with crumbs. When you sprinkle a food with something so it is completely covered, you have coated it with that ingredient. The expression, "**coat a spoon**" means to cook a milk-egg custard mixture until it leaves an even film on a spoon. When you draw a fingertip across the back of the spoon, if the custard doesn't run back into the swath, but instead leaves a clean track, the custard is sufficiently cooked.

**Core:** To remove the center of a fruit or vegetable. Examples of coring include cutting out the seeded center of an apple or the woody center of a head of cabbage.

**Cream:** To beat until light, smooth, and fluffy. Creaming is usually done to fats such as butter or shortening, or to mixtures of fats and sugar in the making of cakes and cookies. You need an electric mixer or food processor to cream butter and sugar. Because this book is written for people without a lot of kitchen equipment, the cake and cookie recipes in this book do not employ creamed fats, but instead call for oils and liquid sweeteners which you can mix together with a spoon.

**Crimp:** To press the edges of two pieces of dough together. If you make ravioli from scratch, you will crimp the edges of the two pieces of pasta together so they securely encase the filling. In pie making, the top crust is cut a little larger than the bottom crust, folded under the bottom crust, and then pressed together with a fork or fluted into a decorative edge with your fingers. (Also see "flute," below).

**Crisp:** To make foods crisp. Salad greens and other vegetables may be crisped by soaking them in cold water. Crackers may be crisped by heating them briefly in the oven.

**Crush:** To pulverize food. Crackers or dry bread can be crushed into crumbs by putting them in a plastic bag and rolling them with a rolling pin. Other ingredients can be made into a paste (as in pesto) or a powder using a mortar and pestle. (This is something you might remember from chemistry lab!)

**Cube:** To cut food into cubes, usually about ½ inch in size. This size is smaller than chopped but larger than diced.

**Curdle:** This is a word you usually don't want to hear when you're cooking! If a food curdles, this means it has separated into liquid and solid particulate parts, which is usually due to overcooking. Adding acid may also cause curdling. If you don't have buttermilk, you may add 1 tablespoon of vinegar or lemon juice to 1 cup of milk, which will curdle it, and then use it as a buttermilk substitute.

**Cut in:** To combine two ingredients, usually a fat with a flour mixture, using a pastry cutter (also called a pastry blender) or food processor. (I've read you can do this with a knife and a fork but never figured out how to do it that way myself!) Put the flour mixture in a bowl and add the solid fat, such as butter or shortening. Push the pastry cutter down through the fat and into the flour repeatedly, shaking off the fat after each push, until the mixture resembles coarse crumbs. This book also contains an oil pastry crust recipe in which the oil and flour mixture are cut together with a pastry cutter.

**Dash:** A small amount, about ¹⁄₁₆ teaspoon, of an ingredient. A "dash" is usually of a seasoning such as salt or pepper and refers to adding a sprinkling of the seasoning to the food.

**Deglaze:** To remove the browned particles which remain in the pan after cooking meat or other foods by adding water, wine, or broth to the pan and then stirring, scraping, and cooking the mixture briefly.

**Degrease:** To remove fat from the surface of a liquid, usually a sauce, soup, stock, or gravy. This is done by carefully spooning the fat from the surface or by chilling the liquid until the fat hardens and then easily removing all of it.

**Dice:** To cut food with a knife into very small cubes about ⅛ to ¼ inch in size.

**Dollop:** About a heaping tablespoon of a soft food such as sour cream, whipped cream, or mashed potatoes. As a verb, dollop means to place a spoonful of a soft food onto another food.

**Dredge:** To coat by dipping. This usually refers to dipping a piece of meat, poultry, or fish in a flour or crumb mixture until it is covered on all sides with the flour or crumbs.

**Drippings:** The melted fat and juices which collect in the bottom of the pan when roasting meat or poultry.

**Drizzle:** To pour a small amount of liquid over a food in a fine stream.

**Dust:** To sprinkle a food lightly with a powder, such as sugar or flour.

**Emulsion:** Here is another chemistry term! An emulsion is a suspension of fine particles of fat in a liquid. Homogenized whole milk is an emulsion. Mayonnaise is an emulsion for which there is a recipe in this book. When you make mayonnaise, you emulsify the oil in the liquid by adding the oil slowly while mixing rapidly. This suspends very small droplets of oil in the egg mixture.

**Fillet:** A flat boneless piece of meat or fish. As a verb, fillet means to cut the bones from meat or fish.

*Flambe:* French for "flamed." When you flambe something, you sprinkle it with liqueur, which is lighted with a match right before serving.

**Flute:** To press or cut in a decorative pattern. To flute vegetables, you cut slashes, grooves and other decorative markings in them. To flute the edge of a pie crust, place your thumb and index finger together on the outside edge of the crust. Then with a finger of your other hand, press the crust in the indentation between your thumb and index finger. Move around the crust, repeating this over and over, until the entire edge of the crust is wavy.

**Fold:** To gently combine a light aerated substance, such as beaten egg whites or whipped cream, with a heavier substance by lifting the mixtures up and over each other. The object of folding is to preserve the aeration in the light substance. If you were to beat or stir rather than fold, you would remove the air.

**Fry:** To cook in hot fat or oil over medium or high heat. In deep fat frying, the food is immersed in hot oil which is deep enough to completely cover the food. The oil should be hot enough to produce a crisp crust while still allowing enough cooking time for the inside of the food to be cooked thoroughly. If the oil is not hot enough, the food will absorb a lot of fat. Even if perfectly cooked, deep fat fried foods are not very healthy, and fires can occur. This book does not include deep fat fried foods. Pan frying is cooking food in a small amount of oil, usually over medium heat. Stir frying is cooking small pieces of food quickly in a small amount of oil over high heat while constantly stirring the food.

**Garnish:** To decorate a completed dish to make it more attractive to the eye. For instance, "garnish with parsley" means to lay a sprig of parsley in an attractive place on the dish.

**Ghee:** Clarified butter. See "clarify," above.

**Glaze:** A glossy coating for foods. For instance, a sugar solution or honey may be brushed on baked goods or beaten egg or egg white may be brushed on bread before baking to produce a shiny surface. Glaze also means to coat a food with a liquid coating, such as when you glaze a sweet bread with a thin icing.

**Grate:** To shred food by rubbing it on a grater, which is a serrated metal surface. Cheese and vegetables are commonly grated foods. A food processor can also be used to grate ingredients.

**Grease:** To rub the surface of a pan with a fat or oil to keep foods from sticking to it. The inner surface of a pan for cake baking is usually greased and floured. After rubbing the surface of the baking pan with a fat or oil, place a small amount of flour in the pan. Then shake and roll the pan around until the bottom and sides are also coated with flour. Shake the excess flour out of the pan.

**Grill:** To cook on a rack directly over an intense heat source, such as a barbecue. Meat, poultry, fish, and vegetables are commonly grilled.

**Julienne:** To cut the food into thin sticks. To julienne a potato, for example, cut it into slices about ⅛ inch thick. Then stack the slices and cut the stack into ⅛ inch strips of potato.

**Knead:** To work dough with your hands using a fold, press, and turn motion. Kneading bread dough by hand is a very satisfying experience. A mixer, food processor, or bread machine can also do this job for you. Bread dough should be kneaded until it is smooth and elastic. When it is sufficiently kneaded, if you poke it with your finger, it will spring back.

**Line:** To cover the bottom of a baking pan or sheet with waxed or parchment paper.

**Macerate:** To soak a food such as fruit in an alcoholic liquid, usually a liqueur such as brandy or rum.

**Marinate:** To soak a food such as meat, poultry, fish, or vegetables in a seasoned liquid which will impart its flavor and, in the case of some meats, tenderize the meat. The liquid which is used for soaking is called a **marinade**. Most marinades contain acid ingredients, so the pan in which you marinate should not be aluminum. (See page 51 for more about this). Keep the food covered and in the refrigerator while it is marinating.

**Mince:** To cut food into extremely small pieces with a knife. Minced food is cut into smaller pieces than chopped food or diced food.

**Pan broil:** To cook food in an ungreased or lightly greased frying pan and pour the rendered fat and drippings off the meat as it cooks.

**Papillote:** French for a pouch made of parchment paper. Foods cooked "en papillote" are usually served in the pouch so the diner can enjoy the aroma when the pouch is opened. To make the pouch, cut a heart shaped piece of parchment paper so half of the heart (folded down the center) is about twice as big as the food you want to wrap. Place the food on the paper near the center fold and fold the heart in half over the food. Beginning at the top center of the heart, fold the edge of the paper inward twice, creasing it well. Then move further along the edge of the heart and fold the paper inward twice again. The second fold anchors the first fold. Repeat this folding process all the way around the heart. When you reach the point at the end, twist the paper to anchor the last fold.

**Parboil:** To boil until the food is only partly cooked. For instance, before "no boil" lasagne pasta was available, the pasta had to be parboiled for a few minutes and then was cooked the rest of the way in the oven with the meat, sauce, and cheese. For stir-frying, you may need to parboil slow-cooking vegetables before adding them to the stir-fry recipe.

**Parchment paper:** A heavy paper used in baking and cooking. It does not contain petrochemical derivatives as waxed paper does. It can be used to line cake and cookie pans for baking, to make disposable baking bags which stand up to moisture longer than if made with waxed paper, and to wrap foods such as fish, meats, and vegetables for baking. (This is referred to cooking "en papillote." See "papillote," above). You can purchase parchment paper at gourmet cooking stores and some supermarkets.

**Pare:** To peel, see below.

**Peel:** To remove the outer skin of fruits and vegetables with a short-bladed knife, called a paring knife, or a vegetable peeler. When purchasing a peeler, look for one with a narrow slit between the blades. A peeler with a wide slit will take off a very thick layer of your fruit or vegetable, thus throwing away much of the most vitamin-rich layer of the food.

**Pastry blender or pastry cutter:** A kitchen tool made of several curved wires attached to a handle. It is used to cut fat into flour when making pie crust.

**Pastry wheel:** A sharp wheel on a handle that is used to cut pastry, cookie, or other dough. The edge of the wheel may be straight or wavy.

**Pinch:** Approximately 1/16 teaspoon of a dry ingredient such as salt or pepper. A pinch is the amount of the ingredient that can be held between the tips of your thumb and forefinger.

**Pipe:** To force a mixture such as frosting, whipped cream, or mashed potatoes through a pasty bag with a decorative tip.

**Plump:** To soak dried foods (usually dried fruits such as raisins) in a liquid until they soften and swell from absorbing the liquid.

**Poach:** To cook in simmering liquid. Poaching is often used for fish; it is cooked in a seasoned liquid which imparts flavor to the fish. Eggs are also commonly poached by breaking them into simmering water gently so they keep their shape. If you like poached eggs and this process is difficult for you, buy an insert for your frying pan that you can use to cook the eggs in cups over boiling water.

**Prick:** To make small holes in the surface of a food, usually with the tines of a fork. Pie crusts are commonly pricked. For a one-crust pie, prick the crust all over before baking to keep it from puffing up from the baking dish. The top crust of a two-crust pie should be pricked to allow steam to escape from the inside of the pie.

**Proof:** To test or prove, as in "proofing" yeast to make sure it is still active. To proof yeast, dissolve it in a small amount of warm liquid, usually containing some sweetener, and set it aside for about 10 minutes to see if it begins to produce bubbles. When the mixture has become bubbly, and thus proved that the yeast is still active, it is added to the rest of the dough ingredients.

**Puree:** To mash foods until they are completely smooth. This is usually done with a food processor or blender. The recipes in this book that require pureeing call for the use of a hand-blender, which is an economical, space-saving tool perfect for the beginning cook's kitchen.

**Render:** To melt solid fat into a liquid by heating it slowly. Fat is often removed from a cut of meat by rendering it or heating the meat slowly and then pouring the fat off.

**Reduce:** To boil a liquid, usually over high heat, until its volume is reduced by evaporation. The resulting liquid, which may be called a reduction, is more intense in flavor and often thicker than it was originally.

**Rice:** To force cooked food, such as boiled potatoes, through a kitchen utensil with holes in it. This utensil is called a ricer. The food may look like rice or like long ribbons of rice when it comes through the ricer. Ricing is a method of mashing potatoes that produces very creamy, non-sticky results.

**Roast:** To cook a food in the oven in an uncovered pan. Meats are commonly roasted to produce a well-browned surface. The poultry or meat that you use for roasting should be a fairly tender cut.

**Roux:** French for a mixture of melted fat or oil and flour that is cooked for a few minutes to remove the starchy taste of the flour. Then liquid is added to the roux to produce a sauce or gravy.

**Sauté:** To cook a food briefly over medium heat in a shallow pan with a small amount of oil or butter. Sautéing is done at a lower temperature and for a shorter time than pan frying. Sautéing seals in and accentuates the flavors of foods.

**Scald:** When this term is used for milk or cream, it means to heat the milk or cream to just below the boiling point. When small bubbles appear at the edge of the pan and the milk or cream is steaming, remove it from the heat before it actually boils. When this term is used for fruits or vegetables, such as peaches or tomatoes, it means to put the food into boiling water, or to pour boiling water over them, to loosen their skins. In this context, scald means the same thing as blanch.

**Score:** To make shallow decorative cuts in the surface of a food such as meat or bread dough.

**Sear:** To brown meat on all sides using high heat. This seals in the meat's juices and produces an attractive surface. Then you finish cooking the meat by another method such as roasting or stewing.

**Season:** To flavor food by the addition of salt or spices.

**Shred:** To cut foods into narrow strips. Fruits and vegetables can be shredded by hand, with a grater or with the shredding disk of a food processor. Cooked meats are shredded by pulling them apart into strands using two forks.

**Sift:** To pass a dry ingredient, usually flour, through a metal mesh for the purpose of lightening the ingredient and/or removing lumps. Not many years ago, flour was always sifted before measuring it prior to making baked goods. Then the flour and other dry ingredients were also usually sifted together to mix them before adding them to the recipe. Now most recipes do not call for sifting the flour. Instead, just stir the flour with a folding motion to lighten and aerate it before measuring. Some dry ingredients, such as carob powder and buttermilk powder, should still be sifted to remove lumps before adding them to a recipe.

**Simmer:** To cook food gently in liquid that is just at or slightly under the boiling point in temperature. A simmering liquid has tiny bubbles breaking the surface, but is not at a full boil.

**Skim:** To remove fat or scum from the surface of the liquid, usually by spooning it off with a large spoon.

**Steam:** To cook over boiling water. Vegetables and fish are commonly steamed by placing them in a perforated metal basket over boiling water in a covered pan.

**Steep:** To soak dry ingredients in a liquid (usually a hot liquid) until their flavor is imparted to the liquid. Tea is made by steeping the tea leaves in boiling water. Ground coffee, herbs, and spices are also commonly steeped in hot or boiling liquid.

**Stew:** To cook food gently in liquid in a covered pan. The liquid should be just at the boiling point, gently simmering, rather than at a full boil.

**Stock:** The flavorful liquid found in the bottom of the pan after cooking meat, poultry, fish, or vegetables, or the liquid produced by cooking meat, poultry, or vegetables in water. Stock is the basis for all soups. The word "stock" is sometimes used interchangeably with the word "broth."

**Sweat:** To cook in a small amount of fat at a low heat, which releases the moisture from the food cooked. Vegetables are commonly cooked this way by oiling them slightly and covering them in foil or parchment paper, then placing them in a pan and tightly covering the pan. They soften without browning and cook in their own flavorful juices.

**Temper:** To heat gently and gradually. In candy-making, chocolate is tempered before dipping. In custard-making, hot milk is commonly added to slightly beaten eggs while whisking the eggs to raise their temperature gently so they don't curdle.

**Test:** Foods are tested for doneness by inserting a fork, knife, toothpick, or cake tester into them. To test fruits and vegetables, pierce them with a fork or knife and notice if they are still hard or if the utensil pierces them easily. To test baked goods for doneness, insert a toothpick or cake tester into them, remove it, and see if the tester is dry or has wet batter on it. The cake, quick bread, or muffins are done baking when the tester comes out dry.

**Toss:** To mix ingredients together, usually salad ingredients, with a light upward motion of the hands or of a fork and spoon.

**Truss:** To tie a turkey, chicken, or roast with string so that the cavity of the bird is closed or the roast holds its shape during cooking.

**Water bath:** A large pan of hot or boiling water that surrounds the food to be cooked. In canning, jars of food are placed in a boiling water bath for sterilization. When you are making custards, small bowls of custard are placed in a shallow pan of hot water and then baked in the oven. A water bath is also called a *bain-marie* in some recipes, which means water bath in French.

**Whip:** To beat rapidly, usually with an electric mixer or whisk, with the goal of incorporating air into the food that is being beaten, thus increasing its volume.

**Whisk:** A kitchen utensil formed of several wires looped on a handle in a teardrop shape. Whisk can also mean to beat with a whisk.

**Zest:** The colored outer layer of citrus fruits that is commonly used as a flavoring ingredient. The zest is the part of the peel that contains the flavorful citrus oils. A zester is a kitchen utensil that is composed of a handle attached a metal blade perforated with tiny sharp holes. When you draw a zester across the surface of a citrus fruit, it removes thin strips of the peel. You can also use a the small holes on a grater to remove the zest from citrus fruits if you are careful not to grate too deeply into the peel. The white part of the peel under the zest, which is called the pith, can be bitter.

# Moving-in Day:
## Equipping Your Dorm Room or Apartment Kitchen

Congratulations on acquiring your first apartment kitchen! (Or maybe your first dorm room!) Now what should you put into it?

Let's assume that your kitchen is already equipped with basic appliances such as a stove and refrigerator and that you have a kitchen sink. We won't discuss how to select these, but there are a few things you should know that will make it easier for you to live with them.

Ovens vary tremendously in their ability to achieve the right temperature and maintain it. You can experiment with your oven and see if the brownie recipe that worked fine in your mom's kitchen at home burns and needs to be cooked at a lower temperature in your apartment, or you can invest in an inexpensive oven thermometer, which will tell you what the temperature in your oven really is. If your apartment manager isn't interested in getting a repairman to fine-tune your oven, you can fiddle with the oven temperature dial until you know where to set it to get the temperature you want. Try to center the food you put in the oven so that it will receive heat from all sides. If your oven has four or five positions for the rack, use the second position from the bottom for baking.

Always broil with the door ajar in an electric oven. Having the door open keeps the heating element on during the entire time you are broiling. Another reason to leave the door open is that the glass in some oven doors may shatter if the heat is too intense, such as it is with broiling. For broiling, if your oven has four or five positions for the rack, use the second position from the top.

Never put metal of any kind in a microwave oven. If you see sparks inside when you start your microwave, open the door immediately and see where the metal is hiding. Some dishes and mugs have metal trim or writing on them which can cause this problem. If you are warming leftovers in a Tupperware™ type of container, be sure to loosen the lid to allow steam to escape before you put your food in the microwave. Never run your microwave oven when it is empty.

Your refrigerator should maintain a temperature of 40°F or lower for your food to be kept safely. It also needs to be able to chill foods in a reasonable amount of time. If you have any doubts as to how well it is working, put a thermometer on the shelf (a room thermometer will work) and check the temperature for yourself. If you put in warm leftovers and the temperature is not back to 40°F an hour later, your refrigerator may need more Freon or other attention from the repairman.

Kitchen sinks, especially those with garbage disposals, are prone to developing odor problems. This is because food may stick to or sit in the pipes and decay, and the smell of that process comes back out into your kitchen! Yuck! A way to remedy this problem is to fill your sink with hot soapy water. Fill both sides if you have a double sink. Pull the plugs from both sides at the same time and let the water run down the drain. If you have a garbage disposal, turn it off and on in bursts of a couple of seconds while the water is running down that side of the sink. This should dislodge any food that is sticking to the disposal blades. Then turn on the cold water and run the disposal for a couple of minutes after all of the water has run down the drain. Put a few tablespoons of baking soda in the drain hole on each side of the sink. Follow this with just a couple of tablespoons of water to get the baking soda down into the pipes. Allow your sink to stand this way, without running any more water down it, for an hour or so. If you have a garbage disposal, whenever you have lemon or orange rinds, be sure to grind them in the garbage disposal rather than throwing them out in the trash. They will help keep your disposal smelling sweet.

## Kitchen Equipment List

To begin cooking in your kitchen, you will need cookware and utensils to cook with and dishes and silverware to eat with. Your mom might have extras of many of the items you will need; go home and see what you can beg or borrow before you buy a lot of them for yourself. You can also hint at the items you'd like to receive for Christmas or birthday gifts while you're at home! If you shop at thrift stores or garage sales you may be able to find many of the items you need for a very low price.

**Tableware:** You will need dishes, glasses, silverware, and possibly a tablecloth. A set (it doesn't have to be matching) of four to six dinner plates, four to six salad or dessert plates, four to six bowls, four to six mugs or cups and saucers, silverware for four to six including two or three large serving spoons, and four to six glasses should keep you eating as long as you wash dishes daily. You will also need a salt shaker and a pepper mill or shaker. A couple of servings bowls, a butter dish, a creamer, a sugar bowl, and possibly some wine glasses might also be nice to have if you plan to have guests for dinner, but you can always use mixing bowls for serving and set the butter on a salad plate in a pinch.

**Cookware:** You will need some pots and pans. You can either buy cheap non-stick coated aluminum pans and plan on replacing them or invest in some good cookware that will last you the rest of your life. I have a set of Revere Ware™ pans that I have been cooking with for 25 years and my mother is still cooking with Revere Ware™ pans she purchased after she was married almost 60 years ago. Stainless steel and glass are the best materials for cookware. Do not cook acid foods in aluminum pans because the aluminum leaches out into the food and will end up in you! I personally avoid aluminum cookware altogether. In addition to the health issues surrounding aluminum, these pans tend to be so lightweight that they are less efficient at heating your food evenly and lead to burnt vegetables and pudding. Cast iron pans require more time and attention than most cookware. They cannot be washed in a dishwasher, and when you wash them, you must dry them quickly and thoroughly or they will rust. For basic beginning cookware, a medium-sized frying pan with a lid, two 2- to 3-quart lidded saucepans, and a large cooking pot with a lid should be enough pots and pans to get you cooking.

Lidded glass casserole dishes are an important addition to your kitchen equipment. They are essential for cooking in a microwave oven and for making casseroles cooked in a conventional oven. Casserole dishes can also double as serving dishes. Most of the microwave recipes and many of the oven recipes in this book call for a 2½ to 3 quart lidded glass casserole dish. A large glass or pyrex baking dish for chicken and other meats is also great to have. Get one that is 9 inches by 13 inches if you have room for it.

**Bakeware:** If you're going to learn to cook, the most fun is learning to bake! Plan to stock your kitchen with at least one or more cookie sheets (which you can use for cookies, pizza, biscuits, and rolls), an 8-inch square cake pan and/or a 13-inch by 9-inch cake pan, a loaf pan, and a muffin tin.

**General cooking equipment and utensils:** You will need some general cooking equipment for basic cooking. The items you will probably want to have include:

Mixing bowls: One 4-cup bowl and one 8-cup bowl will be enough to start with. They can also double as serving bowls.

Measuring cup(s) for liquids: These are glass or see-through plastic. One in a two-cup size should be enough to start with.

Measuring cups for dry ingredients: You will need a set of nested measuring cups in 1-cup, ½-cup, ⅓-cup, and ¼-cup sizes. A ⅛-cup measure is also handy to have. If your set does not come with a ⅛-cup measure, buy a coffee measure which is ⅛ cup.

Measuring spoons: Get a set with 1 tablespoon, 1 teaspoon, ½ teaspoon, ¼ teaspoon, and if possible ⅛ teaspoon sizes.

Mixing spoons: The large serving spoons from your silverware can double here. If you have non-stick pans, you will need plastic or wooden spoons to use with them to prevent scratches.

Rubber spatula – or possibly two – one large spatula and one small narrow spatula

Pancake turner type of spatula: Get a plastic one if you have non-stick pans.

Ladle for soup

Wire whisk

Potato masher

Knives: You will need a paring knife, a serrated knife long enough to slice bread, and a long chef's knife

Peeler for fruits and vegetables

Kitchen scissors

A timer if there is not one on your oven

Potholders

A cutting board: A glass or plastic cutting board is best because it can be thoroughly washed to disinfect it. Wooden cutting boards can harbor bacteria from raw meat and poultry and pass them on to other foods that will be eaten raw.

Strainer or colander

Roasting pan, such as a turkey roaster, and a meat thermometer if you plan to cook turkeys, roasts, or other large pieces of meat

Rolling pin if you plan to make rolled cookies or pies

Yeast thermometer if you plan to make pizza or bread

Manual or electric can opener

**Appliances:** Here's where you can run into money! However, there are a few kitchen appliances which are not terribly expensive that can make your life much easier. A crock pot is a real boon for busy young adults. You can start your dinner in the morning and leave it all day while you work or go to school. When you get home, your dinner will be all ready for you. It's almost as good as having Mom around, and your crock pot will not tell you what to do! A 3 quart crock pot costs $20 or less at a discount department store at the time of this writing or you may be able to get one at a thrift shop or garage sale for a few dollars.

In the recipes in this book, a hand blender substitutes for a mixer, food processor or blender. It can help you overcome the lumps in your first gravy or pudding, make low-fat yet thick salad dressings, and may be your best friend in the kitchen. A hand blender can be purchased at a discount department store for less than $20 and should be even less at thrift shops. An added bonus is that a hand blender takes up very little space in your kitchen.

Coffee drinkers may consider an electric coffee maker to be an essential kitchen appliance. Drip coffee makers are easy to use and maintain.

I consider an electric can opener an essential appliance because I can never get the manual ones to work! However, electric ones may be optional for strong young men.

If you like to cook big breakfasts, you may want an electric pancake griddle and/or waffle iron. Some waffle irons will open flat and have reversible grids so you can use them for pancakes as well. Electric griddles thermostatically control the temperature for you, which makes pancake-making much easier than when you are second-guessing your kitchen range.

If you're really getting into cooking and baking, you may want to ask for an electric mixer, blender, or food processor for your next birthday. A mixer is good for cake mixes, cookies and desserts. These appliances can be pricey and take up a lot of storage space, so consider how often you will use them. All of the dessert recipes in this book can be made with a spoon or a hand blender and do not require an electric mixer. A food processor is handy for chopping vegetables if you are cooking for several people but may be more work to clean than it is worth if you are cooking for only one or two.

A microwave oven is very convenient to have for warming leftovers and making quick meals. Kitchens usually have space for larger models than dorm rooms do. Read "Consumer Reports" magazine and buy a brand with a good repair reputation.

# *Dorm Room Equipment and Pantry List*

The most important items you will need in your dorm room if you intend to cook there are a microwave oven and a small refrigerator. Since most dorm rooms are small and you will probably share your room with a roommate, buy the smallest size appliance that is available but that will still be reliable and meet your needs.

You can do quite a bit of cooking in a small, 0.5 to 0.7 cubic foot oven capacity microwave oven. Be sure it will hold the 2½ to 3 quart casserole in which you will do most of your cooking. (This large-sized casserole is needed to prevent boil-overs in many of the recipes in the "Microwave Marvels" chapter). Small microwave ovens usually have about 700W of power; purchase one with at least 600W. Most microwave ovens made now come with a turntable which insures more even cooking of the food. You can get a good small microwave for less than $100 at a discount appliance store at the time of this writing.

The second appliance you may want for your dorm room, although it is not essential, is a small refrigerator. This will probably also cost you less than $100 at the time of this writing. Be sure to measure the floor space and height of the place where you intend to put the refrigerator in your room before you buy it so you can get one that will fit. When purchasing a small refrigerator, microwave oven or any other appliance (or making any major purchase in general) it is worth your time to go to the library and look up the most recent "Consumer Reports" article on the item you wish to purchase. Buy a brand that has a good repair record. If you have to pay a little more for it, consider it money well spent. Your quality microwave oven, refrigerator, or other appliance will probably last you longer and cause you less grief than some of the off-brands you see on special sales. Also, read the instruction booklets that come with your microwave and refrigerator before you begin using them and follow any grounding and safety guidelines given.

For a dorm room pantry and storage area for your cooking equipment, you may want to purchase an under-bed storage box which is at least six inches deep. The width and length of the box will be determined by how much food you plan to store in it. The cooking equipment and supplies you store in this box or your drawers and closet may include:

One large 2½ to 3 quart glass or pyrex casserole dish with a lid. Make sure the casserole is not too big for your microwave and will turn freely on the turntable.

One hard, dishwasher-safe plastic colander which will fit in the large casserole dish.

Measuring cup for liquid ingredients, 2-cup capacity, made of glass or pyrex if possible so you can cook in it

Measuring cups for dry ingredients: You will need a set of nested measuring cups in 1-cup, ½-cup, ⅓-cup, and ¼-cup sizes.

Measuring spoons, a set with 1 tablespoon, 1 teaspoon, ½ teaspoon, ¼ teaspoon, and if possible ⅛ teaspoon sizes.

Large spoons to use for cooking, one or two

Forks to use for cooking, one or two

Knives, at least one with a 5 inch or longer blade and a straight back

A glass plate, such as ceramic without metal trim or Corelle™, if you have time to wash dishes

Metal silverware, service for one or two, if you have time to wash dishes

Ceramic mug(s) without metal decoration

Soup bowl

Heavy potholders, at least three (two for your hands and one to set a hot dish on)

Can opener
Plastic wrap
Wax paper or parchment paper
Paper towel
Plastic silverware for eating
Paper cups which can be used for hot or cold beverages
Drinking straws for consuming breakfast smoothies on the run
Dishwashing detergent
Dishrags (disposable are most hygienic)
Dishtowel
Plastic bags and containers for food storage

The food you have in your dorm room pantry will vary with the recipes you plan to make and your own food preferences, but might include some of these items:

Dry pasta in medium-sized shapes, such as macaroni, ziti, sea shells, penne rigate, or mostaccioli
Tomato sauce, 8 ounce cans
Tomato paste, 6 ounce cans
Jarred pasta sauce (or if you're really Italian, bring some of Mom's frozen sauce from home)
Non-fat dry powdered milk or powdered goat milk
Evaporated milk, 5.5 ounce cans
Processed cheese in 8 ounce packages (or larger if you can refrigerate unused portions)
Grated Romano or Parmesan cheese – a small amount which you can use up quickly, unless you can refrigerate it for longer storage
Ghee (room temperature stable clarified butter)
Oil, preferably canola
Dried or canned beans, such as 15-ounce cans of kidney beans
Dried vegetable mix
Canned chicken and/or beef broth or bouillon cubes
Honey, Fruit Sweet™, or sugar
Cocoa or carob powder
Cornstarch or arrowroot
Beverage makings – tea bags (herbal or regular), instant coffee, Daco-pa™, cocoa mix, etc.
Oatmeal
Cold breakfast cereal, low-sugar or fruit-sweetened varieties from the health food store

Crackers, nutritious varieties
Microwave popcorn – a low-fat variety
Salt
Pepper
Small bottle of vanilla flavoring
Chili powder
Oregano
Thyme
Sweet basil
Dried minced onion

If you have a refrigerator, you should fill it with nutritious snacks, such as yogurt, fresh fruits and vegetables, dairy products, and ingredients that you will use soon for recipes in the "Microwave Marvels" chapter. Since your refrigerator will be small, you can't keep a lot of staples on hand all the time, but you might want to keep some fresh natural cheeses on hand for casseroles. If you're a microwave pizza fan, keep mozzarella, pepperoni, and a can of crescent roll dough on hand for pizza.

With these items in your dorm room or kitchen, you will be prepared to feed yourself well.

# Economics 201:
## Grocery Shopping

Now that you're ready to cook for yourself, you need to go out and get some food. This chapter will help you learn to grocery shop wisely and to safely store your food once you get it home.

There are three goals to keep in mind when you shop for food. They are economy, nutrition, and time. College students and young people on their own for the first time are usually low on cash and need to make the most of the money they have to spend on food. They want to eat healthily and get the most nutrition for their buck. And there is only so much time to cook! Here is some advice that will help you get the most from your food budget and your time.

Be organized and plan ahead. Once a week, read the newspaper grocery store advertisements. Choosing from the best sales, plan what you want to eat for the next week, and make a grocery list based on your menus. Stick to that list when you shop. Try to do most of your shopping in one weekly trip. Whenever you make a special trip to the store for just one item, you are likely to come home with a whole bag of groceries that you may or may not need. Keep a running list of things you are getting low on, and get them on your weekly shopping trip.

Always eat a meal before you shop. Never go to the grocery store when you are hungry. If you do, you will tempted to buy all the high-priced goodies which are so attractively displayed in prominent places. Buying these types of things on impulse will run your bill up without contributing much to your nutrition or to what you have in the house to cook for dinner.

Shop in the most economical store possible. Small specialty shops, like those within walking distance of many college campuses, tend to be high priced. If you can get to a large supermarket or a bag-your-own warehouse grocery store, you will save money. Learn what things cost and compare prices between stores. Sometimes the warehouse stores are more expensive on some items than a large supermarket is. Stock up on nonperishable items when you make a trip to a more economical store.

Try store brands. They are often as good as name brand items but cost a lot less. However, if you find that you have to use four sheets of a store brand paper towel to do the job that one sheet of Brawny™ can do, buy the Brawny™!

Think when you shop. Read labels and price tags. Is the economy-size box of detergent really a bargain? Are the store brand canned peaches cheaper than name brand? Divide the price by the number of ounces and see for yourself. Read the ingredient lists and nutrition labels on processed foods and skip foods that are not nutrient-dense or that contain partially hydrogenated oil or a lot of sugar.

To save time, do most of your shopping at one store and try to get everything on your one weekly trip. Learn the layout of your favorite store and have a plan when you walk in. Go down the aisles where heavy items are stocked first, such as the canned goods aisle, drink aisle, and detergent aisle. Then shop for other non-perishable items such as paper products before moving on to heavy perishable items, such as dairy products and frozen vegetables. Next pick up meat, poultry, and seafood. Shop for produce towards the end of your trip so you don't smash it in your cart by putting heavy items on top of your tomatoes! Finally, if you are going to buy ice cream, pick it up on your way to the checkout line.

Check freshness and expiration dates, especially on perishable items. Don't buy milk that will expire before you come back to the store next week if there is a newer carton sitting right next to it. If you buy yeast, check the expiration date and use it before it expires. Don't buy produce that is so soft you won't get it eaten before it rots. Throwing groceries away is not economical!

The rest of this chapter will discuss the differences between various foods and help you learn how to choose the best foods you can.

## Pantry Staples

With a well-stocked pantry you can survive almost anything. In an emergency situation (like final exams!) pantry staples will keep you from starving even if you can't make it to the grocery store.

Flour is an important staple to keep in your pantry. If you are not allergic to wheat, unbleached or all purpose flour can be used for almost anything. Unbleached flour and all purpose flour are both refined, meaning that many nutrients have been removed and only some have been added back in the fortification process. Unbleached flour is simply all purpose flour that has not undergone bleaching. It has a slightly darker color, which is quite acceptable considering that it contains fewer chemicals, and can be used in any recipe calling for all purpose flour. Whole wheat flour is also a good staple to keep around. It is very nutritious but can't be used in all types of baking. Baked goods made with whole wheat flour are denser and may not be as popular with your friends as baked goods made with unbleached or all purpose flour. Pastry flour is good for biscuits and pie crusts but you can get good results making these foods using all purpose or unbleached flour. Cake flour is for fragile cakes; the recipes in this book are all for more sturdy cakes and should be made with all purpose or unbleached flour. All purpose or unbleached flour will also work for bread. In fact, these are the best types of flour for pizza if you want to be able to stretch it out to fit your pan easily. However, if you are going to make bread often, especially with a bread machine, keep bread flour on hand. Bread flour has a higher gluten content than does all purpose or unbleached flour. (Gluten is the protein that makes the dough elastic and helps bread rise).

If you are allergic to only one or a few foods (mild food allergies not necessitating a rotation diet) and want to eat nearly "normal" food, the best flour to have in your pantry is white spelt flour. White spelt flour is spelt flour that has been sifted, removing the fibrous elements of the grain, but has not been bleached, bromated, or enriched like commercial wheat flours have. It is produced only by Purity Foods and is available from them or from some health food stores. (See "Sources," page 322). It is the best flour for making light and fluffy non-wheat yeast breads and other baked goods. If you use white spelt flour, "normal" people will not mind eating your food.

Whole spelt flour is also a good pantry staple for those who are allergic to wheat. I have found more variability in whole spelt flour than in any other kind of flour. The only brand that consistently produces good bread is Purity Foods flour. No, this is not an advertisement for a certain brand; I am not being paid to say this! But I do believe their claim that their flour is milled from a European strain of spelt which is higher in gluten and protein than most spelt because it behaves much better and predictably in baking than any other spelt flour I have used. When allergic people call me with baking problems and they are using spelt, the problem is almost always in the brand of flour they are using.

**Note about spelt:** A great deal of confusion has risen concerning spelt recently. The United States Government is now requiring that foods be labeled to indicate whether they contain any of eight food allergens. As part of the implementation of this law, the FDA has declared that spelt is wheat! Although spelt and wheat are indeed closely related, they are two different species in the same genus. Spelt is *Triticum spelta* and wheat is *Triticum aestivum*. When asked why they had decided that spelt is wheat, an FDA official said that it was because spelt contains gluten. (They had no answer to the question of whether rye would also be considered wheat because it contains gluten). Spelt does indeed contain gluten and should not be eaten by anyone who is gluten-sensitive or has celiac disease, but the presence of gluten does not make spelt wheat.

The gluten in spelt behaves differently than the gluten in

wheat in cooking. It is extremely difficult to make seitan from spelt. When making it from wheat, a process of soaking in hot water is used to remove the starch from the protein. If the same process is followed with spelt, the protein structure also dissolves in the hot water. Spelt seitan must be washed by hand very carefully under running cold water.

Because the gluten in spelt is more soluble than wheat gluten, making yeast bread with spelt is also different than making it with wheat. The individual gluten molecules join up more readily to form long chains and sheets that trap the gas produced by yeast. This means that it is possible to over-knead spelt bread. There are some bread machines that work quite well for wheat and even other allergy breads but are unacceptable for spelt bread because they knead so vigorously that they over-develop the gluten.

It is possible that the greater solubility of spelt protein makes it easier to digest than wheat. Undoubtedly, most people have had much less prior exposure to spelt than to wheat resulting in less opportunity to become allergic to spelt. Whatever the reason, there are many people who suffer allergic reactions after eating wheat but do not react to spelt. (I have talked to hundreds of them). Restricting one's diet unnecessarily, as the new law will undoubtedly lead people to do, is counterproductive to good nutrition. Consult your doctor about your own food allergy test results and follow the diet recommended for you, but do not unnecessarily restrict spelt consumption based on faulty government labeling requirements.

If your food allergies are more severe, you should rotate your diet and keep a large variety of flours and grains on hand. Cooking for severe food allergies is beyond the scope of this book. Use this book to learn the basics of cooking and get *The Ultimate Food Allergy Cookbook and Survival Guide* (see the last page of this book) for a rotation diet and recipes that will fit the diet.

Other grains you might like to keep in your pantry include rice, barley, cornmeal, oatmeal, and popcorn. Brown rice is very nutritious and tasty. If you are not rushed on cooking time, brown rice is your best choice for a rice side dish. White rice has had most of the nutrition removed and only part of it added back in the fortification process, but it cooks more quickly than brown rice does. Barley is a great addition to soups. Cornmeal makes good corn bread and polenta. Popcorn is a great snack and is low in fat and salt if you make it "from scratch." And oatmeal is a great breakfast cereal, as well as a nutritious, high-fiber addition to cookies and other baked goods. If you have food allergies, you will probably also want to keep whole spelt, kamut, and other grains around for side dishes.

Other grain products that are good pantry stock include pasta and ready-to-eat cereals. Avoid most grocery store cold cereals; they are loaded with sugar. Make an occasional trip to the health food store and buy fruit sweetened cold cereals if you want them for breakfast. Quick-cooking or instant oatmeal, cream of wheat, and cream of rice are great hot breakfast cereals. If you have allergies, you can find other cereals such as cream of buckwheat or cream of amaranth at health food stores. Pasta is another handy pantry staple. With pasta in your pantry and a few canned items, you can whip up a main dish based on pasta whenever the mood strikes. Keep some spaghetti, macaroni, and sea shell pasta around on a regular basis. Buy some no-boil lasagne pasta when want to make a special meal.

A starch of some kind is a useful ingredient to have in your pantry for when you need to thicken pies, puddings, and sauces. If you do not have allergies, cornstarch is cheap and easy to find. If you are allergic to corn, choose tapioca flour or arrowroot instead. Minute, or granulated, tapioca can also be used to thicken pie fillings, puddings, and stews. For thickening salad dressings, pancake syrup, and sauces without cooking them, Quick Thick™, which is a type of cornstarch, is fantastic. To purchase this, see "Sources," page 324.

Leavening ingredients are essential pantry staples for baking. When you buy baking powder, be sure to choose a brand such as Rumford™ which does not contain aluminum. Most baking powders contain cornstarch. If you are allergic to corn, buy Featherweight™ brand which contains potato starch instead. (See "Source, page 320). If you are allergic to potatoes or are on a rotation diet and do not want to include them in your diet on a daily basis, you can leaven baked good with a combination of baking soda and unbuffered vitamin C powder or crystals instead of baking powder. The recipes in *The Ultimate Food Allergy Cookbook and Survival Guide* are all leavened without the use of baking powder. If you need such recipes, see the last page of this book.

Baking soda is also used to leaven non-yeast baked goods. You may want to keep more than one box of baking soda around because you can use it to absorb odors in the refrigerator, pour down your sink or garbage disposal to make it smell good, and also for general household cleaning.

Yeast does not always go in the pantry for long-term storage but is included here with other leavening agents because it is an essential baking supply if you want to make yeast leavened baked goods. If you make an occasional loaf of bread or pizza, buy individual packets of yeast at your grocery store. Store these packets in the refrigerator. However, if you bake often, it is most economical to purchase your yeast in bulk. SAF instant yeast is very economical; it can cost as little as $3.95 for a whole pound of yeast and is vacuum sealed so it can be stored in the pantry until it is opened. Once you open the package, put a little of the yeast in a jar in the refrigerator and store the rest in the freezer. When your jar is empty, do not allow the frozen yeast to thaw, but instead just pour some into the jar and put the rest back into the freezer. You can make many, many loaves of bread with just $4 worth of yeast if you treat your yeast this way.

Sweeteners are also usually stored in the pantry. The most common sweetener in the American pantry is sugar. The recipes in this book do not contain sugar. Therefore, if you will make only these recipes, you don't need sugar. However, your pantry will contain Fruit Sweet™ (or equivalent sweeteners made by the same company such as Pear Sweet™ or Grape Sweet™) or honey to use in desserts instead. Fruit Sweet™ can be stored at room temperature until it is opened. After that, put the jar in the refrigerator. Honey can be stored in the pantry even after it is opened. Other sweeteners you will find in a sugar-free pantry include date sugar, which is ground dried dates, and Fruit Soure™, a dry granulated fruit and rice sweetener. Frozen fruit juice concentrates can also be used to sweeten desserts, but you will keep them in the freezer, of course! In addition to containing fructose rather than sucrose, some fruit sweeteners are lower in calories for the amount of "sweetness" delivered. Fruit Sweet™, Pear Sweet™, and Grape Sweet™ are sweeter than sugar yet have 30% fewer calories. They also contain fiber and minerals which have been refined out of table sugar. (See pages 42 to 45 for information about blood sugar and weight control). These sweeteners have been featured in the American Dietetic Association's catalogue for use by people with diabetes.

Some oils and fats can be stored in your pantry. However, if you have room to store them in your refrigerator, they will keep longer before they go rancid. The best oil for cooking with moderate or high heat, such as sauteing, is olive oil because it does not break down or become a "damaged fat" when heated. Ghee, or clarified butter, can be stored at room temperature in your pantry and is another good fat for cooking with high heat because it is a saturated fat. Use an oil high in essential fatty acids such as canola oil or walnut oil for salads, serving on cooked vegetables, and baking. Flax oil is the best nutritional oil for providing essential fatty acids and also can be used in salad dressings. Since it is quite fragile, keep it in the refrigerator.

Dry beans are essential residents of a well-stocked pantry. Keep some kidney beans for chili, black beans, lentils, or split peas for soup, and small white beans for making baked beans.

Other items you may want to stock in your pantry include unsweetened baking chocolate, cocoa or carob, coffee, tea, raisins and other dry fruit, unsweetened coconut, carob or chocolate chips, non-fat dry milk or dry goat milk (for when you run out of fresh milk and want to make bread or pudding), cooking wine, vinegar, and seasonings such as salt, pepper, cinnamon, nutmeg, cloves, ginger, vanilla extract, basil, oregano, thyme, bay leaves, chili powder, dry mustard, and paprika.

# Canned and Aseptically Packaged Goods

Having your pantry well stocked with canned goods can save you many an emergency trip to the grocery store. Canned and aseptically packaged products can be stored at room temperature until you open them. After opening, transfer any leftovers to a glass jar or plastic lidded container and put them in the refrigerator. Do not buy canned goods if the ends of the cans are bulging, indicating that the contents are fermenting, or if the can is dented. The fall that dented the can may have broken the seal that preserves the food.

Fruit-juice packed canned fruits are delicious and can be great additions to any meal or the makings of a great dessert. If you want to make an apple crisp in the blink of an eye, keep some water-packed canned apples such as Mussleman's™ apples in your pantry. Read the ingredient list on the fruit cans before you purchase them, and avoid those with added sugar.

Fresh and frozen vegetables are usually tastier than most canned vegetables, but keep a can of corn and a can of french cut green beans around for when you would like to make "Pantry Pasta Casserole" on page 172 or 233. With only pantry ingredients and a little cheese, you can whip up this casserole for a great meal when your refrigerator is empty and you don't have time to go to the grocery store. As with fruits, read the ingredient list on the vegetable cans before you purchase them and avoid those with added sugar.

Tomato products are essential pantry staples. Stock up on diced canned tomatoes, tomato sauce, and tomato paste when they are on sale and have them on hand at all times for casseroles and pizza. When you plan to make spaghetti sauce or lasagne, buy tomato puree. Many people like to keep jarred pasta sauces in their pantry because these sauces can be used to whip up a quick meal. Since our family is Italian, we make our own sauce and keep it in the freezer. Don't let that discourage you, though, from stocking a little pasta sauce in your own pantry!

Canned dried beans are very useful pantry staples. Keep a couple of cans of kidney beans on hand to make chili in a hurry, or keep a variety of beans for side dishes such as three bean salad. Many brands of canned beans contain sugar. Read the can labels; some of the natural or organic brands such as Westbrae™ brand are sugar-free.

Canned broth or bouillon cubes are nice to have in your pantry. Many bouillon cubes contain sugar or MSG. Natural canned broths take up more space but are preferable health-wise to use in casseroles and as bases for other soups. Canned soups are used as base ingredients for casseroles in many "easy" cookbooks. However, they contain such a plethora of chemicals and are so high in salt that it is usually best to leave them in the store and make your own sauces with a little natural canned broth and flour.

Condiments such as mayonnaise, pickles, catsup, and mustard are essential residents of your pantry if you like hamburgers or hot dogs Choose a fruit-juice sweetened catsup such as Westbrae™ brand. Salsa makes a nutritious snack with no-fat corn chips and is a great addition to tacos.

Keep some sandwich fixings in your pantry such as natural peanut butter and all-fruit jam or jelly so you can make a peanut butter and jelly sandwich when you don't have time to cook. If you are allergic to peanuts or just like variety, try cashew, almond, or other natural nut butters; they are a great source of nutritious essential fatty acids. If you like fish salad sandwiches, keep a couple of cans of tuna or salmon around too.

Canned milk and processed cheese are not "the best" but might be things you could keep in a dorm-room pantry where you don't have a refrigerator. Canned milk, processed cheese, and macaroni can be made into macaroni and cheese and can save the day if you're snowed in and have an empty refrigerator. However, processed cheese contains aluminum and should be used only when you cannot use natural cheese.

## Dairy Products

Unless you are allergic to cow's milk, don't bypass the dairy section of your grocery store when you go shopping. Milk is a great source of calcium and protein and, according to Dr. Leo Galland, is not the food "villain" that some have made it out to be. But unless you are a football player during playing season, you may not need the extra calories and fat that whole-fat dairy products contain. Choose 2% or skim milk, low fat cottage cheese and sour cream, and part-skim natural cheeses. Check the expiration dates on dairy products before you buy them, and don't be shy about picking out the freshest carton of milk! All dairy products and eggs should be kept refrigerated at all times.

Natural cheese is an important recipe staple which you will regularly bring home from the dairy section of the grocery store. Cheddar and jack cheese are great to have on hand for sandwiches and casseroles. Keep some grated Romano or Parmesan cheese on hand for pasta or pizza. Grated mozzarella is nice to have on hand when you get the urge to make some pizza. It keeps well in the refrigerator until you open the bag. It also can be stored in the freezer for a long time. Just take it out of the freezer an hour or so before you plan to use it. That's about the time you will start making your dough, and is long enough for the mozzarella to be semi-thawed and ready to throw on your pizza.

Butter is another good food to pick up from the dairy case of your store. It is a safe fat for cooking with moderate or high heat. Instead of margarine, which contains unhealthy trans fats, use butter or EFA-butter (recipe on page 142) for a spread. (See pages 23 to 25 for more about the health advantages of butter and EFA-butter over margarine). Some dairy-sensitive people can tolerate butter, and even more can tolerate ghee, which is butter with the milk solids removed. If you must use margarine due to allergies, chose Earth Balance™ margarine, which does not contain trans fats. (See "Sources," page 322).

The most important food to take home from the dairy section of your grocery store is yogurt. Fermented milks such as yogurt, kefir, and fully fermented acidophilus milk are milk in its most allergically tolerable, digestible, and absorbable form because the milk is partially predigested by the organisms that ferment it. Fermented milks are high in B vitamins and vitamin K. Most importantly, they contain beneficial bacteria that stimulate our immune systems and protect us from the effects of antibi-otics and other chemicals that are part of modern life. Be sure to buy yogurt that contains live cultures of bacteria; pasteurized yogurt should be avoided. If you wish to avoid sugar, buy plain yogurt and stir in your own fruit. However, if you need something to grab as a quick breakfast or snack, choose the brand of fruit yogurt that is lowest in refined sweeten-ers.

If you are allergic to cow's milk, visit a health food store for goat's milk, yogurt, butter, and cheese, sheep's yogurt and cheese, or soy milk, yogurt, and cheese. Making your own yogurt or acidophilus milk from alternative milks is a worthwhile investment in your health. For recipes for fermented milks, see *The Ultimate Food Allergy Cookbook and Survival Guide* as described on the last page of this book.

Eggs also have made a comeback from their recent dietary "villainy." If you plan to use eggs in mayonnaise, Caesar salads, or other recipes where they are not fully cooked, purchase pasteurized eggs which at the time of this writing are available only in certain areas. (See "Sources," page 321, for Davidson's Pasteurized Eggs). If you do not find these eggs at your gro-cery store, call Davidson's and ask where they can be purchased in your area. If you cannot get pasteurized eggs or have been told by your doctor to avoid eggs due to the cholesterol in them, use egg substitutes such as Egg Beaters™ for baking and for making great mayonnaise. However, these substitutes contain egg whites and can contain milk or milk deriva-tives, corn derivatives, wheat gluten, or other common allergens, so many people with food allergies cannot use egg substitutes.

Eggs come in a variety of sizes and colors but their size and color have no effect on their nutritional value. The baking recipes in this book will work best if made with large eggs.

# Bread and Baked Goods

You are probably too young to remember when every kitchen had a bread box. Way back when I was a kid, we used to store homemade bread at room temperature, and, before plastic bags, the bread box kept bread from drying out. Room temperature is still the best storage condition for homemade yeast breads and baked goods. If you have some great hard rolls and don't want them to lose their crisp crust, a properly-functioning breadbox is an ideal place to store them. However, recently it has become harder to find good breadboxes designed for correct moisture content in storage rather than decorative purposes. See *Easy Breadmaking for Special Diets* (as described at the very end of this book)for current breadbox recommendations.

At our house we store loaves of bread in plastic bags because we like a soft crust on bread for sandwiches. The King Arthur Flour Baker's Catalogue sells polyethylene-lined paper bags to use if you don't have a bread box and want your baked goods to retain their crispy crust. Homemade breads also store well in regular plastic bags in the freezer.

The storage of store-bought bread is another story. Due to the chemicals it contains, commercial bread is probably already not really fresh when you buy it. Store it in the refrigerator.

Crackers, cookies, and bakery products are best stored at room temperature. A metal tin is a great place to store cookies. The exception to the "room temperature" rule for bakery items is pastries like eclairs or cream-filled doughnuts. These fillings can spoil, so store such pastries in the refrigerator.

# Meat, Poultry, and Seafood

Animal products can spoil easily so pick them up near the end of your grocery shopping trip and get them home and into the refrigerator as soon as possible. Go for freshness when you buy them; check the expiration date if you purchase them in packages. In a supermarket with a service counter, you may be able to smell your meat, poultry, or seafood before you purchase it to check for freshness, but in most stores you will buy it in a package. If is smells spoiled when you open the package at home, return it to the grocery store.

Look at the color of meat when you buy it. Beef should be a deep, bright red with no brown spots or dried edges. Lamb, pork, and veal should be pink. Buffalo, venison, and game meats should be dark red. The fat on all meats should be white, not yellowish or gray. Ground meat is usually graded by the amount of fat it contains. Meat with more fat may or may not be cheaper in the long run because you pour the fat off when you cook it. Use fresh meat within three days or freeze it. Thaw frozen meat in the refrigerator rather than at room temperature. If you defrost it in the microwave, cook it immediately because parts of the meat will be warm and susceptible to bacterial growth.

Choose poultry that looks bright colored and wholesome. Chicken usually has yellow skin. The skin of most other birds is near-white. The skin should not look dried out. Much poultry is purchased frozen. Thaw it in the refrigerator before cooking it. Large birds, like turkeys, can take several days to thaw in the refrigerator. If you're in a hurry, put your turkey in a sink of cool water for a few hours. Check the bird often by feeling the breast for sponginess and change the water several times. When your turkey is thawed, refrigerate it until it is time to cook it. If there is still ice in the cavity when you are ready to cook it, that is all right. Just remove it when you rinse the body cavity. You cannot defrost a turkey in a microwave oven, even if it will fit in the oven. It is too big to allow the middle to thaw before some parts of the bird are actually cooking. If you thaw a smaller bird in the microwave, cook it immediately. Be sure to remove the giblets from the body and/or neck cavity of your bird before cooking it. Finally, rinse out the body cavity and remove any tissue pieces with your hands before cooking the bird.

Fish is the trickiest animal product to buy. If you live far from an ocean, fish that was frozen shortly after being caught and that you buy frozen may be your best bet. In inland areas, what is sold as "fresh fish" often was frozen and then thawed in the store before being sold. If you have access to actual fresh fish, look for bright eyes rather than cloudy eyes. Shellfish should have tightly closed shells. Fish is highly perishable, so only buy fish that the store received the day you go shopping. Ask the butcher when the fish came in, and if the answer to your question is "yesterday"or earlier, don't buy it. Try to cook the fish the same day you buy it. Waiting one day is all right if you must, but don't wait any longer. If you purchase frozen fish, get it into your freezer as soon as you get home. Thaw it in the refrigerator on the day you want to cook it.

## Frozen Foods

Some frozen foods can save you a lot of time. Frozen vegetables can be much easier and quicker to get to the table than fresh vegetables. If they were frozen shortly after being picked, and the fresh vegetables in your store were shipped many miles and stored for days before you buy them, the frozen vegetables may even contain more nutrients than fresh vegetables. However, locally grown fresh vegetables in season are worth the extra preparation effort when you have time. See the next section for how to choose fresh produce. Frozen fruits, such as berries, are great to stir into yogurt or make into a pie when these fruits are out of season.

Fruit juice concentrates are also great time savers. Frozen orange juice is much quicker to make than freshly squeezed juice. It can also be more nutritious than refrigerated orange juice which has been stored for days. Other fruit juice concentrates are nice to have on hand for juice or to use as a sweetener in baking. If you wish to bake with fruit juice concentrate tomorrow, just set the can in the refrigerator to thaw overnight. If you want to bake now, open the can, pour the juice into a pan, and heat until it is just thawed. Or put it in a microwave safe container or measuring cup and defrost it in the microwave. Don't overheat it either way. It should be cool or at room temperature when you bake with it. If it is hot, it may speed up the leavening process and lead to dense baked goods.

Frozen bread dough is good to have on hand for pizza or if you wish to serve hot bread to guests. However it is so easy to make your own yeast dough or bread, and homemade is so much superior in taste and quality, that you should read pages 242 to 243 and consider making your own bread or pizza dough instead of using frozen dough.

## *Fresh Produce*

Here is what to look for when you shop for common fresh vegetables and fruits. Most vegetables and fruits should be stored in the bins at the bottom of your refrigerator. If your bins have humidity controls, set them to "high" humidity for vegetables and "low" humidity for fruits. Unripe fruit should be stored on the kitchen counter until it ripens. Avocados also should be left at room temperature until they soften and then should be used soon. Potatoes, onions, and garlic should be stored in a cool, dry place, not in the refrigerator..

If you want information about less common vegetables like Jerusalem artichokes and okra, refer to *The Joy of Cooking*. (See "References," page 317). If you are on an allergy diet and want to eat "exotic" vegetables such as fennel, arugula, plantain, taro, or yucca, see *The Ultimate Food Allergy Cookbook and Survival Guide* as described on the last page of this book.

**Apples** should be firm and smooth-skinned with no brown or soft spots. If you bruise them on the way home from the store, a brown spot won't hurt you. Just cut it out before you eat the apple. Apples are best in the fall and may be mealy at other times of the year. Apples may be refrigerated or, if you buy them by the box and don't have that much refrigerator space, kept in a cool, dry basement or porch. My grandpa used to bury apples from his tree in a newspaper-lined hole in the ground to keep them throughout the winter.

**Artichokes:** Look for plump, compact globes. Dark or purple spots on the outer leaves are normal, but the inner leaves should be green. Pull the leaves apart a little so you can look down between them to see the inner leaves. You get more "meat" from larger artichokes, so try to pick the biggest ones. They're usually all the same price (at my store they're sold by "each" rather than by weight) so larger ones are a better buy.

**Asparagus:** Look for bright green spears of medium thickness with firm tips. Very old asparagus will be dull colored and may be getting limp or mushy at the tips. Thicker spears are more flavorful – give them a try. Very thin spears are quite tender but blander in flavor. Extra-long spears are not a great buy because you will break off the woody end before cooking them, and with long spears you just end up throwing more away. Asparagus is very perishable so use it within two to three days of buying it.

**Avocados** are usually purchased hard. Set them on your kitchen counter for a few days to soften. They are ready to eat when they yield to gentle pressure when squeezed. Avocados come in two varieties – thin skinned bright green Fuerte avocados or thick skinned dark green to black Haas avocados. Both are equally nutritious. Avocados are high in vitamins and also in fat, but it is "good" fat. When you cut an avocado open, it will turn black almost immediately. Rub the cut surface with lemon juice, or buy smaller Haas avocados and eat the whole avocado at one sitting.

**Bananas** should be kept at room temperature because they will turn black in the refrigerator. They are green when unripe but will ripen in a few days sitting on your kitchen counter. They are sweetest and best for eating when they are covered with small brown spots. If they turn completely brown and are overripe before you eat them, make banana bread with them or peel them, cut them into chunks, and freeze them to use in smoothies.

**Beans – green or wax:** Look for bright green (or yellow for wax beans) pliable but not limp pods. If they are large, you may want to pull out the strings before cooking. Avoid discolored or shriveled beans or super-large beans which may be pulpy and tough. Since beans are quite perishable, wait until you are ready to cook them to wash them. Cook them within three days of purchasing them.

**Beets:** Look for beets with fresh, unwilted tops and firm, smooth roots. They should be deep magenta in color. The more colorful they are, the more flavorful, usually. Smaller beets are more tender than large ones. Beets keep well in the refrigerator.

**Berries** such as strawberries, raspberries, and blueberries are some of the most delicious treats you will find in the produce section of the grocery store. They are quite perishable and may be expensive, so choose bright colored, plump, firm berries. Don't buy them if they have soft spots or are mushy or moldy. Refrigerate them for only a day or two before you use them.

**Broccoli:** Buy broccoli that is dark green. Avoid bunches that are turning yellow – these are very old. Broccoli with very thick stems is more mature and the stems may be tough. The little balls at the ends of the broccoli florets are actually seeds, which makes broccoli one of the most nutritious of the dark green vegetables. You can store broccoli in a plastic bag in the refrigerator for several days.

**Brussels sprouts:** Look for bright green sprouts with dense, compact heads and no blemishes. You can store Brussels sprouts in a plastic bag in the refrigerator for several days.

**Cabbage – red or green:** Look for firm heads that are heavy for their size. The outer leaves should be free from brown spots, cracks, or bruises. Sometimes green cabbage is sold with many of the outer leaves removed to reveal the inner, lightly colored leaves. The darker leaves contain more nutrients, so if you can find a darker head, buy it. Store in a plastic bag in the refrigerator for up to a week.

**Cabbage – Savoy, Napa, or Chinese:** These cabbages have frilly, leafy leaves. The leaves should not be wilted or blemished. Store in a plastic bag in the refrigerator for up to a week.

**Carrots:** Carrots should be very firm and crisp. Don't buy them if they're getting limp. The darker orange they are, the more beta-carotene they contain, and the more flavorful they are usually. Very large carrots may be woody, so buy small to medium sized, nicely shaped carrots. You can store carrots in the refrigerator for several weeks. If they get limp, just use them in soup or stew.

In our area, some supermarkets have recently begun selling organic carrots for the same price as conventionally raised carrots. A Rutgers University study showed that organic produce offers the advantage of a higher mineral content[1] and the absence of pesticides, but with carrots your can even taste the difference. Organic carrots are much sweeter than conventionally raised carrots. They are also usually much more vividly colored, indicating a higher level of beta-carotene.

**Celery:** Look for crisp stalks without brown spots or blemishes. The white, inner stalks have the best flavor, so if you can get a bunch with more white and less green, choose it.

**Cauliflower:** Look for tightly closed heads with dark green outer leaves. If the ends of the florets are getting black or brown spots, the heads are getting old. However, this happens so quickly with cauliflower that it may happen in your refrigerator if you don't cook what you buy right away! In this case, just trim off the dark spots; they won't hurt you. You can store cauliflower in a plastic bag in the refrigerator for several days.

**Corn:** Look for bright green firm ears of corn with light-colored tassels. Pull down the top of the husk on each ear and check for brownness or worms before purchasing. Corn with very large kernels may be less sweet than corn with smaller kernels. The kernels may be white or yellow. Corn is sweetest when very fresh. If you can purchase it from a farm stand and cook it immediately, do so. You can store corn in the refrigerator for a few days, but it tastes better if you eat it sooner. My grandmother used to put the cooking water on to boil BEFORE she picked corn for dinner; that's how fresh she thought it had to be to taste its best.

**Cucumbers:** Look for firm, dark green cucumbers. Avoid yellowish cucumbers and those with soft ends or mushy spots. You can keep cucumbers about ten days in the vegetable bin of your refrigerator.

**Greens – beet tops, Swiss chard, chicory, collards, escarole, kale, or mustard greens:** These are the most nutritious vegetables around; give them a try! Look for brightly colored or dark green leaves. Smaller leaves indicate younger greens which are more delicately flavored. The leaves should not be wilted. You can store greens for two or three days in the refrigerator.

**Eggplant:** Look for dark purple, glossy, smooth-skinned eggplant without any mold on the cap or stem. Avoid eggplant with rust spots or blemishes. Chose an eggplant that feels heavy in your hand and is the right size for its intended use. You can keep eggplant for up to one week in the refrigerator.

**Fennel** is a celery-like vegetable that has a bulbous root end and a faint licorice taste. Select firm white bulbs without blemishes and with unwilted leafy tops. Fennel is a real treat raw but also can be cooked. It will keep in the refrigerator for several days.

**Garlic:** Chose firm heads without any black rust spots. Avoid heads that contain dried out cloves. (Cloves are the small individual sections that make up a head of garlic). Garlic should be kept at room temperature in a cool dry place and will keep for several weeks.

**Grapes** are available year round now. They come from South America during the winter and may contain large amounts of pesticides at that time of the year. Chose grapes with fresh looking stems which are not rotten or discolored. The grapes should be solidly attached to the stems. They will keep for several days in the refrigerator before you wash them. Wash them right before eating them.

**Kohlrabi:** At our house, kohlrabi has been called the vegetable from outer space because of its unusual appearance. It tastes great raw or cooked, so give it a try! Small and medium sized bulbs have the best flavor and texture; very large bulbs may be woody. Look for smooth bulbs with no blemishes. Keep kohlrabi in the refrigerator for up to a week.

**Leeks:** Look for white bulbs and crisp green tops. Smaller bulbs are the most tender. Leeks will keep for several days in the refrigerator.

**Lemons** should have smooth, shiny skins without blemishes. Thin-skinned ones will yield the most juice. Avoid soft lemons or those with soft spots. Lemons will keep in the refrigerator for a few weeks.

**Lettuce:** Lettuce comes in many varieties; try some of the ones that are new to you! Iceberg lettuce contains the least nutrition. When purchasing lettuce, look for firm heads that are heavy for their size. Avoid heads with rusty outer leaves or stems. Leaf lettuce should be dark green or reddish brown. Pick heads with brightly colored leaves that are not wilted. The more darkly colored the leaves are, the more nutrition they contain. Lettuce will keep in the refrigerator for several days. Wash leaf lettuce in several changes of cool water in the sink to remove all dirt. Dry it with a salad spinner or by laying it on a paper towel on your kitchen counter. Washed and dried lettuce is best stored in perforated plastic bags. Zippered perforated bags recently disappeared from the market, but tie-top perforated bags are available from the King Arthur Flour Baker's Catalogue. (See "Sources," page 323). Tupperware™ makes lettuce storage containers that will keep washed and dried lettuce in great condition.

**Limes:** Look for limes with smooth, unblemished skins without brown spots or soft spots. Heavier limes will give you more juice. You can keep limes in the refrigerator for up to a month.

**Melons – cantaloupe, honeydew, Crenshaw, Persian, etc.:** These can be tricky to pick. Feel the ends of the melon; they should give slightly but not be soft. Smell the melons also. The most fragrant ones are usually the sweetest. However, don't buy melons that smell yeasty or spoiled. Keep underripe melons on the kitchen counter for a few days to ripen. Once they are ripe, you can refrigerate them for two to three days.

**Mushrooms:** Look for clean, firm, tan to light brown caps which are closed around the stem. Do not buy mushrooms that are soft and limp; they are getting old. Avoid excessively dirty mushrooms. Unwashed mushrooms will keep up to a week in the refrigerator. Right before you will cook them, rinse them under running water.

**Nectarines and peaches** are some of the most delicious summer fruits. Shop for and store them in the same way. Nectarines are somewhat sturdier than peaches, bruise less easily, and will keep longer. Get golden yellow to red nectarines or peaches with pink or red tones on the skin. When they are ripe, they will smell good and give a little when squeezed. Store under-ripe nectarines and peaches on the kitchen counter until they ripen. Once ripe, they will keep in the refrigerator for about a week.

**Onions:** Look for firm onions with papery skin. Avoid those that are starting to sprout. They may be white, yellow, or purple in color. Purple

(Bermuda) onions are best for salads. Peel onions under running water to avoid tears. Store onions in a paper bag in a cool, dry place at room temperature for up to a month.

**Oranges** come in several varieties. In the winter, you can get seedless navel oranges; juice or Valencia oranges are available year-round. Look for oranges which are heavy for their size and without soft spots. If the skin is smooth and shiny, there is more orange and less peel, although thick-skinned oranges can also taste good. Oranges will keep in the refrigerator for several weeks.

**Parsnips:** Look for firm unblemished parsnips. Avoid those that are not firm or are very large. Very large parsnips may have woody centers. Parsnips will keep in the refrigerator for about a week before they get limp.

**Pea pods, Chinese:** Look for crisp, bright green pods that are not too large. Avoid limp or yellow pods. These are very perishable so try to use them the same day you buy them.

**Peas:** Look for crisp, bright green pods with medium-sized peas in them. Very large peas may be woody and less sweet than smaller ones. Don't buy limp or yellow pods. Remove the peas from the pods by squeezing the end of the pod in to snap it open and then breaking the peas free from their stems with your finger. Since peas are very perishable, try to use them the same day you buy them or the next day.

**Peppers:** Look for firm, shiny, bright colored peppers. Avoid those with soft spots, bruises, or wrinkles. Bell peppers may be green, red, yellow, or orange. Red bell peppers are the sweetest. There are also many varieties of hot peppers. Ask the produce clerk to help you pick a pepper of the right degree of heat for your intended use. Peppers can be stored in a paper bag in the refrigerator for up to two weeks.

**Pineapples:** To choose a ripe pineapple, squeeze the fruit gently. It should yield slightly to the pressure. Smell it too and see if it smells delicious and sweet but not yeasty. Avoid pineapples with soft or rotten bottoms. Once pineapples are picked from the plant, they will not ripen any more, so buy them ripe and eat them within a day or two. Store your pineapple in a plastic bag in the refrigerator until you are ready to eat it. You can twist the top off before you put it in the refrigerator. However, if you have a lot of space, it's all right to leave the top on. When it's time to eat the pineapple, lay the pineapple on its side on a cutting board. Use a sharp knife to take a slice of the spiny outer skin off the bottom of the pineapple. Then set the pineapple upright on its flat-sliced bottom on a cutting board and cut down from the top to the bottom, slicing off the skin, and making successive cuts moving around the pineapple. When the sides have been peeled, set it on its side again and take a slice off the top to remove the skin there. Cut the pineapple in half and then in quarters lengthwise and remove the core. Pineapple is a fair amount of work to peel. If you live inland where fresh pineapples are not that great, just buy canned pineapple packed in its own juice.

**Plums** are summer fruit. While they may be available in the winter, usually the price is high and the quality is low then. Choose brightly colored plums that yield slightly to pressure but are not too soft. If you buy them underripe, store them in a paper bag on the kitchen counter until they ripen. Then refrigerate them for up to a week.

**Potatoes, sweet:** Look for firm, smooth potatoes with unblemished skins. Brown spots may be the beginning of decay. Store them at room temperature in a cool, dry place. Sweet potatoes get moldy easily so use them within a week or two after purchase.

**Potatoes, white:** Choose potatoes that are firm and large. (It's less work to peel a pound of potatoes if they are large). Avoid potatoes that have a greenish cast under their skin, are soft or starting to shrivel, have moldy or soft spots, or are starting to sprout. White potatoes may have thin red skins or brown skins. The red skinned ones, including very small ones, are usually used for boiling and may be served without peeling. Brown skinned potatoes such as russets are best for baking, but they also make great mashed potatoes. Store potatoes in a paper bag in a cool (best if it's about 50°F), dry place. If it is very cool in their storage spot, they will keep several weeks. If it's warm, they may start sprouting in a week or two. When they begin to sprout, just break the sprouts off and use the potatoes soon. Don't store potatoes in the refrigerator or they will turn brown when cooked. To wash them, scrub them with a brush or scrubbing pad under running water.

**Radishes:** Choose medium-sized or small radishes that are firm and unblemished. Very large radishes can be tough and very hot in flavor. Radishes will keep well in a plastic bag in the refrigerator for a week.

**Spinach:** Look for brightly colored or dark green leaves. Smaller leaves indicate younger greens which are more delicately flavored. Spinach with medium-sized leaves is also good and can be less work to clean and wash. The leaves should not be wilted or yellow. Spinach with huge leaves will be tough and strong-tasting. Wash spinach in several changes of water. It can be quite sandy and take lots of washing to remove all of the dirt. If you don't have time to wash spinach, you can buy it pre-washed in plastic bags. Store unwashed spinach in a plastic bag in the refrigerator for two to three days. After washing it, if you want to use it for salad, dry it with a salad spinner or by laying it on paper towel on your kitchen counter. Washed and dried spinach is best stored in perforated plastic bags. Zippered perforated bags recently disappeared from the market, but tie-top perforated bags are available from the King Arthur Flour Baker's Catalogue. (See "Sources," page 323). Tupperware™ makes lettuce storage containers that will keep washed and dried spinach in great condition for several days after washing. Don't miss out on this great salad vegetable and source of nutrition!

**Squash, spaghetti:** Look for dark yellow colored squash with hard rinds. Buy squash that are heavy for their size – you get more spaghetti and less seeds. Avoid spaghetti squash with blemishes or soft spots. Just rinse squash before baking them. Store spaghetti squash in a cool dry place. It will keep for weeks or even months.

**Squash, summer (zucchini, crookneck, etc.):** Look for firm, glossy squash that are heavy for their size. Crookneck squash often has brown spots; pick the ones that are the brightest yellow with the least number of spots or no spots, if possible. Avoid squash with soft spots or bruises. Small or medium-sized squash are more flavorful than very large summer squashes which can be woody. Store summer squash in a plastic bag in the refrigerator for up to five days.

**Squash, winter (Hubbard, acorn, butternut, etc.):** Look for firm squash which are heavy for their size, have no soft spots, and have hard, tough rinds. If the squash is cut (Hubbard often is), look for dark orange flesh. Acorn squash with yellow or orange patches on the skin may have been ripened on the vine longer than all-green squash and may be a little sweeter. Avoid winter squash with bruises, soft spots, or gouges. Store whole squash at room temperature for one or two weeks. Store cut squash in a plastic bag or plastic wrap in the refrigerator for 3 to 4 days before cooking it. If you have a cool dry place to store whole winter squash from a garden, they can last for months.

**Tangerines:** Look for bright orange tangerines with bright orange, smooth, loose skin and no bruises. Heavier tangerines are juicier than light ones. Some varieties are seedless. Tangerines can be stored in the fruit bin of your refrigerator for a few weeks.

**Tomatoes:** Look for heavy tomatoes with dark red skins, no bruises, mold or soft spots, and a texture that gives a little but is not mushy to the touch. Roma tomatoes are often a good buy and very flavorful. Slightly underripe tomatoes will ripen on the kitchen counter. When they are ripe, use them immediately or refrigerate them for up to three days. If you cook tomatoes, use a little oil because the oil helps you to better utilize the antioxidants (specifically the lycopenes) in the tomatoes.

**Turnips and rutabagas:** Look for globes that are smooth and firm. Smaller ones will have a milder taste. Soft turnips and rutabagas may be old. Keep them in a plastic bag in the refrigerator for up to a week.

## Footnotes

1. McHerron, Elena, "Eating Organic Means More Minerals," *Organic Living,* Volume 57, Late Spring, 1996, page 6.

# Time Management 203

Learning to manage your time effectively is an important skill that applies to all areas of life. If you are on your own for the first time, up until now your parents, teachers, and other adults in your life may have been making sure you got up on time, got to school on time, knew when you needed to be someplace, and transported you there. These same adults may have also imposed their values of good nutrition on you, if only by not bringing a lot of junk food home from the grocery store and preparing you healthy meals. Now that you are on your own, you are in charge of your own time and your own diet.

Our lives and our health are the greatest gifts we have; it is "good stewardship" to value and protect them. Our lives are made up of small increments of time. We each have only 24 hours in each day, and we have a finite number of days, so we must learn to use our time wisely. Time is of greatest value if you are healthy enough to use it productively. You must get enough sleep and good nutrition to be optimally healthy. If you are reading this book, you have probably realized that your health is important and that eating junk food all the time is not optimal nutrition. You have already begun to set some priorities that are the basis of good time management and optimal health.

Budget your time like you budget your money. Make a list of your goals and then budget your time so you can meet those goals. Staying out late and eating junk food occasionally can fill the goal of having good relationships with your friends, but if done too often these things can interfere with the goals of being a good student or responsible employee and maintaining good health. You must decide which things are most important to you and then use your time wisely to reach these goals.

After you have set your goals, how do you go about using your time to fulfill them? Get organized! Buy a calendar with big squares for each day in which you can write your schedule or a notebook such as a DayRunner™ and use it to record everything you need to do and when you need to do it. Look at it daily or several times a day so that you do not forget anything. When your calendar starts getting too full, make some hard choices and eliminate those activities that are least important to reaching your goals. Do not over commit yourself to the extent that you start missing sleep.

Feeding yourself nutritiously does not have to take a lot of time. If you eat out in "sit down" restaurants regularly, you may spend more time eating out than you would spend cooking and eating at home as well as spending more money for your meals. You can feed yourself nutritiously and economically and do the other things you need to do as well. It's all a matter of planning and organization.

Once a week, plan your menus. To save money, do this while reading the weekly grocery advertisements so you can plan to use the best buys in your meals for the next week. Shop once a week at a familiar store so you don't have to spend time looking for things. If you can shop at an "off" time when the store is not crowded, you will be able to zip up and down the aisles and have a short wait in the check-out line.

Make the best use of your appliances. For some things, like cooking pasta, a conventional stove cooks more quickly than a microwave oven. If you are cooking a large meal, cook some of it in the microwave and some conventionally to save time, rather than cooking dishes one after another in the microwave. Oven meals are great to make when you will be spending the afternoon at home studying. Just put all the components of the meal into the oven and let things cook while you work. For oven vegetable and side dish recipes, see pages 204 and 209 to 213. Put a roast, ham, or chicken into the oven with these dishes, and you will have a complete meal. A week's worth of sample oven meal menus is found at the end of this chapter.

Make good use of your crock pot. Peel vegetables and prepare other ingredients for the crock pot in the evening, and in the morning before you go to school or work just throw them in the pot and start it cooking. When you get home, add a salad, bread, and some fruit and you will have a great meal.

The best way to save time is to make large batches of main dishes and freeze the leftovers in individual serving sized portions. You may have noticed that most of the recipes in this book are not for one or two servings. That is because as long as you are going to do the work of cooking a meal, you may as well make that work count for several meals.

I asked our nephew recently if he cooked for himself much. He said he cooked occasionally but then ended up eating the leftovers for several days in a row. This is *not* the way to make a large batch of an entree serve for several meals for many reasons. The most obvious is that if you make a batch of stew on Saturday and intend to eat it for several meals, by Tuesday you will be so tired of it that you can't face it, and you will stop for fast food on the way home instead. Another reason to avoid eating this way is because the best nutrition comes from eating a variety of foods, not eating the same foods day after day.

Here is an example of a plan for cooking ahead and freezing meals. On Friday make a large batch of chili and freeze the leftovers in individual portions. You will be able to take out leftovers once a week for a month or more. On Saturday make a large batch of soup or lasagne (or both) and freeze the leftovers in individual portions. The next weekend make stew and a casserole or two. After doing this for a few weekends, you will have a variety of small meals in your freezer so you don't have to repeat any of them more than once a week. Reserve most of your freezer space for these meals. There's no need to keep several flavors of ice cream, a dozen packages of vegetables (buy just enough for the week on your regular weekly shopping trip), or anything that you will probably never eat. To save freezer space, freeze the meals in zippered plastic bags, clearly labeled with the contents and date, or in rectangular containers. If your freezer meals are packaged in uniformly sized and shaped containers, you can get a lot of them into the top freezer section of a conventional refrigerator. Cook on the weekends and take things out of the freezer on the weekdays. You will eat healthily and save a lot of time and money.

Organize your kitchen for efficiency. Put the silverware and dishes near the table, if possible. Put the utensils you use for cooking near the stove. Group similar types of ingredients together in an organized fashion so you don't have to spend a lot of time looking for something when you want to cook.

Keep your cooking and your life simple. What is important is not always what you do but who you are. Who you are and your character will be reflected in how you do whatever you do. Especially when entertaining, remember that people are important. Feed your guests something simple and take time to talk to them and enjoy their company. Use food as a tool to build relationships because relationships are what life is all about. Your friends will not remember how fancy the food you prepared was as long as they will remember what kind of a person you are and how welcome they felt in your home.

# Oven Meal Menus

*Serve each of these menus with a tossed salad and bread if desired.*

## Sunday's Roast Beef Dinner:

Beef Roast, p.156
Baked Potatoes, p.200
Oven Carrots, p.209
Easy Fruit Tapioca made
  with peaches, p.265

## Monday's Easy Pork Dinner:

Pork Chop and
  Rice Dinner, p.160
Oven Cabbage, p.209
Baked Apples, p.266

## Tuesday's Oven Chicken Dinner:

Oven Fried Chicken, p.162
Oven Millet, p.205
Oven Beans, p.210
Easy Fruit Tapioca made
  with cherries, p.265

## Wednesday's Pepper Steak Dinner:

Pepper Steak, p.158
Oven Brown Rice or
  Barley, p.204
Oven Carrots, p.209
Baked Pears, p.266

## Thursday's Easy Lamb Dinner:

Lamb Roast, p.156
Oven Brown Rice, p.204
Baked Winter Squash, p.201
Baked Pears, p.266

## Friday's Company Best Ham Dinner:

Baked Ham with Pineapple, p.297
Scalloped Potatoes, p.213, or
  Baked Sweet Potatoes, p.199
Oven Peas, p.210
Easy Fruit Tapioca made
  with cherries, p.265

## Saturday's Cabbage and Hot Dogs Dinner:

Oven Cabbage and
  Hot Dogs, p.163
Baked Potatoes, p.200
Baked Apples, p.266

# Entertaining 205

By the time you have read this far in this book and have made some of the recipes, you will have taught yourself a valuable new life skill – cooking! Now it is time to consider sharing the fruits of your labors with people you care about. As Marion Cunningham said in the April, 2001 *Saveur* magazine, "Coming together at the table is a reminder that you are part of something bigger than yourself. You are exposed to ... (people) ... in a very real way, sitting at a table, facing one another. It's a metaphor for life....Nothing seems to bring people closer together than the act of sharing food." When you cook for your friends or family, you give yourself and your love to them in a very real, tangible way.

The goal of cooking for and sharing a meal with others is to build relationships. Today's families are so busy that time is often at a premium, but try to let mealtimes be unhurried and keep the conversation pleasant. When you cook for guests, you should pay more attention to the guests than to the food. Do as much of the food preparation as possible before they arrive. Keep the menu simple and consider serving foods which can be prepared ahead of time so you can spend your time enjoying the company of your guests. They will remember being made welcome more than they will remember a difficult-to-make dish which you served.

Never try a new recipe when you are having guests – always make things that you have made more than once before. Even with old familiar recipes, you are bound to have a "flop" when you cook for company occasionally. Don't be too upset about it yourself, and your guests will not be either.

Make as many "do-ahead" dishes as possible. Lasagne, page 308, is very impressive and can be made ahead of time so all you have to do on the day of your party is put it in the oven. Bake the dessert and mix the salad dressing ahead. If you want to make a "show stopper" recipe such as a very tricky sauce or a flaming dessert, only do ONE per party.

Plan your menu carefully. Think about colors and textures and strive for contrast. Your guests may fall asleep if you serve them white fish, mashed potatoes, and cauliflower! If you are serving a buffet dinner which your guests will eat sitting in your living room without benefit of a table, make sure the food is pre-cut. Serve casseroles rather than a roast which must be cut with a fork and knife.

Write the menu out and refer to it often as you are preparing for your party. I have more than once served a meal to guests and then discovered a salad I forgot to serve hiding in the refrigerator. It is helpful to include beverages and condiments on your menu list as well so you don't forget to make the coffee or put out the butter.

Inventory your recipe ingredients, supplies, and serving pieces a day or two ahead of the party, especially the first few times you have company. This will help you avoid last minute trips to the grocery store and ending up with more foods to serve than you have serving dishes. If you're using "real" silverware, check it a week or so before your party so you have plenty of time to polish it if necessary.

Don't forget the ice. Make a good supply of ice cubes a day or two before your party and store them in plastic bags in the freezer.

When you cook for a really large crowd, it may be better to make several double or triple batches of your favorite recipes than to multiply the recipe by 10 or 12. For some unknown reason, just multiplying often does not work for quantity cooking. In addition, you may not own pans and bowls big enough to mix up a 10 or 12-fold batch.

Finally, remember that your family is the most significant group of people for whom you will ever prepare a meal. The "important" guests from work or school whom you have over a few times may not even remember you a few years from now. However, spouses, children, parents, and siblings are the most important people in your life. What you do for your family and how you treat them on a routine basis can influence them – and you – for the rest of your lives.

## What To Cook?

What should you feed your guests? That depends on how many guests you will have and who they are. If your college roommate is coming to visit alone, make pizza and take him or her into the kitchen with you while you prepare it. Maybe the two of you can work together while you talk. If you're having 20 people to dinner in a small apartment, you should probably serve buffet-style, and your guests can sit and eat anywhere they can find a spot. A sit-down, family style dinner is good for a group of four to eight people, or as many as your table will seat.

Here are some ideas for parties. Each menu consists mainly of foods which can be prepared ahead of time so you can relax and enjoy your guests' company. Don't let these menus limit you – any dinner from this book can be served to guests. Just keep it simple, especially the first few times, and plan ahead.

# Menus for Entertaining

## Easy Breakfast for Guests

Having overnight guests and feeding them breakfast in the morning does not have to be a lot of work. You can enjoy their company early in the morning if you plan ahead and make the French toast the evening before you plan to serve it. Pop the bacon into the microwave while the French toast is in the oven.

Make-ahead French Toast, page 116
Blueberry Pancake Syrup, page 113, or Fruit Sauce, page 115
Microwave Bacon, page 122
Fresh fruit
Beverages such as orange juice, coffee (page 294), and tea (page 294)

## Sweetheart Dinner for Two

This menu is for that special girl or guy. When I was a girl we were told, "The way to a man's heart is through his stomach." I think it works both ways! Today's young women are very impressed by a man who can cook. Sometimes you can buy sweetheart steaks for Valentine's Day, which are two rib eye steaks joined in the center to form a heart shape. If not, any high quality steak will do.

Broiled Steaks, page 157
Baked potatoes, page 200, with sour cream and/or butter
Broccoli, page 187 or other green vegetable
Dinner rolls, page 262, muffins, pages 244 to 247, or biscuits, page 247
    to 248, with red jelly or raspberry jam
Caesar Salad, page 312
Strawberry shortcake, page 269. If you have a heart-shaped cake pan or
    can buy a foil heart-shaped pan, use it to bake the shortcake for a
    romantic dessert.
Beverages

# Saint Patrick's Day Feast

Crock Pot Corned Beef Dinner, page 217: Cook the carrots and pota-
toes in the crock pot with the meat and cook the cabbage separately
in the oven.
Oven Cabbage, page 209
Make Ahead Tossed Salad, page 311
Biscuits, pages 247 to 248
Chocolate Cake, page 278
Beverages

# Easter Oven Dinner

*Make the sauce, muffins, pie, and salad ahead of time, put the rest of the
dinner in the oven, and enjoy your guests! Use this easy meal for other occasions as well.*

Baked Ham, page 297
Cherry Sauce, page 115
Scalloped Potatoes, page 213
Oven Peas, page 210
Blueberry Muffins, pages 244 to 247
Make Ahead Tossed Salad, page 311
Apple Pie, page 270, or other dessert
Beverages

# Graduation Gala

*This is great for a "just family" graduation party of several to a dozen peo-
ple. You can make the lasagne a day or two ahead and refrigerate it, or make
it a week or two before your party and freeze it. Move it from the freezer to the
refrigerator the day before your party. If you're feeding a large crowd, see the
next menu below.*

Lasagne, page 308, made ahead
Italian beans: Buy frozen beans and cook them (directions on page 184)
right before your guests arrive.
Dinner Rolls, page 262
Make Ahead Tossed Salad, page 311
Graduation cake: Get one from the bakery with the student's name on it,
or make Carrot Cake with cream cheese frosting, page 279, if you
want to avoid sugar.
Beverages

# After-Event Reception

*Serve this menu for a large graduation party or a reception after a wedding. The menu can come completely from the store and is good for a large crowd. If you have more money than time you can have the meat, cheese, and relish trays prepared by your grocery store or delicatessen.*

Breads, several varieties, sliced
Cold cuts including ham, turkey, roast beef, and luncheon meats
Cheese of several varieties, sliced
Mayonnaise, mustard, or other sandwich spreads
Relishes such as carrot sticks, celery sticks, radishes, olives, etc.
Potato chips and/or corn chips
Coffee
Punch
Bakery sheet cake

# July 4th Picnic

Hamburgers cooked outside on the grill, page 129, or hot dogs boiled in
     a large pot on the kitchen stove, page 131
Hamburger or hot dog buns: Buy these at the store or make them using
     the recipe on page 261
Catsup, mustard, pickles, lettuce, sliced tomato, pickle relish, and
     whatever other condiments you enjoy
Crock Pot Baked Beans, page 226
Potato chips or Potato Salad, page 139
Relishes such as carrot sticks, celery sticks, radishes, olives, etc.
Ice cream and cookies: The cookies can come from the bakery or be made
     using any of the recipes on pages 283 to 289
Cold beverages

# Chili Supper For a Crowd

Economy Chili For a Crowd, page 220.
Toppings for the chili such as grated cheese or sour cream
Dinner Rolls, page 262 or buy rolls at the store
Apple Crisp, page 266
Beverages

# Make-Your-Own Pizza Party

*Make the pizza dough to be risen and ready when your friends arrive. Have your guests make individual pizzas in cake pans, or use a pizza pan for two people, with each person embellishing half of it with their chosen toppings. Then enjoy each other's company while the pizza bakes.*

Pizza Dough, page 178 or 179
Pizza Sauce, page 178
Toppings: Mozzarella cheese, Romano or Parmesan cheese, pepperoni, cooked ground beef, olives, mushrooms, sliced green peppers, onions, and whatever else your guests may like. (I once served this for a birthday party for children, and one of the kids asked, "Do you have any pineapple for the pizza? Sure enough, we had some!)
Make Ahead Tossed Salad, page 311
Spumoni ice cream from the store or Pineapple Sorbet, page 264
Beverages

# Pasta Dinner

*Spaghetti is not a "do-ahead" dish, but you can have the vegetables ready to go and everything else prepared in advance.*

Spaghetti or Mostaccioli with "Pasta Sauce with Meatballs," page 304: Make the sauce a week or two ahead of the party and freeze it. Move it from the freezer to the refrigerator the day before the party.
Italian beans, green beans, page 184, or other green vegetable. Cook the vegetable right before your guests arrive and reheat it at dinner time.
Cloverleaf Rolls, page 262
Make Ahead Tossed Salad, page 311
Baked Pears, page 266.
Beverages

# Crock Pot Roast Beef Supper

Crock Pot Roast, page 216.
Potatoes and carrots cooked with the roast
Natural juice from the roast
Spinach Salad, page 133
Dinner Rolls, page 262, or buy them at the bakery
Brownies, page 288, or Oatmeal Bars, page 287.
Beverages

# Cozy Cold Weather Buffet

*Put your crock pot on the buffet table to keep this meal warm for second helpings.*

Crock Pot Stew, page 220, or any hearty crock pot soup, pages 221 to 226
Dinner Rolls, page 262, or get them from the bakery
Make Ahead Tossed Salad, page 311
Any fruit cobbler, page 268, still warm from the oven. Prepare the cobbler
    right before your guests arrive and have it baking while they eat
    dinner.
Whipped Cream, page 281, or vanilla ice cream to serve
    on top of the cobbler
Beverages

# The Little Bird Dinner

*This is almost as impressive as the big bird dinner but a lot less work.*

Stuffed Cornish Hens, page 302
Oven Beans, page 210.
Baked Potatoes, page 200, or Sweet and Spicy Rice, page 208 (optional)
Make Ahead Tossed Salad, page 311
Blueberry Pie, page 270
Beverages

# The Big Bird Dinner

*Wait until you've had guests a few times to cook this meal, and if you can recruit your mom to come over and help, do so! Make the stuffing the day before Thanksgiving or the "big occasion" and have it ready to go into the oven in a casserole dish. Make the sweet potatoes a day ahead and reheat them most of the way in the microwave; pop them into the oven to "finish" when the turkey is resting. Let your guests bring the salad, relishes, and maybe even the pie. You can do it! Go for it!*

Roast Turkey, page 298
Gravy, page 299.
Bread Stuffing, page 300
Mashed Potatoes, page 214
Broccoli or other green vegetable, page 187
Oven Sweet Potatoes, page 212 (optional)
Dinner Rolls, page 262, or buy them at the bakery
Cranberry Sauce, page 301
Relishes such as carrot sticks, celery sticks, pickles, olives, etc.
Make Ahead Tossed Salad, page 311
Pumpkin Pie, page 273
Beverages

# Recipes

The previous chapters were a lecture course. Now it is time to put your knowledge into action in the "lab" section. The rest of this book is your "lab manual" and contains recipes to help you cook in a healthy, nutritious way. The next two pages explain how to use the nutritional analysis figures in this "lab manual."

A nutritional analysis is included with each recipe in the following chapters. Please use these analyses to guide your food choices by comparing a recipe with another recipe from this book or with the "Nutrition Facts" label on a similar commercially prepared food. Do not become consumed with counting calories or grams of fat. Avoid the fallacy of thinking that calories are all that count for weight control, especially since counting calories is much more likely to drive you crazy and waste your time than to result in permanent weight loss. (See pages 42 to 45 for more about this and about weight control in general).

Diabetics, however, are an exception to the "don't count" rule. If you are diabetic, follow the diet plan your doctor or nutritionist has prescribed and eat the proper number of diabetic exchanges at each meal or snack. It is vitally important that you balance your food intake with your insulin intake or production and your energy expenditures.

You may remember learning about significant figures in your general science class. When you performed a laboratory exercise, your final answer was only as "good" as or only had as many significant figures as the numbers from which the answer was calculated. Just as in that science class, the numbers given in the nutritional analyses of these recipes are derived from data that may not be exact. There may very well be variations between the ingredients you use and those that were tested to get the data on which the nutritional calculations were based. For example, a freshly picked organic carrot will contain much more of the vitamin A precursor beta-carotene than a conventionally grown carrot that has been sitting in cold storage for several months. Therefore, nutritional analyses should be taken as approximations.

In some of the recipes, the nutritional analyses are also approximate because you are given ingredient choices or because the ingredient amount is given as a range. When such choices exist in a recipe in this book, the nutritional analyses were calculated* using the first ingredient given in a list where there is a choice, the first amount given when there is a range in the amounts you might use, and with any optional ingredients omitted.

*Note: The nutritional analyses of the recipes in this book were calculated using Food Processor for Windows, Version 7.7, by ESHA Research, Inc., P.O. Box 13028, Salem, OR 97309.

In most cases, the recipes have been divided into servings in a way that yields close-to-whole numbers of diabetic exchanges with the total number of exchanges per serving adding up to a number of calories which is very close to the number of calories provided by one serving of the recipe. The diabetic exchanges have been "rounded" to the nearest whole number or simple fraction whenever possible. This is consistent with the significant figure concept and also makes these recipes easier for diabetics to use in their diets. For an example of this rounding process, consider the "Barbecue Sauce" recipe. The computer program figures that one serving of barbecue sauce, or the amount that would be used in one barbecued beef sandwich, is 0.39833 other (not bread/starch) carbohydrate exchange, 0.633 fruit exchange, and 0.12268 vegetable exchange. Your science teacher would tell you that, given the accuracy of the nutritional data that was used to make this calculation, there is no way that we have the accuracy in the number of exchanges implied by five significant figures! Therefore, the exchanges for one serving of barbecue sauce given in the recipe are ⅓ other carbohydrates exchange and ⅔ fruit exchange.

The mathematically-minded reader may be adding together numbers from some of the sub-categories of nutrients on the nutritional analyses and wondering what the main categories in the nutritional analyses include. The total fats figure includes monounsaturated fats and polyunsaturated fats as well as the three individual fat categories which are listed. The individual types of fat that are listed in the nutritional analyses are essential fatty acids, or omega-3 fatty acids and omega-6 fatty acids, and saturated fats. The total carbohydrates include sugars. These sugars may be – as they are in this book – healthy sugars such as fructose or lactose in milk products. On the nutritional analyses on packages of commercially prepared foods, this category includes refined sugars as well as natural sugars. All types of vitamin A are lumped together in the nutritional analyses. Both preformed vitamin A, or retinol, and beta-carotene, which is a precursor of vitamin A, are put together and listed as Retinol Equivalents (RE). Both soluble and insoluble fiber are included in the amount of fiber listed in the nutritional analyses.

It is not an oversight that this book does not contain a table listing the recommended daily allowances (RDA) of the various nutrients listed in the nutritional analyses. Since each person's need for various nutrients is a very individual matter, these tables are of little value. The RDA tables imply that you should add up, for example, the vitamin A in all the foods you consume in a day's time and compare that total to the RDA for vitamin A. Instead, just choose the most nutrient-dense foods you can find.

You may need considerably more than the RDA of many nutrients, and it is nearly impossible to get too much of any vitamin or mineral from food sources.

Now you're ready to cook with the recipes that follow. Use the nutritional analyses to maximize your intake of the nutrients you need. Go for it! Have fun learning the skill and art of cooking and, best of all, enjoy eating whatever you make.

# Breakfasts

Mom was right when she said, "Breakfast is the most important meal of the day." After you've been sleeping all night, breakfast is the meal that "breaks your fast" and gives you energy for the day. If you don't eat breakfast, your blood glucose levels may be low all morning, making it difficult to concentrate. Educational experts agree with Mom – the Iowa Breakfast Studies showed that children who ate breakfast did better on standardized tests.

Skipping breakfast is not a good way to lose weight. Eating breakfast "jump starts" your metabolism so you actually burn calories faster in general if you are a regular breakfast eater. A Mayo Clinic study showed that breakfast eaters start their day with a higher metabolic rate than breakfast skippers. This results in burning an extra 150 calories every 24 hours.[1] Furthermore, people who skip breakfast tend to make up for it by eating more later in the day. If you find that eating breakfast makes you hungrier, it is because your body has been overcompensating to make up for habitually not eating breakfast. Keep eating breakfast for two weeks and this hunger problem will disappear. As a regular breakfast eater, you will be better able to control your appetite throughout the day.

As good for your health as breakfast is, don't fall into the trap of thinking to yourself on a regular basis, "Breakfast will help me lose weight; I'll just drive into this fast food restaurant for a breakfast sandwich." In this situation, your breakfast is likely to be so high in calories and saturated fat that it's almost a toss-up as to whether some breakfast is better for your weight control than none. Sugar-laden cold cereals also might be worse for you than no breakfast at all. The sugar high they can cause may lead to mid-morning low blood glucose and a lack of energy, poor concentration, and the inability to resist unhealthy mid-morning snacks. If you like cold cereal for breakfast, make yourself a big batch of homemade granola, page 109, on the weekend or buy fruit-sweetened cold cereals at a health food store.

Breakfast doesn't have to be complicated or take a lot of time to make. If you don't have time to cook on work or school days, but do have time for a breakfast that requires chewing, keep natural nut butters on hand and spread them on a bagel or English muffin. They'll give you a good dose of protein to keep up your strength all morning long and will help you resist the mid-morning doughnuts. If you're in too much of a rush to take time to chew, try "On the Go Smoothie," below. A low-calorie, protein-rich, high energy breakfast such as this smoothie or a bagel with nut butter really *will* help you control your weight.

# On the Go Smoothie

1 8 ounce carton of low fat fruit yogurt
1 straw
-OR-
1 cup low fat plain yogurt (cow, soy, goat, or sheep)
¼ to ⅓ cup fruit, pureed
1 tablespoon Fruit Sweet™ or honey (optional)
1 straw

If you are using the fruit yogurt, simply shake or stir it until the yogurt is thin, put the straw into it, and take it along to drink on the way to work or school.

If you are using the plain yogurt, puree the fruit with a hand blender. Add the yogurt and optional sweetener and blend until smooth. You can even use baby food fruit, which is already pureed for you, and just stir a half jar or whole jar into plain yogurt. The whole purpose of mixing the yogurt and fruit yourself is to avoid sugar, so read the jar label and be sure you're getting unsweetened baby fruit. Put in your straw and take off! Makes one serving.

**Nutritional Analysis per serving:** 1 serving per recipe
**Made with commercial low fat fruit yogurt:**

| | | |
|---|---|---|
| Calories: 258 | Total fat: 3.45 g | Calcium: 414 mg |
| Protein: 12 g | Saturated fat: 2.23 g | Magnesium: 40 mg |
| Carbohydrate: 46 g | Omega-3 fatty acids: 0.03 g | Potassium: 530 mg |
| Sugars: 46 g | Omega-6 fatty acids: 0.07 g | Sodium: 159 mg |
| Fiber (total): 0 g | Cholesterol: 13 mg | Iron: 0.2 mg |
| Vitamin C: 2 mg | Vitamin A: 37 RE | Zinc: 2 mg |

Diabetic exchanges: 1 serving equals 1 low fat milk exchange, 1 fruit exchange, 1 other carbohydrate exchange

**Made with plain low fat yogurt:**

| | | |
|---|---|---|
| Calories: 181 | Total fat: 3.83 g | Calcium: 449 mg |
| Protein: 13 g | Saturated fat: 2.45 g | Magnesium: 45 mg |
| Carbohydrate: 24 g | Omega-3 fatty acids: 0.03 g | Potassium: 619 mg |
| Sugars: 23 g | Omega-6 fatty acids: 0.08 g | Sodium: 173 mg |
| Fiber (total): 1 g | Cholesterol: 15 mg | Iron: 0.3 mg |
| Vitamin C: 3 mg | Vitamin A: 41 RE | Zinc: 2 mg |

Diabetic exchanges: 1 serving equals 1 low fat milk exchange, 1 fruit exchange

# Banana Breakfast Smoothie

*This is a good way to use up those over-ripe bananas. Just peel them, break them into chunks, put the chunks in a plastic bag, and pop them into the freezer. They'll be ready for breakfast when you are.*

1 cup (1 8 ounce carton) low fat plain or fruit yogurt (cow, soy, goat, or sheep)
1 frozen banana, cut into chunks
½ cup milk
1 to 2 tablespoons Fruit Sweet™ or honey, to taste
        (optional, but nice to have with plain yogurt)
1 teaspoon vanilla (optional)

Put all of the ingredients into a 4-cup measuring cup or the cup that came with your hand blender. Hand blend – or blend in a blender or food processor – and drink. Makes one large or two small servings.

**Nutritional Analysis per serving:** 2 servings per recipe

| | | |
|---|---|---|
| Calories: .........................153 | Total fat:.............................2.29 g | Calcium:...........................303 mg |
| Protein:............................9 g | Saturated fat: ...............1.41 g | Magnesium:...................45 mg |
| Carbohydrate:................25 g | Omega-3 fatty acids:...0.04 g | Potassium: ....................621 mg |
| Sugars: ..........................23 g | Omega-6 fatty acids: ..0.07 g | Sodium: ..........................118 mg |
| Fiber (total):......................2 g | Cholesterol: .....................9 mg | Iron: ................................0.3 mg |
| Vitamin C:........................7 mg | Vitamin A:.........................62 RE | Zinc: ...............................1 mg |

Diabetic exchanges: 1 serving equals 1 low fat milk exchange, 1 fruit exchange

# Berry-Orange Breakfast Smoothie

1 cup (1 8 ounce carton) low-fat plain or fruit yogurt (cow, soy, goat, or sheep)
1½ cups frozen unsweetened strawberries, blueberries, raspberries, or blackberries
½ cup orange juice
2 to 4 tablespoons Fruit Sweet™ or honey, to taste
    (optional, but nice to have with plain yogurt)

Put all of the ingredients into a 4-cup measuring cup or the cup that came with your hand blender. Hand blend – or blend in a blender or food processor – and drink. Makes one large or two small servings.

**Nutritional Analysis per serving:** 2 servings per recipe

| | | |
|---|---|---|
| Calories: .........................143 | Total fat:.............................2 g | Calcium:...........................247 mg |
| Protein:............................7 g | Saturated fat: ...............1 g | Magnesium:...................41 mg |
| Carbohydrate:................25 | Omega-3 fatty acids:...0.05 g | Potassium: ....................561 mg |
| Sugars:...........................22 g | Omega-6 fatty acids: ..0.09 g | Sodium: ..........................89 mg |
| Fiber (total):......................2 g | Cholesterol: .....................7 mg | Iron:................................1 mg |
| Vitamin C:........................68 mg | Vitamin A:.........................35 RE | Zinc: ...............................1 mg |

Diabetic exchanges: 1 serving equals ¾ low fat milk exchange, 1 fruit exchange

# Healthy Homemade Granola

*This recipe avoids the sugar, hydrogenated saturated fats, and high calorie count of many store-bought granolas. Instead you get quick-energy carbohydrates, a little healthy fat, and pro-tein from the nuts, seeds, and coconut. For granola made with other grains, see pages 178-179 of* The Ultimate Food Allergy Cookbook and Survival Guide.

3 cups rolled oatmeal, regular or quick-cooking (not instant oatmeal)
½ cup all purpose, unbleached, white spelt, or oat flour
½ cup chopped almonds, walnuts, or other nuts
½ cup sunflower or pumpkin seeds
½ cup unsweetened coconut
1 teaspooon cinnamon
¼ cup walnut, canola, or other oil
¼ cup Fruit Sweet™ or honey
½ cup unsweetened applesauce, pureed banana (about one banana), or other
    pureed fruit
⅔ cup TOTAL raisins, chopped dates, or other chopped dried fruit in any
    combination

Preheat your oven to 300°F. Lightly oil a 15-inch by 11-inch jelly roll pan or two 13-inch by 9-inch cake pans. (You may also use any other combination of pans you have that will hold the granola in a thin layer).

In a large bowl, stir together the oatmeal, flour, nuts, seeds, and cinnamon. In a separate bowl or cup, combine the pureed fruit, oil, and sweetener. Stir the liquid ingredients into the dry ingredients until they are thoroughly mixed.

Spread the granola mixture in the prepared pan(s) and bake it for 35 to 45 minutes, stirring every 10 to 15 minutes. When the granola is golden brown, remove it from the oven and allow it to cool completely in the pan(s). Stir in the dried fruit. Store the granola in an airtight container at room temperature, or to maintain freshness for a long time, store it in the freezer. Makes 6 to 7 cups of granola, or 12 to 14 half-cup servings.

**Nutritional Analysis per serving:** 13 servings per recipe

| | | |
|---|---|---|
| Calories: .....................242 | Total fat: ..........................12 g | Calcium: ...........................31 mg |
| Protein:................................6 g | Saturated fat: ...............3 g | Magnesium: ...................34 mg |
| Carbohydrate:................28 g | Omega-3 fatty acids:...0.46 g | Potassium: ....................194 mg |
| Sugars:................................9 g | Omega-6 fatty acids:...3.3 g | Sodium: ................................5 mg |
| Fiber (total):.....................4 g | Cholesterol: ....................0 mg | Iron:.....................................2 mg |
| Vitamin C: ...........................2 mg | Vitamin A:..........................2 RE | Zinc:.....................................1 mg |

Diabetic exchanges: 1 serving equals 1 starch exchange, ¼ other carbohydrate exchange, ½ fruit exchange, ½ lean meat exchange, 2 fat exchanges

# Creamy Oatmeal

*Hot cereals are a delicious, homey way to start your day, especially when the weather is chilly. There is a good selection of unsweetened instant cereals on most grocery store shelves which are great for those mornings when you are in a hurry. But the "real thing" cooked from scratch is especially delicious and economical. Try it; you'll like it! To cook other hot cereals, such as kamut, barley, rye and spelt, see page 98 of* The Ultimate Food Allergy Cookbook and Survival Guide.

2½ cups water, skim milk, whole milk, or goat milk OR 1¼ cups each of water and milk
¼ teaspoon salt
1 cup oatmeal, regular or quick-cooking
½ cup raisins or other cut up dried fruit (optional)

Combine the water and/or milk and salt in a saucepan. Bring the liquid to a boil, add the oatmeal and raisins, return the mixture to a boil over medium heat, and then turn the heat down to low. Cover the pan and simmer the oatmeal for about 15 to 20 minutes for regular oatmeal or for 5 to 10 minutes for quick-cooking oatmeal, stirring often to make sure it doesn't stick to the bottom of the pan. Serve with milk or cream, butter, honey, cinnamon, or whatever you like. Makes 2 to 4 servings. This recipe can be halved or quartered if you are feeding one person. If you find the oatmeal is too thick or too thin for your preference, add more or less water and/or milk the next time you make it.

**Nutritional Analysis per serving:** 4 servings per recipe

| | | |
|---|---|---|
| Calories: .....................78 | Total fat: ..........................1 g | Calcium:...........................11 mg |
| Protein:................................3 g | Saturated fat: ...............0 g | Magnesium:...................30 mg |
| Carbohydrate:................14 g | Omega-3 fatty acids:...0.02 g | Potassium: ........................71 mg |
| Sugars:................................0.4 g | Omega-6 fatty acids: ..0.45 g | Sodium:..........................147 mg |
| Fiber (total):.....................2 g | Cholesterol: ....................0 mg | Iron:.....................................1 mg |
| Vitamin C:...........................0 mg | Vitamin A:..........................2 RE | Zinc:.....................................1 mg |

Diabetic exchanges: 1 serving equals 1 starch exchange

# *Pancakes*

2 cups unbleached or all purpose flour
3 teaspoons baking powder*
½ teaspoon salt (optional)
1 large egg**
1⅞ cups (1¾ cups plus 2 tablespoons) water or milk
2 tablespoons Fruit Sweet™ or honey***
3 tablespoons oil

Lightly oil a griddle. Heat it over medium heat until a drop of water dances on the surface, or heat an electric griddle to 350°F.

Mix together the flour, baking powder, and salt in a large bowl. Beat the egg lightly with a fork. Combine the egg, water or milk, sweetener, and oil in a separate bowl. Stir the liquid ingredients into the flour mixture with a wire whisk, adding a tablespoon or two of additional water if necessary to make the batter the right consistency for pancakes. The batter may thicken as it stands and you may need to add another tablespoon or two of water after part of the pancakes have been cooked.

When the griddle is ready, pour about ¼ cup of batter on the griddle for each pancake. Let the pancakes cook until the bubbles have popped on the top surface and the pancakes are beginning to look dry around the edges. Then turn them with a spatula and cook until the other side is light brown. Makes about 2 dozen 4 inch pancakes.

* Note on baking powder: Use Featherweight™ brand baking powder if you are allergic to corn. It contains potato starch instead of cornstarch.

**Note on egg: If you are allergic to eggs, you may substitute an additional ¼ cup of water or milk for the egg.

***Note on sweetener: If you would like to use a fruit sweetener and don't have Fruit Sweet™, decrease the water or milk to 1¾ cups and use ¼ cup thawed apple juice concentrate for the sweetener – or substitute 1 cup of regular apple juice (not concentrate) for ⅞ cup of the water or milk.

**Nutritional Analysis per serving:** 12 servings per recipe, 2 pancakes per serving

| | | |
|---|---|---|
| Calories: ........................108 | Total fat:............................4 g | Calcium:............................92 mg |
| Protein:.............................3 g | Saturated fat:................0.4 g | Magnesium:........................1 mg |
| Carbohydrate:.................16 g | Omega-3 fatty acids:...0.32 g | Potassium: ..........................5 mg |
| Sugars: .............................1 g | Omega-6 fatty acids: ..0.75 g | Sodium:............................194 mg |
| Fiber (total): ...................0.6 g | Cholesterol: ....................18 mg | Iron:......................................1 mg |
| Vitamin C:.........................0 mg | Vitamin A: ...........................7 RE | Zinc:.....................................0 mg |

Diabetic exchanges: 1 serving equals 1 starch exchange, ½ fat exchange

# Wheat-free Pancakes

*These pancakes are so "normal" your guests will never know they don't contain wheat! For pancakes made with other non-wheat grains and without milk or eggs, see pages 172 to 174 of* The Ultimate Food Allergy Cookbook and Survival Guide.

2¼ cups white spelt flour
3 teaspoons baking powder*
½ teaspoon salt (optional)
1 large egg**
1¾ cups water or milk
2 tablespoons Fruit Sweet™ or honey***
3 tablespoons oil

Lightly oil a griddle. Heat it over medium heat until a drop of water dances on the surface, or heat an electric griddle to 350°F.

Mix together the flour, baking powder, and salt in a large bowl. Beat the egg lightly with a fork. Combine the egg, water or milk, sweetener, and oil in a separate bowl. Stir the liquid ingredients into the flour mixture with a wire whisk, adding a tablespoon or two of additional water if necessary to make the batter the right consistency for pancakes. The batter may thicken as it stands and you may need to add another tablespoon or two of water after part of the pancakes have been cooked.

When the griddle is ready, pour about ¼ cup of batter on the griddle for each pancake. Let the pancakes cook until the bubbles have popped on the top surface and the pancakes are beginning to look dry around the edges. Then turn them with a spatula and cook until the other side is light brown. Makes about 24 to 26 4 inch pancakes.

* Note on baking powder: Use Featherweight™ brand baking powder if you are allergic to corn. It contains potato starch instead of cornstarch.

**Note on egg: If you are allergic to eggs, you may substitute an additional ¼ cup of water for the egg.

***Note on sweetener: If you would like to use a fruit sweetener and don't have Fruit Sweet™, decrease the water to 1⅝ cups (1½ cups plus 2 tablespoons) and use ¼ cup thawed apple juice concentrate for the sweetener – or substitute 1 cup of regular apple juice (not concentrate) for ⅞ cup of the water or milk.

**Nutritional Analysis per serving:** 13 servings per recipe, 2 pancakes per serving

| | | |
|---|---|---|
| Calories: ...........................108 | Total fat:.............................4 g | Calcium:...............................84 mg |
| Protein:................................3 g | Saturated fat:................0.4 g | Magnesium: ..........................1 mg |
| Carbohydrate:.................16 g | Omega-3 fatty acids:...0.3 g | Potassium: ............................5 mg |
| Sugars:................................2 g | Omega-6 fatty acids: ..0.69 g | Sodium:...............................190 mg |
| Fiber (total): .....................0.8 g | Cholesterol: ....................16 mg | Iron:.......................................1 mg |
| Vitamin C:...........................0 mg | Vitamin A: .........................6 RE | Zinc:.......................................0 mg |

Diabetic exchanges: 1 serving equals 1 starch exchange, ½ fat exchange

# Weight Wise Pancake Syrup

*If you love pancakes, waffles, and French toast with syrup but hate the calories or unsettling effect of syrup on your blood sugar, here are some alternative syrups you can make for yourself. The maple-flavored varieties are lower in calories than real maple syrup. However, they have their drawbacks. Artificial sweeteners may not be great for your health, and you may not like the way the herb stevia tastes. The fruit-flavored variety will not save you a lot of calories but may be better for weight control because the fructose in this syrup is metabolized more slowly than the sucrose in maple syrup, leading to better blood sugar control. (See pages 22 to 23 for more about this). Quick Thick™ is a corn derivative similar to cornstarch but doesn't need to be cooked. To order it, see "Sources," page 324.*

## Maple-flavored syrup:

2 tablespoons plus 1 teaspoon Quick Thick™
1 cup water
Non-nutritive sweetener equivalent to 12 teaspoons of sugar – ⅛ teaspoon white
    stevia powder OR 1 to 1¼ teaspoons liquid saccharin, to taste, or an equiva-
    lent amount of any other non-nutritive sweetener which you're willing to risk
    (See note on non-nutritive sweeteners below).
½ teaspoon maple flavoring
½ teaspoon vanilla extract

Combine the Quick Thick™ and water in a large cup. Blend with a hand blender for a minute or two until they are thoroughly combined into a syrupy liquid. Mix in the sweetener and flavorings. Store any syrup you do not use immediately in a jar in the refrigerator. Shake it up before serving it again. Makes about 1 cup of syrup, or 8 two-tablespoon servings.

## Fruit-flavored syrup:

½ pound fresh or frozen blueberries, strawberries, or raspberries (about 2 cups of
    fresh berries)
¾ cup orange, apple, or pineapple juice
⅓ cup Fruit Sweet™ or honey
1 to 2 tablespoons Quick Thick™

Combine the fruit, juice, and sweetener in a bowl. Blend with a hand blender until smooth. (Or blend them using a blender or food processor). Pour the blended mixture into a sieve or strainer which has been set over a bowl or measuring cup. Allow the mixture to stand for several minutes or until it has finished draining. Reserve the liquid and discard the seeds, skins, etc. that remain in the sieve. Add 1 tablespoon of Quick Thick™ to the reserved liquid, blend it, and let it stand a couple of minutes. If it is not thick enough for you, add the second tablespoon of Quick Thick™ and blend it. (How much Quick Thick™ you need depends on the amount of pulp from the fruit that passed through your sieve and also on how thick you prefer your syrup). Serve immediately or store any syrup you do not use right away in a jar in the refrigerator. Shake it up before serving it again. Makes about 1¾ to 2 cups of syrup, or about 16 two-tablespoon servings.

Note on non-nutritive sweeteners: Most non-nutritive sweeteners do not taste like sugar, and those that taste the best have the most health drawbacks. Stevia is a potently sweet herb which has been used in Japan in diet foods for 40 years and for centuries in

South America. It has a long track record of safety, but it has a pronounced licorice-like aftertaste that many children and young people don't like. Saccharin has also been around many years. Dr. William Crook, author of the well known series of *Yeast Connection* books, feels that saccharin is all right in moderation and has a place in a low-yeast diet. Aspartame (Nutrasweet™) is a relative newcomer. It has a history of causing headaches in quite a number of people and is possibly implicated in even more serious problems when used in large amounts. However, it tastes normal. As in the decision about eating sushi and risking parasites, you are an adult and this decision is yours. If aspartame does not bother you and you use it rarely, you can substitute 6 packages of Nutrasweet™ for the stevia or saccharin in this recipe.

**Maple-flavored syrup:**
**Nutritional Analysis per serving:** *8 servings per recipe, 2 tablespoons per serving*

| | | |
|---|---|---|
| Calories: .............................8 | Total fat: ............................0 g | Calcium:................................0 mg |
| Protein:.............................0 g | Saturated fat:.............0 g | Magnesium:........................0 mg |
| Carbohydrate: ..................2 g | Omega-3 fatty acids:...0 g | Potassium: ........................0 mg |
| Sugars:..............................0 g | Omega-6 fatty acids: ..0 g | Sodium:..............................0 mg |
| Fiber (total): ....................0 g | Cholesterol: ....................0 mg | Iron:....................................0 mg |
| Vitamin C:.........................0 mg | Vitamin A: .........................0 RE | Zinc:....................................0 mg |

Diabetic exchanges: 1 serving equals 0 exchanges

**Fruit-flavored syrup:**
**Nutritional Analysis per serving:** *16 servings per recipe, 2 tablespoons per serving*

| | | |
|---|---|---|
| Calories: ..........................23 | Total fat: ............................0 g | Calcium: .............................12 mg |
| Protein:.............................0 g | Saturated fat:.............0 g | Magnesium: ........................2 mg |
| Carbohydrate:..................6 g | Omega-3 fatty acids:...0 g | Potassium:........................31 mg |
| Sugars:..............................5 g | Omega-6 fatty acids: ..0 g | Sodium:..............................1 mg |
| Fiber (total):....................1 g | Cholesterol: ....................0 mg | Iron: ...................................0 mg |
| Vitamin C:.........................6 mg | Vitamin A:.........................3 RE | Zinc:....................................0 mg |

Diabetic exchanges: 1 serving equals ⅓ fruit exchange

# Fruit Sauce

*Not only is this sauce good on pancakes, waffles, and French toast, it is great on ice cream or frozen yogurt, or you can even use it as a topping on cake.*

## Apple or Peach Sauce:

3 cups peeled and diced apple (2 large apples) or peaches (4 to 6 peaches)
¾ teaspoon cinnamon
⅞ cup (¾ cup plus 2 tablespoons) thawed apple juice concentrate, divided
2 teaspoons cornstarch, arrowroot, or tapioca starch

## Berry Sauce:

1 pound fresh or unsweetened frozen blueberries, raspberries, or sliced strawberries
½ cup apple juice concentrate, thawed
2 teaspoons cornstarch, arrowroot, or tapioca starch

## Pineapple Sauce:

 1 8 ounce can crushed pineapple packed in its own juice or ¾ cup finely chopped
    fresh pineapple
 1 cup pineapple juice (part may be from the can above)
 2 teaspoons cornstarch, arrowroot, or tapioca starch

## Cherry Sauce:

 1 16 ounce can tart pie cherries, packed in water
 ½ cup cherry juice, drained from the can above
 1 cup apple or pineapple juice concentrate, thawed
 4 teaspoons cornstarch, arrowroot, or tapioca starch

Chose one of the above sets of ingredients. If you are making the apple or peach sauce, combine the diced apples or peaches, cinnamon, and ¾ cup of the apple juice concentrate in a saucepan and bring them to a boil. Reduce the heat and simmer for 5 to 10 minutes for the peaches or 15 to 20 minutes for the apples or until the fruit is tender. Stir the remaining 2 tablespoons of juice into the starch, and then stir this into the fruit mixture. Cook over medium heat, stirring often, until the sauce thickens and boils. Serve and store as below.

If you are making pineapple or cherry sauce, drain the fruit from the juice, and reserve ½ cup of the cherry juice or all of the pineapple juice. For the pineapple sauce, add additional pineapple juice to the reserved juice to get 1 cup of juice in all.

For all the kinds of sauce except apple or peach, stir together the starch and juice(s) in a saucepan. Add the fruit to the pan. Cook the mixture over medium heat, stirring often until the sauce thickens and boils. Remove the pan from the heat and serve the sauce immediately or refrigerate it overnight. The cherry sauce is best after overnight refrigeration, which allows the flavors to blend. You can reheat it in a saucepan over low heat or in the microwave if you wish to serve it warm. Makes about 2 cups of sauce or 8 to 12 servings.

### Apple fruit sauce:
**Nutritional Analysis per serving:** 12 servings per recipe, ¼ cup per serving

| | | |
|---|---|---|
| Calories: 57 | Total fat: 0 g | Calcium: 7 mg |
| Protein: 0 g | Saturated fat: 0 g | Magnesium: 5 mg |
| Carbohydrate: 14 g | Omega-3 fatty acids: 0 g | Potassium: 132 mg |
| Sugars: 12 g | Omega-6 fatty acids: 0 g | Sodium: 5 mg |
| Fiber (total): 1 g | Cholesterol: 0 mg | Iron: 0 mg |
| Vitamin C: 2 mg | Vitamin A: 2 RE | Zinc: 0 mg |

Diabetic exchanges: 1 serving equals 1 fruit exchange

### Berry fruit sauce:
**Nutritional Analysis per serving:** 8 servings per recipe, ¼ cup per serving

| | | |
|---|---|---|
| Calories: 61 | Total fat: 0 g | Calcium: 8 mg |
| Protein: 0 g | Saturated fat: 0 g | Magnesium: 6 mg |
| Carbohydrate: 15 g | Omega-3 fatty acids: 0 g | Potassium: 109 mg |
| Sugars: 12 g | Omega-6 fatty acids: 0 g | Sodium: 5 mg |
| Fiber (total): 2 g | Cholesterol: 0 mg | Iron: 0 mg |
| Vitamin C: 2 mg | Vitamin A: 5 RE | Zinc: 0 mg |

Diabetic exchanges: 1 serving equals 1 fruit exchange

**Pineapple fruit sauce:**
**Nutritional Analysis per serving:** 8 servings per recipe, ¼ cup per serving

| | | |
|---|---|---|
| Calories: ...........................28 | Total fat: ............................0 g | Calcium: ...............................7 mg |
| Protein:...........................0 g | Saturated fat:................0 g | Magnesium: .......................6 mg |
| Carbohydrate:....................7 g | Omega-3 fatty acids:...0 g | Potassium: .......................56 mg |
| Sugars:............................6 g | Omega-6 fatty acids: ..0 g | Sodium:................................1 mg |
| Fiber (total): ......................0 g | Cholesterol: ......................0 mg | Iron: ....................................0 mg |
| Vitamin C:..........................6 mg | Vitamin A: ...........................1 RE | Zinc:....................................0 mg |

Diabetic exchanges: 1 serving equals ½ fruit exchange

**Cherry fruit sauce:**
**Nutritional Analysis per serving:** 12 servings per recipe, ⅙ cup per serving

| | | |
|---|---|---|
| Calories: ...........................56 | Total fat: ............................0 g | Calcium:................................9 mg |
| Protein:...........................0 g | Saturated fat:................0 g | Magnesium: .......................6 mg |
| Carbohydrate:..................14 g | Omega-3 fatty acids:...0 g | Potassium: .....................142 mg |
| Sugars:............................12 g | Omega-6 fatty acids: ..0 g | Sodium:................................9 mg |
| Fiber (total):......................1 g | Cholesterol: ......................0 mg | Iron:....................................1 mg |
| Vitamin C: .........................1 mg | Vitamin A:.........................28 RE | Zinc:....................................0 mg |

Diabetic exchanges: 1 serving equals 1 fruit exchange

# Make Ahead French Toast

4 to 5 slices of bread – whole wheat, whole spelt, white, or white spelt
3 eggs
½ cup skim, whole, or goat milk
1 teaspoon Fruit Sweet™ or honey (optional)
1 teaspoon vanilla extract
Dash of salt
1½ tablespoons butter, goat butter, or Earth Balance™ margarine, plus additional
      for greasing the baking dish

Toast the bread lightly, allow it to cool, and butter it on both sides. Lightly butter
a 9 by 13 inch baking pan, preferably made of glass. Arrange the toast in the pan; if the
slices don't quite fit, piece in partial slices so the whole pan bottom is covered. Beat the
eggs lightly. Then add the milk, sweetener, vanilla, and salt to the beaten eggs and mix.
Pour this mixture over the toast in the baking pan and refrigerate for at least four hours,
or up to 36 hours. Preheat your oven to 350°F. Bake for 35 to 45 minutes, or until the
French toast is browned and puffed up. Makes 2 to 5 servings.

**Nutritional Analysis per serving:** 5 servings per recipe

| | | |
|---|---|---|
| Calories: ...........................149 | Total fat: ............................8 g | Calcium:..............................69 mg |
| Protein:...........................6 g | Saturated fat: ................2 g | Magnesium:.......................11 mg |
| Carbohydrate:..................13 g | Omega-3 fatty acids:...0.09 g | Potassium: .....................102 mg |
| Sugars: ............................2 g | Omega-6 fatty acids:....1.08 g | Sodium: ...........................221 mg |
| Fiber (total):......................1 g | Cholesterol: ....................113 mg | Iron:....................................1 mg |
| Vitamin C:..........................0 mg | Vitamin A:.........................59 RE | Zinc: ...................................1 mg |

Diabetic exchanges: 1 serving equals 1 starch exchange, ½ lean meat exchange, 1
fat exchange

# Traditional French Toast

2 eggs
½ cup skim, whole, or goat milk if bread is thinly sliced or ⅔ cup milk if the bread
    is large or thickly sliced
1 teaspoon vanilla extract (optional)
Dash of salt
1½ to 2 tablespoons butter or oil, preferably olive oil
4 slices of bread, preferably whole grain, thickly sliced and not too fresh if possible

In a flat-bottomed large bowl, slightly beat the eggs with a fork. Add the milk, vanilla, and salt and beat again. Melt one tablespoon of the butter or heat one tablespoon of the oil over medium heat in a frying pan. If you have a pan that is large enough to hold two slices of bread side by side at the same time, that's the one to use. Dip the bread, one slice at a time, into the egg mixture, allowing it to stand in the egg mixture briefly so that some of the mixture soaks into the bread. Turn it over, and dip and soak the other side of the bread. Add the bread to the heated oil or butter in the frying pan. Cook the French toast until it is golden brown on the first side, about 2 to 3 minutes. Then turn it and cook it until the second side is also browned nicely, which will take another 2 to 3 minutes. If necessary, add more butter or oil to the pan as you cook subsequent slices of French toast. Serve with pancake syrup (page 112), fruit sauce (page 114), or all-fruit jam. Makes two to four servings. If you need only one or two servings, divide the amounts of all of the ingredients in half.

### Nutritional Analysis per serving: 4 servings per recipe

| | | |
|---|---|---|
| Calories: .........................167 | Total fat: .............................9 g | Calcium: ...........................75 mg |
| Protein: ................................7 g | Saturated fat: ................2 g | Magnesium: .....................31 mg |
| Carbohydrate:.................15 g | Omega-3 fatty acids:....0.09 g | Potassium: .....................159 mg |
| Sugars:.............................3 g | Omega-6 fatty acids:....1.02 g | Sodium:..........................261 mg |
| Fiber (total):.....................2 g | Cholesterol: ..................126 mg | Iron:.........................................1 mg |
| Vitamin C:..........................0 mg | Vitamin A:........................64 RE | Zinc: .......................................1 mg |

Diabetic exchanges: 1 serving equals 1 starch exchange, ½ medium-fat meat exchange, 1 fat exchange

# Traditional Waffles

*This is a good recipe for beginning waffle makers. The challenge with waffles may be to get them out of the iron, and this recipe contains eggs, which strengthen the structure of the waffles, and butter, which makes them less likely to stick than if you use oil. To avoid the scenario of half of your waffle stuck on the top half of the iron and the other half stuck on the bottom half of the iron, resist the temptation to peek into the iron early. Wait until the time is up and the waffle has stopped steaming to open the iron.*

2 cups all purpose or unbleached flour
2 teaspoons baking powder
½ teaspoon baking soda
½ teaspoon salt
2 cups skim or whole milk or water
¼ cup lemon juice
¼ cup melted butter, plus a little more for greasing the iron.
2 eggs, slightly beaten

Brush the grids of the waffle iron with melted butter. Plug the iron in and preheat it as directed in the instruction booklet. Do not begin baking waffles until the iron is completely heated. For most irons, the preheating time is about 10 to 15 minutes at a medium-high setting.

In a large bowl, stir together the flour, baking powder, baking soda, and salt. In another bowl or cup, stir together the milk or water, lemon juice, melted butter, and eggs. Add the liquid ingredients to the dry ingredients and stir until just mixed. Do not over-mix waffle batter; it is all right if some small dry lumps of flour remain.

Read the directions for your waffle iron to see how much batter to add for each waffle and how long to cook it. When the iron is completely pre-heated, add the correct amount of batter to the iron. (The batter will not cover the whole iron at this point but it will expand as it cooks. Overfilling the iron makes it harder to remove the waffles). Cook until steam stops coming out of the iron and until the cooking time given in your instruction booklet has elapsed, which will probably be about 5 to 7 minutes. Do not open the iron early or the waffle may split down the middle.

When the proper time has elapsed, gently open the iron. If the waffle is pale, close the iron again for another minute or two. Make a note to cook subsequent waffles longer. If the waffle is golden brown, remove it with two forks. If it is very dark, remove it and decrease the cooking time by one to two minutes for the next waffle. If the light has come back on after removing the waffle, indicating that the iron is heating, close the iron and let it reheat. When the iron is hot again, cook another waffle.

This recipe makes about 18 four-inch square waffles. They freeze well and can be reheated in a toaster for a quick, healthy breakfast.

**Nutritional Analysis per serving:** 18 servings per recipe, 1 waffle per serving

| | | |
|---|---|---|
| Calories: ...........................92 | Total fat:............................3 g | Calcium:.............................77 mg |
| Protein:............................3 g | Saturated fat: ...............2 g | Magnesium: .......................7 mg |
| Carbohydrate:..................12 g | Omega-3 fatty acids:...0.04 g | Potassium: ........................72 mg |
| Sugars: ............................2 g | Omega-6 fatty acids: ..0.19 g | Sodium: ...........................188 mg |
| Fiber (total): .....................0.4 g | Cholesterol: ....................31 mg | Iron:....................................1 mg |
| Vitamin C: .........................2 mg | Vitamin A: .........................51 RE | Zinc:....................................0 mg |

Diabetic exchanges: 1 serving equals ¾ starch exchange, ¹⁄₁₀ medium-fat meat exchange, ½ fat exchange

# No Allergy Waffles

*These waffles contain no milk or eggs and can be made wheat-free using white spelt flour. For waffles made with other grains, such as kamut, rye, barley, teff, whole spelt, buckwheat, arrowroot, or tapioca flour see pages 175 to 177 of* The Ultimate Food Allergy Cookbook and Survival Guide. *If you have trouble with these waffles sticking to the iron, substitute melted butter, ghee, or coconut oil for the oil in this recipe.*

2¼ cups all purpose or unbleached flour or 2¾ cups white spelt flour
2 teaspoons baking powder*
½ teaspoon salt
¼ cup oil, plus a little more for greasing the iron
2 cups water or 1¾ cups water plus ¼ cup apple juice concentrate, thawed

Brush your waffle iron with oil. Plug the iron in and preheat it as directed in the instruction booklet. Do not begin baking waffles until the iron is completely heated. For most irons, the preheating time is about 10 to 15 minutes at a medium-high setting.

In a large bowl, stir together the flour, baking powder, and salt. In another bowl or cup, stir together the water, optional apple juice concentrate, and oil. Add the liquid ingredients to the dry ingredients and stir until just mixed. Do not over-mix waffle batter; it is all right if some small dry lumps of flour remain.

Read the directions for your waffle iron to see how much batter to add for each waffle. When the iron is completely pre-heated, add the correct amount of batter to the iron. (The batter will not cover the whole iron at this point but it will expand as it cooks. Overfilling the iron makes it harder to remove the waffles). Cook for 6 to 10 minutes. This seems like a long time, but egg-free waffles must be thoroughly cooked to insure you can remove them from the iron without splitting them. Do not open the iron too early; wait until the light has gone off and the steaming has stopped. If your first waffle is too brown, you can try decreasing the cooking time a little on subsequent waffles.

When the cooking time has elapsed, gently open the iron. If the waffle is pale, close the iron again for another minute or two. If it is golden brown, remove the waffle with two forks. If the light has come back on after removing the waffle, indicating that the iron is heating, close the iron and let it reheat. When it is hot again, cook another waffle.

This recipe makes about 16 four-inch square waffles. They freeze well and can be reheated in a toaster for a quick, healthy breakfast.

* Note on baking powder: Use Featherweight™ brand baking powder if you are allergic to corn. It contains potato starch instead of cornstarch.

**Nutritional Analysis per serving:** 16 servings per recipe, 1 waffle per serving

| | | |
|---|---|---|
| Calories: .........................94 | Total fat:............................4 g | Calcium:..........................45 mg |
| Protein: ...............................2 g | Saturated fat:...............0.3 g | Magnesium:.......................4 mg |
| Carbohydrate:.................14 g | Omega-3 fatty acids:...0.32 g | Potassium:.........................19 mg |
| Sugars:..............................0.3 g | Omega-6 fatty acids: ..0.76 g | Sodium:.............................85 mg |
| Fiber (total): ....................0.5 g | Cholesterol: ......................0 mg | Iron:.......................................1 mg |
| Vitamin C:.........................0 mg | Vitamin A: .........................0 RE | Zinc:......................................0 mg |

Diabetic exchanges: 1 serving equals ⅞ starch exchange, ½ fat exchange

# Hard-Cooked Eggs

*Eggs today should be thoroughly cooked because they can transmit the bacteria <u>Salmo-nella</u>. However, pasteurized eggs are available in some areas of the country. (See "Sources, page 321). If you like soft-cooked eggs and can find pasteurized eggs in your grocery store, just follow this recipe but boil the eggs for only 4 or 5 minutes.*

Unshelled eggs
Cold water

Place the eggs in a saucepan and cover them with cold water to a depth of at least one inch above the eggs. Put the saucepan on the burner of your stove, turn the heat to high, and bring the eggs to a rolling boil. Then turn the heat down to medium and begin timing 15 minutes. (This is how long it takes to cook eggs straight from the refrigerator. Way back when, we could start with the eggs near room temperature and cook them for 10 minutes, but that's not considered safe any more). After the 15 minutes are up, drain the hot water from the pan and place it in the sink under running cold water for a few minutes. This stops the cooking process and keeps the egg yolks from becoming discolored. Serve the eggs immediately or refrigerate them for use in other recipes.

Years ago I learned a trick from a man who never cooked, which is probably heresy in the world of gourmet cooking, but it works. Before boiling eggs, if you use a pin to bore one or two small holes in the shell at the rounder end of the eggs, the shells will not break during cooking. There is an air pocket at the rounder end of the egg, and the holes go into that pocket. If you use this method and watch the eggs as the water is coming to a boil, you will see small bubbles of air occasionally escaping from the holes.

**Nutritional Analysis per serving:** 1 large egg per serving

| | | |
|---|---|---|
| Calories: ...........................77 | Total fat:............................5 g | Calcium: ...........................25 mg |
| Protein:...............................6 g | Saturated fat: ................2 g | Magnesium:.......................5 mg |
| Carbohydrate: ..................0.6 g | Omega-3 fatty acids:...0.04 g | Potassium: ........................63 mg |
| Sugars:.............................0.6 g | Omega-6 fatty acids: ..0.67 g | Sodium: ............................62 mg |
| Fiber (total): ....................0 g | Cholesterol: ..................212 mg | Iron:...................................1 mg |
| Vitamin C:..........................0 mg | Vitamin A:.......................84 RE | Zinc:...................................1 mg |

Diabetic exchanges: 1 serving equals 1 medium-fat meat exchange

# Scrambled Eggs

*If you're in a rush, stuff these into a pita bread and take them along to eat on the way to work or school.*

2 to 3 teaspoons butter or oil, preferably olive oil
4 eggs
¼ cup milk (optional – may be omitted if you are allergic to milk)
¼ teaspoon salt
Dash of pepper (optional)

Melt the butter or heat the oil in a frying pan over medium heat until it just begins to sizzle. (Don't let it get any hotter than this or it will begin to burn). While the fat is heating, beat together the rest of the ingredients with a wire whisk or fork. Pour the egg mixture into the pan and cook for a minute or so without stirring. When the eggs begin to set, stir them gently with a spoon or break them into shreds with a fork. When they are set throughout, serve them immediately. Makes two servings for hungry college students or four servings for middle-aged weight watchers. This recipe can be halved or quartered for one person. If you're in the mood for some excitement, try adding some chopped fresh oregano, basil or dill, grated cheese, chopped sauteed onion or green pepper, crumbled bacon, or lox to your eggs before cooking them.

**Nutritional Analysis per serving:** 4 servings per recipe

| | | |
|---|---|---|
| Calories: ........................110 | Total fat: ..........................76 g | Calcium: ...........................29 mg |
| Protein: ..............................7 g | Saturated fat: ............20 g | Magnesium: ........................6 mg |
| Carbohydrate: ..................0 g | Omega-3 fatty acids:...0.06 g | Potassium: ........................73 mg |
| Sugars:...............................0 g | Omega-6 fatty acids: ..0.95 g | Sodium: ...........................219 mg |
| Fiber (total): ......................0 g | Cholesterol: ..................246 m | Iron:......................................1 mg |
| Vitamin C:...........................0 mg | Vitamin A: ........................97 RE | Zinc: .....................................1 mg |

Diabetic exchanges: 1 serving equals 1 medium-fat meat exchange, ½ fat exchange

# Breakfast Sausage

*Sausages should be cooked thoroughly. If you're watching your weight, try turkey sausage. To make your own sausage from any kind of meat see the recipe on page 77 of* The Ultimate Food Allergy Cookbook and Survival Guide.

1 pound sausage links, preferably turkey sausage
½ cup boiling water

Cut the sausage links apart into individual sausages and prick them each in several places with a pin. Put them in a skillet with the water, bring them to a boil over medium heat, and then reduce the heat to low or medium-low so the sausages are simmering gently. Cover the pan with its lid and cook for 10 minutes. Uncover the pan and continue cooking until the liquid has evaporated. Watch the sausages carefully, and turn them so they brown on all sides. Drain any fat from the sausages and serve. Makes 6 servings for hungry college students or 12 servings for middle-aged weight watchers.

**Nutritional Analysis per serving:** 12 servings per recipe

| | | |
|---|---|---|
| Calories: ..........................62 | Total fat:..............................4 g | Calcium:................................3 mg |
| Protein: ..............................7 g | Saturated fat: ................1 g | Magnesium:..........................8 mg |
| Carbohydrate:..................0 g | Omega-3 fatty acids:...0.03 g | Potassium: ......................107 mg |
| Sugars:...............................0 g | Omega-6 fatty acids: ..0.82 g | Sodium:.............................313 mg |
| Fiber (total): ......................0 g | Cholesterol: ..................29 mg | Iron:......................................1 mg |
| Vitamin C:...........................0 mg | Vitamin A: ..........................0 RE | Zinc: .....................................1 mg |

Diabetic exchanges: 1 serving equals 1 lean meat exchange

# Bacon

*A microwave oven is a wonderful appliance for cooking bacon easily and safely. If you don't want to use a lot of paper towels, invest in a Bacon Wave™ microwave bacon cooker. This ingenious device allows you to stand 14 slices of bacon up on edge for cooking, and the fat drains into the bottom of the tray.*

## Stove-top method for cooking bacon:

Lay bacon in a frying pan in a single layer. Put the pan on the burner of your stove and turn on the heat to "medium." As the bacon cooks, pour off the fat into a can. This helps the bacon cook more easily and quickly. If you are coordinated, you can hold the slices in the pan with a spatula while you pour the grease off into a can. If not, you can use a metal turkey baster to remove the grease from the pan. (Bacon grease is very hot and may melt a plastic baster). When the bacon is crisp, drain it on paper towels for a minute or two and then serve it.

## Microwave paper towel method for cooking bacon:

Put two layers of paper towel in the bottom of a glass baking dish or dinner dish. Do not use melamine or styrofoam dishes because they will melt! Lay four strips of bacon on the paper towel. Add another layer of paper towel and another layer of bacon. Lay the bacon in a direction parallel to the bacon in the first layer. Repeat layers until you have as much bacon as you want to cook in the dish. Top with one last sheet of paper towel. Microwave on high for ½ to 1½ minutes per strip of bacon. Start with the minimum time and check the bacon every 30 seconds after that. The time will vary with the thickness of the bacon, the power of your microwave, and how much sweetener was used in the curing process. (Different brands of bacon microwave differently because of the sweetener). When the bacon is cooked to almost-crisp throughout the dish, remove it from the paper towels. It may stick to the towels if it is allowed to cool on them. The bacon will continue to cook and gain crispness for a minute or two after it is removed from the microwave oven.

## Bacon Wave™ Microwave Bacon Cooker method for cooking bacon:

If you don't want to waste a lot of paper towels cooking bacon, order a Bacon Wave™ Microwave Bacon Cooker. (See "Sources," page 323). Set up to 14 strips of bacon on edge in the slots in the cooker. For most brands of bacon, this is a full pound. If you want to cook less than a pound, just use fewer of the slots. When cooking less than a pound, space the bacon evenly throughout the cooker. Place the cooker in your microwave oven and microwave on high for ½ to 1½ minutes per strip of bacon. Start with the minimum time. After the minimum cooking time, pour off the grease from the bottom of the cooker into a can. Continue cooking the bacon on high power. Check the bacon every 30 seconds if you are cooking a few slices and every 1 to 2 minutes if you are cooking a full pound of bacon. The cooking time will vary with the thickness of the bacon, the power of your microwave, and how much sweetener was used in the curing process. (Different brands of bacon microwave differently because of the sweetener). When the bacon is cooked to almost-crisp throughout the dish, remove it from microwave oven and drain off the grease into a can. Wait a few minutes to serve it; it will continue to cook and crisp for a minute or two.

**Nutritional Analysis per serving:**
15 to 20 servings per recipe, 1 slice of bacon per serving

| | | |
|---|---|---|
| Calories: ...........................36 | Total fat:..............................3 g | Calcium: ................................1 mg |
| Protein: ...............................2 g | Saturated fat: ................1 g | Magnesium: ........................2 mg |
| Carbohydrate: ................0.04 g | Omega-3 fatty acids:...0.05 g | Potassium: .........................31 mg |
| Sugars:.............................0.04 g | Omega-6 fatty acids: ..0.32 g | Sodium: ............................101 mg |
| Fiber (total): .....................0 g | Cholesterol: .........................5 mg | Iron: .....................................0 mg |
| Vitamin C: ..........................0 mg | Vitamin A: ..........................0 RE | Zinc:......................................0 mg |

Diabetic exchanges: 1 serving equals ½ fat exchange, ¼ lean meat exchange. Some diabetic exchange tables consider one slice of bacon one fat exchange.

# Ann Fisk's Gourmet Brunch

*This is such a versatile recipe that is was hard to determine where to put it in the book! Perhaps it belongs in "Recipes to Impress," because it will delight guests. Serve this dish for breakfast, brunch, lunch, or a light dinner entree.*

1 bagel, sliced, preferably whole grain
1 to 2 tablespoons low-fat cream cheese
¼ to ⅓ cup flaked leftover cooked fish of any kind
1 to 2 teaspoons capers

Spread the cut surface of both halves of the bagel with the cream cheese. Top the cream cheese on the bottom half with the fish and capers. Press down the top half of the bagel firmly. Enjoy! Makes one serving.

**Nutritional Analysis per serving:** 1 servings per recipe

| | | |
|---|---|---|
| Calories: ........................239 | Total fat:..............................2 g | Calcium:................................39 mg |
| Protein: .............................20 g | Saturated fat: ................2 g | Magnesium:........................75 mg |
| Carbohydrate:................32 g | Omega-3 fatty acids:..0.04 g | Potassium: .....................459 mg |
| Sugars: ..............................2 g | Omega-6 fatty acids: ..0.06 g | Sodium:............................471 mg |
| Fiber (total):.....................5 g | Cholesterol: ...................35 mg | Iron:......................................2 mg |
| Vitamin C: ..........................2 mg | Vitamin A:......................38 RE | Zinc:......................................2 mg |

Diabetic exchanges: 1 serving equals 2 starch exchanges, 1½ lean meat exchanges

Footnotes

1. Thornton, Jim, "Fast-Break Breakfasts," *Cooking Light*, March, 2000, page 38.

# Sandwiches and Salads

This chapter contains the makings of some great lunches, light dinners, or salads to go along with soups. Don't limit yourself to the sandwich recipes in this chapter or old standbys like ham and cheese sandwiches. Use your imagination to create new sandwich combinations.

Salads can be powerhouses of nutrition. Dark leafy greens are some of the most nutrient-dense foods known. However, don't drown your salads in high-fat commercial salad dressings. Instead, try some of the healthy dressing recipes at the end of this chapter.

# Sandwiches

## Bacon, Lettuce, and Tomato Sandwich

2 slices of bread, preferably whole grain
3 to 5 slices of cooked bacon
1 small or ½ large tomato (a single Roma tomato works well)
1 leaf of lettuce
2 teaspoons of mayonnaise

Cook the bacon as directed on page 122 of this book. Slice the tomato. Toast the bread, if desired, and spread it with the mayonnaise. Layer the bacon, tomato, and lettuce between the slices of bread. Makes one serving.

**Nutritional Analysis per serving:** 1 serving per recipe

| | | |
|---|---|---|
| Calories: ......................328 | Total fat: ...........................19 g | Calcium: ............................54 mg |
| Protein:.............................12 g | Saturated fat: ...............5 g | Magnesium: .....................61 mg |
| Carbohydrate: ................30 g | Omega-3 fatty acids:...0.58 g | Potassium: ....................401 mg |
| Sugars:.............................4 g | Omega-6 fatty acids:...4.99 g | Sodium:..........................657 mg |
| Fiber (total):.....................5 g | Cholesterol: ...................22 mg | Iron: .......................................3 mg |
| Vitamin C:.........................14 mg | Vitamin A:......................65 RE | Zinc: .......................................2 mg |

Diabetic exchanges: 1 serving equals 2 starch exchanges, 1 high-fat meat exchange, ½ vegetable exchange, 1¼ fat exchanges

## Club Sandwich

2 to 3 slices of bread, preferably whole grain
3 strips of cooked bacon
2 to 3 ounces of sliced cooked chicken or turkey
1 ounce of sliced cheddar or American cheese (optional)
1 small or ½ large tomato (a single Roma tomato works well)
1 leaf of lettuce
2 to 3 teaspoons of mayonnaise

Cook the bacon as directed on page 122 of this book. Slice the tomato. Toast the bread, if desired, and spread it with the mayonnaise. Layer the bacon, tomato, and lettuce on one slice of bread or toast. Top with a second slice. Put the chicken or turkey and cheese between the middle and top slices of bread or toast. If you want to save on calories, just put everything between two slices of bread. Makes one serving.

**Nutritional Analysis per serving:** 1 serving per recipe

| | | |
|---|---|---|
| Calories: .................440 | Total fat: ....................24 g | Calcium: ...................62 mg |
| Protein: ....................29 g | Saturated fat: .............6 g | Magnesium: .............76 mg |
| Carbohydrate:..........29 g | Omega-3 fatty acids:...0.63 g | Potassium:...............540 mg |
| Sugars:......................4 g | Omega-6 fatty acids:...5.83 g | Sodium:.....................697 mg |
| Fiber (total):...............5 g | Cholesterol: ...............69 mg | Iron: ...........................3 mg |
| Vitamin C:................14 mg | Vitamin A: ..................80 RE | Zinc: ...........................2 mg |

Diabetic exchanges: 1 serving equals 2 starch exchanges, 1 high-fat meat exchange, 2 lean meat exchanges, ½ vegetable exchange, 1¼ fat exchanges

# Turkey and Cranberry Sandwich

2 slices of bread, preferably whole grain
2 to 3 ounces of sliced cooked turkey
2 tablespoons of cranberry sauce

Toast the bread if desired. Spread one slice of it with the cranberry sauce. Layer the turkey on top of the cranberries. Top with the second slice of bread or toast. Serve immediately to keep the cranberry sauce from soaking into the bread too much. Makes one serving.

**Nutritional Analysis per serving:** 1 serving per recipe

| | | |
|---|---|---|
| Calories: .................297 | Total fat: ....................7 g | Calcium: ...................54 mg |
| Protein:....................22 g | Saturated fat: .............2 g | Magnesium:.............65 mg |
| Carbohydrate: ..........39 g | Omega-3 fatty acids:...0.10 g | Potassium: ...............313 mg |
| Sugars:....................15 g | Omega-6 fatty acids:....1.46 g | Sodium: ...................341 mg |
| Fiber (total):...............4 g | Cholesterol: ...............42 mg | Iron: ...........................3 mg |
| Vitamin C: ..................1 mg | Vitamin A: ....................1 RE | Zinc: ...........................2 mg |

Diabetic exchanges: 1 serving equals 2 starch exchanges, 2 lean meat exchanges, ½ fruit exchange

# Poultry, Meat, Egg or Fish Salad Sandwiches

2 slices of bread, preferably whole grain
⅓ cup chicken, turkey, beef, egg, tuna, or fish salad (recipes on pages 136 to 138 of this book)
1 leaf of lettuce or a few leaves of spinach (optional)
Sliced tomato (optional)

Make the salad as directed in the recipe. Toast the bread if desired. Spread about ⅓ cup of the salad on one piece of the bread or toast. Layer with the optional vegetables. Top with the other piece of bread or toast. Makes one serving.

**Nutritional Analysis per serving:** 1 serving per recipe

| | | |
|---|---|---|
| Calories: .................328 | Total fat:.....................2 g | Calcium: ...................57 mg |
| Protein: ....................19 g | Saturated fat: .............3 g | Magnesium:.............62 mg |
| Carbohydrate: ..........27 g | Omega-3 fatty acids:...0.66 g | Potassium:...............311 mg |
| Sugars:......................3 g | Omega-6 fatty acids: ..6.42 g | Sodium: ...................412 mg |
| Fiber (total):...............4 g | Cholesterol: ...............43 mg | Iron: ...........................3 mg |
| Vitamin C: ..................1 mg | Vitamin A: ..................13 RE | Zinc: ...........................2 mg |

Diabetic exchanges: 1 serving equals 2 starch exchanges, 2 lean meat exchanges, 1⅓ fat exchanges

# Grilled Cheese Sandwich

*This is a sandwich that most of you already know how to make. However, the consensus at our house was that this recipe should be in* Easy Cooking for Special Diets *anyway because, "You burn toasted cheese sandwiches sometimes, Mom."*

2 slices of bread, preferably whole grain
2 to 3 one-ounce slices of cheddar, American, Monterey jack, Swiss, Colby, soy,
    or goat cheese
1 to 2 teaspoons of EFA-butter (recipe on page 142), softened butter or
    goat butter, or Earth Balance™ margarine

Spread one side of each piece of bread with EFA-butter, butter or margarine. Put one slice of the bread into a frying pan buttered side down. Lay the cheese on top of it. Top the sandwich with the second slice of bread buttered side up. Place the pan on the burner of your stove and turn the heat up to low, medium-low, or medium. (You will have to find the setting on your stove that produces the perfect grilled cheese sandwich by trial and error). Cover the pan with a lid; this helps the cheese melt. Cook the sandwich for 2 to 5 minutes, or until the bottom side is golden-brown. (With experience you will soon learn what the ideal cooking time is for your stove). Turn the sandwich over and cook it until the other side is also golden-brown. The secret to a perfectly done (not burnt) sandwich is to pay attention and not get distracted while you are cooking it. Serve the sandwich immediately after it is cooked. Makes one serving.

**Nutritional Analysis per serving:** 1 serving per recipe

| | | |
|---|---|---|
| Calories: .......................403 | Vitamin C: .......................0 mg | Vitamin A: .......................175 RE |
| Protein: .......................20 g | Total fat: .......................25 g | Magnesium: .......................64 mg |
| Carbohydrate: .................27 g | Saturated fat: .............14 g | Potassium: .......................198 mg |
| Sugars: .........................3 g | Omega-3 fatty acids:...0.47 g | Sodium: .......................666 mg |
| Calcium: ....................450 mg | Omega-6 fatty acids:....1.37 g | Iron: .......................2 mg |
| Fiber (total): ....................4 g | Cholesterol: ..................65 mg | Zinc: .......................3 mg |

Diabetic exchanges: 1 serving equals 2 starch exchanges, 2 high-fat meat exchanges, 1 fat exchange

# French Dip Sandwich

1 hard roll, preferably whole grain, sliced
2 ounces of leftover roast beef
½ cup leftover juice from "Crock Pot Roast Beef Dinner," page 216

Warm the juice in a small pan or in a glass cup or bowl in the microwave oven. If desired, warm the roast beef. Put the roast beef into the roll. Serve the sandwich with the warm juice for dipping. Makes one serving.

**Nutritional Analysis per serving:** 1 serving per recipe

| | | |
|---|---|---|
| Calories: .......................255 | Vitamin C: .......................0 mg | Vitamin A: .......................0.04 RE |
| Protein: .......................25 g | Total fat: .......................8 g | Magnesium: .......................34 mg |
| Carbohydrate: .................20 g | Saturated fat: .............3 g | Potassium: .......................336 mg |
| Sugars: .........................2 g | Omega-3 fatty acids:...0.04 g | Sodium: .......................270 mg |
| Calcium: ....................51 mg | Omega-6 fatty acids: ..0.64 g | Iron: .......................4 mg |
| Fiber (total): ....................2 g | Cholesterol: ..................57 mg | Zinc: .......................5 mg |

Diabetic exchanges: 1 serving equals 1¼ starch exchanges, 2 medium-fat meat exchanges

# Hot Roast Beef Sandwich

1 to 2 slices of bread, preferably whole grain
2 ounces of leftover roast beef
⅓ cup leftover juice from "Crock Pot Roast Beef Dinner," page 216
2 teaspoons all purpose, unbleached, or white spelt flour

Combine the flour and juice in a small pan or glass bowl with a hand blender. Heat the ingredients in the pan over medium heat on the stove, stirring constantly, until the gravy thickens. If you combined the ingredients in a glass bowl, heat them on "high" in the microwave oven, stirring every minute or two until the gravy thickens. If the gravy gets lumpy, blend it again with the hand blender. Warm the roast beef by heating it in a microwave oven, or wrap it in foil and put it in a 350°F oven for about 15 minutes. Toast the bread if desired. Put the bread or toast on a plate. Top with the roast beef and gravy. Makes one serving.

**Nutritional Analysis per serving:** 1 serving per recipe

| | | |
|---|---|---|
| Calories: ...................223 | Total fat: ...................6 g | Vitamin A: ...................0 RE |
| Protein: ...................24 g | Saturated fat: ...............2 g | Magnesium: ...................40 mg |
| Carbohydrate: ...............17 g | Omega-3 fatty acids:...0.03 g | Potassium: ...................308 mg |
| Sugars: ...................2 g | Omega-6 fatty acids: ..0.46 g | Sodium: ...................209 mg |
| Fiber (total): ...............2 g | Cholesterol: ...............57 mg | Iron: ...................3 mg |
| Vitamin C: ...............0 mg | Calcium: ...................29 mg | Zinc: ...................6 mg |

Diabetic exchanges: 1 serving equals 1 starch exchange, 2 medium-fat meat exchanges

# Barbecued Beef Sandwiches

*This is a great dish to take along in a thermos when you are going to a game or on a picnic. If you are in a rush, you can use store-bought barbecue sauce, but be aware that it is usually loaded with sugar.*

1 batch (about 2 cups) of "Barbecue Sauce," page 142, or 2 cups
        commercial barbecue sauce
12 ounces of leftover sliced roast beef
4 to 6 hard rolls, preferably whole grain, sliced

Make the barbecue sauce, or if you are using commercial sauce, put it in a saucepan and heat it to the boiling point. Add the roast beef to the saucepan and simmer it in the sauce for a few minutes until it is heated through. If you want to take barbecued beef sandwiches on an outing, put the hot beef and sauce in a thermos. Serve on hard rolls. Makes 4 to 6 servings.

**Nutritional Analysis per serving:** 6 servings per recipe

| | | |
|---|---|---|
| Calories: ...................329 | Total fat: ...................7 g | Calcium: ...................173 mg |
| Protein: ...................24 g | Saturated fat: ...............2 g | Magnesium: ...................35 mg |
| Carbohydrate: ...............46 g | Omega-3 fatty acids:...0.44 g | Potassium: ...................564 mg |
| Sugars: ...................15 g | Omega-6 fatty acids: ..0.26 g | Sodium: ...................781 mg |
| Fiber (total): ...............6 g | Cholesterol: ...............57 mg | Iron: ...................5 mg |
| Vitamin C: ...............17 mg | Vitamin A: ...................72 RE | Zinc: ...................5 mg |

Diabetic exchanges: 1 serving equals 2¼ starch/other carbohydrate exchanges, 2 lean meat exchanges, ⅔ fruit exchange

# Sloppy Joe Sandwiches

1 batch (about 2 cups) of "Barbecue Sauce," page 142, or use commercial
    barbecue sauce
½ pound of lean ground beef
4 to 6 hard rolls, preferably whole grain, sliced

Place the ground beef in a frying pan. Heat it over medium heat, and break it up
with a fork and stir it until it is no longer pink. Cook it for an additional five minutes.
Drain the grease from the pan. Put the cooked meat on paper towels, if desired, to remove
a little more fat from the meat. Make the barbecue sauce, or if you are using commercial
sauce, put it in a saucepan and heat it to the boiling point. Add the cooked ground beef
to the saucepan and simmer it in the sauce for a few minutes until it is heated through.
Serve on hard rolls. Makes 4 to 6 servings.

**Nutritional Analysis per serving:** 6 servings per recipe

| | | |
|---|---|---|
| Calories: .................313 | Total fat: .................10 g | Calcium: .................172 mg |
| Protein: .................15 g | Saturated fat: .................3 g | Magnesium: .................29 mg |
| Carbohydrate: .................46 g | Omega-3 fatty acids:...0.46 g | Potassium: .................511 mg |
| Sugars: .................15 g | Omega-6 fatty acids: ..0.32 g | Sodium: .................772 mg |
| Fiber (total): .................6 g | Cholesterol: .................36 mg | Iron: .................3 mg |
| Vitamin C: .................17 mg | Vitamin A: .................72 RE | Zinc: .................2 mg |

Diabetic exchanges: 1 serving equals 2 starch exchanges, 2 lean meat exchanges, ⅔
fruit exchange

# Reuben Sandwich

2 slices of bread, preferably whole grain
1 to 2 one-ounce slices of Swiss cheese
1 slice (about 1 ounce) of cooked corned beef
3 tablespoons (about 1½ ounces) of canned sauerkraut, drained
1 to 2 teaspoons of EFA-butter (recipe on page 142) or softened butter

Spread one side of each piece of bread with EFA-butter or softened butter. Press the
sauerkraut between two pieces of paper towel to remove the moisture from it. Put one
slice of the bread into a frying pan buttered side down. Put the cheese on top of it. Lay
the corned beef on top of the cheese. Put the sauerkraut on top of the corned beef. Top
the sandwich with the second slice of bread buttered side up. Place the pan on the burner of your stove and turn the heat up to low or medium-low. (You will have to find by
trial and error the setting on your stove that produces a Reuben sandwich that contains
melted cheese and is warm all the way through without being burned on the outside).
Cover the pan with a lid; this helps the cheese melt. Cook the sandwich for 3 to 6 minutes, or until the bottom side is golden-brown. (With experience you will soon learn what
the ideal cooking time is for your stove). Turn the sandwich over and cook it for another 3 to 6 minutes until the other side is also golden-brown. Serve immediately. Makes
one serving.

**Nutritional Analysis per serving:** 1 serving per recipe

| | | |
|---|---|---|
| Calories: ...............361 | Total fat:...............20 g | Calcium: ...............328 mg |
| Protein: ...............19 g | Saturated fat:...............9 g | Magnesium: ...............67 mg |
| Carbohydrate:...............29 g | Omega-3 fatty acids:...0.41 g | Potassium: ...............287 mg |
| Sugars: ...............4 g | Omega-6 fatty acids: ....1.38 g | Sodium:...............991 mg |
| Fiber (total):...............5 g | Cholesterol: ...............59 mg | Iron: ...............3 mg |
| Vitamin C:...............6 mg | Vitamin A:...............90 RE | Zinc:...............4 mg |

Diabetic exchanges: 1 serving equals 2 starch exchanges, 1 high-fat meat exchange, 1 medium-fat meat exchange, ⅓ vegetable exchange, ½ fat exchange

# All-Meat Hamburgers

*If you wish to make hamburgers using ground buffalo or other game meats, you may want to braise rather than broil them so they can be well done without being tough. See the recipe for braised game burgers on page 77 of* The Ultimate Food Allergy Cookbook and Survival Guide.

1 pound lean ground beef or ground turkey
½ teaspoon salt
Dash of pepper (optional)
4 hamburger buns, preferably whole grain
Optional toppings – sliced cheese, tomatoes, lettuce, pickles, catsup, mustard, etc.

Mix the beef, salt, and pepper with your hands. Lightly shape the mixture into four patties. Place the patties on a broiler pan and broil at 500°F about 3 to 4 inches from the heat. Broil the burgers for 10 minutes, then turn them and broil the other side for 10 minutes. Cut one of the burgers to make sure the inside is no longer pink before serving. These burgers will be well done and should not give you an *E. coli* infection. If you shorten the broiling time, you will do so at your own risk! Serve the burgers on split buns with the toppings of your choice. Makes four servings.

**Nutritional Analysis per serving:** 4 servings per recipe

| | | |
|---|---|---|
| Calories: ...............394 | Total fat:...............17 g | Calcium: ...............159 mg |
| Protein: ...............31 g | Saturated fat:...............6 g | Magnesium: ...............24 mg |
| Carbohydrate: ...............30 g | Omega-3 fatty acids:...0.49 g | Potassium:...............354 mg |
| Sugars:...............4 g | Omega-6 fatty acids: ..0.48 g | Sodium:...............492 mg |
| Fiber (total):...............5 g | Cholesterol: ...............95 mg | Iron: ...............4 mg |
| Vitamin C:...............0 mg | Vitamin A: ...............0 RE | Zinc:...............6 mg |

Diabetic exchanges: 1 serving equals 2 starch exchanges and 3 medium-fat meat exchanges if made with beef. (The nutritional values above are for beef hamburgers). Each serving contains 2 starch exchanges, 3 lean meat exchanges and 333 calories if made with turkey.

# Vegetarian Burgers

1 8 ounce can of tomato sauce
¾ cup textured vegetable protein (dry flakes)
¾ cup uncooked oatmeal, regular or quick-cooking (not instant oatmeal)
1 large egg or ¼ cup egg substitute
½ teaspoon salt
¼ teaspoon pepper
1 tablespoon chopped onion OR 1 teaspoon dry minced onion flakes (optional)
6 hamburger buns, preferably whole grain
Optional toppings – sliced cheese, tomatoes, lettuce, pickles, catsup, mustard, etc.

Put the tomato sauce in a saucepan, put the pan on the stove, and bring the sauce to a boil over medium heat. Stir in the textured vegetable protein, remove the pan from the heat, and allow it to stand for 5 to 10 minutes or until all of the liquid is absorbed. Mix in the oatmeal, egg, salt, pepper and onion with your hands. Form the mixture into six patties. Lightly oil a non-stick skillet and put it on the burner of your stove over medium heat. Place the patties (as many as will fit at one time) into the skillet. Cook them until they brown on the bottom side; then turn them over and cook until the other side is also brown. Serve them immediately on split hamburger buns with the toppings of your choice. Makes 6 servings. If you're not feeding six people, you can freeze the leftover burgers for future meals either before or after cooking them.

**Nutritional Analysis per serving:** 6 servings per recipe

| | | |
|---|---|---|
| Calories: ......................234 | Total fat:............................4 g | Calcium: ............................199 mg |
| Protein: ..........................13 g | Saturated fat:................0 g | Magnesium:..................30 mg |
| Carbohydrate:................43 g | Omega-3 fatty acids:...0.44 g | Potassium: ....................293 mg |
| Sugars: ............................7 g | Omega-6 fatty acids: ..0.38 g | Sodium:........................576 mg |
| Fiber (total): ....................8 g | Cholesterol: ....................41 mg | Iron: ....................................3 mg |
| Vitamin C: ........................5 mg | Vitamin A:..........................71 RE | Zinc:....................................3 mg |

Diabetic exchanges: 1 serving equals 2⅓ starch exchanges, ½ lean meat exchange, 1 vegetable exchange

# Heart-Healthy Burgers

8 ounces of ground turkey
4 ounces of ground buffalo
½ cup cooked rice or other cooked grain of any kind
½ cup cooked vegetables, any kind or combination (peas, carrots, beans, or a
        combination of these vegetables are good)
½ teaspoon salt (optional)
¼ teaspoon pepper
5 hamburger buns, preferably whole grain
Optional toppings – sliced cheese, tomatoes, lettuce, pickles, catsup, mustard, etc.

Put the cooked vegetables and grain in a food processor or blender and puree, or puree them with a hand blender. To do this with a hand blender, puree the vegetables first. Then add the grain and blend the mixture some more. It does not have to be perfectly liquified; a few chunks remaining in the burgers are nice. Combine the puree with the meats and seasonings. Form the mixture into 5 patties. Place the patties on a broiler pan and broil at 500°F about 3 to 4 inches from the heat. Broil the burgers for 8 minutes, then turn them and broil the other side for 8 minutes. Cut one of the burgers to make sure the inside is no longer pink before serving. Serve the burgers on split buns with the toppings of your choice. Makes 5 servings. If you are not feeding five people, these burgers freeze well, either before or after cooking.

**Nutritional Analysis per serving:** 5 servings per recipe

| | | |
|---|---|---|
| Calories: ......................273 | Total fat: ...........................7 g | Calcium:............................161 mg |
| Protein: ............................18 g | Saturated fat:.....................1 g | Magnesium:.......................17 mg |
| Carbohydrate: ................38 g | Omega-3 fatty acids:....0.47 g | Potassium: ......................154 mg |
| Sugars: ..............................5 g | Omega-6 fatty acids:....0.88 g | Sodium: ..........................408 mg |
| Fiber (total): ....................6 g | Cholesterol: ...................47 mg | Iron: .....................................3 mg |
| Vitamin C: .........................2 mg | Vitamin A:.........................11 RE | Zinc: ....................................2 mg |

Diabetic exchanges: 1 serving equals 2⅓ starch exchanges, 1 lean meat exchange, 1 very lean meat exchange

# Hot Dogs

*Hot dogs, as purchased, are already fully cooked. You just need to heat them through before serving them – and I'm sure you already know how to do that! This recipe is just here to remind you of another good choice you have for lunch.*

Hot dogs (Use turkey dogs for a healthy, low-fat treat).
Water
Hot dog buns, preferably whole grain
Optional toppings – warmed chili (recipes, pages 175, 176, 220 and 236), grated cheese, mustard, ketchup, pickles, etc.

Bring a saucepan of water to a boil. Drop the hot dogs into the water, return it to a boil, reduce the heat to medium, and boil the hot dogs for five minutes. Serve in the buns with whatever toppings you desire. Hot dogs may also be warmed in a microwave oven by heating them on "high" for about one minute per hot dog.

**Nutritional Analysis per serving:** 1 serving per recipe

| | | |
|---|---|---|
| Calories: ......................208 | Total fat: ...........................6 g | Calcium:............................161 mg |
| Protein: ............................10 g | Saturated fat: ...................1 g | Magnesium:.........................9 mg |
| Carbohydrate:................32 g | Omega-3 fatty acids:...0.53 g | Potassium: ........................85 mg |
| Sugars:..............................5 g | Omega-6 fatty acids: ....1.03 g | Sodium: ...........................511 mg |
| Fiber (total):....................5 g | Cholesterol: ...................27 mg | Iron:......................................2 mg |
| Vitamin C:.........................0 mg | Vitamin A: ..........................0 RE | Zinc: ....................................1 mg |

Diabetic exchanges: 1 serving equals 2 starch exchanges, 1 lean meat exchange if you have a turkey dog.

# Vegetable Salads

## Grandpa Capraro's Salad

2 medium-sized cucumbers
2 regular or 4 to 6 Roma tomatoes
⅛ teaspoon salt
⅛ teaspoon pepper
2 tablespoons vinegar or lemon juice
1½ to 2 tablespoons oil, preferably canola oil, walnut oil, or another oil high in
    essential fatty acids

Peel and slice the cucumbers and put them in a large serving bowl. Slice the tomatoes and add them to the cucumbers. In a separate small bowl, stir together the salt, pepper, vinegar or lemon juice, and oil. Pour the dressing over the vegetables and mix. Makes 2 to 4 servings. Serve with crusty bread to sop up the juice.

**Nutritional Analysis per serving:** 4 servings per recipe

| | | |
|---|---|---|
| Calories: ...........................71 | Total fat:...........................5 g | Calcium: .........................18 mg |
| Protein: .............................1 g | Saturated fat: ...............0 g | Magnesium:....................21 mg |
| Carbohydrate:...................6 g | Omega-3 fatty acids:...0.52 g | Potassium: ...................294 mg |
| Sugars:...............................2 g | Omega-6 fatty acids: ....1.14 g | Sodium:...........................81 mg |
| Fiber (total):.....................1 g | Cholesterol: ...................0 mg | Iron: ..................................0 mg |
| Vitamin C:........................15 mg | Vitamin A: .......................45 RE | Zinc:...................................0 mg |

Diabetic exchanges: 1 serving equals 1 vegetable exchange, 1 fat exchange

## Tossed Salad

*This salad is a powerhouse of nutrition when made with greens or lettuce other than iceberg lettuce. The more darkly colored the greens, the more nutritious they are. Try red leaf lettuce, red bibb lettuce, endive, and a little arugula in this salad.*

4 cups of leaf lettuce or other greens, any variety or combination, torn into bite-
    sized pieces
¼ to ½ cup sliced carrots, cucumbers, and/or radishes
1 medium or large tomato, cut into eight to twelve pieces
¼ to ⅓ cup of any salad dressing on pages 143 to 147
Optional additions to make the salad more substantial:
    ⅓ cup croutons or ¼ cup crumbled crackers
    2 tablespoons chopped nuts
    2 tablespoons crumbled or grated cheese
    ⅓ cup cooked beans, such as garbanzo beans, drained

Tear the lettuce or greens into bite sized pieces and put them in a large salad bowl. Slice the cucumbers, carrots, or radishes and cut up the tomato; add them to the salad bowl and toss. Add the dressing and toss. Sprinkle the top of the salad with the optional additions such as croutons, nuts, beans, or cheese. Serve immediately. Makes 2 to 3 servings.

**Nutritional Analysis per serving for the salad only (no dressing):** 3 servings per recipe

| | | |
|---|---|---|
| Calories: ...........................26 | Total fat: ...........................0 g | Calcium:..........................40 mg |
| Protein: .............................1 g | Saturated fat: ...............0 g | Magnesium: .....................6 mg |
| Carbohydrate:...................6 g | Omega-3 fatty acids:...0 g | Potassium:....................329 mg |
| Sugars:...............................4 g | Omega-6 fatty acids: ..0.06 g | Sodium: ...........................34 mg |
| Fiber (total):.....................3 g | Cholesterol: ...................0 mg | Iron: ..................................0 mg |
| Vitamin C:........................13 mg | Vitamin A:....................489 RE | Zinc:...................................0 mg |

Diabetic exchanges for the salad vegetables only: 1 serving equals 1 vegetable exchange. Add the exchanges for whatever dressing you choose to use to the exchanges for this salad.

# Spinach Salad

4 cups of spinach leaves, washed, dried, and torn into bite-sized pieces
1 cup diced or sliced cooked beets or 1 avocado, peeled, seeded, and cut into bite-sized pieces (optional)
2 slices of bacon, cooked until crisp and crumbled (optional)
¼ cup of "Oil and Vinegar Dressing," page 143
⅓ cup croutons or ¼ cup broken crackers (optional)

Tear the spinach into bite sized pieces and put it in a large salad bowl. Slice or cut up the beets or avocado and add the pieces to the salad bowl. Crumble the bacon, add it to the salad bowl and toss the salad. Add the dressing and toss. Sprinkle the top of the salad with the croutons or crackers if desired. Serve immediately. Makes 2 to 3 servings.

**Nutritional Analysis per serving:** 3 servings per recipe

| | | |
|---|---|---|
| Calories: ...........................104 | Total fat:.............................11 g | Calcium:.............................40 mg |
| Protein: ................................1 g | Saturated fat: ................1 g | Magnesium:.......................33 mg |
| Carbohydrate: ...................2 g | Omega-3 fatty acids: ....1.16 g | Potassium: .......................231 mg |
| Sugars:.................................1 g | Omega-6 fatty acids:...5.68 g | Sodium:..............................143 mg |
| Fiber (total):.........................1 g | Cholesterol: .......................0 mg | Iron:........................................1 mg |
| Vitamin C:...........................11 mg | Vitamin A:......................269 RE | Zinc:.......................................0 mg |

Diabetic exchanges: 1 serving equals ½ vegetable exchange, 2 fat exchanges

# Coleslaw

1 pound of cabbage, about half of a large head
¼ cup chopped onion (optional)
1 small carrot, shredded
¼ teaspoon salt (optional)
¾ cup mayonnaise (preferably homemade, page 140, or made with canola oil) or super smooth sauce, page 141
2 tablespoons lemon juice

Wash and core the cabbage. Cut it into wedges and slice each wedge crosswise as thinly as possible. Put the cabbage strips into a large salad bowl. Shred the carrot and chop the onion, and add them to the salad bowl. Stir together the salt, mayonnaise, and lemon juice in a separate bowl. Add them to the cabbage mixture and toss throughly until the cabbage is completely coated with the dressing. Makes 6 to 8 servings. Keeps well in the refrigerator.

**Nutritional Analysis per serving:** 8 servings per recipe

| | | |
|---|---|---|
| Calories: ...........................147 | Total fat: ............................14 g | Calcium:.............................32 mg |
| Protein: ................................1 g | Saturated fat: ................1 g | Magnesium:.........................9 mg |
| Carbohydrate: ...................5 g | Omega-3 fatty acids: ....1.34 g | Potassium:.......................197 mg |
| Sugars:.................................2 g | Omega-6 fatty acids:...2.92 g | Sodium:..............................172 mg |
| Fiber (total):.........................2 g | Cholesterol: .......................0 mg | Iron:........................................0 mg |
| Vitamin C:...........................22 mg | Vitamin A:......................185 RE | Zinc:.......................................0 mg |

Diabetic exchanges: 1 serving equals 1 vegetable exchange, 2⅔ fat exchanges

# Sweet Carrot Slaw

1 pound of carrots (about 5 carrots)
¼ cup raisins (optional)
1 tablespoon of Fruit Sweet™ or honey OR 2 tablespoons of apple or pineapple
    juice concentrate, thawed
¾ cup mayonnaise (preferably homemade, page 140, or made with canola oil) or
    super smooth sauce, page 141

Peel the carrots. Grate them using the coarse holes of a cheese grater. Put them in a large salad bowl, and add the raisins. Stir together the mayonnaise and sweetener in a separate bowl. Then stir the dressing into the carrots until they are completely coated. Makes 6 to 8 servings. Keeps well in the refrigerator.

**Nutritional Analysis per serving:** 8 servings per recipe

| | | |
|---|---|---|
| Calories: ...157 | Vitamin C: ...6 mg | Vitamin A: ...990 RE |
| Protein: ...1 g | Total fat: ...14 g | Magnesium: ...1 mg |
| Carbohydrate: ...7 g | Saturated fat: ...9 g | Potassium: ...220 mg |
| Sugars: ...5 g | Omega-3 fatty acids: ...1.3 g | Sodium: ...187 mg |
| Calcium: ...21 mg | Omega-6 fatty acids: ...2.89 g | Iron: ...0 mg |
| Fiber (total): ...2 g | Cholesterol: ...0 mg | Zinc: ...0 mg |

Diabetic exchanges: 1 serving equals 1 vegetable exchange, ⅙ fruit exchange, 2⅔ fat exchanges

# Jicama Slaw

1 large jicama weighing about 1½ to 2 pounds
¾ cup mayonnaise (preferably homemade, page 140, or made with canola oil) or
    super smooth sauce, page 141
1 tablespoon lemon juice

Peel the jicama. Grate it using the coarse holes of a cheese grater. Put it in a large salad bowl. Stir together the mayonnaise and lemon juice in a separate cup or bowl. Then stir the dressing into the jicama until it is completely coated. Makes 6 to 8 servings. Keeps well in the refrigerator.

**Nutritional Analysis per serving:** 8 servings per recipe

| | | |
|---|---|---|
| Calories: ...166 | Total fat: ...14 g | Calcium: ...15 mg |
| Protein: ...1 g | Saturated fat: ...1 g | Magnesium: ...13 mg |
| Carbohydrate: ...9 g | Omega-3 fatty acids: ...1.3 g | Potassium: ...168 mg |
| Sugars: ...2 g | Omega-6 fatty acids: ...2.89 g | Sodium: ...161 mg |
| Fiber (total): ...5 g | Cholesterol: ...0 mg | Iron: ...1 mg |
| Vitamin C: ...22 mg | Vitamin A: ...11 RE | Zinc: ...0 mg |

Diabetic exchanges: 1 serving equals 1¾ vegetable exchanges, 2⅔ fat exchanges

# Waldorf Salad

1 large apple, preferably red, diced to make about 1½ cups diced apple
½ cup diced celery, about one large stalk
¼ cup chopped walnuts or other nuts
3 tablespoons raisins
¼ to ⅓ cup mayonnaise or super smooth sauce, page 141
2 teaspoons apple juice concentrate, thawed (optional)

Core the apple but do not peel it. Dice the apple and the celery and put them in a large bowl. Add the nuts and raisins and mix. In a separate bowl or cup, stir together the mayonnaise and apple juice concentrate. (If you don't have apple juice concentrate, you can substitute a little apple juice, thin the mayonnaise slightly with milk, or just use it "as is"). Stir the dressing into the apple mixture until it is completely coated. Serve immediately. Makes 3 to 6 servings. Store any leftovers in the refrigerator.

**Nutritional Analysis per serving:** 6 servings per recipe

| | | |
|---|---|---|
| Calories: ........................185 | Total fat:............................16 g | Calcium:.............................16 mg |
| Protein: ................................1 g | Saturated fat: ................1 g | Magnesium: ......................13 mg |
| Carbohydrate: ....................11 g | Omega-3 fatty acids: ....1.62 g | Potassium: ......................153 mg |
| Sugars:................................9 g | Omega-6 fatty acids:...4.52 g | Sodium:...........................150 mg |
| Fiber (total):......................2 g | Cholesterol: ....................0 mg | Iron:....................................0 mg |
| Vitamin C: ..........................4 mg | Vitamin A:..........................11 RE | Zinc:....................................0 mg |

Diabetic exchanges: 1 serving equals ⅓ lean meat exchanges, ⅔ fruit exchanges, 3 fat exchanges

# Anything Goes Fruit Salad

*Use your imagination – and clean out your refrigerator – when you make this salad.*

Fresh fruit of several varieties – try an apple, a banana, a peach, and 1 cup of strawberries and/or grapes
Canned fruit lurking in your pantry or refrigerator – try 1 cup of pineapple chunks, sliced peaches, and/or canned pears
2 teaspoons lemon juice
1½ tablespoons Fruit Sweet™ or honey or 2 tablespoons of frozen apple or pineapple juice concentrate, thawed

Cut the fresh or canned fruit into bite-sized pieces. Put it in a large salad bowl. Stir together the lemon juice and sweetener in a cup. Pour it over the fruit in the bowl and combine thoroughly. How many servings you get depends on how much fruit you started with, but if all the fruits above are used, this recipe makes about 8 half-cup servings. Keeps well in the refrigerator.

**Nutritional Analysis per serving:** 8 servings per recipe

| | | |
|---|---|---|
| Calories: ........................58 | Total fat: ............................0 g | Calcium:.............................10 mg |
| Protein:................................0 g | Saturated fat:................0 g | Magnesium: ......................7 mg |
| Carbohydrate:....................15 g | Omega-3 fatty acids:...0.02 g | Potassium:......................137 mg |
| Sugars:................................12 g | Omega-6 fatty acids: ..0.03 g | Sodium: ............................3 mg |
| Zinc:....................................0 mg | Cholesterol: ....................0 mg | Iron: ...................................0 mg |
| Vitamin C: ..........................17 mg | Vitamin A: ..........................10 RE | Zinc:....................................0 mg |

Diabetic exchanges: 1 serving equals 1 fruit exchange

# Main Course Salads

These salads are fairly substantial and contain protein foods. Served on a bed of lettuce with some bread, they make a nice lunch or light dinner. The egg, fish, and meat salads are also great as sandwich fillings. See the recipe for these sandwiches on page 125.

## Egg Salad

2 to 3 hard-cooked eggs, chopped
¼ cup finely chopped celery (about half of a stalk)
1 teaspoon minced onion (optional)
3 tablespoons mayonnaise or more to taste
Dash of salt (optional)
Dash of pepper (optional)

Cut up the eggs and vegetables. Add the rest of the ingredients and stir until well mixed. Makes enough egg salad for two sandwiches or two servings. This recipe may be halved if you only need one serving, or you may refrigerate the leftovers for tomorrow's lunch.

**Nutritional Analysis per serving:** 2 servings per recipe

| | | |
|---|---|---|
| Calories: ........................198 | Total fat: ...........................19 g | Calcium: ..............................31 mg |
| Protein:...............................6 g | Saturated fat: ................2 g | Magnesium: .......................7 mg |
| Carbohydrate:......................1 g | Omega-3 fatty acids: ....1.34 g | Potassium:.........................115 mg |
| Sugars: ..............................1 g | Omega-6 fatty acids:...3.48 g | Sodium:.............................342 mg |
| Fiber (total): ...................0 g | Cholesterol: ..................187 mg | Iron:...........................................1 mg |
| Vitamin C: .........................2 mg | Vitamin A:.......................85 RE | Zinc:..........................................1 mg |

Diabetic exchanges: 1 serving equals 1 medium-fat meat exchange, 2¾ fat exchanges

## Chicken or Turkey Salad

⅔ cup chopped cooked chicken or turkey
¼ cup chopped celery (about half of a stalk)
3 tablespoons mayonnaise or super smooth sauce, page 141
Dash of salt (optional)
Dash of pepper (optional)

Cut up the poultry and celery. Add the rest of the ingredients and stir until well mixed. Makes enough chicken or turkey salad for two to three sandwiches or two servings as a salad. This recipe may be halved if you only need one serving, or you may refrigerate the leftovers for tomorrow's lunch.

**Nutritional Analysis per serving:** 3 servings per recipe

| | | |
|---|---|---|
| Calories: ........................190 | Total fat: ...........................14 g | Calcium: ..............................16 mg |
| Protein:.............................14 g | Saturated fat: ................3 g | Magnesium: .......................14 mg |
| Carbohydrate:......................1 g | Omega-3 fatty acids:...0.63 g | Potassium:.........................169 mg |
| Sugars:..............................0 g | Omega-6 fatty acids:...5.89 g | Sodium:.............................117 mg |
| Fiber (total): ...................0 g | Cholesterol: ..................43 mg | Iron:...........................................1 mg |
| Vitamin C: .........................1 mg | Vitamin A: .......................13 RE | Zinc:..........................................1 mg |

Diabetic exchanges: 1 serving equals 2 lean meat exchanges, 1¾ fat exchanges

# Chopped Beef Salad Sandwich Filling

⅔ cup chopped leftover roast
¼ cup chopped celery
1 tablespoon minced onion (optional)
3 tablespoons mayonnaise or super smooth sauce, page 141
Dash of salt (optional)
Dash of pepper (optional)

Cut up the roast and vegetables. Add the rest of the ingredients and stir until well mixed. Makes enough filling for two sandwiches. This recipe may be halved if you only need one serving, or you may refrigerate the leftovers for tomorrow's lunch.

**Nutritional Analysis per serving:** 2 servings per recipe

| | | |
|---|---|---|
| Calories: ......................283 | Total fat:...........................20 g | Calcium: ...........................15 mg |
| Protein: ............................24 g | Saturated fat: ..............3 g | Magnesium: .......................19 mg |
| Carbohydrate:.....................1 g | Omega-3 fatty acids: ....1.32 g | Potassium:....................265 mg |
| Sugars:............................0 g | Omega-6 fatty acids:...3.11 g | Sodium:...........................334 mg |
| Fiber (total): ....................0 g | Cholesterol: ...................72 mg | Iron: .................................3 mg |
| Vitamin C: ..........................2 mg | Vitamin A:..........................11 RE | Zinc:................................6 mg |

Diabetic exchanges: 1 serving equals 3 lean meat exchanges, 2⅔ fat exchanges

# Tuna Salad

1 7 ounce can of water packed tuna, drained
⅓ cup chopped celery (about one small stalk)
1 tablespoon minced onion (optional)
¼ to ⅓ cup mayonnaise or super smooth sauce, page 141
Dash of salt (optional)
Dash of pepper (optional)

Chop the vegetables. Drain the tuna and break it into small chunks with a fork. Combine the tuna and vegetables with the rest of the ingredients and stir until well mixed. Makes enough tuna salad for three to four sandwiches or three servings as a salad. The leftovers refrigerate well.

**Nutritional Analysis per serving:** 4 servings per recipe

| | | |
|---|---|---|
| Calories: ......................219 | Total fat:...........................19 g | Calcium: ...........................12 mg |
| Protein:............................11 g | Saturated fat: ................1 g | Magnesium: .......................13 mg |
| Carbohydrate:.....................1 g | Omega-3 fatty acids: ....1.85 g | Potassium:....................149 mg |
| Sugars:............................0 g | Omega-6 fatty acids:...3.87 g | Sodium:...........................416 mg |
| Fiber (total): ....................0 g | Cholesterol: ...................12 mg | Iron:.................................1 mg |
| Vitamin C: ..........................2 mg | Vitamin A:..........................20 RE | Zinc:................................0 mg |

Diabetic exchanges: 1 serving equals 2 lean meat exchanges, 2½ fat exchanges

# Fish Salad

*Wondering what to do with the fish leftover from last night's dinner? Here's your answer! This is great made with leftover grilled salmon.*

1 to 1¼ cups leftover cooked fish, about ½ pound
¼ cup chopped celery, about half of a stalk
3 to 4 tablespoons mayonnaise or super smooth sauce, page 141
Dash of salt (optional)
Dash of pepper (optional)

Chop the celery. Break the fish into chunks with a fork. Combine the fish and celery with the rest of the ingredients and stir until well mixed. Makes enough fish salad for two generous sandwiches or two servings as a salad. This recipe may be halved if you only need one serving, or you may refrigerate the leftovers for tomorrow's lunch.

**Nutritional Analysis per serving:** 2 servings per recipe

| | | |
|---|---|---|
| Calories: ........................246 | Total fat: ...........................15 g | Calcium: ...........................19 mg |
| Protein: ...........................26 g | Saturated fat: ................1 g | Magnesium: ....................33 mg |
| Carbohydrate: ....................1 g | Omega-3 fatty acids: ....1.30 g | Potassium: .....................546 mg |
| Sugars: ..............................0 g | Omega-6 fatty acids: ...2.90 g | Sodium: ..........................378 mg |
| Fiber (total): .....................0 g | Cholesterol: ....................52 mg | Iron: ......................................1 mg |
| Vitamin C: ..........................5 mg | Vitamin A: ........................20 RE | Zinc: ......................................1 mg |

Diabetic exchanges: 1 serving equals 3¾ lean meat exchanges, 1 fat exchange

# Three Bean Salad

2 cups of cooked kidney beans or a 1 pound can of kidney beans, drained
2 cups of cooked garbanzo beans or a 1 pound can of garbanzo beans, drained
2 cups of cooked green beans or a 1 pound can of green beans, drained
3 tablespoons chopped onion (optional)
⅔ cup chopped green pepper
¼ teaspoon salt
⅛ teaspoon pepper
2 tablespoons Fruit Sweet™ or honey or ¼ cup apple juice concentrate, thawed
½ to ⅔ cup vinegar or lemon juice, to taste
⅓ cup oil

Combine the beans, onion, and pepper in a large bowl. In a small bowl stir together the salt, pepper, sweetener, ½ cup of the lemon juice or vinegar, and the oil. Pour this dressing over the beans, mix the salad, and taste it. If you like it tangier, add the additional lemon juice or vinegar. Refrigerate to blend flavors for a few hours before serving. Makes 10 to 12 servings. Leftovers keep well for several days refrigerated.

**Nutritional Analysis per serving:** 12 servings per recipe

| | | |
|---|---|---|
| Calories: ........................156 | Total fat: .............................7 g | Calcium: ...........................29 mg |
| Protein: .............................6 g | Saturated fat: ................0 g | Magnesium: ....................35 mg |
| Carbohydrate: ..................19 g | Omega-3 fatty acids: ...0.65 g | Potassium: .......................87 mg |
| Sugars: ..............................4 g | Omega-6 fatty acids: ...1.28 g | Sodium: ..........................226 mg |
| Fiber (total): .....................6 g | Cholesterol: ....................0 mg | Iron: ......................................1 mg |
| Vitamin C: ..........................9 mg | Vitamin A: ........................19 RE | Zinc: ......................................0 mg |

Diabetic exchanges: 1 serving equals 1 starch exchange, 1 vegetable exchange, 1¼ fat exchanges

# Potato Salad

1 pound potatoes, about 2 large or 3 small
2 to 3 hard cooked eggs (See page 120 or 230).
¼ cup diced celery, about half of a stalk
1 to 2 tablespoons minced onion (optional)
¼ teaspoon salt
⅛ teaspoon pepper
1 tablespoon lemon juice or vinegar
⅓ cup mayonnaise, or more to taste

Peel the potatoes. Put them in a pan with water and bring them to a boil over high heat. Reduce the heat to medium and cook until the potatoes are tender when pierced with a fork, about 30 to 45 minutes. Cut the potatoes into cubes and put them in a large bowl. Peel the hard cooked eggs. Cut them into small pieces and add them to the potatoes. Add the celery and onion to the potatoes and stir to mix. In a small bowl, stir together the salt, pepper, lemon juice or vinegar, and mayonnaise. Add this dressing to the large bowl and stir until the potatoes, eggs, and vegetables are well coated with the dressing. If you like your potato salad quite creamy, add more mayonnaise to taste. Chill before serving to allow the flavors to blend. Makes 4 to 8 servings. Store refrigerated.

### Nutritional Analysis per serving: 8 servings per recipe

| | | |
|---|---|---|
| Calories: ...........................211 | Total fat: ...........................14 g | Calcium:..............................17 mg |
| Protein:................................4 g | Saturated fat: ................1 g | Magnesium: ....................23 mg |
| Carbohydrate:.................19 g | Omega-3 fatty acids: ....1.17 g | Potassium:..........................4 mg |
| Sugars: ...........................2 g | Omega-6 fatty acids: ...2.73 g | Sodium:.............................235 mg |
| Fiber (total):.....................2 g | Cholesterol: ...................47 mg | Iron:.......................................1 mg |
| Vitamin C: .......................18 mg | Vitamin A:.......................27 RE | Zinc:......................................1 mg |

Diabetic exchanges: 1 serving equals 1 starch exchange, ⅓ medium-fat meat exchange, 2⅓ fat exchanges

# Sauces and Dressings for Sandwiches and Salads

## Mayonnaise

*Once you get used to homemade mayonnaise, you will never want to eat store-bought mayonnaise again. It is not at all hard to make using a food processor or blender, and if you're careful – or have an extra set of helping hands – you can even do it with a hand blender. Do not use "regular" raw eggs in this recipe. They can be contaminated with <u>Salmonella</u>.*

¼ cup egg substitute such as EggBeaters™ or 1 pasteurized egg
1 teaspoon dry ground mustard
1 teaspoon salt
Dash of pepper
1 teaspoon Fruit Sweet™ or honey (optional)
1 cup oil, divided, preferably a type of oil high in essential fatty acids such as canola
     or walnut oil
3 tablespoons lemon juice

Combine the egg or egg substitute, mustard, salt, pepper, sweetener, and ¼ cup of the oil in the bowl of a food processor or blender or in the cup that came with your hand blender. Turn on the food processor or blender or begin mixing with the hand blender. After the ingredients are thoroughly mixed (this takes just a few seconds), very slowly, pouring in a trickle, add half of the remaining oil while processing continuously. At this point, you may stop processing. Add the lemon juice and begin processing again. After the lemon juice is mixed in (again, this takes just a few seconds), very slowly, pouring in a trickle, add the rest of the oil while processing continuously. Makes about 1½ cups of mayonnaise, or 48 1½ teaspoon servings. Store in the refrigerator.

Note: If you are making this with a hand blender and don't have a helper to pour the oil while you blend, you may have to add a little oil, stop and blend, then add a little more oil, stop and blend, etc. If the mayonnaise starts to separate with a tablespoon or two of the oil remaining to be added, just stop adding oil, blend the mayonnaise very well, and quit while you're ahead.

**Nutritional Analysis per serving:** 48 servings per recipe

| | | |
|---|---|---|
| Calories: ...........................41 | Total fat:............................5 g | Magnesium:...................0 mg |
| Protein:...........................0 g | Saturated fat:...............0.3 g | Calcium: ...........................1 mg |
| Carbohydrate:..................0 g | Omega-3 fatty acids:...0.42 g | Potassium: ...................6 mg |
| Sugars:............................0 g | Omega-6 fatty acids: ..0.94 g | Sodium:.......................51 mg |
| Fiber (total): .....................0 g | Cholesterol: .......................0.01 mg | Iron:.................................0 mg |
| Vitamin C:..........................0 mg | Vitamin A:..........................3 RE | Zinc:................................0 mg |

Diabetic exchanges: 1 serving equals 1 fat exchange

# Super-Smooth Sauce

*This sauce is made from natural nut butters and "good" oils. It is a great source of essential fatty acids and a good substitute for mayonnaise for those who are allergic to eggs. Several variations on the recipe are given as well as an alternative way to add tart flavor for those who are allergic to lemon or lime juice.*

## Cashew sauce:

¼ cup cashew butter
¼ cup lemon or lime juice or ¼ cup water plus 1½ teaspoons tart-tasting
    unbuffered vitamin C powder or crystals
⅛ teaspoon salt
¼ cup oil high in essential fatty acids such as walnut or canola oil

## Almond sauce:

¼ cup almond butter
¼ cup lemon or lime juice or ¼ cup water plus 1 teaspoon tart-tasting
    unbuffered vitamin C powder or crystals
⅛ teaspoon salt
¼ cup oil high in essential fatty acids such as walnut, canola, or almond oil

## Macadamia sauce:

¼ cup macadamia nut butter
¼ cup lemon or lime juice or ¼ cup water plus 1 teaspoon tart-tasting unbuffered
    vitamin C powder or crystals
⅛ teaspoon salt
¼ cup oil high in essential fatty acids such as walnut or canola oil

Chose one set of ingredients from the list above. Combine the nut butter, lemon or lime juice or water plus vitamin C, and salt in a 2-cup glass measuring cup or the tall narrow cup that came with your hand blender. Turn on the blender and blend until the ingredients are thoroughly combined. (You can use a standard blender of food processor instead if you have one). With the blender running, add the oil very gradually in a thin steam until it has all been added and the sauce is thick, smooth, and creamy. Makes about ¾ cup of sauce or 18 two teaspoon servings. Store in the refrigerator.

**Nutritional Analysis per serving:** 18 servings per recipe

| | | |
|---|---|---|
| Calories: ....................48 | Saturated fat:...................1 g | Calcium:............................2 mg |
| Protein: .....................1 g | Omega-3 fatty acids: ....0.32 g | Magnesium:.....................9 mg |
| Carbohydrate:.................1 g | Omega-6 fatty acids: .....1.89 g | Potassium:........................24 mg |
| Sugars:.........................0 g | Cholesterol: ....................0 mg | Sodium: ............................17 mg |
| Fiber (total): ................0 g | Vitamin A: ..........................0 RE | Iron: .................................0 mg |
| Total fat:.....................5 g | Vitamin C: ..........................2 mg | Zinc:..................................0 mg |

Diabetic exchanges: 1 serving equals 1 fat exchange

# EFA-Butter
(Essential Fatty Acid-Butter)

*This is a great spread for toast and sandwiches, tasty to put on vegetables, and an all-around easy-to-spread good substitute for butter or margarine. Don't try to use it in baking though! With EFA-butter, you get the taste of butter and the essential fatty acids of walnut or canola oil for good health.*

½ cup walnut or canola oil
½ cup (1 stick) butter or goat butter at room temperature

Allow the butter to come to room temperature. If you forget to take it out of the refrigerator in time and like to live dangerously, you can try microwaving it for 5 to 10 seconds. Don't let it melt! Put the oil and butter in a 2-cup glass measuring cup or small bowl. Combine them with a hand blender until thoroughly mixed. (You can use a standard blender of food processor instead if you have one). Pour the EFA-butter into a jar and refrigerate it. Makes a little over 1 cup of EFA-butter or 40 1¼ teaspoon servings.

**Nutritional Analysis per serving:** 40 servings per recipe

| | | |
|---|---|---|
| Calories: ...........................44 | Total fat:............................5 g | Calcium: ...................................1 mg |
| Protein:................................0 g | Saturated fat: ................2 g | Magnesium:.........................0 mg |
| Carbohydrate:.....................0 g | Omega-3 fatty acids:...0.32 g | Potassium:.............................1 mg |
| Sugars:................................0 g | Omega-6 fatty acids:....1.49 g | Sodium:.................................23 mg |
| Fiber (total): .....................0 g | Cholesterol: .....................6 mg | Iron: ......................................0 mg |
| Vitamin C:.........................0 mg | Vitamin A: ........................21 RE | Zinc:......................................0 mg |

Diabetic exchanges: 1 serving equals 1 fat exchange

# Barbecue Sauce

*Use this sauce for "Barbecued Beef Sandwiches" or "Sloppy Joes," pages 127 and 128, or brush it on meats you are grilling outside. This sauce has all of the flavor of commercial barbecue sauces without the sugar.*

1 6 ounce can of tomato paste
¼ cup water
½ cup apple juice concentrate, thawed
¼ cup vinegar
2 whole cloves
1 teaspoon salt
¼ teaspoon pepper
¼ cup chopped green pepper
2 tablespoons minced celery
1 tablespoon minced onion (optional)

Combine all of the ingredients in a saucepan. Bring them to a boil and simmer over low heat for 35 to 45 minutes, stirring every 10 minutes to keep the sauce from sticking to the bottom of the pan. If you can find them, remove the cloves from the sauce before serving it. Makes about 2 cups of barbecue sauce or 6 ⅓ cup servings.

**Nutritional Analysis per serving:** 6 servings per recipe

| | | |
|---|---|---|
| Calories: ...........................66 | Total fat: ............................0 g | Calcium: ...............................18 mg |
| Protein: ...............................1 g | Saturated fat:..................0 g | Magnesium: .......................22 mg |
| Carbohydrate:...................16 g | Omega-3 fatty acids:...0 g | Potassium: ......................400 mg |
| Sugars:................................11 g | Omega-6 fatty acids: ..0 g | Sodium: ............................623 mg |
| Fiber (total):.......................1 g | Cholesterol: .....................0 mg | Iron: .......................................1 mg |
| Vitamin C: ........................17 mg | Vitamin A:........................72 RE | Zinc:......................................0 mg |

Diabetic exchanges: 1 serving equals ⅓ other carbohydrate exchange,
⅔ fruit exchange

# Oil and Vinegar Salad Dressing

*Salad dressings are a great place to add "good" oils to your diet. Canola and walnut oils are good sources of omega-3 fatty acids which most of our diets lack in sufficient quantities. See pages 23 to 25 for more about the nutritional aspects of oils.*

½ cup oil, preferably walnut, canola, flax*,
    or another oil high in essential fatty acids
1 clove of garlic, crushed (optional)
2 teaspoons finely chopped fresh oregano, sweet basil or parsley or
    ½ teaspoon dried oregano, sweet basil or parsley (optional)
½ teaspoon salt
Dash of pepper
⅓ cup vinegar or lemon juice

If you wish to use the garlic, crush it and put it and the oil in a glass jar. Refrigerate at least overnight. Remove the garlic from the oil and discard it. Combine the rest of the ingredients with the oil in the jar. Shake the dressing to thoroughly mix it right before pouring the dressing on your salad. Makes 1 scant cup of dressing or about 22 two teaspoon servings. Refrigerate leftover dressing.

*Note on flax oil: Flax oil is so fragile that it goes rancid quickly after opening it even if you store it in the refrigerator. Be sure to use oil that is freshly purchased.

**Nutritional Analysis per serving:** 22 servings per recipe

| | | |
|---|---|---|
| Calories: ...........44 | Total fat:............5 g | Calcium:............0 mg |
| Protein:............0 g | Saturated fat:......0 g | Magnesium:..........0 mg |
| Carbohydrate:......0 g | Omega-3 fatty acids:...0.52 g | Potassium:..........4 mg |
| Sugars:............0 g | Omega-6 fatty acids:...2.62 g | Sodium: ............3 mg |
| Fiber (total):.....0 g | Cholesterol: .......0 mg | Iron: .............0 mg |
| Vitamin C:.........0 mg | Vitamin A: .........0 RE | Zinc:..............0 mg |

Diabetic exchanges: 1 serving equals 1 fat exchange

# Sweet Vinaigrette

½ cup oil, preferably walnut, canola, flax*,
    or another oil high in essential fatty acids
½ teaspoon salt
Dash of pepper (optional)
⅓ cup vinegar or lemon juice
2 tablespoons thawed fruit juice concentrate (apple, pineapple, orange, or white
    grape) or 1 tablespoon Fruit Sweet™ or honey

Combine all of the ingredients in a glass jar. Shake the dressing thoroughly to mix it right before pouring the dressing on your salad. Makes about 1 cup of dressing or 24 two teaspoon servings. Refrigerate leftover dressing.

*Note on flax oil: Flax oil is so fragile that it goes rancid quickly after opening it even if you store it in the refrigerator. Be sure to use oil that is freshly purchased.

**Nutritional Analysis per serving:** 24 servings per recipe

| | | |
|---|---|---|
| Calories: ...........43 | Total fat:............5 g | Calcium: ...........1 mg |
| Protein:............0 g | Saturated fat:......0 g | Magnesium: .........1 mg |
| Carbohydrate:......1 g | Omega-3 fatty acids:...0.47 g | Potassium:..........10 mg |
| Sugars: ...........1 g | Omega-6 fatty acids:...2.40 g | Sodium: ............49 mg |
| Fiber (total):.....0 g | Cholesterol: .......0 mg | Iron: .............0 mg |
| Vitamin C:.........0 mg | Vitamin A: .........0 RE | Zinc:..............0 mg |

Diabetic exchanges: 1 serving equals 1 fat exchange

# Creamy French Dressing

¼ cup water
2 teaspoons cornstarch, tapioca starch, or arrowroot
        or 1 tablespoon of Quick Thick™
⅓ cup vinegar or lemon juice
2 teaspoons Fruit Sweet™ or honey
1 tablespoon paprika
1 teaspoon salt
Dash of pepper
1 cup oil, preferably walnut, canola, flax*, or another oil high in essential fatty acids

If you are using the cornstarch, tapioca starch, or arrowroot, combine it with the ¼ cup of water in a saucepan. Cook the mixture over medium heat until it reaches the boiling point, becomes thick, and clears somewhat. Allow it to cool slightly. Put the cooked starch mixture or the ¼ cup water and Quick Thick™ in a large measuring cup or the tall container that came with your hand blender. (You can use a standard blender of food processor instead if you have one). Add the vinegar or lemon juice, sweetener, paprika, salt, and pepper. Blend until thoroughly mixed. While you continue blending, add the oil gradually in a slow stream. Serve immediately on salad or refrigerate it. Refrigerate any leftover dressing. Makes about 1⅔ cups of dressing or 40 two teaspoon servings.

**Lower fat variation:** Use ¾ cup water in place of the ¼ cup water, 3 tablespoons of cornstarch, tapioca starch or arrowroot or ¼ cup Quick Thick™, and ½ cup of oil.

*Note on flax oil: Flax oil is so fragile that it goes rancid quickly after opening it even if you store it in the refrigerator. Be sure to use oil that is freshly purchased.

**Nutritional Analysis per serving:** 40 servings per recipe

## "Regular" variation:

| | | |
|---|---|---|
| Calories: ............49 | Total fat:............5 g | Calcium: ............1 mg |
| Protein:............0 g | Saturated fat:............0 g | Magnesium: ............1 mg |
| Carbohydrate:............0 g | Omega-3 fatty acids:...0.57 g | Potassium:............2 mg |
| Sugars:............0 g | Omega-6 fatty acids:...2.88 g | Sodium: ............59 mg |
| Fiber (total): ............0 g | Cholesterol: ............0 mg | Iron: ............0 mg |
| Vitamin C:............0 mg | Vitamin A: ............0 RE | Zinc:............0 mg |

Diabetic exchanges: 1 serving equals 1 fat exchange

## Lower fat variation:

| | | |
|---|---|---|
| Calories: ............25 | Total fat:............2.7 g | Calcium: ............1 mg |
| Protein:............0 g | Saturated fat:............0 g | Magnesium: ............1 mg |
| Carbohydrate:............0 g | Omega-3 fatty acids:...0.28 g | Potassium:............2 mg |
| Sugars:............0 g | Omega-6 fatty acids:....1.44 g | Sodium: ............59 mg |
| Fiber (total): ............0 g | Cholesterol: ............0 mg | Iron: ............0 mg |
| Vitamin C:............0 mg | Vitamin A: ............0 RE | Zinc:............0 mg |

Diabetic exchanges: 1 serving equals ½ fat exchange

# Low Fat Blue Cheese Dressing

One 16 ounce container of non-fat sour cream
2 tablespoons vinegar
1 tablespoon lemon juice
2 tablespoons minced fresh or dried parsley
½ teaspoon salt or garlic salt
2 ounces blue cheese

Put the sour cream, vinegar, lemon juice, parsley, and salt in a bowl and stir throughly or blend them with a hand blender. Crumble the blue cheese and stir it into the dressing. Serve it immediately on salad or refrigerate it. Refrigerate any leftover dressing. Makes about 2½ cups of dressing or 40 two tablespoon servings.

**Nutritional Analysis per serving:** 40 servings per recipe

| | | |
|---|---|---|
| Calories: ...........................15 | Total fat: ...........................0.4 g | Calcium: ...........................28 mg |
| Protein: ...........................1 g | Saturated fat: ...............0 g | Magnesium: ...........................1 mg |
| Carbohydrate: ...................2 g | Omega-3 fatty acids:...0 g | Potassium: ...........................37 mg |
| Sugars: ...........................1 g | Omega-6 fatty acids: ..0 g | Sodium: ...........................60 mg |
| Fiber (total): ...................0 g | Cholesterol: ...........................1 mg | Iron: ...........................0 mg |
| Vitamin C: ...........................0 mg | Vitamin A: ...........................3 RE | Zinc: ...........................0 mg |

Diabetic exchanges: 1 serving equals ¹⁄₁₀ skim milk exchange, ¹⁄₁₀ fat exchange

# Avocado Dressing

*This dressing is delicious on spinach or sliced cucumbers.*

1 large ripe avocado (about ½ to ¾ pound in weight)
2 tablespoons vinegar or lemon juice, or more to taste
⅛ teaspoon salt
Dash of pepper
Water

Peel and seed the avocado. Put the avocado flesh in a 2-cup or larger glass measuring cup and mash it slightly or blend it with a hand blender. You should have about ⅔ cup of avocado flesh. Add the lemon juice or vinegar, salt, and pepper to the cup. Add water to the 1 cup mark. Puree with a hand blender until the dressing is smooth. (You can use a standard blender of food processor instead if you have one). Serve immediately. This dressing may darken if it stands for very long. Makes 1 cup of dressing or 16 one tablespoon servings.

**Nutritional Analysis per serving:** 16 servings per recipe

| | | |
|---|---|---|
| Calories: ...........................20 | Total fat: ...........................2 g | Calcium: ...........................2 mg |
| Protein: ...........................0 g | Saturated fat: ...............0 g | Magnesium: ...........................5 mg |
| Carbohydrate: ...................1 g | Omega-3 fatty acids:...0.01 g | Potassium: ...........................77 mg |
| Sugars: ...........................0 g | Omega-6 fatty acids: ..0.23 g | Sodium: ...........................20 mg |
| Fiber (total): ...................1 g | Cholesterol: ...........................0 mg | Iron: ...........................0 mg |
| Vitamin C: ...........................1 mg | Vitamin A: ...........................8 RE | Zinc: ...........................0 mg |

Diabetic exchanges: 1 serving equals ½ fat exchange

# Sweet Yogurt Dressing

1 cup plain low fat yogurt (cow, goat, or sheep)
2 tablespoons lemon juice
¼ cup apple or pineapple juice concentrate, thawed, or 2 tablespoons of Fruit
   Sweet™ or honey
¼ teaspoon salt
1 teaspoon poppy seeds (optional)

Thoroughly combine all of the ingredients. Serve immediately or refrigerate.
Refrigerate any leftover dressing. Makes about 1⅓ cups of dressing or 22 one tablespoon
servings.

**Nutritional Analysis per serving:** 22 servings per recipe

| | | |
|---|---|---|
| Calories: ...........................17 | Total fat: ...........................0 g | Calcium: ...........................20 mg |
| Protein: ...........................1 g | Saturated fat: ...............0 g | Magnesium: ........................2 mg |
| Carbohydrate: ...................3 g | Omega-3 fatty acids:...0 g | Potassium: ......................40 mg |
| Sugars: ...........................3 g | Omega-6 fatty acids: ..0 g | Sodium: ...........................35 mg |
| Fiber (total): .....................0 g | Cholesterol: ........................1 mg | Iron: ...................................0 mg |
| Vitamin C: ..........................0 mg | Vitamin A: ..........................2 RE | Zinc: ...................................0 mg |

Diabetic exchanges: 1 serving equals ¼ fruit exchange

# Herbed Yogurt Dressing

1 cup of plain low fat yogurt (cow, goat, or sheep)
2 tablespoons of lemon juice
⅛ to ¼ teaspoon pepper, or to taste
¼ teaspoon salt
1 tablespoon fresh chopped oregano or sweet basil or 1 teaspoon dry oregano or
   sweet basil

Stir together all of the ingredients until they are thoroughly combined. Serve immediately or refrigerate. Refrigerate any leftover dressing. Makes about 1⅛ cups of dressing
or 18 one tablespoon servings.

**Nutritional Analysis per serving:** 18 servings per recipe

| | | |
|---|---|---|
| Calories: ...........................9 | Total fat: ...........................0 g | Calcium: ...........................25 mg |
| Protein: ...........................1 g | Saturated fat: ...............0 g | Magnesium: ........................2 mg |
| Carbohydrate: ...................1 g | Omega-3 fatty acids:...0 g | Potassium: ......................34 mg |
| Sugars: ...........................1 g | Omega-6 fatty acids: ..0 g | Sodium: ...........................42 mg |
| Fiber (total): .....................0 g | Cholesterol: ........................1 mg | Iron: ...................................0 mg |
| Vitamin C: ..........................0 mg | Vitamin A: ..........................2 RE | Zinc: ...................................0 mg |

Diabetic exchanges: 1 serving equals ¹⁄₁₀ skim milk exchange

# Health Dressing

*If you make this dressing with flax oil, it is a powerhouse of omega-3 essential fatty acids. The combination of flax oil with yogurt is reputed to have amazing health-enhancing properties.*

1 cup of plain low fat yogurt (cow, goat, or sheep)
½ cup oil, preferably flax*, walnut, canola,
    or another oil high in essential fatty acids
¼ to ½ teaspoon salt, to taste
Dash of pepper
1 to 2 tablespoons fresh chopped oregano or sweet basil or 1 to 2 teaspoons dry
    oregano or sweet basil

Stir together all of the ingredients until they are thoroughly combined. Serve immediately or refrigerate. Refrigerate any leftover dressing. Makes about 1½ cups of dressing or 24 one tablespoon servings.

*Note on flax oil: Flax oil is so fragile that it goes rancid quickly after opening it even if you store it in the refrigerator. Be sure to use oil that is freshly purchased.

**Nutritional Analysis per serving:** 24 servings per recipe

| | | |
|---|---|---|
| Calories: .........................46 | Total fat:.............................5 g | Calcium: ............................19 mg |
| Protein: ...............................1 g | Saturated fat: .................1 g | Magnesium:.........................2 mg |
| Carbohydrate:.....................1 g | Omega-3 fatty acids: ...2.51 g | Potassium:.........................24 mg |
| Sugars: ..............................1 g | Omega-6 fatty acids: ..0.61 g | Sodium:..............................32 mg |
| Fiber (total): .....................0 g | Cholesterol: .........................1 mg | Iron: ....................................0 mg |
| Vitamin C:...........................0 mg | Vitamin A:............................2 RE | Zinc:.....................................0 mg |

Diabetic exchanges: 1 serving equals 1 fat exchange

# Soups and Stews

Soup or stew is almost a meal! Just add a salad, bread, and some fruit for dessert, and dinner is ready. Soups and stews can cook nearly unattended while you do other things, so they fit well into a busy lifestyle. They also contain nutritious ingredients, thoroughly cooked, so they are easily digested and the nutrients are well absorbed. Soups and stews can be made almost effortlessly with a crock pot. See the "Crock Pot Creations" chapter for more recipes for vegetable soups, bean soups, and hearty stews.

## Lentil-Barley Soup

*This vegetarian soup can be made from ingredients which you have in your pantry. If you have a few carrots and some celery in the refrigerator, they're nutritious additions.*

1⅓ cups of lentils (about ½ pound)
Water
½ cup pearled barley
2 stalks of celery, sliced (optional, but use them if you have them on hand)
2 carrots, sliced (optional, but use them if you have them on hand)
1 14 ounce can diced tomatoes
1 teaspoon salt
¼ teaspoon pepper
¾ teaspoon dried sweet basil or 2 teaspoons fresh chopped sweet basil

The night before you wish to make this soup, rinse and sort over the lentils, discarding any that are shriveled or bad-looking. Combine them with at least 5 cups of water in a saucepan and let them soak overnight. The next day, drain the water and replace it with fresh cool water three times. (The overnight soak and rinsing removes indigestible carbohydrates from the lentils which cause "gas"). To the drained lentils add 8 cups of water, the barley, the sliced carrots, and the celery. Bring the pan to a boil over medium to medium-high heat. Reduce the heat and simmer the soup for one hour. Check it occasionally as it is cooking and add additional water if it becomes too thick. At the end of the hour add the tomatoes, salt, pepper, sweet basil, and 1 to 2 additional cups of water if the soup is getting too thick. Simmer the soup another 15 to 30 minutes and serve. Makes 4 to 6 servings.

**Nutritional Analysis per serving:** 6 servings per recipe

| | | |
|---|---|---|
| Calories: ...................213 | Saturated fat:................0 g | Calcium:....................58 mg |
| Protein: ...........................13 g | Omega-3 fatty acids:...0.05 g | Magnesium:..................65 mg |
| Carbohydrate:................41 g | Omega-6 fatty acids: ..0.27 g | Potassium: ....................671 mg |
| Sugars:...........................6 g | Cholesterol: ......................O mg | Sodium:.......................519 mg |
| Fiber (total):.................16 g | Vitamin A:......................718 RE | Iron: ............................4 mg |
| Total fat:..........................1 g | Vitamin C:.......................15 mg | Zinc:..............................2 mg |

Diabetic exchanges: 1 serving equals 2 starch exchanges, ½ very lean meat exchange, 1⅓ vegetable exchanges

# Corn Chowder

*This soup is quick, easy, and flavorful. If you're adventurous, add the chili pepper.*

2 tablespoons oil
¼ cup finely diced celery
¼ cup minced onion or an additional ¼ cup finely diced celery
4 cups of chicken broth (homemade, canned, or made from bouillon cubes)
1 tablespoon lemon juice
1 teaspoon salt (optional)
⅛ to ¼ teaspoon pepper, to taste
3 cups finely diced potatoes (1 large or 2 small potatoes)
3 cups fresh or 1 pound frozen corn, preferably white corn
2 to 4 tablespoons chopped green chili pepper, to taste (optional)

Combine the oil, celery, and onion in a saucepan. Cook them over medium heat until the vegetables are soft. Peel and dice the potatoes. Dice the optional chili pepper. If the type of pepper you are using is very hot, be sure not to touch your eyes. Make the chicken broth from 4 cups of water plus 4 bouillon cubes or two cans of chicken broth plus water to make 4 cups, or you may use homemade broth. When the celery and onions are cooked, add the rest of the ingredients to the pan with them and bring the soup to a boil over medium or medium-high heat. Reduce the heat and simmer the soup for 10 to 15 minutes or until the potatoes are tender. Remove about 3 cups of the soup and puree it with a hand blender. Return it to the pot and reheat the soup before serving it. Makes 4 to 6 servings. This soup does not freeze well. If you cannot eat this large of a batch in a few days, halve the amounts of all of the ingredients.

**Nutritional Analysis per serving:** 6 servings per recipe

| | | |
|---|---|---|
| Calories: ........................185 | Total fat: ............................7 g | Calcium: ...........................19 mg |
| Protein: .............................5 g | Saturated fat: ................1 g | Magnesium: ....................35 mg |
| Carbohydrate: ...............30 g | Omega-3 fatty acids:...0.44 g | Potassium:....................364 mg |
| Sugars: ........................3 g | Omega-6 fatty acids: ....1.39 g | Sodium:..........................482 mg |
| Fiber (total):....................3 g | Cholesterol: ........................3 mg | Iron:........................................1 mg |
| Vitamin C:..........................0 mg | Vitamin A: ...........................1 RE | Zinc:.......................................1 mg |

Diabetic exchanges: 1 serving equals 1¾ starch exchanges, 1 fat exchange

# Cauliflower and Cottage Cheese Soup

*The cottage cheese and milk in this soup are great sources of protein yet the fat content of this soup is very low.*

1 tablespoon oil (optional)
1 small onion, chopped (optional)
3 to 4 cups of chopped cauliflower
2 cups chicken broth (homemade, canned, or made from bouillon cubes)
1 cup skim, low fat, or whole milk
1 cup low fat cottage cheese
Dash of salt and pepper, to taste

If you wish to use the onion, combine it with the oil in a saucepan. Cook it over medium heat until the onion is soft, about 3 minutes. Make the chicken broth from 2 cups of water plus 2 bouillon cubes or one can of chicken broth plus water to make 2 cups, or you may use homemade broth. When the onion is cooked, add the cauliflower and broth to the pan and bring it to a boil over medium to high heat. Reduce the heat and simmer the soup for ten minutes or until the cauliflower is tender. While the cauliflower is cooking, combine the cottage cheese and milk. Puree them with a hand blender until they are smooth. (You can use a standard blender of food processor instead if you have one). When the cauliflower is cooked, remove about half of the cauliflower and a little of the broth from the pot and puree them with a blender. Return the pureed cauliflower to the pot and add the cottage cheese puree. Reheat the soup carefully over low heat, stirring frequently, until it is just under the boiling point. Do not let it boil! Taste the soup and season with pepper and, if needed, salt to taste. Makes 4 servings.

**Nutritional Analysis per serving:** 4 servings per recipe

| | | |
|---|---|---|
| Calories: ........................105 | Total fat:...........................2 g | Calcium: ..........................158 mg |
| Protein: ...........................13 g | Saturated fat: ................1 g | Magnesium: ....................24 mg |
| Carbohydrate:..................12 g | Omega-3 fatty acids:...0.09 g | Potassium:.....................510 mg |
| Sugars:...............................8 g | Omega-6 fatty acids: ..0.03 g | Sodium: ..........................368 mg |
| Fiber (total):.....................3 g | Cholesterol: .....................11 mg | Iron:.......................................1 mg |
| Vitamin C: ......................53 mg | Vitamin A:.........................40 RE | Zinc:......................................1 mg |

Diabetic exchanges: 1 serving equals 1½ vegetable exchanges, 1 lean meat exchange, ¼ skim milk exchange

# Cream of Broccoli and Vegetable Soup

1 pound frozen chopped broccoli or a 1¼ pound head of fresh broccoli
1 cup peeled and sliced carrots (1 large or 2 small)
1 cup sliced celery (1½ to 2 stalks)
3 cups water or chicken broth (homemade, canned, or made from bouillon cubes)
½ to 1 teaspoon of salt only if you use water rather than broth
⅛ teaspoon pepper
2 cups skim, whole, or goat milk
6 tablespoons of all-purpose, unbleached, or white spelt flour (optional)

Peel and slice the carrots. Slice the celery. If you are using fresh broccoli, wash it and chop it, discarding the woody large stems, so that you end up with about a pound of chopped broccoli. Put the vegetables in a large pan. If you are using bouillon cubes, make the chicken broth from 3 cups of water plus 3 bouillon cubes. Use broth (homemade, canned, or made from bouillon cubes) or use 3 cups of water plus ½ to 1 teaspoon of salt. Add the broth or water, salt (if you are using the water), and pepper to the pan with the vegetables. Bring the soup to a boil over medium to high heat. Reduce the heat and simmer the soup for 15 to 20 minutes or until the vegetables are tender. If you like thick soup, thoroughly combine the flour with the milk. (A hand blender works well for this). Stir the milk or milk-flour mixture into the pan with the vegetables and reheat the soup to just below the boiling point. Serve immediately. Makes 4 servings.

**Nutritional Analysis per serving:** 4 servings per recipe

| | | |
|---|---|---|
| Calories: ........................92 | Total fat: ..........................0.4 g | Calcium:............................221 mg |
| Protein:...............................8 g | Saturated fat: ..............0 g | Magnesium: ....................42 mg |
| Carbohydrate:..................16 g | Omega-3 fatty acids:...0.05 g | Potassium:.....................496 mg |
| Sugars: ............................10 g | Omega-6 fatty acids: ..0.05 g | Sodium:...........................501 mg |
| Fiber (total):.....................5 g | Cholesterol: .....................2 mg | Iron:.......................................1 mg |
| Vitamin C: ......................48 mg | Vitamin A: ...................1247 RE | Zinc:......................................1 mg |

Diabetic exchanges: 1 serving equals 2 vegetable exchanges, ½ skim milk exchange

# Potato Soup

*You can make this soup without the milk if you are allergic to dairy products.*

2 medium potatoes, about 1 pound
1 small onion, chopped (optional)
1¾ cups water or 1 cup water plus ¾ cup skim, whole, or goat milk
¾ teaspoon salt
⅛ teaspoon pepper
Chopped parsley for garnish (optional)

Peel the potatoes. Cut one potato into quarters and the other into ½-inch cubes. Combine the potatoes and onion with the water in a saucepan. Bring them to a boil over medium or high heat; then reduce the heat and simmer them until they are tender, about 20 to 30 minutes. Remove the potato quarters and about ½ cup of the water from the pan and puree them with a hand blender until smooth. (You can use a standard blender of food processor instead if you have one). Add the potato puree, milk (if you are using it), salt, and pepper to the pan with the potato cubes. Reheat the soup carefully over low heat, stirring frequently, until it is just under the boiling point. If you have used the milk, do not let the soup boil. Serve immediately. Makes 2 servings. This recipe may be doubled or tripled to serve more people.

## Nutritional Analysis per serving: 2 servings per recipe

| | | |
|---|---|---|
| Calories: ...............154 | Total fat: ..................0 g | Calcium:......................9 mg |
| Protein: ...................3 g | Saturated fat:.........0 g | Magnesium:.............42 mg |
| Carbohydrate: ........36 g | Omega-3 fatty acids:...0 g | Potassium:...............649 mg |
| Sugars:....................3 g | Omega-6 fatty acids: ..0 g | Sodium:...................888 mg |
| Fiber (total):............2 g | Cholesterol: ............0 mg | Iron:...........................1 mg |
| Vitamin C:..............21 mg | Vitamin A: ...............0 RE | Zinc:...........................0 mg |

Diabetic exchanges: 1 serving equals 2 starch exchanges if this soup is made without the milk. If skim milk is used, 1 serving contains 2 starch exchanges, ⅓ skim milk exchange, and 186 calories.

# Potato Cheese Soup

*Although processed cheese is not an ideal ingredient health-wise, in a soup like this using processed rather than natural cheese produces a smooth soup and eliminates problems with reheating leftovers.*

2 to 3 large potatoes, peeled and chopped
½ onion, finely chopped (optional)
½ cup finely chopped carrot, about 1 small carrot (use if possible for the vitamin A)
½ cup finely chopped celery, about 1 stalk of celery (optional)
3 cups water or chicken broth (homemade, canned, or made from bouillon cubes)
½ to 1 teaspoon of salt only if you use water rather than broth
⅛ teaspoon of pepper
1 cup skim, low-fat, whole, or goat milk
8 ounces of low-fat processed cheese or natural cheddar cheese or goat cheese

Peel and chop the potatoes into ½ inch cubes. You should have 2½ to 3 cups of cubes, or up to 3½ cups of cubes if you will not be using the other vegetables. Chop the optional vegetables. If you are using bouillon cubes, make the chicken broth from 3 cups of water plus 3 bouillon cubes. Use broth (homemade, canned, or made from bouillon cubes) or use 3 cups of water plus ½ to 1 teaspoon of salt. Combine the vegetables, broth or water, salt (if you are using the water), and pepper in a large pot. Bring the soup to a boil over medium to high heat. Reduce the heat and simmer the soup for 15 minutes or until the vegetables are tender. While the vegetables are cooking, cut the cheese into cubes. Stir the milk and cheese cubes into the pan with the vegetables and reheat the soup over low heat, stirring frequently, to just below the boiling point. Serve immediately. Makes 6 servings.

**Nutritional Analysis per serving:** 6 servings per recipe

| | | |
|---|---|---|
| Calories: ....................162 | Total fat: .....................4 g | Calcium: .....................280 mg |
| Protein: ....................10 g | Saturated fat: ...............3 g | Magnesium: ....................21 mg |
| Carbohydrate: ................21 g | Omega-3 fatty acids: ...0.01 g | Potassium: ....................481 mg |
| Sugars: ......................7 g | Omega-6 fatty acids: ..0.04 g | Sodium: ......................832 mg |
| Fiber (total): .................2 g | Cholesterol: .................17 mg | Iron: ...........................0 mg |
| Vitamin C: ....................7 mg | Vitamin A: ....................418 RE | Zinc: ...........................1 mg |

Diabetic exchanges: 1 serving equals 1 starch exchange, 1 lean meat exchange, 1 vegetable exchange

# Quick and Easy Vegetable Soup

*This makes a big batch of soup, but it freezes well. Considering how quick and easy it is to make this soup, if you freeze leftovers for several meals you will be spending just a few minutes of cooking time per meal.*

6 cups of beef broth (homemade, canned, or made from bouillon cubes)
1 14 to 16 ounce can of diced tomatoes
¼ cup quick-cooking barley
1 10 ounce package of frozen mixed vegetables (peas, beans, carrots, and corn)
1 small stalk of celery, sliced (optional)
1 small onion, chopped (optional)
¼ head of cabbage, chopped
2 to 3 cups of cubed cooked beef, such as leftover roast

If you are using bouillon cubes, combine 6 cups of water and 6 bouillon cubes in a large saucepot, or use canned or homemade beef broth. Add the tomatoes and quick cooking barley to the broth in the pot and bring the soup to a boil over medium or high heat. Reduce the heat to low and boil the soup gently for 5 minutes. Add the frozen vegetables, celery, and onion, raise the heat, and bring the soup back to a boil. Boil the soup gently for another 10 minutes. Add the cabbage and beef and bring the soup back to a boil. Boil gently for another 5 minutes. Makes 8 to 10 servings.

**Nutritional Analysis per serving:** 10 servings per recipe

| | | |
|---|---|---|
| Calories: ....................126 | Total fat: .....................3 g | Calcium: .....................40 mg |
| Protein: ....................13 g | Saturated fat: ...............1 g | Magnesium: ....................0 mg |
| Carbohydrate: ................12 g | Omega-3 fatty acids: ...0.04 g | Potassium: ....................401 mg |
| Sugars: ......................3 g | Omega-6 fatty acids: ..0.15 g | Sodium: ......................138 mg |
| Fiber (total): .................3 g | Cholesterol: .................23 mg | Iron: ..........................2 mg |
| Vitamin C: ....................15 mg | Vitamin A: ....................167 RE | Zinc: ...........................2 mg |

Diabetic exchanges: 1 serving equals ½ starch exchange, 1⅓ lean meat exchanges, ½ vegetable exchange

# Homemade Chicken Soup or Broth

*This is the ultimate comfort food. It has even been shown to mollify the symptoms of the common cold. It's not as much work as you would think to make. If you can get an older (large) chicken, your soup will be more flavorful.*

1 large (3½ to 4 pound) chicken, or an equivalent weight of smaller chickens
3 quarts (12 cups) water
5 to 7 carrots, about 1 to 1½ pounds
3 stalks of celery
1 small or ½ medium sized onion
4 teaspoons salt
¼ teaspoon pepper
2 to 3 cups of additional soup ingredients (optional) such as:
    1 to 2 cups of peas or beans (fresh or frozen), chopped cabbage, or other vegetables
    1 cup of cooked pasta, rice, or barley

Clean out the cavity of the chicken. Put it into a large kettle with the water. Bring the chicken and water to a boil on high heat, reduce the heat, and simmer for 30 minutes. Skim the foam from the top of the soup while it is simmering. While the soup is cooking, peel the carrots and slice them. Slice the celery and chop the onion. (If you wish to make broth, not soup, cut the vegetables in half rather than smaller pieces so you can remove them from the liquid easily). Add the carrots, celery, onion, salt, and pepper to the soup, return it to a boil, and simmer it for 2 hours. Cool the soup slightly. Pour it through a strainer to remove the vegetables, meat, skin, and bones. The broth will be cloudy due to calcium leaching out of the bones. Don't worry about it – it's excellent nutrition! Skim the fat from the top of the broth with a spoon. (If you wish to remove all of the fat, refrigerate the broth and lift the fat off the top after it hardens). If you want broth rather than soup, this is the end of the recipe; use the cooked chicken in sandwiches or salads. If you want soup, return the vegetables to the broth. Pick the chicken meat from the bones and skin and cut it into small pieces. Return the meat to the pot. If you wish to use the optional vegetables, add them at this point. Return the soup to a boil, reduce the heat, and simmer it until the optional vegetables are tender. Add the pasta, rice, or barley and simmer the soup for a few more minutes until they are heated through. Serve immediately. Non-wheat pasta may fall apart if it is left in hot soup for a long time. Makes 10 to 15 servings.

**Nutritional Analysis per serving:** 15 servings per recipe

| | | |
|---|---|---|
| Calories: ......................165 | Total fat:............................5 g | Calcium:............................26 mg |
| Protein: ..........................23 g | Saturated fat: ...............2 g | Magnesium: .......................18 mg |
| Carbohydrate: ..................5 g | Omega-3 fatty acids:...0.09 g | Potassium: .....................314 mg |
| Sugars:..............................3 g | Omega-6 fatty acids: ....1.11 g | Sodium:...........................709 mg |
| Fiber (total): .....................1 g | Cholesterol: ...................68 mg | Iron:.......................................1 mg |
| Vitamin C: ..........................4 mg | Vitamin A: ...................668 RE | Zinc:.....................................2 mg |

Diabetic exchanges: 1 serving equals 2 lean meat exchanges, 1 very lean meat exchange, 1 vegetable exchange

# Meatball Soup

    1 pound extra-lean ground beef, buffalo, or other mild-tasting red game meat
    1½ teaspoons salt, divided
    ½ teaspoon pepper, divided (optional)
    2 teaspoons oil (optional)
    2 to 3 stalks of celery, sliced
    4 to 5 carrots, peeled and sliced
    8 cups water

Mix together the ground meat, ½ teaspoon of the salt, and ¼ teaspoon of the pepper. Form it into 1 inch meatballs. If you are using very lean game meat, put the oil into a large pot. For beef, omit the oil. Put the meatballs into the bottom of the pot and brown them over medium heat, turning them until they are browned on all sides. Drain off and discard the fat. Add the vegetables, the remaining 1 teaspoon of salt, the remaining ¼ teaspoon of pepper, and the water to the pot. Bring the soup to a boil over medium to high heat, reduce the heat, and simmer the soup for 1½ hours. Makes 6 to 8 servings.

**Nutritional Analysis per serving:** 8 servings per recipe

| | | |
|---|---|---|
| Calories: ...........................115 | Total fat:...........................5 g | Calcium: ...............................19 mg |
| Protein:.............................12 g | Saturated fat: ...............2 g | Magnesium: ......................14 mg |
| Carbohydrate: ...................4 g | Omega-3 fatty acids:...0 g | Potassium:....................346 mg |
| Sugars:................................3 g | Omega-6 fatty acids: ..0.01 g | Sodium:...........................510 mg |
| Fiber (total):.......................1 g | Cholesterol: ......................21 mg | Iron:......................................1 mg |
| Vitamin C: ...........................4 mg | Vitamin A:......................676 RE | Zinc:.......................................3 mg |

Diabetic exchanges: 1 serving equals 1⅔ lean meat exchanges, 1 vegetable exchange

# Oven Stew

    2 pounds beef round or chuck steak cut into 1 to 2 inch cubes
    1 onion cut into eighths (optional)
    4 carrots, peeled and cut into quarters
    4 celery stalks cut into quarters
    1 green bell pepper cut into one-inch squares
    ¼ cup quick-cooking ("minute") tapioca
    1 to 2 cups fresh or 1 8 ounce (drained weight) can of mushrooms, drained
        (optional)
    1 teaspoon salt
    ¼ teaspoon pepper
    1 28 ounce can of peeled tomatoes, undrained
    1 cup dry red wine or water

Thoroughly stir together all of the ingredients in a large casserole dish with a tight fitting lid, or if you don't have a dish that is large enough, divide the ingredients into two 2½ to 3 quart casserole dishes with lids. Bake at 300°F, covered, for 4 hours. Resist the impulse to open the oven and uncover the stew to check it until near the end of the cooking time. Do check it at about 3 hours after you put it into the oven and add a little more water if needed. Makes 8 to 10 servings. Leftovers freeze well.

**Nutritional Analysis per serving:** 10 servings per recipe

| | | |
|---|---|---|
| Calories: ........................213 | Total fat: ...........................7 g | Calcium: ...........................45 mg |
| Protein: ...........................65 g | Saturated fat: ...............3 g | Magnesium: .....................42 mg |
| Carbohydrate: ..................12 g | Omega-3 fatty acids:...0.08 g | Potassium: ......................699 mg |
| Sugars: ..............................4 g | Omega-6 fatty acids: ..0.30 g | Sodium: ...........................423 mg |
| Fiber (total): .......................1 g | Cholesterol: ...................54 mg | Iron: ...................................3 mg |
| Vitamin C: .......................30 mg | Vitamin A: .....................870 RE | Zinc: ...................................3 mg |

Diabetic exchanges: 1 serving equals 3 lean meat exchanges, 2 vegetable exchanges

# Grandma's Zucchini Stew

*My grandma made this with ground beef, but if you are eating a low-fat diet or are allergic to beef, try ground turkey, buffalo, or other game meat. This is one of the rare recipes in which zucchini freezes well. If you have an overflow of zucchini from your garden, double the recipe and freeze the leftovers.*

2 tablespoons finely chopped onion (optional)
1 tablespoon oil (optional)
1 pound lean ground beef, turkey, buffalo, or other game meat
1 1 pound can of peeled tomatoes
1 8 ounce can of tomato sauce or 6 tablespoons of tomato paste plus ¼ cup water
½ teaspoon salt
¼ teaspoon pepper (optional)
2 to 2½ pounds of zucchini, sliced about ⅜ inch thick

If you wish to use the onion, combine it with the oil in a saucepan and cook it over medium heat, stirring occasionally, until the onion begins to brown. Add the meat and brown it, stirring occasionally. Pour off the fat. Add the tomatoes, tomato sauce or tomato paste plus water, salt, and pepper. Return the mixture to a boil over medium to high heat. Reduce the heat and simmer it for about 15 minutes. Add the zucchini, return the stew to a boil, reduce the heat, and simmer it for an additional 10 to 15 minutes, or until the zucchini is just tender. (Large zucchinis take longer to cook than small ones). Add an additional ¼ cup of water if the stew begins to dry out or is thicker than you prefer it to be. Makes 4 to 8 servings.

**Nutritional Analysis per serving:** 8 servings per recipe

| | | |
|---|---|---|
| Calories: ........................132 | Total fat:............................5 g | Calcium: ...........................43 mg |
| Protein:...........................14 g | Saturated fat: ...............2 g | Magnesium:......................50 mg |
| Carbohydrate: ....................8 g | Omega-3 fatty acids:...0.04 g | Potassium: ......................697 mg |
| Sugars: ..............................4 g | Omega-6 fatty acids: ..0.07 g | Sodium: ...........................460 mg |
| Fiber (total):........................2 g | Cholesterol: ...................21 mg | Iron:....................................2 mg |
| Vitamin C:........................22 mg | Vitamin A: .....................103 RE | Zinc:....................................3 mg |

Diabetic exchanges: 1 serving equals 2 lean meat exchanges, 1 vegetable exchange

# Main Dishes

This chapter contains recipes for conventionally-made main dishes. There are also some great main dish recipes in the "Crock Pot Creations" and "Microwave Marvels" chapters.

## Roast Beef, Lamb, or Pork

*The best way to tell if a roast is done is with a meat thermometer. This kitchen tool is a worthy investment because it will ensure both good results in cooking and the safety of what you are eating. Pork should always be cooked "well done" to kill any eggs of the parasite Trichinella which may be present. Roasting should be used as a cooking method only with tender cuts of meat. The less tender cuts may be stewed or cooked in a crock pot for good results.*

Roast of beef, lamb, or pork
Dash of salt
Dash of pepper

Place the meat fat side up on a rack in a roasting pan. Season the meat with salt and/or pepper. Turn the oven on to 350°F and put the roast into the center of the oven. Estimate the cooking time at 20 to 30 minutes per pound for beef, depending on how well done you like it, at 30 to 35 minutes per pound for lamb, or at 40 minutes per pound for pork, which should always be cooked well-done. The actual roasting time depends on the shape of the roast and the fat content of the meat. Therefore, you will need to test your roast with a meat thermometer to see when it is cooked to your preference. Insert the thermometer into the center of the thickest part of the roast, but don't let it touch bone. The final thermometer readings should be:

Beef – rare: 140°F
Beef – medium: 160°F
Beef – well done: 170°F
Lamb: 160 to 180°F
Pork: 170 to 180°F

Remove the roast from the oven when it has reached the right internal temperature. Allow it to stand for about 10 to 15 minutes for easier carving.

**Nutritional Analysis per serving: Beef rib roast:** 1 serving per 3 ounce portion

| | | |
|---|---|---|
| Calories: 286 | Saturated fat: 9 g | Calcium: 9 mg |
| Protein: 20 g | Omega-3 fatty acids: 0.25 g | Magnesium: 17 mg |
| Carbohydrate: 0 g | Omega-6 fatty acids: 0.55 g | Potassium: 260 mg |
| Sugars: 0 g | Cholesterol: 71 mg | Sodium: 172 mg |
| Fiber (total): 0 g | Vitamin A: 0 RE | Iron: 2 mg |
| Total fat: 23 g | Vitamin C: 0 mg | Zinc: 5 mg |

Diabetic exchanges: one 3 ounce serving equals 3 high-fat meat exchanges

**Lamb leg roast:** 1 serving per 3 ounce portion

| | | |
|---|---|---|
| Calories: ...191 | Saturated fat: ...4 g | Calcium:...9 mg |
| Protein:...22 g | Omega-3 fatty acids:...0.14 g | Magnesium:...21 mg |
| Carbohydrate:...0 g | Omega-6 fatty acids: ..0.61 g | Potassium:...277 mg |
| Sugars:...0 g | Cholesterol: ...77 mg | Sodium:...172 mg |
| Fiber (total): ...0 g | Vitamin A: ...0 RE | Iron:...2 mg |
| Total fat: ...11 g | Vitamin C:...0 mg | Zinc:...4 mg |

Diabetic exchanges: one 3 ounce serving equals 1 medium-fat meat exchange plus 2 lean meat exchanges

**Pork loin roast:** 1 serving per 3 ounce portion

| | | |
|---|---|---|
| Calories: ...210 | Saturated fat: ...5 g | Calcium:...16 mg |
| Protein:...23 g | Omega-3 fatty acids:...0.03 g | Magnesium:...22 mg |
| Carbohydrate:...0 g | Omega-6 fatty acids: ..0.96 g | Potassium:...347 mg |
| Sugars:...0 g | Cholesterol: ...70 mg | Sodium:...167 mg |
| Fiber (total): ...0 g | Vitamin A: ...0 RE | Iron:...1 mg |
| Total fat: ...12 g | Vitamin C:...0 mg | Zinc:...2 mg |

Diabetic exchanges: one 3 ounce serving equals 3 medium-fat meat exchanges

# Broiled Beef or Lamb Steak or Chops

The "rules" for cooking solid cuts of meat, such as beef or lamb steaks, chops, and roasts, differ from those for cooking ground meats. If you broil a hamburger, it should be cooked thoroughly to the very center of the meat because it contains bacteria all the way into the center of the meat. However, solid cuts of beef and lamb should be sterile on the inside. Only the outside needs to be thoroughly cooked to make them safe to eat. Therefore, instructions are given here for cooking steaks and chops to your preference, whether that is well-done or medium-rare.

Tender cuts of beef steak (T-bone, New York, etc.) or lamb chops
Dash of salt
Dash of pepper

Trim any excess fat from the meat. Score it with a knife at 2-inch intervals around the outside edge to keep it from curling up as it cooks. Place it on a broiler pan. Set the pan in the stove about 3 to 4 inches from the heating unit. Turn the broiler on to 500°F or 550°F or to "broil." Broil the steak(s) or chop(s) until the top of the meat is well-browned. Then turn the meat and broil the other side. For a thin chop or steak to be well done, or a 1-inch thick steak to be medium-well, broil the meat for 10 minutes on each side. Season the meat with salt and/or pepper right before serving it. The way to gain experience with how long it takes your stove to cook your meat to the degree you prefer is to cut the meat during the broiling process and take a look at the inside of the meat. When you've cooked the "perfect" steak or chop, write down the thickness of the meat and the cooking time for future reference.

**Nutritional Analysis per serving:** 1 serving per 3 ounce portion

| | | |
|---|---|---|
| Calories: ...210 | Saturated fat: ...5 g | Calcium: ...6 mg |
| Protein:...21 g | Omega-3 fatty acids:...0.14 g | Magnesium:...21 mg |
| Carbohydrate:...0 g | Omega-6 fatty acids: ..0.37 g | Potassium:...296 mg |
| Sugars:...0 g | Cholesterol: ...48 mg | Sodium:...174 mg |
| Fiber (total): ...0 g | Vitamin A: ...0 RE | Iron:...2 mg |
| Total fat: ...14 g | Vitamin C:...0 mg | Zinc:...4 mg |

Diabetic exchanges: one 3 ounce serving equals 3 medium-fat meat exchanges

# Pepper Steak

1 pound beef or game round steak, cut into serving-size pieces
1 to 2 bell peppers
Dash of salt
Dash of pepper
Water

Remove the stems and seeds from the peppers and slice them into strips. Place the steak pieces into a glass baking dish. Add water almost to the top of the meat. Sprinkle the meat with salt and pepper and top it with the bell pepper strips. Cover the dish with its lid or with foil and bake it at 350°F for 2 hours. Watch the steak as it is cooking and add more water if necessary to keep it from drying out completely. The water should have almost completely evaporated by serving time. If it seems to be evaporating too slowly, remove the lid during the last half hour of baking so that the water evaporates and the meat will brown. Makes 4 to 6 servings.

## Nutritional Analysis per serving: 6 servings per recipe

| | | |
|---|---|---|
| Calories: ...........................131 | Saturated fat: ...............2 g | Calcium:...............................5 mg |
| Protein:................................17 g | Omega-3 fatty acids:...0.06 g | Magnesium:......................21 mg |
| Carbohydrate: ....................2 g | Omega-6 fatty acids: ..0.20 g | Potassium: ....................322 mg |
| Sugars: ...............................1 g | Cholesterol: ......................45 mg | Sodium: ............................77 mg |
| Fiber (total): .....................0.5 g | Vitamin A:..........................17 RE | Iron:.......................................2 mg |
| Total fat: ............................6 g | Vitamin C:..........................24 mg | Zinc:......................................2 mg |

Diabetic exchanges: 1 serving equals 2¼ lean meat exchanges, ⅓ vegetable exchange

# Meatloaf

1 pound lean ground beef, game meat, turkey, or other ground meat of any kind
1 cup grated or finely shredded vegetables such as carrots, cabbage, spinach, or
      summer squash
¼ small onion, finely chopped (optional)
⅓ cup finely chopped green pepper (optional)
¾ teaspoon salt
¼ teaspoon pepper
¼ teaspoon dry mustard (optional)
¼ cup water
¼ cup catsup, preferably fruit sweetened (optional)

Put the meat, vegetables, and seasonings in a bowl and mix them together thoroughly with your hands. Shape the mixture into a loaf. Add the water to a 2 to 3 quart casserole dish. Put the meatloaf in the casserole dish and cover it with its lid or with foil. Turn the oven on to 350°F. Bake the meatloaf for 45 minutes. Then uncover it and bake it for another 30 minutes to brown it. If you wish, you may top it with the catsup for the last 15 minutes of the baking time. Slice and serve. Makes 6 servings.

**Nutritional Analysis per serving:** 6 servings per recipe

| | | |
|---|---|---|
| Calories: ........................137 | Saturated fat: ...............4 g | Calcium: ............................12 mg |
| Protein: ...........................16 g | Omega-3 fatty acids:...0.00 g | Magnesium:.....................20 mg |
| Carbohydrate: ...................2 g | Omega-6 fatty acids: ..0.01 g | Potassium:....................303 mg |
| Sugars: ............................1 g | Cholesterol: ....................28 mg | Sodium:.........................355 mg |
| Fiber (total): ......................1 g | Vitamin A:.....................572 RE | Iron:...................................2 mg |
| Total fat: .............................7 g | Vitamin C: .......................2 mg | Zinc:...................................3 mg |

Diabetic exchanges: 1 serving equals 2½ lean meat exchanges

# Pork Chops

*I know that the producers of pork say that things are different nowadays, but I still think that pork should always be cooked thoroughly to eliminate any possibility of transmission of the parasite <u>Trichinella</u>. Therefore, I do not recommend broiling pork chops. By the time I would consider them cooked long enough to be safe if broiled, they would also be tough. Instead, cook your pork chops in a frying pan or the oven as directed in this recipe. They'll be tasty, juicy, and definitely safe to eat!*

Pork chops
Dash of salt
Dash of pepper
Water

Chose a frying pan that is large enough to hold your pork chops in a single layer. Rub the inside of the pan with the fat edge of one of the chops. Then trim the excess fat from the chops and score the edges to keep the chops from curling as they cook. Lay the pork chops in the pan and place the pan on the burner of your stove. Turn the heat to medium. Cook the chops until they are nicely browned on one side, about 8 to 10 minutes. Turn them over and cook until the other side is also nicely browned, or for another 8 to 10 minutes. Season the meat with salt and/or pepper. Add water to the frying pan to the depth of the pork chops. When it comes to a boil, reduce the heat, cover the pan with a lid, and simmer for 45 minutes. If necessary, add water to the pan to keep it from drying out during the cooking time. At the end of the cooking time, uncover the pan and allow the water to dry out. Turn the pork chops several times to coat them with the pan juices. Drain any fat from the pan. Serve immediately.

**Oven Pork Chops Variation:** This will save you from having to "tend" the pork chops as they cook. After browning the chops, place them in a glass baking dish. Sprinkle them with salt and/or pepper. (If you wish to prepare this dish ahead of serving time, you may refrigerate it at this point). Add boiling water to the baking dish to a depth of about ½ inch. Cover the dish with its lid or with aluminum foil. Bake it at 350°F for 1 hour, adding more water if necessary during baking to keep the chops from drying out completely. If necessary, remover the lid from the casserole dish at the end of the hour to allow the water to evaporate and the chops to brown a little more.

**Nutritional Analysis per serving:** 1 serving per 3 ounce portion

| | | |
|---|---|---|
| Calories: ........................217 | Saturated fat: ...............5 g | Calcium:...............................4 mg |
| Protein:............................22 g | Omega-3 fatty acids:...0.03 g | Magnesium: ....................14 mg |
| Carbohydrate: ...................0 g | Omega-6 fatty acids: ....1.06 g | Potassium:....................329 mg |
| Sugars: ............................0 g | Cholesterol: ....................62 mg | Sodium: .........................151 mg |
| Fiber (total): ......................0 g | Vitamin A:...........................2 RE | Iron:...................................1 mg |
| Total fat: ...........................13 g | Vitamin C: .......................0 mg | Zinc:...................................2 mg |

Diabetic exchanges: one 3 ounce serving equals 3 medium-fat meat exchanges

# Pork Chop and Rice Dinner

4 medium pork chops or 8 small pork chops, about 1½ to 2 pounds
1 cup brown rice, uncooked
2½ cups boiling water
½ teaspoon salt
½ small onion, chopped (optional)
½ green pepper, chopped (optional)
¼ cup water
Additional water as necessary

Combine the rice, 2½ cups boiling water, and salt in a 7 inch by 10 inch baking dish and allow the mixture to stand while browning the chops. Rub the inside of a frying pan with the fat edge of one of the chops. Then trim the excess fat from the chops and score the edges to keep the chops from curling as they cook. Lay the pork chops in the pan and place the pan on the burner of your stove. Turn the heat to medium. Cook the chops until they are nicely browned on one side, about 8 to 10 minutes. Turn them over and cook until the other side is also nicely browned, or for another 8 to 10 minutes. Remove the pork chops from the frying pan and set them aside. Add the chopped vegetables to the pan and cook them until they are soft. Stir them into the rice mixture. Drain any fat from the pan. Add ¼ cup water to the frying pan and bring it to a boil, stirring it to allow the water to absorb the brown glaze from the pan. Add this water to the rice mixture and stir it to combine. Lay the pork chops on top of the rice. (They will be partially submerged). Cover the dish with foil or a lid. You can refrigerate this dish at this point if you want to make it ahead of time. Bake the dish at 350°F for 1½ hours if freshly prepared or for 2 hours if refrigerated. Add more water if it gets too dry during the baking time. Makes 4 to 8 servings. Leftovers keep well refrigerated or can be frozen for future meals.

**Nutritional Analysis per serving:** 8 servings per recipe

| | | |
|---|---|---|
| Calories: .......................302 | Saturated fat: ..............5 g | Calcium: ...........................10 mg |
| Protein: .............................24 g | Omega-3 fatty acids:...0.04 g | Magnesium:......................48 mg |
| Carbohydrate:.................18 g | Omega-6 fatty acids: ....1.29 g | Potassium:.......................381 mg |
| Sugars:..............................0 g | Cholesterol: ....................62 mg | Sodium:...........................182 mg |
| Fiber (total):......................1 g | Vitamin A:..........................2 RE | Iron:.......................................1 mg |
| Total fat: ..........................14 g | Vitamin C:...........................0 mg | Zinc:.......................................2 mg |

Diabetic exchanges: 1 serving equals 3 medium-fat meat exchanges, 1 starch exchange

# Sauerkraut and Pork Chops

*This is a good recipe to make when you will be home for the day working around the house or studying.*

2 16 ounce cans of sauerkraut, undrained
1½ pounds of pork chops or cut-up pork roast
1 teaspoon Fruit Sweet™ or honey OR 1 tablespoon apple juice concentrate,
    thawed, OR 3 tablespoons of apple juice

Start making this recipe a little over three hours before you want to serve it. Pour the sauerkraut into a 3-quart casserole dish. Stir in the sweetener. Lay the pork chops on top of the sauerkraut in a single layer. Cover the casserole dish and bake it at 350°F for one hour. Uncover it and bake it for another 45 minutes or until the pork chops are brown on top. Turn the pork chops over and bake another 45 minutes or until the other side of the pork chops is also browned. Cut up the pork chops into bite-sized pieces, removing the bones as you do so, and stir the pieces into the sauerkraut. Bake the casserole for an additional half hour. Serve with mashed potatoes. Makes 4 to 8 servings. If you want to serve this to a crowd or have plenty for your freezer, you can triple the batch and cook it in a turkey roaster.

**Nutritional Analysis per serving:** 8 servings per recipe

| | | |
|---|---|---|
| Calories: 240 | Saturated fat: 5 g | Calcium: 40 mg |
| Protein: 23 g | Omega-3 fatty acids: 0.06 g | Magnesium: 29 mg |
| Carbohydrate: 5 g | Omega-6 fatty acids: 1.09 g | Potassium: 522 mg |
| Sugars: 1 g | Cholesterol: 62 mg | Sodium: 784 mg |
| Fiber (total): 3 g | Vitamin A: 4 RE | Iron: 2 mg |
| Total fat: 14 g | Vitamin C: 17 mg | Zinc: 2 mg |

Diabetic exchanges: 1 serving equals 3 medium-fat meat exchanges, 1 vegetable exchange

# Chicken Marsala

*A little wine adds a lot of class to this receipe and "Turkey Piccata" on page 162.*

2 whole skinless boned chicken breasts
1 tablespoon olive oil or butter
¼ cup all purpose, white spelt, or any other kind of flour
Dash of salt
Dash of pepper
1 2 ounce can mushrooms, not drained
½ cup Marsala wine

Pound the chicken breasts with a meat pounder until they are thin. Mix the flour, salt, and pepper together and dip the breasts into it so both sides are coated. Heat the oil or melt the butter in a large frying pan over medium heat. Add the breasts and brown them on one side. Turn them over and brown them on the other side. Add the mushrooms with their juice and the Marsala to the pan. Cover the pan and bring the liquid to a boil. Reduce the heat and simmer for 30 minutes. Check the pan often and add more water or wine if the liquid is drying out. If necessary, at the end of the cooking time remove the lid and simmer until the sauce is thick. Serve immediately. Makes 4 servings.

**Nutritional Analysis per serving:** 4 servings per recipe

| | | |
|---|---|---|
| Calories: 213 | Saturated fat: 1 g | Calcium: 18 mg |
| Protein: 28 g | Omega-3 fatty acids: 0.06 g | Magnesium: 41 mg |
| Carbohydrate: 7 g | Omega-6 fatty acids: 0.56 g | Potassium: 253 mg |
| Sugars: 0 g | Cholesterol: 68 mg | Sodium: 197 mg |
| Fiber (total): 1 g | Vitamin A: 7 RE | Iron: 1 mg |
| Total fat: 5 g | Vitamin C: 1 mg | Zinc: 1 mg |

Diabetic exchanges: 1 serving equals 3 lean meat exchanges, 1 very lean meat exchange, ¼ starch exchange

# Oven Fried Chicken

3 pounds of skinless chicken breasts or parts of any kind
½ to ¾ cup all purpose, white spelt, or other flour of any kind
¼ teaspoon salt
⅛ teaspoon pepper

Skin the chicken and cut it into serving-sized pieces. Combine the flour, salt, and pepper in a plastic bag. Put the chicken pieces into the flour one or two at a time and shake the bag to coat the chicken thoroughly. Put the chicken into a baking dish in a single layer. Turn your oven on to 350°F. Bake the chicken, uncovered, for one hour. Remove the pan from the oven and tilt it to allow the fat to run to one corner of the pan. Use a spoon or baster to pick up the fat and dribble it over the poultry. (If you wish, you can baste the chicken with oil instead of pan drippings). Return the chicken to the oven and bake it for another hour, for a total cooking time of 2 hours. Remove it from the oven when it is browned and crisp. Makes 6 to 12 servings.

**Nutritional Analysis per serving:** 12 servings per recipe

| | | |
|---|---|---|
| Calories: ...........................123 | Saturated fat: ...............0.3 g | Calcium: ...............................11 mg |
| Protein: ..........................22 g | Omega-3 fatty acids:...0.03 g | Magnesium: .....................28 mg |
| Carbohydrate: ...................4 g | Omega-6 fatty acids: ..0.22 g | Potassium: .....................247 mg |
| Sugars: ............................0 g | Cholesterol: ...................55 mg | Sodium: ............................110 mg |
| Fiber (total): ....................0 g | Vitamin A: .........................6 RE | Iron: ........................................1 mg |
| Total fat: ...........................1 g | Vitamin C: ..........................1 mg | Zinc: .......................................1 mg |

Diabetic exchanges: 1 serving equals 3 very lean meat exchanges, ¼ starch exchange

# Turkey Piccata

1 pound of sliced turkey breast
2 to 3 tablespoons olive oil or 1 tablespoon olive oil plus 1 to 2 tablespoons butter
¼ cup all purpose, white spelt, or other kind of flour
½ teaspoon salt
Dash of pepper
Juice of one lemon
½ cup white wine

Mix the flour, salt, and pepper together and dip the turkey slices into it so both sides are coated. Heat the oil and butter (if you are using it) in a large frying pan over medium heat. Add the turkey breast slices and brown them on one side. Turn them over and brown them on the other side. Add the lemon juice and wine to the pan. Cover the pan and bring the liquid to a boil. Reduce the heat and simmer for 30 minutes. Check the pan often and add more water or wine if the liquid is drying out. If necessary, at the end of the cooking time, remove the lid and simmer until the sauce is thick. Serve immediately. Makes 4 to 5 servings.

**Nutritional Analysis per serving:** 5 servings per recipe

| | | |
|---|---|---|
| Calories: ...........................190 | Saturated fat: ....................1 g | Calcium: ...............................13 mg |
| Protein: ..........................23 g | Omega-3 fatty acids:...0.04 g | Magnesium: .....................30 mg |
| Carbohydrate: ...................6 g | Omega-6 fatty acids: ..0.57 g | Potassium: .....................307 mg |
| Sugars: ............................1 g | Cholesterol: ...................56 mg | Sodium: ...........................280 mg |
| Fiber (total): ....................0 g | Vitamin A: .........................0 RE | Iron: ........................................1 mg |
| Total fat: ...........................6 g | Vitamin C: ..........................6 mg | Zinc: .......................................1 mg |

Diabetic exchanges: 1 serving equals 3 lean meat exchanges, ⅓ starch exchange

# Oven Cabbage and Hot Dogs

1 small head of cabbage weighing 1½ to 1¾ pounds
¼ teaspoon salt
¼ teaspoon pepper (optional)
¾ cup water
2 tablespoons oil
4 hot dogs weighing about 6 ounces, preferably turkey dogs or other low-fat variety

Wash, quarter, and core the head of cabbage. Cut it into pieces of cabbage that are about 1 to 2 inches square. Put the cabbage pieces into a 3 quart casserole dish which has a lid. Sprinkle it with the salt and pepper, pour the water over it, and drizzle it with the oil. Cover the dish with its lid and bake at 350°F for 45 minutes to 1 hour. Cut the hot dogs into pieces and stir them into the cabbage. Bake for another 30 to 45 minutes. Makes 4 servings.

**Nutritional Analysis per serving:** 4 servings per recipe

| | | |
|---|---|---|
| Calories: ............................172 | Saturated fat: ................2 g | Calcium:............................84 mg |
| Protein: ...............................10 g | Omega-3 fatty acids:...0.79 g | Magnesium:.....................35 mg |
| Carbohydrate: ....................9 g | Omega-6 fatty acids:...2.4 g | Potassium:.....................539 mg |
| Sugars:..................................4 g | Cholesterol: ....................32 mg | Sodium: .........................676 mg |
| Fiber (total):.......................4 g | Vitamin A: .......................22 RE | Iron:......................................2 mg |
| Total fat: ...........................12 g | Vitamin C: .......................55 mg | Zinc:.......................................1 mg |

Diabetic exchanges: 1 serving equals 1½ medium-fat meat exchanges, 2 vegetable exchanges, ¼ fat exchange

# Broiled Fish

*Do you know those skinless salmon filets you can buy for twice the price of "regular" salmon? Well, you can make your own with this recipe. Served with "Super Smooth Sauce," page 141, you have a dish loaded with essentil fatty acids and fit for a king!*

Fish fillet(s) or steak(s), any kind
Dash of salt.

Put the fish on a broiler pan. Set the pan in the broiler unit of your oven about 3 to 4 inches from the heating unit. Turn the broiler on to 500°F or 550°F or to "broil." Broil skinless filets or steaks for five minutes. Turn the fish with a spatula and broil the other side for five minutes. If the fish is thicker than one inch, increase the broiling time so that it totals at least 10 minutes per inch of thickness of the fish. Filets with skin may be broiled skin side down for the whole cooking time. When the broiling time is up, pierce the fish with a fork to see if it is opaque throughout and flakes easily. If it flakes easily, it is done. Remove it from the broiler pan and serve it immediately.

**Skinless salmon variation:** For skinless salmon, place a fillet with skin on the broiler pan skin side down. Broil for 8 minutes. Turn it with a spatula. Use a sharp knife to remove the skin. Broil it on the second side for another 5 minutes, or until it is opaque throughout and flakes easily when pierced with a fork. Serve immediately.

**Nutritional Analysis per serving (based on salmon):** one 3 ounce (cooked weight) serving per portion

| | | |
|---|---|---|
| Calories: ............................161 | Saturated fat: ................1 g | Calcium: ............................14 mg |
| Protein:...............................22 g | Omega-3 fatty acids: ....1.97 g | Magnesium:.....................33 mg |
| Carbohydrate: ....................0 g | Omega-6 fatty acids: ..0.50 g | Potassium:.....................556 mg |
| Sugars:..................................0 g | Cholesterol: ....................62 mg | Sodium: .........................167 mg |
| Fiber (total): ......................0 g | Vitamin A: .......................14 RE | Iron:......................................1 mg |
| Total fat: .............................7 g | Vitamin C:..........................0 mg | Zinc:.......................................1 mg |

Diabetic exchanges: one 3 ounce serving equals 3 lean meat exchanges

# Crispy Fish

1 pound fillets of white fish such as cod, haddock, turbot, or halibut
2 to 3 teaspoons oil
Dash of salt
⅓ cup fine cracker or bread crumbs

Brush oil on both sides of the fish. Sprinkle the fish with salt. Pat the cracker or bread crumbs onto both sides of the fish. Put the fish on a broiler pan. Turn the broiler on to 450°F. Broil the fish for 5 minutes; turn it with a spatula and broil the other side for 5 minutes. If the fish is thicker than one inch thick, increase the broiling time so that the total time is 10 minutes per inch of thickness of the fish. When the broiling time is up, pierce the fish with a fork to see if it flakes easily and is opaque throughout. If it is, remove it from the broiler pan and serve it immediately. Makes 2 to 4 servings.

**Nutritional Analysis per serving:** 4 servings per recipe

| | | |
|---|---|---|
| Calories: ...................207 | Saturated fat: ................1 g | Calcium:..........................50 mg |
| Protein: ......................23 g | Omega-3 fatty acids: ....1.85 g | Magnesium: ...................42 mg |
| Carbohydrate:...............6 g | Omega-6 fatty acids: ....1.12 g | Potassium: ...................379 mg |
| Sugars:............................0 g | Cholesterol: ...................68 mg | Sodium: ..........................141 mg |
| Fiber (total): ...................0 g | Vitamin A: .........................41 RE | Iron:.....................................1 mg |
| Total fat): .....................9 g | Vitamin C:...........................0 mg | Zinc:.....................................1 mg |

Diabetic exchanges: 1 serving equals 3 lean meat exchanges, ¼ starch exchange, ½ fat exchange

# Ann Fisk's Baked Fish

1 pound fillets of orange roughy, tilapia, or other fish of your choice
2 to 4 teaspoons of olive oil, other oil, butter, or ghee
Dash of paprika (optional)
Salt and pepper to taste (optional)

Preheat your oven to 400°F. Lay the fish in a single layer in a glass baking dish. If the fillets have skin, lay them skin side down. Dot the fish with the butter or ghee or drizzle it with the oil. To give the fish an appealing color, sprinkle it with paprika. Put it into the oven and bake it until it is opaque throughout and flakes easily with a fork. The cooking time will be about 5 minutes "warm up" time plus 10 minutes per inch of thickness of the fish. Sprinkle the fish with salt and pepper if desired. Serve immediately. Makes 3 to 4 servings.

**Sweet salmon variation:** Use salmon for the fish and drizzle it with 2 tablespoons of orange juice and 2 teaspoons of honey in addition to the oil.

**Orange roughy variation:**

**Nutritional Analysis per serving:** 4 servings per recipe

| | | |
|---|---|---|
| Calories: ...........................98 | Saturated fat:................0 g | Calcium:..........................34 mg |
| Protein:............................17 g | Omega-3 fatty acids:...0.02 g | Magnesium: ...................34 mg |
| Carbohydrate:...................0 g | Omega-6 fatty acids: ..0.18 g | Potassium:....................340 mg |
| Sugars:............................0 g | Cholesterol: ...................23 mg | Sodium: ............................71 mg |
| Fiber (total): ...................0 g | Vitamin A: .........................24 RE | Iron:.....................................0 mg |
| Total fat):.........................3 g | Vitamin C:...........................0 mg | Zinc:.....................................1 mg |

Diabetic exchanges: one 3 ounce serving equals 2½ very lean meat exchanges, ¼ fat exchange

**Salmon variation:**
**Nutritional Analysis per serving:** 4 servings per recipe

| | | |
|---|---|---|
| Calories: ............195 | Saturated fat: ..........1 g | Calcium: ............15 mg |
| Protein: ............23 g | Omega-3 fatty acids: ....1.98 g | Magnesium: ............34 mg |
| Carbohydrate: ............4 g | Omega-6 fatty acids: ..0.68 g | Potassium: ............573 mg |
| Sugars: ............4 g | Cholesterol: ............62 mg | Sodium: ............50 mg |
| Fiber (total): ............0 g | Vitamin A: ............15 RE | Iron: ............1 mg |
| Total fat: ............9 g | Vitamin C: ............4 mg | Zinc: ............1 mg |

Diabetic exchanges: 1 serving equals 3 lean meat exchanges, ¼ other carbohydrate exchange, ¼ fat exchange

# Poached Fish

Fish fillet(s) or steak(s), any kind (Orange roughy is good prepared this way).
Water
Dash of salt

Add water to a covered skillet to a depth of ½ to 1 inch, depending on the thickness of the fish. Salt the water lightly and bring it to a boil over high heat. Add the fish, put the cover back on the skillet and let the water return to a boil. Turn the heat down to medium or low and simmer the fish until it is opaque throughout and flakes easily when pierced with a fork. This will take about 10 minutes per inch of thickness of the fish. Serve immediately.

**Nutritional Analysis per serving:** 1 serving per 3 ounce (cooked weight) portion

| | | |
|---|---|---|
| Calories: ............98 | Saturated fat: ..........0 g | Calcium: ............43 mg |
| Protein: ............21 g | Omega-3 fatty acids: ..0.00 g | Magnesium: ............43 mg |
| Carbohydrate: ............0 g | Omega-6 fatty acids: ..0.01 g | Potassium: ............425 mg |
| Sugars: ............0 g | Cholesterol: ............28 mg | Sodium: ............207 mg |
| Fiber (total): ............0 g | Vitamin A: ............30 RE | Iron: ............0 mg |
| Total fat: ............1 g | Vitamin C: ............0 mg | Zinc: ............1 mg |

Diabetic exchanges: 1 serving equals 3 very lean meat exchanges

# Oven Poached Fish

Fish fillet(s) or steak(s), any kind (Orange roughy is good prepared this way).
Water
Dash of salt

Place the fish in a single layer in a glass baking dish. Add water to a depth of ½" and salt to taste. Cover the dish with its lid or foil. Bake at 350°F for 15 to 25 minutes (longer for thicker fish), or until the fish flakes easily. Serve immediately.

**Nutritional Analysis per serving:** 1 serving per 3 ounce (cooked weight) portion

| | | |
|---|---|---|
| Calories: ............98 | Saturated fat: ..........0 g | Calcium: ............43 mg |
| Protein: ............21 g | Omega-3 fatty acids: ..0.00 g | Magnesium: ............43 mg |
| Carbohydrate: ............0 g | Omega-6 fatty acids: ..0.01 g | Potassium: ............425 mg |
| Sugars: ............0 g | Cholesterol: ............28 mg | Sodium: ............207 mg |
| Fiber (total): ............0 g | Vitamin A: ............30 RE | Iron: ............0 mg |
| Total fat: ............1 g | Vitamin C: ............0 mg | Zinc: ............1 mg |

Diabetic exchanges: 1 serving equals 3 very lean meat exchanges

# Fish in Papillote

*This is an incredibly delicious, no-dirty-dishes meal. To make it healthfully, cook the fish and vegetables in a parchment paper pouch. Don't be frightened off by the detailed directions for making the pouch – it's really easy to do and results in great flavor. If you must, you can substitute aluminum foil.*

⅓ to ½ pound fish fillets per serving, preferably a mild tasting fish such as orange roughy, tilapia, etc.
Vegetable of your choice, such as 8 to 10 spears of asparagus, 1 to 2 carrots, or a small piece of broccoli per serving
1 teaspoon oil or butter per serving, optional
1 teaspoon lemon juice per serving, optional
Dash of salt
Dash of pepper, optional
Dash of paprika, optional

For each serving, cut a piece of parchment paper about twice as long and four times as wide as the fillet of fish. Fold it in half (so it is now twice as long and twice as wide as the fish) and cut it so it will be the shape of a plump heart when opened. Rub the center of the paper with a little of the butter or oil, if you are using it. If you prefer not to use butter or oil, the fish will still taste good, but it might stick to the paper a little.

Peel the carrots, if you are using them. Cut each carrot into about six thin strips lengthwise. If you are using the broccoli, cut it into thin lengthwise strips. Break off the woody stem ends of the asparagus.

Lay the fish on the parchment paper about ½ inch from the fold. Sprinkle the fish with the optional paprika. Lay the vegetable strips on top of the fish. Drizzle the fish and vegetables with the oil and lemon juice and sprinkle them with the salt and pepper.

Fold the top half of the parchment paper over the fish and vegetables along the crease that you made to cut the heart shape. Starting at the top center of the half-heart, hold the two cut edges of paper together, fold ½ inch of the edge toward the center of the heart and crease it. Fold this small section of the edge toward the center of the heart and crease it again. Then move a little farther along the edge of the half-heart and fold another small section of the edge of the paper toward the center of the heart twice in the same manner. Each double-folded section should overlap the previous section a little. Keep moving around the heart and folding small sections so that each section anchors the previous section until you reach the point at the bottom of the heart. Twist the paper at the point to lock the whole edge in place. When you are nearing the end of the wrapping process, preheat your oven to 400°F.

Put the parchment pouches on a baking sheet. Bake them for about 30 minutes if you are using thin fillets of fish. If you are using thick fillets, open one pouch and make sure the fish is opaque and flakes easily with a fork before serving it; if it is not done, cook it longer. Serve each person's fish and vegetables in the pouch.

## Nutritional Analysis per serving: 1 serving per recipe

| | | |
|---|---|---|
| Calories: ...........132 | Saturated fat: ..........0 g | Calcium: ..........69 mg |
| Protein: ...........25 g | Omega-3 fatty acids: ...0.01 g | Magnesium: ..........57 mg |
| Carbohydrate: ..........5 g | Omega-6 fatty acids: ..0.17 g | Potassium: ..........641 mg |
| Sugars: ..........2 g | Cholesterol: ..........30 mg | Sodium: ..........225 mg |
| Fiber (total): ..........2 g | Vitamin A: ..........96 RE | Iron: ..........1 mg |
| Total fat: ..........1 g | Vitamin C: ..........13 mg | Zinc: ..........2 mg |

Diabetic exchanges: 1 serving equals 3 very lean meat exchanges, 1 vegetable exchange

# Basil Roughy

1 pound orange roughy fillets
1½ to 2 tablespoons oil or melted butter or margarine
1 tablespoon lemon juice
⅛ teaspoon salt, or to taste
Dash of paprika (optional)
½ teaspoon dry sweet basil or 1 teaspoon chopped fresh sweet basil

Combine the oil or melted butter or margarine with the lemon juice in a 9" by 13" glass baking dish. Put the fillets into the dish and turn them over so they are coated on both sides. Sprinkle them with the salt, paprika, and basil. Bake at 350°F for 10 to 15 minutes, or until the fish flakes easily with a fork. Makes 2 to 4 servings.

**Nutritional Analysis per serving:** 3 servings per recipe

| | | |
|---|---|---|
| Calories: ......................166 | Saturated fat: ................1 g | Calcium:............................46 mg |
| Protein:...........................22 g | Omega-3 fatty acids:....0.64 g | Magnesium:......................46 mg |
| Carbohydrate:...................0 g | Omega-6 fatty acids: ....1.40 g | Potassium: ......................461 mg |
| Sugars:...........................0 g | Cholesterol: ...................30 mg | Sodium:...........................193 mg |
| Fiber (total): ....................0 g | Vitamin A:.........................33 RE | Iron: ...................................0 mg |
| Total fat: ..........................8 g | Vitamin C:...........................0 mg | Zinc: ....................................1 mg |

Diabetic exchanges: 1 serving equals 3 lean meat exchanges

# Baked Stuffed Peppers

*Stuffed peppers make a tasty meal made either with meat or in the vegetarian version. The options given in the vegetarian stuffed peppers recipe makes this a good recipe for people with food allergies.*

### Traditional Stuffed Peppers:

6 large bell peppers
Water
12 ounces to 1 pound lean ground beef, buffalo, or other red game meat
1 tablespoon chopped onion (optional)
¼ teaspoon dry or 1 teaspoon chopped fresh sweet basil
1 teaspoon salt
1 cup cooked rice or other grain
1 15 ounce can tomato sauce

Wash, core, and seed the peppers. Bring a large pan of water to a boil over high heat. Add the pepper shells and return the water to a boil. Lower the heat to medium or low and simmer the peppers for 5 minutes. Drain off most of the boiling water and replace it with cold water to stop the cooking of the peppers.

In a frying pan, brown the ground meat with the onion, stirring occasionally, until all traces of pink in the meat are gone. Drain off the fat. Add the sweet basil, salt, rice, and 1 cup of the tomato sauce.

Remove the pepper shells from the cold water and drain any water that remains inside of them. Stuff the meat mixture into the pepper shells. Stand the peppers upright in a casserole dish. Pour the remaining tomato sauce over and around them. Cover the dish with its lid or with aluminum foil. Bake at 350°F for 45 minutes. Uncover the dish and bake the peppers an additional 15 minutes. Makes 6 servings. Any leftover peppers freeze well.

## Vegetarian Stuffed Peppers:

6 large bell peppers
Water
3 cups of cooked grain of any kind – rice, quinoa, barley, spelt, buckwheat, etc.
1 10 ounce package frozen chopped spinach or ¾ to 1 pound of shredded carrots
　　or chopped fresh spinach, Swiss chard, collards or kale
2 tablespoons oil
2 teaspoons salt
¾ teaspoon pepper
1 tablespoon dry or 3 tablespoons fresh chopped sweet basil
2 tablespoons paprika (optional – for color) or ¼ cup tomato sauce
¾ cup additional tomato sauce (optional)

Wash, core, and seed the peppers. Bring a large pan of water to a boil over high heat. Add the pepper shells and return the water to a boil. Lower the heat to medium or low and simmer the peppers for 5 minutes. Drain off most of the boiling water and replace it with cold water to stop the cooking of the peppers.

Put the oil into a saucepan. Add the vegetables and saute them, stirring often, until they are barely tender, about 5 to 10 minutes. For fresh green vegetables, the wash water clinging to their leaves will be enough liquid in which to cook them. The frozen spinach likewise needs no added water. Add 2 tablespoons of water to the pan if you are using the carrots or if the fresh green vegetables you are using are dry.

When the vegetables are cooked, drain any liquid from the pan. Add the grain, salt, pepper, sweet basil, and paprika or ¼ cup tomato sauce to the vegetables.

Remove the pepper shells from the cold water and drain any water that remains inside of them. Stuff the grain mixture into the pepper shells. If you are not using the tomato sauce, oil the casserole dish lightly to keep the peppers from sticking. Stand the peppers upright in a casserole dish. Pour the remaining tomato sauce over and around them. Cover the dish with its lid or with aluminum foil. Bake at 350°F for 45 minutes. Makes 6 servings. Any leftover peppers freeze well.

### Traditional stuffed peppers variation:
**Nutritional Analysis per serving:** 6 servings per recipe

| | | |
|---|---|---|
| Calories: 199 | Saturated fat: 2 g | Calcium: 34 mg |
| Protein: 15 g | Omega-3 fatty acids: 0.02 g | Magnesium: 58 mg |
| Carbohydrate: 24 g | Omega-6 fatty acids: 0.30 g | Potassium: 766 mg |
| Sugars: 7 g | Cholesterol: 21 mg | Sodium: 900 mg |
| Fiber (total): 5 g | Vitamin A: 179 RE | Iron: 3 mg |
| Total fat: 6 g | Vitamin C: 157 mg | Zinc: 3 mg |

Diabetic exchanges: 1 serving equals 1 lean meat exchange, 1 very lean meat exchange, ½ starch exchange, 3 vegetable exchanges

### Vegetarian stuffed peppers variation:
**Nutritional Analysis per serving:** 6 servings per recipe

| | | |
|---|---|---|
| Calories: 204 | Saturated fat: 0.5 g | Calcium: 60 mg |
| Protein: 5 g | Omega-3 fatty acids: 0.45 g | Magnesium: 59 mg |
| Carbohydrate: 35 g | Omega-6 fatty acids: 1.38 g | Potassium: 335 mg |
| Sugars: 5 g | Cholesterol: 0 mg | Sodium: 854 mg |
| Fiber (total): 6 g | Vitamin A: 439 RE | Iron: 1 mg |
| Total fat: 6 g | Vitamin C: 150 mg | Zinc: 1 mg |

Diabetic exchanges: 1 serving equals 1⅓ starch exchanges, 2½ vegetable exchanges 1 fat exchange

# How to Cook Pasta

*Pasta is a most versatile main or side dish. If you are allergic to wheat, there are many delicious wheat-free pastas on the market. How you cook your pasta can either bring out the best in it or turn it to mush, so follow these basic instructions for cooking it on the stove-top. To cook pasta in a microwave oven, see page 231.*

> 10 ounces to 1 pound of pasta – R & F™ brand, Purity Foods™ white spelt pasta,
>    or other variety
> 3 to 6 quarts of water
> ½ to 1 teaspoon salt

Put the water and salt in a large pot. (The purpose of the salt is to increase the boiling temperature of the water slightly). Bring the water to a rolling boil over high heat. Add the pasta and stir to keep it from sticking together. If you are cooking spaghetti and it is too long for the pan, don't break it. Just put one end into the pan, let it soften a little, and then stir it all in. Return the water to a boil and then reduce the heat slightly to keep the pasta from boiling over while maintaining a good boil. Begin timing the cooking of the pasta from the time the water returns to a boil. Set a large colander in your kitchen sink so you will be ready to drain the pasta when the right time comes.

The best estimate of how long to cook the pasta will be what the package says for cooking time. This varies with the size and shape of the pasta, the type of flour it is made from, and the altitude at which you are cooking. At the minimum cooking time given on the package, take a piece of pasta from the pan and taste it. It should be *"al dente"* when you bite into it, or offer some resistance to the tooth, without being hard. If it is not done, continue to boil it, retesting it at one to two minutes intervals, until it is done. Then immediately pour it though the colander to drain. Do not run cold water on it! After draining the pasta, put it back into the pan or a serving bowl and toss it with sauce or a little oil or butter to keep it from sticking together. Serve immediately. Makes 4 to 6 servings.

**Nutritional Analysis per serving:** 6 servings per recipe

| | | |
|---|---|---|
| Calories: ......................185 | Saturated fat:................0 g | Calcium:..............................9 mg |
| Protein:................................6 g | Omega-3 fatty acids:...0.03 g | Magnesium: .....................24 mg |
| Carbohydrate:.................37 g | Omega-6 fatty acids: ..0.33 g | Potassium: .......................41 mg |
| Sugars: ...........................2 g | Cholesterol: ....................0 mg | Sodium:.............................41 mg |
| Fiber (total):.....................2 g | Vitamin A: .........................0 RE | Iron:.......................................2 mg |
| Total fat: ..........................1 g | Vitamin C:..........................0 mg | Zinc: ....................................1 mg |

Diabetic exchanges: 1 serving equals 2⅓ starch exchanges if a 10 ounce package of pasta is used

# Macaroni and Cheese

*This is one "conventional" recipe that it is nice to make in the microwave, and there are fewer dirty dishes to wash when you're finished.*

8 ounces elbow macaroni, wheat or spelt
Dash of salt
Water, about 2 quarts
1¾ cup skim, whole, or goat milk
¼ cup Quick Thick™ or flour (unbleached, all-purpose, or white spelt)
8 ounces grated sharp cheddar cheese or goat cheese

**Conventional method:** Bring about 2 quarts of water to a boil and add the salt. Add the macaroni to the water and stir. When it returns to a boil, reduce the heat and simmer the macaroni for a couple of minutes less than the cooking time given on the package.

While the macaroni is cooking, thoroughly stir together or use a hand blender to combine the milk with the flour or Quick Thick™ in a saucepan. Heat over medium heat, stirring often, until the mixture begins to boil and thicken. If the sauce forms lumps, remove them by blending with the hand blender. After the sauce comes to a boil, remove it from the heat and stir in the grated cheese. Combine the cheese sauce and cooked macaroni in a large casserole dish. Bake at 350°F for 30 minutes or until it is bubbly. Makes 4 to 8 servings. Leftovers keep well in the refrigerator or can be frozen.

**Microwave method:** Put 3 cups of water in a 2½ to 3 quart casserole dish. Place it in your microwave, uncovered, and heat it on "high" until it comes to a boil. Add the macaroni to the casserole dish and microwave on high for 5 minutes.

If you are using the Quick Thick™, while the macaroni is cooking, combine the milk and Quick Thick™ in a bowl or 4-cup measuring cup and stir it thoroughly or blend it with a hand blender until all the lumps are gone. If you are using the flour, combine the milk and flour in a bowl or 4-cup measuring cup.

Drain the water from the macaroni using a strainer. If you are using flour to thicken your macaroni and cheese, put the milk-flour mixture into the same casserole you used to cook the macaroni, put it into the microwave, and heat it on "high" for 3 to 5 minutes, stirring every minute, until it is thick and bubbly. If the sauce forms lumps, use a hand blender to remove them. Add the cooked macaroni to the sauce and cook the casserole on high for 5 to 9 minutes, stirring every 2 minutes until the pasta is completely cooked and the sauce is bubbling.

If you are using the Quick Thick™, combine the cooked macaroni with the milk-Quick Thick™ mixture in the casserole dish, cover it, and return it to the microwave oven. Cook it on high for 5 to 9 minutes, stirring every 2 minutes, until the sauce is thick and bubbly and the pasta is cooked.

Stir in the grated cheese into the macaroni-milk mixture about a cup at a time until it is melted. Serve immediately. Makes 4 to 8 servings.

**Nutritional Analysis per serving:** *8 servings per recipe*

| | | |
|---|---|---|
| Calories: 281 | Saturated fat: 6 g | Calcium: 279 mg |
| Protein: 16 g | Omega-3 fatty acids: 0.11 g | Magnesium: 39 mg |
| Carbohydrate: 31 g | Omega-6 fatty acids: 0.25 g | Potassium: 155 mg |
| Sugars: 4 g | Cholesterol: 31 mg | Sodium: 237 mg |
| Fiber (total): 1 g | Vitamin A: 112 RE | Iron: 1 mg |
| Total fat: 10 g | Vitamin C: 1 mg | Zinc: 2 mg |

Diabetic exchanges: 1 serving equals 2 starch exchanges, 1 high-fat meat exchange, ¼ skim milk exchange

# Sea Shell Casserole

1 pound lean ground beef or buffalo
1 16 ounce can tomato sauce
½ of a 6 ounce can of tomato paste
½ pound of medium sized sea shell pasta or white spelt macaroni
Water, about 2 quarts
¼ teaspoon salt
8 ounces of grated cheddar cheese or goat cheese, about 2 to 3 cups

Crumble the ground meat into a frying pan. Cook it over medium heat, stirring often, until no pink color remains. Then cook it for an additional five minutes. Drain off the fat and set it aside.

In a large pot, bring the water and salt to a boil. Add the pasta and cook it as directed in "How to Cook Pasta," page 169. Cook it for about 2 minutes less than the package directs, and drain it when it is still a little on the hard side. With medium sized wheat sea shell pasta, it takes about 10 minutes to cook to the "slightly hard" stage, and spelt macaroni takes about 5 minutes. However, read the package and test it when you cook it yourself because your cooking time may vary.

Stir together the tomato sauce and tomato paste in a 3-quart casserole dish. Freeze the remaining half-can of tomato paste to use the next time you make this casserole. Stir in the cooked meat, cooked pasta, and all but ¼ cup of the cheese. Sprinkle the remaining cheese on top. If you wish, you can refrigerate the casserole at this point. Bake at 350°F for 30 minutes if freshly made or for 45-55 minutes if it has been refrigerated, or until it is hot throughout. Makes 4 to 8 servings. Leftovers freeze well for future meals.

## Nutritional Analysis per serving: 8 servings per recipe

| | | |
|---|---|---|
| Calories: 337 | Saturated fat: 8 g | Calcium: 226 mg |
| Protein: 24 g | Omega-3 fatty acids: 0.11 g | Magnesium: 50 mg |
| Carbohydrate: 27 g | Omega-6 fatty acids: 0.22 g | Potassium: 568 mg |
| Sugars: 4 g | Cholesterol: 50 mg | Sodium: 600 mg |
| Fiber (total): 2 g | Vitamin A: 160 RE | Iron: 3 mg |
| Total fat: 15 g | Vitamin C: 12 mg | Zinc: 4 mg |

Diabetic exchanges: 1 serving equals 1⅓ starch exchanges, 3 lean meat exchanges, 1 vegetable exchange, 1 fat exchange

# Pantry Pasta Casserole

8 ounces of pasta such as rotini, gnocchi, or white spelt macaroni
¼ teaspoon salt
Water, about 2 quarts
1 14.5 ounce can diced tomatoes or 1 14.5 ounce can Italian-flavor diced tomatoes
¼ teaspoon dry or 1 teaspoon fresh sweet basil (omit if you use the flavored diced
tomatoes)
¼ teaspoon dry or 1 teaspoon fresh oregano (omit if you use the flavored diced
tomatoes)
1 15 ounce can of plain corn, drained
1 15 ounce can french cut green beans, drained
1½ cups chicken broth* – homemade, canned, or made from 1½ cups water plus
1½ chicken bouillon cubes
¼ cup all purpose, unbleached, or white spelt flour*
2 to 3 cups, or about 8 ounces, shredded Monterey jack cheese or goat cheese

Bring the water and salt to a boil in a large pot. Add the pasta, return the water to
a boil, and cook it until about 2 minutes before the package recommended cooking time
is up. It should be slightly on the hard side. (This cooking time will probably be about
5 to 8 minutes, depending on what kind of pasta you use). Drain the pasta and put it in
a 3-quart casserole dish. Add the tomatoes, spices, corn, and beans.

If you are using bouillon cubes, make the broth by dissolving the cubes in ½ cup
of boiling water. Add 1 cup of cold water to the broth. Make a sauce of the chicken broth
and flour as below. *(Or you can substitute a 10.5 ounce can of cream of celery, cream
of chicken, or cream of mushroom soup for the broth and flour in this step. The canned
soup contains some strange chemicals and is not as healthy, but is quicker). Combine the
broth and flour with a hand blender. Heat in a saucepan or microwave oven, stirring
often, until it thickens and boils. Blend it again with the hand blender if lumps form in
the sauce.

Add the sauce or soup and all but ¼ cup of the cheese to the casserole dish and stir
everything together. Sprinkle the remaining cheese on top. If you wish, you can refrigerate the casserole at this point. Bake at 350°F for 30 minutes if freshly made or for 45-55
minutes if it has been refrigerated, or until it is hot throughout. Makes 4 to 8 servings.
Leftovers freeze well for future meals.

**Nutritional Analysis per serving:** 8 servings per recipe

| | | |
|---|---|---|
| Calories: 292 | Saturated fat: 5 g | Calcium: 271 mg |
| Protein: 13 g | Omega-3 fatty acids: 0.10 g | Magnesium: 43 mg |
| Carbohydrate: 39 g | Omega-6 fatty acids: 0.62 g | Potassium: 246 mg |
| Sugars: 7 g | Cholesterol: 25 mg | Sodium: 644 mg |
| Fiber (total): 4 g | Vitamin A: 114 RE | Iron: 3 mg |
| Total fat: 10 g | Vitamin C: 16 mg | Zinc: 1 mg |

Diabetic exchanges: 1 serving equals 2 starch exchanges, 1 lean meat exchange, 1⅓
vegetable exchanges, 1 fat exchange

# Dumpling Pie

## Filling Ingredients:

½ cup chopped celery (about one large stalk)
¼ cup chopped onion or additional chopped celery
2 tablespoons oil
3 tablespoons all purpose, unbleached, or white spelt flour
¼ teaspoon dry sweet basil or 1 teaspoon chopped fresh sweet basil
¼ teaspoon pepper
1½ cups chicken or turkey broth
1½ cups peas, fresh or frozen
2 cups cubed cooked chicken or turkey

## Topping Ingredients:

1 cup all purpose, unbleached, or white spelt flour
1 teaspoon baking powder*
¼ teaspoon salt
¼ teaspoon dry sweet basil or 1 teaspoon chopped fresh sweet basil
2 tablespoons oil
⅓ cup water

To make the filling, saute the celery and onion in 2 tablespoons of oil until the vegetables begin to brown. Add the 3 tablespoons of flour and stir and cook one minute. Add the sweet basil, pepper, and broth. Bring the mixture to a boil and cook it over medium heat for a few minutes until it is thickened. Stir in the peas and chicken or turkey. Put the filling into a 2½ to 3 quart casserole dish. Preheat your oven to 400°F.

To make the topping, put the 1 cup flour, baking powder, salt, and sweet basil into a large bowl. In a cup, mix the oil and water. Pour the liquid ingredients into the flour mixture and stir until just mixed. Drop this dumpling topping on top of the filling in the casserole dish by large spoonfuls. Bake the casserole for 30 to 35 minutes or until the topping browns. Makes 6 servings. Leftovers freeze well.

* Note on baking powder: Use Featherweight™ brand baking powder if you are allergic to corn. It contains potato starch instead of cornstarch.

## Nutritional Analysis per serving: servings per recipe

| | | |
|---|---|---|
| Calories: ....................262 | Total fat:............................11 g | Calcium: ............................81 mg |
| Protein: ............................16 g | Saturated fat: ................1 g | Magnesium: ......................26 mg |
| Carbohydrate:................24 g | Omega-3 fatty acids:...0.88 g | Potassium:........................212 mg |
| Sugars:............................3 g | Omega-6 fatty acids:...2.26 g | Sodium:............................19 mg |
| Fiber (total):....................2 g | Cholesterol: ....................32 mg | Iron:....................................2 mg |
| Vitamin C:..........................6 mg | Vitamin A:........................27 RE | Zinc: ....................................1 mg |

Diabetic exchanges: 1 serving equals 1½ starch exchanges, 1⅔ lean meat exchanges, ⅓ vegetable exchange, 1 fat exchange

# Tamale Pie

## Filling ingredients:

¼ cup chopped bell pepper (about ½ of a pepper)
½ small onion chopped (optional)
1 tablespoon oil
1 15 ounce can tomatoes
1 teaspoon chili powder
1 4 ounce can sliced mushrooms, drained
1 14 ounce can black beans, drained
1 cup cubed chicken or turkey

## Topping ingredients:

½ cup all purpose, unbleached, or white spelt flour
½ cup yellow cornmeal
2 teaspoons baking powder
¼ teaspoon salt
2 tablespoons oil
½ cup water

To make the filling, saute the pepper and onion in the oil until they begin to brown. Coarsely cut up the tomatoes and add them and their juice to the saucepan with the pepper and onion. Stir in the chili powder, mushrooms, beans, and chicken or turkey and bring the mixture to a boil. Pour it into a 2½ to 3 quart casserole dish. Preheat your oven to 350°F.

To make the topping, put the flour, cornmeal, baking powder, and salt into a large bowl. In a cup, mix the oil and water. Pour the liquid ingredients into the flour mixture and stir until just mixed. Spread this batter on top of the filling in the casserole dish. Bake the casserole for 30 to 35 minutes or until the topping browns. Makes 6 servings. Leftovers freeze well.

### Nutritional Analysis per serving: 6 servings per recipe

| | | |
|---|---|---|
| Calories: ..........................241 | Total fat: ............................8 g | Calcium:............................167 mg |
| Protein:.............................12 g | Saturated fat: ................1 g | Magnesium: ....................32 mg |
| Carbohydrate: ................33 g | Omega-3 fatty acids:...0.66 g | Potassium:....................530 mg |
| Sugars: .............................1 g | Omega-6 fatty acids: ....1.76 g | Sodium: ..........................682 mg |
| Fiber (total): ....................6 g | Cholesterol: ......................16 mg | Iron: ......................................3 mg |
| Vitamin C: .......................20 mg | Vitamin A: ........................79 RE | Zinc: ........................................1 mg |

Diabetic exchanges: 1 serving equals 1½ starch exchanges, 1 lean meat exchange, 1 vegetable exchange, 1 fat exchange

# Mexican Strata

3 to 4 slices of bread of any kind, preferably whole grain
1 pound fresh or frozen corn kernels
2 pounds zucchini or crookneck squash, thinly sliced
1 4 ounce can diced green chili peppers, drained
4 ounces low fat or regular Monterey jack cheese or goat cheese, coarsely grated
3 eggs
1¾ cup skim, whole, or goat milk
½ teaspoon salt
⅛ teaspoon pepper

Cut and piece the bread to fit the bottom of an 11 inch by 7 inch baking dish. Spread the corn on top of the bread. Cover it with the squash. Spread the chili pepers on top of the squash. Sprinkle the whole dish with the grated cheese. Beat together the eggs, milk, salt and pepper and pour them over the whole dish. At this point you can refrigerate this casserole a few hours or overnight if desired. Bake, uncovered, at 375°F for 30 to 40 minutes, or until it puffs up and begins to brown. Makes 6 servings.

**Nutritional Analysis per serving:** *6 servings per recipe*

| | | |
|---|---|---|
| Calories: .....................250 | Total fat: ............................8 g | Calcium:...........................314 mg |
| Protein: .............................19 g | Saturated fat: ...............4 g | Magnesium:.....................89 mg |
| Carbohydrate:................32 g | Omega-3 fatty acids:...0.19 g | Potassium:..................1080 mg |
| Sugars: ..............................9 g | Omega-6 fatty acids: ..0.80 g | Sodium: ...........................710 mg |
| Fiber (total):...................5 g | Cholesterol: ..................108 mg | Iron:.......................................2 mg |
| Vitamin C:........................70 mg | Vitamin A: .....................253 RE | Zinc:.......................................3 mg |

Diabetic exchanges: 1 serving equals 1⅓ starch exchanges, 1¼ medium-fat meat exchanges, ¼ skim milk exchange, 1 vegetable exchange

# Quick and Easy Chili

1 pound lean ground beef lean, ground buffalo, or any red game meat
½ small onion, chopped (optional)
1 27 ounce can plus 1 16 ounce can kidney beans
2 16 ounce cans tomato sauce
¼ teaspoon salt
½ to 1 teaspoon chili powder, or to taste

Crumble the ground beef into a large saucepan. Cook it over medium heat, stirring often, until no pink color remains. Then cook it for an additional five minutes. Drain off the fat. Add the onion to the pan and cook it for a few more minutes. Drain the beans. Add the beans, tomato sauce, salt, and chili powder to the pan and heat to boiling. Reduce the heat and simmer it for 20 to 30 minutes. Makes 6 to 10 servings. Leftovers freeze well.

**Nutritional Analysis per serving:** *10 servings per recipe*

| | | |
|---|---|---|
| Calories: .....................248 | Total fat:............................5 g | Calcium:...........................17 mg |
| Protein: .............................19 g | Saturated fat: ...............2 g | Magnesium:.....................75 mg |
| Carbohydrate: ...............33 g | Omega-3 fatty acids:...0.20 g | Potassium: ..................480 mg |
| Sugars: ..............................2 g | Omega-6 fatty acids: ..0.13 g | Sodium:...........................103 mg |
| Fiber (total): ..................12 g | Cholesterol: ....................17 mg | Iron:.......................................2 mg |
| Vitamin C:........................12 mg | Vitamin A: .......................94 RE | Zinc:.......................................3 mg |

Diabetic exchanges: 1 serving equals 1¾ starch/other carbohydrate exchanges, 1½ lean meat exchanges, 1 vegetable exchange

# Economy Chili

*You can also make this chili very easily and with less "tending" using a crock pot. For the recipe, see page 220.*

1 pound dry kidney beans
Water
1½ to 2 pounds of lean ground beef, ground buffalo, or any red game meat
1 12 ounce can tomato paste
1 16 ounce can tomato sauce
1 small onion, chopped (optional)
1 teaspoon salt
1 to 3 teaspoons of chili powder, to taste

The night before you plan to serve this chili, sort over and rinse the beans. Put the beans into a 3 to 5 quart pan. Cover the beans with cold water and allow them to soak overnight. In the morning, drain the water from the beans, add fresh water to the pan, and drain the water again. Rinse the beans this way three times. (This soaking and draining process removes difficult-to-digest carbohydrates from the beans, which can cause "gas"). Add enough water to the beans to cover them. Bring them to a boil over high heat; then reduce the heat so they boil gently. Cook them for 2 to 2½ hours or until they are tender. Check the beans every half hour and replenish the water as needed. (Use boiling water if you don't want to fuss with bringing them back to a boil after adding water). In a separate pan, brown the ground meat. Drain and discard the fat. Add the onion and cook for a few minutes more. When the beans are tender, drain the water until it is an inch or so below the level of the beans in the pot. Stir the tomato paste into the pot thoroughly. Add the cooked meat, tomato sauce, and seasonings and stir. Cook the chili for another half hour or until it is thoroughly heated. Makes 8 to 10 servings. Leftover chili freezes well and is great for quick meals on days when you don't have time to cook.

### Nutritional Analysis per serving: 10 servings per recipe

| | | |
|---|---|---|
| Calories: ....................291 | Total fat: ....................7 g | Calcium:....................96 mg |
| Protein: ....................26 g | Saturated fat: ....................2 g | Magnesium:....................93 mg |
| Carbohydrate:....................34 g | Omega-3 fatty acids:...0.04 g | Potassium:....................1156 mg |
| Sugars:....................3 g | Omega-6 fatty acids: ..0.11 g | Sodium:....................325 mg |
| Fiber (total): ....................12 g | Cholesterol: ....................25 mg | Iron: ....................6 mg |
| Vitamin C:....................22 mg | Vitamin A:....................137 RE | Zinc:....................4 mg |

Diabetic exchanges: 1 serving equals 1¾ starch exchanges, 2 lean meat exchanges, 1½ vegetable exchanges

# *Tacos*

1 pound lean ground beef
2 16 ounce cans of kidney beans
½ to 1 teaspoon chili powder, to taste
3 tomatoes, chopped
1 onion, chopped
1 cup of chopped lettuce
1 cup of shredded cheddar cheese or goat cheese
1 cup of low-fat plain yogurt, goat yogurt, or sour cream (non-fat, low-fat, or regular sour cream)
1 16 ounce jar of salsa
8 large or 12 small taco shells

Crumble the ground beef into a frying pan. Cook it over medium heat, stirring often, until no pink color remains. Then cook it for an additional five minutes and drain off the fat.

While the meat is cooking, drain the kidney beans and put them in a saucepan. Put the pan on the stove and heat the beans over medium heat. While heating them, mash them and stir in the chili powder.

Chop the vegetables and put them in serving bowls. Then put the cheese, yogurt or sour cream, and salsa in serving bowls. When the meat is cooked and the beans are hot, have your guests make themselves tacos with meat, beans, and their choice of toppings. Makes 4 to 6 two-taco servings or 8 to 12 1-taco servings.

**Nutritional Analysis per serving:** 12 servings per recipe

| | | |
|---|---|---|
| Calories: ......................270 | Total fat: ..........................9 g | Calcium: ............................141 mg |
| Protein: ...............................18 g | Saturated fat: ...............4 g | Magnesium:....................63 mg |
| Carbohydrate:.................29 g | Omega-3 fatty acids:...0.21 g | Potassium: ....................378 mg |
| Sugars:...........................5 g | Omega-6 fatty acids: ..0.93 g | Sodium:..........................324 mg |
| Fiber (total):.....................9 g | Cholesterol: ...................25 mg | Iron:.......................................2 mg |
| Vitamin C:...........................13 mg | Vitamin A: .......................76 RE | Zinc:.......................................3 mg |

Diabetic exchanges: 1 serving of 1 small taco equals 1½ starch exchanges, 1½ medium-fat meat exchanges, 1 vegetable exchange, ¼ fat exchange

# Pizza

*Making homemade pizza is really not all that difficult, and it will impress that special guy or girl in your life! The old saying, "The way to a man's heart is through his stomach," applies to women too! Making the sauce is a snap; the homemade dough requires a little more work, but easy store-bought options are also given below.*

## Pizza toppings for one pizza:

2 to 3 ounces low fat or part-skim mozzarella cheese or goat cheese

2 tablespoons grated Romano cheese, Parmesan cheese, or all-sheep milk
   Romano cheese

½ cup chopped vegetables of your choice, such as green peppers, mushrooms,
   olives, etc.

2 ounces cooked meat such as lean ground beef, pepperoni, etc.

## Pizza sauce for two pizzas:

1 6 ounce can tomato paste

1 8 ounce can tomato sauce

⅓ cup water

1 teaspoon dry oregano or 1 tablespoon chopped fresh oregano

½ teaspoon dry thyme or 1 teaspoon chopped fresh thyme

½ teaspoon dry sweet basil or 1 teaspoon chopped fresh sweet basil

1 tablespoon olive oil (optional)

Combine the sauce ingredients in a saucepan. Put them on the burner of your stove and heat on medium heat until the sauce begins to boil. Reduce the heat to low and simmer the sauce for 30 to 40 minutes, stirring every ten minutes to keep the sauce from sticking to the bottom of the pan. This makes enough sauce for two pizzas. You can either freeze half of the sauce for future use or double the amounts of dough and toppings you use and have two pizzas. If you don't eat both of them, the leftover one will freeze well.

## Pizza dough option #1 – standard homemade dough for one pizza:

¾ cup water at about 115°F

1½ tablespoons Fruit Sweet™ or honey

1 tablespoon oil

½ teaspoon salt

2¼ to 2¾ cups all purpose or unbleached flour

1¼ teaspoons active dry or quick rise yeast

To make this dough in a bread machine, add the ingredients to the pan in the order listed and start the dough cycle. Check the dough after several minutes of kneading and adjust the consistency of the dough by adding a little more flour or water if needed.

To make the dough by hand, mix together the water and sweetener in a large bowl. Sprinkle the surface of the liquid with the yeast, then stir the yeast in. Allow it to stand for about 10 minutes until it begins to get foamy. Stir in the oil, salt, and about half of the flour. Add the remaining flour a little at a time until you've added as much of the flour as you can stir in by hand. Spread a little of the remaining flour on your kitchen counter. Put the dough on the counter and knead in as much of the remaining flour as it takes to make a soft, yet smooth and elastic dough. Pizza dough should be softer than most bread dough and is also made with all-purpose or unbleached rather than bread flour so that it will be easier to stretch out in the pizza pan. (See the procedure for making yeast breads on pages 242 to 243 for more about making yeast dough). Knead the dough for 10 minutes.

While you are kneading the dough, unless you have a very cozy (85 to 90°F) corner in your kitchen, begin to prepare your oven to be a rising spot for the dough. If you have a gas oven, the pilot light will probably keep the oven at just about the right temperature, 85 to 90°F. If you have an electric oven, turn it on to 350°F and let it preheat. Then turn it off, open the oven, and let it cool for 8 to 10 minutes until the temperature inside the oven is about 85 to 90°F. Then close the oven door.

When the dough is well kneaded, wash out the mixing bowl you used to make the dough and dry it. Rub the inside of the bowl generously with oil. Put the dough into the bowl and turn it over so the top side of the dough is also oiled. Cover the dough with plastic wrap. Place the bowl in your pre-warmed oven or a warm spot in your kitchen and let it rise until doubled. This will take about an hour if you used active dry yeast or about 40 minutes if you used quick rise yeast. Then punch the dough down by plunging your fist into the middle of it. Let it rest for about five minutes before shaping it into a pizza.

If you made your dough in a bread machine, let it rest for a few minutes at the end of the cycle.

While the dough is resting, very lightly oil a baking sheet or 12 inch pizza pan by putting a teaspoon or less of oil on a paper towel and rubbing the paper towel on the baking sheet or all around the bottom and edges of the pizza pan.

Turn the dough out onto your kitchen counter. The oil on the dough should be sufficient to keep it from sticking to the counter. Stretch or roll it out into a 12-inch circle. Transfer the dough to the baking sheet or pizza pan. You may have to push and stretch it with your hands to get it to fit all the way to the edges of the pan. If you want a "thin crust" pizza, top it immediately as directed below. If you want a "thick crust" pizza, place the pizza in the pre-warmed oven or in a warm spot in your kitchen and let the dough rise for 15 to 20 minutes. Remove the pizza from the oven and preheat your oven to 400°F. While the oven is heating, spread the pizza with sauce for one pizza (half of what you made above) and the desired toppings. Bake it for 20 to 25 minutes or until the edge is golden brown. Makes one 12 inch pizza.

## Pizza dough option #2 – white spelt homemade dough for one pizza:

⅔ cup water at about 115°F
2½ tablespoons apple juice concentrate, thawed, or 1 tablespoon Fruit Sweet™ or
    honey plus 1½ tablespoons water
1 tablespoon oil
½ teaspoon salt
2¼ to 2½ cups white spelt flour
1¼ teaspoons active dry or quick rise yeast

To make this dough in a bread machine, add the ingredients to the pan in the order listed and start the dough cycle. Check the dough after several minutes of kneading and adjust the consistency of the dough by adding a little more flour or water if needed.

To make the dough by hand, mix together the water and sweetener in a large bowl. Sprinkle the surface of the liquid with the yeast, then stir the yeast in. Allow it to stand for about 10 minutes until it begins to get foamy. Stir in the oil, salt, and about half of the flour. Add the remaining flour a little at a time until you've added as much of the flour as you can stir in by hand. Spread a little of the remaining flour on your kitchen counter. Put the dough on the counter and knead in as much of the remaining flour as it takes to make a soft, yet smooth and elastic dough. Pizza dough should be softer than most bread dough so that it will be easier to stretch out in the pizza pan. (See the procedure for making yeast breads on pages 242 to 243 for more about making yeast dough). Knead the dough for 10 minutes.

While you are kneading the dough, unless you have a very cozy (85 to 90°F) corner in your kitchen, begin to prepare your oven to be a rising spot for the dough. If you have a gas oven, the pilot light will probably keep the oven at just about the right temperature, 85 to 90°F. If you have an electric oven, turn it on to 350°F and let it preheat. Then turn it off, open the oven, and let it cool for 8 to 10 minutes until the temperature inside the oven is about 85 to 90°F. Then close the oven door.

When the dough is well kneaded, wash out the mixing bowl you used to make it and dry it. Rub the inside of the bowl generously with oil. Put the dough into the bowl and turn it over so the top side of the dough is also oiled. Cover the dough with plastic wrap. Place the bowl in your pre-warmed oven or a warm spot in your kitchen and let it rise until doubled. This will take about an hour if you used active dry yeast or about 40 minutes if you used quick rise yeast. Then punch the dough down by plunging your fist into the middle of it. Let it rest for about five minutes before shaping it into a pizza.

If you made your dough in a bread machine, let it rest for a few minutes at the end of the cycle.

While the dough is resting, very lightly oil a baking sheet or 12 inch pizza pan by putting a teaspoon or less of oil on a paper towel and rubbing the paper towel on the baking sheet or all around the bottom and edges of the pizza pan

Turn the dough out onto your kitchen counter. The oil on the dough should be sufficient to keep it from sticking to the counter. Stretch or roll it out into a 12-inch circle. Transfer the dough to the baking sheet or pizza pan. You may have to push and stretch it with your hands to get it to fit all the way to the edges of the pan. If you want a "thin crust" pizza, top it immediately as directed below. If you want a "thick crust" pizza, place the pizza in the pre-warmed oven or in a warm spot in your kitchen and let the dough rise for 15 to 20 minutes. Remove the pizza from the oven and preheat your oven to 400°F. While the oven is heating, spread the pizza with sauce for one pizza (half of what you made above) and the desired toppings. Bake it for 20 to 25 minutes or until the edge is golden brown. Makes one 12 inch pizza.

## Pizza dough option #3 – frozen bread dough as a crust for one pizza

  1 1 pound loaf of Rhodes White Bread Dough™, which can be found in the freezer section of your grocery store

Remove one loaf of the bread dough from the package and put it in a plastic bag. Thaw it for 2 to 4 hours at room temperature or for 6 to 12 hours in the refrigerator. Unless you have a warm spot (85 to 90°F) in your kitchen, about an hour and fifteen minutes before you wish to serve the pizza, prepare your oven to be a "rising spot" as in pizza dough option #1, above. VERY lightly oil a 12 inch pizza pan by putting a little oil on a piece of paper towel and rubbing the pan. (If you use too much oil, it will be very difficult to get this dough to stay stretched out in the pan). Also rub the paper towel on your rolling pin and kitchen counter. Put the dough on the counter and roll it out to a 12-inch circle. Transfer the dough to the pizza pan. You may have to push and stretch it with your hands more than once to get it to fit all the way to the edges of the pan. Place the pizza in the pre-warmed oven or in a warm spot in your kitchen and let the dough rise for 20 to 30 minutes or until it begins to puff up. Remove the pizza from the oven and preheat your oven to 400°F. While the oven is heating, spread the pizza with sauce for one pizza (half of what you made above) and the desired toppings. Bake it for 20 to 25 minutes or until the edge is golden brown. Makes one 12 inch pizza.

## Pizza dough option #4 – refrigerator pizza crust for one pizza

1 10-ounce can of Pillsbury Pizza Crust™, which can be found in the refrigerator section of your grocery store

Preheat your oven to 425°F. Lightly oil a baking sheet or a 12 inch pizza pan. Open the can of dough and unroll it. Place it on the baking sheet or pizza pan and press and stretch it to fit the pan. Bake it (the crust only) for 7 minutes or until it just begins to brown. Spread it with sauce for one pizza (half of what you made above) and top it with the desired toppings. Bake it for another 6 to 10 minutes or until the edge of the crust is well browned. Makes one 12 inch pizza.

**Nutritional Analysis per serving:**
**Pizza made with standard wheat or white spelt homemade dough:** 8 servings per pizza

| | | |
|---|---|---|
| Calories: ........................201 | Total fat:............................4 g | Calcium:............................85 mg |
| Protein:................................8 g | Saturated fat: ................1 g | Magnesium: ....................22 mg |
| Carbohydrate:................32 g | Omega-3 fatty acids:...0.19 g | Potassium: ....................251 mg |
| Sugars: ..............................2 g | Omega-6 fatty acids: ..0.54 g | Sodium:..........................216 mg |
| Fiber (total):......................1 g | Cholesterol: ......................8 mg | Iron: ....................................3 mg |
| Vitamin C:........................13 mg | Vitamin A:........................62 RE | Zinc: ....................................1 mg |

Diabetic exchanges: 1 serving equals 1¾ starch exchanges, ½ medium-fat meat exchange, ½ vegetable exchange, ¼ fat exchange

**Pizza made with frozen bread dough:** 8 servings per pizza

| | | |
|---|---|---|
| Calories: ........................209 | Total fat:............................5 g | Calcium:............................90 mg |
| Protein:..............................10 g | Saturated fat: ................1 g | Magnesium: ....................14 mg |
| Carbohydrate: ................33 g | Omega-3 fatty acids:...0.03 g | Potassium: ....................201 mg |
| Sugars:...............................3 g | Omega-6 fatty acids: ..0.06 g | Sodium:..........................384 mg |
| Fiber (total):......................3 g | Cholesterol: ......................8 mg | Iron: ....................................3 mg |
| Vitamin C:........................13 mg | Vitamin A:........................62 RE | Zinc: ....................................1 mg |

Diabetic exchanges: 1 serving equals 1¾ starch exchanges, ½ medium-fat meat exchange, ½ vegetable exchange, ½ fat exchange

**Pizza made with refrigerator pizza crust dough:** 6 servings per pizza

| | | |
|---|---|---|
| Calories: ........................194 | Total fat:............................5 g | Calcium:..........................101 mg |
| Protein: ..............................10 g | Saturated fat: ................2 g | Magnesium: ....................18 mg |
| Carbohydrate: ................28 g | Omega-3 fatty acids:...0.03 g | Potassium:......................268 mg |
| Sugars:...............................3 g | Omega-6 fatty acids: ..0.08 g | Sodium: ..........................406 mg |
| Fiber (total):......................2 g | Cholesterol: ....................11 mg | Iron:......................................2 mg |
| Vitamin C: ........................17 mg | Vitamin A:........................82 RE | Zinc: ....................................1 mg |

Diabetic exchanges: 1 serving equals 1½ starch exchanges, ⅔ lean meat exchange, ½ vegetable exchange, ½ fat exchange

# A Vegetable Primer

Vegetables are nutritional powerhouses. They are great sources of complex carbohydrates, vitamins, and minerals. Some even contain a good quantity of protein and all vegetables are very low in fat. If you can include vegetables in your diet, you can get along very well nutritionally even if you have dietary limitations. People who eat five servings of vegetables or fruits per day have a 30% less risk of having a stroke than people who do not.[1] Obviously, vegetables are foods you will want to eat as often as possible for good health. This chapter will teach you basic techniques to prepare and cook vegetables by either conventional or microwave methods. For special vegetable recipes, see the next chapter.

There are several schools of thought on the "best" way to eat your vegetables. Some advocate eating them raw or very lightly steamed. This preserves the vitamin content of your vegetables because a short cooking time or no cooking keeps the vitamins from either being destroyed (some of them are very heat-sensitive) or leaching out into the cooking water. However, people with digestive problems may not be able to eat many vegetables if they are raw or lightly cooked. It's much better for you to eat them "well done" than not at all! So ranges of cooking times are given in this chapter; cook them to fit your personal needs and preferences.

Before you eat vegetables raw, you may wish to soak them in a disinfecting solution such as grapefruit seed extract to kill any parasites or harmful bacteria that might have contaminated them. See page 13 for more about this.

## Artichokes

*These are fun to eat! Try them. You'll like them!*

**Preparation:** Remove any bad leaves and the small leaves at the bottom of the artichoke and cut off the stem flush with the base of the artichoke. If are having guests for dinner or have sensitive fingers, slice off the top inch of the artichoke and cut the spines off of the leaf tips. If you are cooking the artichokes just for yourself, you can omit this step. Just be careful about how you handle the spines when you eat your artichoke. Wash the artichokes thoroughly with cold water, running water between the leaves to remove any dirt.

**Conventional cooking:** If you have a steamer basket, place the artichokes in the basket with ½ inch of water in the bottom of the saucepan. If not, place them in a pan with water to cover. Bring the water to a boil, reduce the heat, and simmer (or steam) for 20 to 40 minutes or until the stem end is tender when pierced with a fork.

**Microwave cooking:** Place ½ cup water and one large or two small artichokes in a glass casserole dish. Cover with the lid or plastic wrap. Microwave for 10 to 15 minutes on high or until the leaves pull out easily and the base is tender when pierced with a fork.

**Eating the artichoke:** To eat an artichoke, peel off each leaf and, if you wish, dip the end opposite the spine into a dip, such as mayonnaise or melted butter. Hold onto the spine end of the leaf, put the other end between your front teeth and pull off the edible part with your teeth. This is a socially acceptable way of playing with your food!

**Serving suggestions:** Serve plain or with melted butter, mayonnaise, or other sauces for dipping.

**Nutritional Analysis per serving:** 1 medium artichoke per serving

| | | |
|---|---|---|
| Calories: ........................60 | Total fat: ........................0.2 g | Calcium: ........................54 mg |
| Protein: ........................4 g | Saturated fat: ..............0 g | Magnesium: ....................72 mg |
| Carbohydrate: ................13 g | Omega-3 fatty acids:...0.02 g | Potassium: ....................425 mg |
| Sugars: ........................1 g | Omega-6 fatty acids: ..0.06 g | Sodium: ........................114 mg |
| Fiber (total): ..................7 g | Cholesterol: ..................0 mg | Iron: ..............................2 mg |
| Vitamin C: ....................12 mg | Vitamin A: ....................22 RE | Zinc: ..............................1 mg |

Diabetic exchanges: 1 medium artichoke equals 2½ vegetable exchanges

# Asparagus

**Preparation:** Hold both ends of each asparagus stalk and bend. The stalk will break between the woody root end and the tender tip end. Discard the root end. Swish the stalks in a sink of cold water, allowing a little soaking time to loosen any dirt that might be hiding in the tip. Swish again, and if you think there might still be some dirt left, hold the tips under running water. Remove the stalks from the water. If desired, cut them into one-inch pieces.

**Conventional cooking:** To steam, put asparagus in a steamer basket or in a saucepan with a little boiling water. Or put the asparagus in a pan with water and bring it to a boil. Steam or simmer the asparagus until it is done to your preference. To cook it to tenderness will take 10 to 15 minutes. Drain and serve.

**Microwave cooking:** For whole spears, arrange them in a glass baking dish with the tip ends lined up down the center of the dish. Add ¼ cup of water. Cover with a lid or plastic wrap and microwave on high for 6 to 9 minutes for 1½ pounds (purchased weight rather than prepared weight) of asparagus. Let stand one minute; drain and serve.

For one inch pieces, put the asparagus in a glass casserole. Add ¼ cup of water. Cover and microwave for 6 to 9 minutes for 1½ pounds of asparagus, stirring every 3 minutes.

**Serving suggestions:** Serve plain or with a little butter or oil and salt.

**Nutritional Analysis per serving:** About 8 spears or 4 ounces per serving

| | | |
|---|---|---|
| Calories: ........................28 | Total fat: ........................0.4 g | Calcium: ........................24 mg |
| Protein: ........................3 g | Saturated fat: ..............0 g | Magnesium: ....................12 mg |
| Carbohydrate: ................5 g | Omega-3 fatty acids:...0.01 g | Potassium: ....................192 mg |
| Sugars: ........................2 g | Omega-6 fatty acids: ..0.15 g | Sodium: ........................13 mg |
| Fiber (total): ..................2 g | Cholesterol: ..................0 mg | Iron: ..............................1 mg |
| Vitamin C: ....................13 mg | Vitamin A: ....................65 RE | Zinc: ..............................0.5 mg |

Diabetic exchanges: 1 serving equals 1 vegetable exchange

# Beans – Green, Wax, or Italian Beans

**Preparation:** Break off the ends of the beans. If the strings down the sides of the beans stay attached to the ends when you snap them off, pull the strings out. Italian beans should have the strings removed in this way. Wash the beans in cool water. Cook the beans whole or break them into small sections.

**Conventional stove top cooking:** Bring about ½ inch of water to boil in a saucepan or in the bottom of a steamer. Add the beans and steam, or return the water to a boil and simmer the beans until they are tender, about 10 to 20 minutes, or until they are done to your preference. Cook frozen green or Italian beans in the same way for the time directed on the package or until they are done to your preference.

**Oven cooking:** Green beans can be a great part of an oven dinner. See page 210 for the recipe.

**Microwave cooking:** Break the beans into one inch pieces. For 1 pound of beans, put the beans, ½ cup of water, and a generous sprinkling of salt in a casserole dish and cover with the lid or plastic wrap. Microwave on high 10 to 15 minutes, stirring every 5 minutes. Let the beans stand for 5 more minutes. Drain before serving.

**Serving suggestions:** Serve green or wax beans plain or with butter or oil and salt. Serve Italian beans with olive oil and salt.

**Nutritional Analysis per serving:** About 3 ounces or 1 cup beans per serving

| | | |
|---|---|---|
| Calories: ...................25 | Total fat: ..........................0 g | Calcium: ...........................40 mg |
| Protein: ..........................1 g | Saturated fat: ...............0 g | Magnesium: .....................24 mg |
| Carbohydrate: ................5 g | Omega-3 fatty acids:...0 g | Potassium: ...................200 mg |
| Sugars: ...........................2 g | Omega-6 fatty acids: ..0 g | Sodium: .............................0 mg |
| Fiber (total): ..................3 g | Cholesterol: ....................0 mg | Iron: ..................................0.4 mg |
| Vitamin C: .......................6 mg | Vitamin A: .......................20 RE | Zinc: ....................................0 mg |

Diabetic exchanges: 1 serving equals 1 vegetable exchange

# Beans – Lima Beans

**Preparation:** Wash and shuck lima beans just before cooking them. To shuck them, squeeze the tip towards the body of the pod to pop the pod open. Then remove the beans by running your finger down the inside of the pod. You may also use frozen lima beans.

**Conventional stove top cooking:** Bring about ½ inch of water to boil in a saucepan. Add the beans, return the water to a boil and simmer until tender, about 15 to 20 minutes, or until they are done to your preference.

**Oven cooking:** Lima beans can be a great part of an oven dinner. See page 210 for the recipe.

**Microwave cooking:** Place one 10 ounce package of frozen lima beans in a glass casserole with 2 tablespoons of water and a generous sprinkling of salt. Cover with the lid or plastic wrap and microwave on high for 10 to 12 minutes, stirring every 3 minutes, until the beans are tender.

**Serving suggestions:** Serve plain or with a little butter or oil and salt.

**Nutritional Analysis per serving:** About 3 ounces or a scant ½ cup per serving

| | | |
|---|---|---|
| Calories: ..........................79 | Total fat: ...........................0 g | Calcium: ...........................21 mg |
| Protein: ............................5 g | Saturated fat: ..............0 g | Magnesium: .....................42 mg |
| Carbohydrate: ................15 g | Omega-3 fatty acids:...0 g | Potassium:........................311 mg |
| Sugars: ...........................2 g | Omega-6 fatty acids: ..0 g | Sodium:.............................22 mg |
| Fiber (total):....................5 g | Cholesterol: ......................0 mg | Iron:....................................1 mg |
| Vitamin C: ........................4 mg | Vitamin A: .........................13 RE | Zinc:...................................0 mg |

Diabetic exchanges: 1 serving equals 1 starch exchange

# Beans – Dried Beans, Split Peas, Lentils, etc.

Dried legumes are nutritional dynamite, very economical, and easy to prepare, especially using a crock pot. There is one thing to watch out for, however. Do not salt or season your legumes before cooking them or they may never soften. Salt, acid foods, and some seasonings interfere with the ability of the beans to absorb water.

**Preparation:** The night before you plan to serve dried legumes, pick out any shriveled looking beans. Put the rest of the beans in a strainer and wash them under running water to remove any dirt that might be on them. Put them in a large pan or crock pot with about twice their volume of water. Let them soak overnight. In the morning, drain them and add cool water back to the pan or crock pot three times. (This rinsing removes most of the indigestible carbohydrates responsible for "gas"). Each pound of dried legumes will make about 2½ cups of cooked legumes, or about 5 servings.

**Conventional cooking:** DO NOT SALT OR SEASON DRIED LEGUMES BEFORE COOKING! Cover the legumes with water to a depth of an inch or two above the top of the beans in the pot, or add the amount of water specified in the recipe or about 3 to 4 cups of water per pound of beans. (Smaller varieties of beans may require less water than larger varieties). Bring the pan to a boil on the stove, reduce the heat, and simmer for the time specified in the recipe or below. Replenish the water during cooking if needed. Taste the beans to see if they are tender after this time; if not, cook them longer. When they are tender, drain any excess water and add salt, tomatoes, and other seasonings and simmer them for ½ hour more.

## Approximate cooking times for dried beans are:

| | |
|---|---|
| Adzuki beans: 2 to 2½ hours | Lentils: 1 to 2 hours |
| Anasazi beans: 2 to 2½ hours | Lima beans: 1 to 1½ hours |
| Black-eyed peas: 1½ to 2 hours | Navy (small white) beans: 3 to 3½ |
| Black beans: 2 to 2½ hours | hours |
| Canellini beans: 1½ to 2 hours | Pinto beans: 2 to 2½ hours |
| Cranberry beans: 1½ to 2 hours | Red beans: 2 to 2½ hours |
| Garbanzo beans: 3 to 3½ hours | Soybeans: 3½ to 4½ hours |
| Great northern beans: 2 to 2½ hours | Split peas: 1 to 2 hours |
| Kidney beans: 2½ to 3 hours | |

These times may vary with the age of the beans, the hardness of your water, the altitude, etc. Occasionally you may get a very old batch of beans that seems to take forever to soften. It has nothing to do with you; it's just the beans!

**Crockpot cooking:** Soak and rinse the beans as above. DO NOT SALT OR SEASON DRIED LEGUMES BEFORE COOKING! Cover the legumes with water to a depth an inch or two above the top of the beans in the pot, or add the amount of water specified in the recipe or about 4 cups of water per pound of beans. Cook on high for 4 to 6 hours, on low for 8 to 10 hours, or for the time specified in the recipe. Drain any excess water and add salt, tomatoes, and other seasonings to the pot and continue to cook for an additional hour or longer on high.

**Microwave cooking:** Most dried legumes do not soften enough to be easily digestible when cooked in a microwave. If you live in a dorm room and don't have a stove with which to cook your dried beans, invest in a crock pot.

**Serving suggestions:** Cooked dried beans are great served plain with a little oil. You also can freeze them for use in other recipes. See the recipes for chili, legume soups and baked beans on pages 175, 176, 220, and 222 to 227.

**Nutritional Analysis per serving:** About ⅜ cup per serving

| | | |
|---|---|---|
| Calories: ...........................82 | Total fat: ...........................0 g | Calcium: ...........................44 mg |
| Protein: ...........................6 g | Saturated fat: ...............0 g | Magnesium: ...................32 mg |
| Carbohydrate: ...............15 g | Omega-3 fatty acids:...0 g | Potassium: ...................278 mg |
| Sugars: ...........................1 g | Omega-6 fatty acids: ..0 g | Sodium: ...........................3 mg |
| Fiber (total): ...................6 g | Cholesterol: ...................0 mg | Iron: ...........................2 mg |
| Vitamin C: ...........................1 mg | Vitamin A: ...........................0 RE | Zinc: ...........................1 mg |

Diabetic exchanges: 1 serving equals 1 starch exchange

# Beets

**Preparation:** Cut off the beet tops about 1 inch from the beet. Wash the beets in cool water to remove the dirt from them.

**Conventional cooking:** Put the beets in a saucepan with water to cover. Bring them to a boil, reduce the heat, and simmer until the beets are tender when pierced with a fork. This time can vary greatly depending on the size of the beets. Small beets can take 20 minutes to cook and very large beets can take an hour. Just keep testing them until they are done. When they are tender, drain the water from the pan. If they are too hot to touch, run cold water over the beets to cool them enough so you can handle them. Slip the skins off with your fingers. Slice them if desired, and reheat them if necessary.

**Microwave cooking:** Pierce each beet with a knife. For 1 pound of beets, place the beets and ½ cup of water in a glass casserole dish and cover it with the lid or plastic wrap. Microwave on high for 20 to 30 minutes, stirring every 5 minutes, or until they are tender when pierced with a fork. Let them stand for 5 minutes. If they are too hot to touch, run cold water over the beets to cool them enough so you can handle them. Slip the skins off with your fingers. Slice them if desired, and reheat them if necessary.

**Serving suggestions:** Serve plain with a little oil or butter and salt, or chill them and serve them with vinegar as a salad.

**Nutritional Analysis per serving:** About 2½ ounces or a scant ½ cup of slices per serving

| | | |
|---|---|---|
| Calories: ...........................27 | Total fat: ...........................0 g | Calcium: ...........................11 mg |
| Protein: ...........................1 g | Saturated fat: ...............0 g | Magnesium: ...................16 mg |
| Carbohydrate: ...............6 g | Omega-3 fatty acids:...0 g | Potassium: ...................207 mg |
| Sugars: ...........................3 g | Omega-6 fatty acids: ..0 g | Sodium: ...........................194 mg |
| Fiber (total): ...................1 g | Cholesterol: ...................0 mg | Iron: ...........................1 mg |
| Vitamin C: ...........................2 mg | Vitamin A: ...........................3 RE | Zinc: ...........................0 mg |

Diabetic exchanges: 1 serving equals 1 vegetable exchange

# Broccoli

**Preparation:** Trim off any leaves and cut the stems to about 4 inches in length. Wash the broccoli and cut it into spears by cutting downward between the stalks. For microwave cooking, be sure that the stalks are not thicker than ½ inch. If desired, cut off the florets and cut the stalks into one inch pieces.

**Conventional cooking:** Bring about ½ inch of water to boil in a saucepan or the bottom of a steamer. Add the broccoli and steam, or return the water to a boil and simmer the broccoli until it is tender, about 10 to 15 minutes, or until it is done to your preference. Cook frozen broccoli in the same way for the time directed on the package or until it is done to your preference.

**Microwave cooking:** To cook spears, arrange the broccoli in a baking dish with the florets lined up down the center of the dish. Add 1 cup of water for 1½ pounds of broccoli. Cover the dish with plastic wrap and microwave on high for 10 to 14 minutes or until the broccoli is tender or almost tender. Let it stand for 5 minutes, drain the water, and serve.

To cook broccoli pieces, put the pieces in a casserole dish and add 1 cup of water for 1½ pounds of broccoli. Cover the dish with plastic wrap and microwave on high for 10 to 14 minutes or until the broccoli is tender or almost tender. Let it stand for 5 minutes, drain and serve. For one to two servings, use about 5 to 6 ounces of broccoli, ½ cup of water, microwave on high for 5 to 7 minutes, let it stand for 5 minutes, drain, and serve.

**Serving suggestions:** Sprinkle it with salt and/or pepper. Add a little butter or oil if desired.

**Nutritional Analysis per serving:** About 3 ounces, ½ medium stalk or ½ cup chopped broccoli per serving

| | | |
|---|---|---|
| Calories: .........................25 | Total fat: ..........................0 g | Calcium: ...........................42 mg |
| Protein: ...........................3 g | Saturated fat: ...............0 g | Magnesium: .....................22 mg |
| Carbohydrate: ...............5 g | Omega-3 fatty acids:...0 g | Potassium:....................286 mg |
| Sugars: .........................2 g | Omega-6 fatty acids: ..0 g | Sodium:...........................24 mg |
| Fiber (total):..................3 g | Cholesterol: ....................0 mg | Iron:....................................1 mg |
| Vitamin C: ....................82 mg | Vitamin A: ...................136 RE | Zinc:....................................0 mg |

Diabetic exchanges: 1 serving equals 1 vegetable exchange

# Brussels Sprouts

**Preparation:** Pull off any loose outer leaves and trim off any stem left on the brussels sprouts. Put them in a sink of cool water and swish them around.

**Conventional cooking:** Bring about ½ inch of water to boil in a saucepan or the bottom of a steamer. Add the brussels sprouts and steam, or return the water to a boil and simmer the sprouts until they are tender, about 10 to 14 minutes, or until they are done to your preference. Cook frozen brussels sprouts in the same way for the time directed on the package or until they are done to your preference.

**Microwave cooking:** Put ¼ cup water and about 1 pound of brussels sprouts in a 2 quart casserole dish. Cover the dish with its lid or plastic wrap. Microwave on high for 5 minutes, stir, and microwave another 4 to 6 minutes or until the sprouts are tender when pierced with a fork or done to your preference. Let stand for 5 minutes, drain, and serve.

**Serving suggestions:** Serve plain or with a little butter or oil and salt.

**Nutritional Analysis per serving:** About 3 whole or ⅜ cup chopped brussels sprouts per serving

| | | |
|---|---|---|
| Calories: ............................25 | Total fat: .............................0 g | Calcium: ............................23 mg |
| Protein: ...............................2 g | Saturated fat: ................0 g | Magnesium: ......................13 mg |
| Carbohydrate: ..................5 g | Omega-3 fatty acids:...0 g | Potassium:.....................200 mg |
| Sugars:...............................3 g | Omega-6 fatty acids: ..0 g | Sodium:................................13 mg |
| Fiber (total):......................2 g | Cholesterol: .......................0 mg | Iron:........................................1 mg |
| Vitamin C: .......................39 mg | Vitamin A: .......................45 RE | Zinc:.......................................0 mg |

Diabetic exchanges: 1 serving equals 1 vegetable exchange

# Cabbage – Red or Green

**Preparation:** Wash the cabbage. Quarter the head, core it, and cut the leaves into small squares or strips. To cook the cabbage in wedges, do not core it; just cut the head into 6 to 8 wedges for cooking. For coleslaw, slice each cored quarter into thin strips perpendicular to the long axis of the wedge.

**Conventional stove top cooking:** In a saucepan, heat one inch of water and ½ teaspoon of salt to the boiling point. Add the cabbage. Cover and bring the water back to a boil. Lower the heat and simmer cabbage wedges about 15 minutes for green cabbage or 20 minutes for red cabbage. Simmer chopped or shredded cabbage about 5 to 10 minutes, or until it is done to your preference. You may also put the cabbage in a steamer basket over boiling water and steam for 10 to 20 minutes or until it is done to your preference.

**Oven cooking:** Cabbage is extremely well-suited to being cooked in the oven as part of an oven meal. It is so tasty prepared this way that I never cook it any other way! To prepare it in the oven, see the "Oven Cabbage" recipe on page 209.

**Microwave cooking:** Cut a small (¾ to 1 pound) head of cabbage into wedges or core it and shred it. Put it in a 2 quart casserole dish with ¼ cup of water and ½ teaspoon of salt. Cover it and microwave it on high for 6 minutes. Stir the shredded cabbage or rearrange the cabbage wedges so that what was in the center of the casserole is at the edge. Cover and microwave the cabbage on high until it is done – another 4 to 8 minutes. Let it stand for 3 to 5 minutes. Drain and serve.

**Serving suggestions:** Serve plain or with a little butter or oil and salt.

**Nutritional Analysis per serving:** About 1 cup raw or ¾ cup shredded cooked cabbage per serving

| | | |
|---|---|---|
| Calories: ...........................25 | Total fat: ...........................0 g | Calcium:...........................35 mg |
| Protein: ...............................1 g | Saturated fat:................0 g | Magnesium:......................9 mg |
| Carbohydrate: ....................5 g | Omega-3 fatty acids:...0 g | Potassium:.....................109 mg |
| Sugars: ...........................2 g | Omega-6 fatty acids: ..0 g | Sodium: ...............................9 mg |
| Fiber (total):.....................3 g | Cholesterol: ...................0 mg | Iron: .......................................0 mg |
| Vitamin C: ......................23 mg | Vitamin A: .........................15 RE | Zinc:......................................0 mg |

Diabetic exchanges: 1 serving equals 1 vegetable exchange

# Cabbage – Savoy or Chinese

**Preparation:** Wash the cabbage, quarter and core the head, and cut the cabbage into small squares.

**Conventional cooking:** Put the cabbage squares in a saucepan. For one medium head weighing about 1½ pounds, add ¾ cup of water, ¼ teaspoon of salt, and 2 tablespoons of oil. Bring the pan to a boil, reduce the heat, and simmer for 15 to 20 minutes, stirring every 5 minutes. The water will be almost gone; cook it longer with the lid off to evaporate any remaining water if necessary.

**Microwave cooking:** Prepare and cook as for shredded red or green cabbage, above.

**Serving suggestions:** Serve plain or with some butter or oil and salt. If this cabbage is braised as in the "conventional cooking" method above, it is great served over a baked potato as a meal!

**Nutritional Analysis per serving:** About ¾ cup cooked shredded cabbage per serving

| | | |
|---|---|---|
| Calories: ...........................25 | Total fat: ...........................0 g | Calcium:...........................33 mg |
| Protein: ...............................2 g | Saturated fat:................0 g | Magnesium:....................26 mg |
| Carbohydrate: ....................6 g | Omega-3 fatty acids:...0 g | Potassium:.....................200 mg |
| Sugars: ...........................2 g | Omega-6 fatty acids: ..0 g | Sodium: .............................26 mg |
| Fiber (total):.....................3 g | Cholesterol: ...................0 mg | Iron: .......................................0 mg |
| Vitamin C: ......................18 mg | Vitamin A: .........................97 RE | Zinc:......................................0 mg |

Diabetic exchanges: 1 serving equals 1 vegetable exchange. Add ⅔ fat exchange and 30 calories if cooked with the oil.

# Carrots

**Preparation:** Peel the carrots and cut off the ends. Cut them crosswise into ¼ inch thick slices or lengthwise in half, and then cut the halves into quarters or strips. Small baby carrots may be cooked whole.

**Conventional stove top cooking:** In a saucepan, heat one inch of water and ½ teaspoon of salt to the boiling point. Add the carrots. Cover and bring the water back to a boil. Lower the heat and simmer about 25 minutes for whole baby carrots, 20 minutes for lengthwise strips, or 15 minutes for crosswise slices, or until the carrots are tender or done to your preference. You may also put carrot slices in a steamer basket and steam them for 15 to 18 minutes or until they are tender.

**Oven cooking:** Carrots are delicious when cooked in the oven as part of an oven meal. The natural sugars in the carrots caramelize, giving them a great taste! To cook carrots in the oven, see the "Oven Carrots" recipe on page 209.

**Microwave cooking:** Peel 1 pound of carrots and cut them crosswise. Put them in a 1 quart casserole with ¼ cup of water and ¼ teaspoon of salt. Cover and microwave on high for 5 minutes. Stir, cover, and microwave until tender, another 4 to 8 minutes. Drain and serve.

**Serving suggestions:** Serve plain or with a little butter or oil and salt. Stir in 1 to 2 tablespoons of chopped fresh parsley if desired.

**Nutritional Analysis per serving:** About ⅜ cup cooked carrot slices per serving

| | | |
|---|---|---|
| Calories: ...25 | Total fat: ...0 g | Calcium: ...16 mg |
| Protein: ...1 g | Saturated fat: ...0 g | Magnesium: ...9 mg |
| Carbohydrate: ...6 g | Omega-3 fatty acids: ...0 g | Potassium: ...189 mg |
| Sugars: ...4 g | Omega-6 fatty acids: ..0 g | Sodium: ...20 mg |
| Fiber (total): ...2 g | Cholesterol: ...0 mg | Iron: ...0 mg |
| Vitamin C: ...2 mg | Vitamin A: ...1483 RE | Zinc: ...0 mg |

Diabetic exchanges: 1 serving equals 1 vegetable exchange

# Cauliflower

**Preparation:** Wash the cauliflower and remove the outer leaves. Cut off any dark spots from the florets. Cut the florets from the center core.

**Conventional stove top cooking:** In a saucepan, heat one inch of water and ½ teaspoon of salt to the boiling point. Add the cauliflower. Cover and bring the water back to a boil. Lower the heat and simmer about 20 to 25 minutes for a whole head of cauliflower or 10 to 13 minutes for florets, or until the cauliflower is done to your preference. You may also put the cauliflower florets in a steamer basket over boiling water and steam for 10 to 12 minutes or until they are tender.

**Oven cooking:** Cauliflower is a vegetable that is well-suited to being cooked in the oven as part of an oven meal. To do this, substitute a head of cauliflower, cut into florets, for the cabbage in the "Oven Cabbage" recipe on page 209.

**Microwave cooking:** Put the florets from one medium (about 1 pound) head of cauliflower in a 1½ quart casserole dish with ¼ cup of water and ¼ teaspoon of salt. Cover and microwave on high for 5 minutes. Stir, cover, and microwave until tender, another 4 to 8 minutes. Drain and serve.

**Serving suggestions:** Serve plain or with a little butter or oil and salt.

**Nutritional Analysis per serving:** About ⅞ cup cauliflower florets per serving

| | | |
|---|---|---|
| Calories: ...25 | Total fat: ...0 g | Calcium: ...17 mg |
| Protein: ...2 g | Saturated fat: ...0 g | Magnesium: ...10 mg |
| Carbohydrate: ...4 g | Omega-3 fatty acids: ...0 g | Potassium: ...154 mg |
| Sugars: ...1 g | Omega-6 fatty acids: ..0 g | Sodium: ...16 mg |
| Fiber (total): ...3 g | Cholesterol: ...0 mg | Iron: ...0 mg |
| Vitamin C: ...48 mg | Vitamin A: ...2 RE | Zinc: ...0 mg |

Diabetic exchanges: 1 serving equals 1 vegetable exchange

# Celery

**Preparation:** Trim off the leaves and root ends from each stalk. Wash thoroughly. Eat the celery raw or, for cooking, cut it into 1 inch pieces.

**Conventional cooking:** In a saucepan, heat one inch of water and ½ teaspoon of salt to the boiling point. Add the celery slices. Cover and bring the water back to a boil. Lower the heat and simmer about 15 to 20 minutes or until the celery is tender or done to your preference, or you may put celery slices in a steamer basket and steam for 5 to 10 minutes or until they are tender.

**Microwave cooking:** Prepare about 4 cups of celery pieces. Place them in a 1½ quart casserole dish with 2 tablespoons of water and ¼ teaspoon of salt. Cover and microwave on high for 5 minutes. Stir, cover, and microwave until tender, another 3 to 5 minutes. Allow the celery to stand for three minutes. Drain and serve.

**Serving suggestions:** Serve cooked celery plain or with a little butter or oil and salt. Serve raw celery ribs plain or with the center cavity of the stalk filled with cream cheese or peanut butter or drizzled with a little olive oil and sprinkled with salt and pepper.

**Nutritional Analysis per serving:** About 4 stalks or 1 cup chopped cooked celery per serving

| | | |
|---|---|---|
| Calories: ...........................24 | Total fat: ..............................0 g | Calcium: ............................60 mg |
| Protein: ................................1 g | Saturated fat: ...............0 g | Magnesium: ........................17 mg |
| Carbohydrate: ..................5 g | Omega-3 fatty acids:...0 g | Potassium: ......................432 mg |
| Sugars: ...........................1 g | Omega-6 fatty acids: ..0 g | Sodium: ............................131 mg |
| Fiber (total):......................3 g | Cholesterol: .....................0 mg | Iron: ....................................0 mg |
| Vitamin C: ........................9 mg | Vitamin A: .........................19 RE | Zinc:....................................0 mg |

Diabetic exchanges: 1 serving equals 1 vegetable exchange

# Corn on the Cob

**Preparation:** Remove the husks from fresh corn. Break or cut off the stem end. Remove any tassel strings that cling to the corn. Rinse each ear. Dry the ears and refrigerate them in a plastic bag until you want to eat the corn. Corn on the cob is best very fresh. As it sits after being picked, the natural sugars begin to convert to starch. My grandma always picked the corn from their farm right before dinner, put the water on to boil, husked the corn while the water was coming to a boil, and then cooked the corn immediately. Field-to-table time had to be less than a half hour for her to consider corn good. Frozen corn on the cob is definitely inferior to fresh corn. I suggest eating your corn OFF the cob in the winter. However, if you want to eat frozen corn on the cob, follow the cooking directions given on the package.

**Conventional cooking:** Bring a large pot of water to a boil. Add the corn. Return the water to a boil and cook for five minutes. Drain and serve.

**Microwave cooking:** Cut off a 12 inch by 14 inch piece of plastic wrap. Lay rinsed and still wet corn on the wrap diagonally. If the corn had been washed previously and is now dry, add about 1 teaspoon of water to the plastic. Fold one corner of the wrap over the corn, fold down the corners near the ends of the ear, and roll the corn up in the remaining plastic wrap. Put it on the turntable of the microwave and microwave on high for 3 minutes for one ear, 5 minutes for two ears, or 8 minutes for four ears. If you cook four ears at once, half-way through the cooking time, rearrange them on the turntable so that the ears that were in the center are on the outside and the ears that were on the outside are in the center. Let the corn stand for a minute or so before eating it. The cooking time for corn can vary with the power of your microwave, altitude, etc. If the cob seems mushy, decrease your cooking time next time. If the corn is not done, microwave it a minute or two longer and increase your cooking time next time.

**Serving suggestions:** Serve plain or with a little butter and salt.

**Nutritional Analysis per serving:** One medium (about 3 ounce ear) per serving

| | | |
|---|---|---|
| Calories: ...........................83 | Total fat: ..............................1 g | Calcium: ...............................2 mg |
| Protein: ..............................3 g | Saturated fat: ...............0 g | Magnesium: ...................25 mg |
| Carbohydrate: ...................19 g | Omega-3 fatty acids: ...0.01 g | Potassium: ....................192 mg |
| Sugars: ............................2 g | Omega-6 fatty acids: ..0.45 g | Sodium: ...............................13 mg |
| Fiber (total): ....................2 g | Cholesterol: ....................0 mg | Iron: ....................................0 mg |
| Vitamin C: .........................5 mg | Vitamin A: ......................17 RE | Zinc: ....................................0 mg |

Diabetic exchanges: 1 serving equals 1 starch exchange

# Corn Kernels

**Preparation:** For fresh corn, husk and rinse the ears. Cut the kernels from the cob. If it is winter or you want to save time, use frozen corn kernels.

**Conventional cooking:** Put corn kernels and a minimal amount of unsalted water (just enough to cover the bottom of the pan) into a saucepan. Over medium heat, bring the corn to a boil and simmer it for five minutes. Season with salt to taste after cooking it. Add a little oil or butter if desired.

**Microwave cooking:** Put two cups of fresh corn kernels or a 10 ounce package of frozen corn into a 1½ quart casserole dish with 2 tablespoons of water and ¼ teaspoon of salt. Cover and microwave on high for 3 minutes. Stir, cover, and microwave until tender, another 3 to 5 minutes. Drain and serve.

**Serving suggestions:** Serve plain or with a little butter or oil and salt.

**Nutritional Analysis per serving:** A scant ½ cup per serving

| | | |
|---|---|---|
| Calories: ...........................80 | Total fat: ..............................1 g | Calcium: ...............................1 mg |
| Protein: ..............................2 g | Saturated fat: ...............0 g | Magnesium: ...................24 mg |
| Carbohydrate: ...................19 g | Omega-3 fatty acids: ...0.01 g | Potassium: ....................184 mg |
| Sugars: ............................2 g | Omega-6 fatty acids: ..0.43 g | Sodium: ...............................13 mg |
| Fiber (total): ....................2 g | Cholesterol: ....................0 mg | Iron: ....................................0 mg |
| Vitamin C: .........................5 mg | Vitamin A: ......................16 RE | Zinc: ....................................0 mg |

Diabetic exchanges: 1 serving equals 1 starch exchange

# Eggplant

**Preparation:** Wash the eggplant well and peel if desired. You may steam the eggplant whole. To cook it in the microwave or to boil it, cut it into ½ inch cubes or ¼ inch slices.

**Conventional cooking:** To steam eggplant, put a whole, unpeeled eggplant into the top of a steamer basket over ½ inch of water. Cover tightly and steam it for 12 to 20 minutes or until it is tender when pierced with a fork.

To boil eggplant, put about ½ inch of water in a saucepan and bring it to a boil. Add eggplant cubes or slices and ½ teaspoon of salt to the water. Cover and return to a boil. Cook on medium heat for 5 to 8 minutes or until the eggplant is tender when pierced with a fork.

**Microwave cooking:** Cut a medium (1½ pound) eggplant into cubes. Put it into a 1½ quart casserole dish with 2 tablespoons of water and ½ teaspoon of salt. Cover and microwave on high, stopping the microwave and stirring the eggplant at one minute intervals, for 6 to 10 minutes or until tender. Drain and serve.

**Serving suggestions:** Serve plain or with a little butter or oil and salt. Sprinkle with Parmesan cheese if desired.

**Nutritional Analysis per serving:** About 1 cup boiled cubed eggplant per serving

| | | |
|---|---|---|
| Calories: ............................27 | Total fat: ............................0 g | Calcium: ..............................6 mg |
| Protein: ................................1 g | Saturated fat:................0 g | Magnesium: ......................13 mg |
| Carbohydrate:....................7 g | Omega-3 fatty acids:...0 g | Potassium:.....................246 mg |
| Sugars:..............................4 g | Omega-6 fatty acids: ..0 g | Sodium: ...............................3 mg |
| Fiber (total):......................2 g | Cholesterol: ....................0 mg | Iron: .....................................0 mg |
| Vitamin C: ..........................1 mg | Vitamin A: ..........................6 RE | Zinc:.....................................0 mg |

Diabetic exchanges: 1 serving equals 1 vegetable exchange

# Greens — Spinach, Beet Tops, Swiss Chard, Chicory, Collards, Escarole, Kale, or Mustard Greens

**Preparation:** Remove the stem ends from the greens. Put them in a sink filled with cool water and swish them around. Lift them out into the other side of the sink, fill the sink with water, and swish them again. Repeat this several times until there is no more dirt left in the water when you lift the greens out.

**Conventional cooking:** Put the greens into a large pan with the water still clinging to the leaves. Heat over medium heat, stirring occasionally, until the greens come to a boil. Cook for 5 to 10 minutes or until they are done to your preference.

**Microwave cooking:** For 1 pound of greens, place them in a 3 quart casserole dish with the water from washing them still clinging to the leaves. Cover and microwave on high for 3 minutes. Stir, cover, and microwave until tender, another 3 to 5 minutes. Let stand 3 minutes. Drain and serve.

**Serving suggestions:** Serve plain or with a little butter or oil and salt.

**Nutritional Analysis per serving:** About 3 ½ cups fresh or ½ to ⅔ cup cooked greens per serving

| | | |
|---|---|---|
| Calories: ............................25 | Total fat: ............................0 g | Calcium:..............................147 mg |
| Protein:................................3 g | Saturated fat:................0 g | Magnesium:......................94 mg |
| Carbohydrate: ..................4 g | Omega-3 fatty acids:...0 g | Potassium:.....................503 mg |
| Sugars:..............................0 g | Omega-6 fatty acids: ..0 g | Sodium:..............................76 mg |
| Fiber (total):......................3 g | Cholesterol: ....................0 mg | Iron: .....................................4 mg |
| Vitamin C: ..........................11 mg | Vitamin A:....................885 RE | Zinc: ....................................1 mg |

Diabetic exchanges: 1 serving equals 1 vegetable exchange

# Kohlrabi

**Preparation:** Trim off the root ends and stems coming from the sides of bulb. Wash and pare the kohlrabi. Slice them into ¼ inch thick slices. They are great eaten raw!

**Conventional cooking:** Bring 3 to 4 inches of water to a boil in a saucepan. Add the kohlrabi, return the water to a boil, and simmer them for 10 to 20 minutes or until they are tender or done to your preference. Old kohlrabi take longer to cook than small young kohlrabi. You may also put them in a steamer over boiling water and steam for 10 to 20 minutes or until they are tender.

**Microwave cooking:** Put slices from 6 to 8 medium kohlrabi (about 1 pound) into a 1 quart casserole with ¼ cup water and ¼ teaspoon salt. Cover and microwave on high for 3 minutes. Stir, cover, and microwave until tender, another 3 to 5 minutes. Let stand for 2 minutes. Drain and serve.

**Serving suggestions:** Serve plain or with a little butter or oil and salt.

**Nutritional Analysis per serving:** About 5 slices raw or ½ cup boiled chopped kohlrabi per serving

| | | |
|---|---|---|
| Calories: 25 | Total fat: 0 g | Calcium: 21 mg |
| Protein: 1 g | Saturated fat: 0 g | Magnesium: 16 mg |
| Carbohydrate: 6 g | Omega-3 fatty acids: 0 g | Potassium: 281 mg |
| Sugars: 4 g | Omega-6 fatty acids: 0 g | Sodium: 17 mg |
| Fiber (total): 1 g | Cholesterol: 0 mg | Iron: 0 mg |
| Vitamin C: 45 mg | Vitamin A: 3 RE | Zinc: 0 mg |

Diabetic exchanges: 1 serving equals 1 vegetable exchange

# Leeks

**Preparation:** Cut the roots from the leeks and cut off the green tops to about 2 inches from the white part. Peel the outside layer off the bulbs. Cut lengthwise into fourths. Wash thoroughly, spreading the bulbs apart to remove the dirt between the leaves. The green tops of leeks can be saved for use in soups or to sprinkle on baked potatoes.

**Conventional cooking:** Leeks taste best when sauteed. Cut the fourths into ¼ inch slices and put them in a frying pan with a little olive oil. Heat over medium heat for 10 to 20 minutes until they are tender or done to your preference. If you prefer to cook them without any oil, put one inch of water and ½ teaspoon of salt in a saucepan and bring them to a boil. Add the leeks. Cover the pan and bring the water back to a boil. Lower the heat and simmer about 12 to 15 minutes or until the leeks are tender or done to your preference.

**Microwave cooking:** Prepare 2 pound of leeks (purchased weight rather than prepared weight) as directed above. Put the quarters into a 1½ quart casserole dish with ¼ cup water and ½ teaspoon salt. Cover and microwave on high for 3 minutes. Stir the leeks and microwave until tender, another 3 to 5 minutes. Let stand for 2 minutes. Drain and serve.

**Serving suggestions:** Serve plain, with a little butter or oil and salt, or sprinkled with cheese.

**Nutritional Analysis per serving:** About ½ whole raw leek or I cup boiled leeks per serving

| | | |
|---|---|---|
| Calories: ......................25 | Total fat: ...........................0 g | Calcium: ........................23 mg |
| Protein: .............................1 g | Saturated fat: ...............0 g | Magnesium: ....................11 mg |
| Carbohydrate: ................6 g | Omega-3 fatty acids:...0 g | Potassium: .....................68 mg |
| Sugars: ............................1 g | Omega-6 fatty acids: ..0 g | Sodium: .........................192 mg |
| Fiber (total): .....................1 g | Cholesterol: ...................0 mg | Iron: ..................................0 mg |
| Vitamin C: .......................3 mg | Vitamin A: ......................4 RE | Zinc: ..................................0 mg |

Diabetic exchanges: 1 serving equals 1 vegetable exchange

# *Mushrooms*

**Preparation:** Mushrooms are very sensitive vegetables – so sensitive that some people advocate not washing them! However, I feel that anything which will be eaten raw should not only be washed but should be soaked in a disinfecting solution. (See page 13 for more about this). If you intend to eat them raw in a salad and like to play it safe, soak them as on page 13; they *do* grow in the dirt in dark places! If you are going to cook them, right before you are going to use them, hold them under running water to wash them. Cut off the end of the stem. If you do not wish to use them whole, slice them parallel to the stem.

**Conventional cooking:** Wash and slice the mushrooms. Heat 1 tablespoon of olive oil over medium heat in a large skillet. Add about ¼ pound of the mushroom to the skillet at a time and cook them for about 4 minutes turning them once midway through the cooking time. Remove them to a serving dish and keep them warm. Add another table-spoon of oil to the skillet and then another ¼ pound of mushrooms until you have cooked all of the mushrooms.

**Microwave cooking:** Wash and slice 1 pound of mushrooms. Put them in a casserole dish with only the washing water that is still clinging to them. Cover and microwave on high for 2 minutes. Stir them and microwave until tender, another 2 to 3 minutes. Let stand for 2 minutes. Drain, add 1 tablespoon of oil, and serve.

**Serving suggestions:** Serve plain or with oil and salt. (Oil has already been added in cook-ing if cooked conventionally).

**Nutritional Analysis per serving:** About 3½ ounces or ⅜ cup cooked mushrooms per serving

| | | |
|---|---|---|
| Calories: ......................25 | Total fat: ...........................0 g | Calcium: ..........................6 mg |
| Protein: .............................2 g | Saturated fat: ...............0 g | Magnesium: ....................11 mg |
| Carbohydrate: ................5 g | Omega-3 fatty acids:...0 g | Potassium: ...................333 mg |
| Sugars: ............................0 g | Omega-6 fatty acids: ..0 g | Sodium: .........................223 mg |
| Fiber (total): .....................5 g | Cholesterol: ...................0 mg | Iron: ..................................2 mg |
| Vitamin C: .......................4 mg | Vitamin A: ......................0 RE | Zinc: ..................................1 mg |

Diabetic exchanges: 1 serving equals 1 vegetable exchange. If sauteed with olive oil, 1 serving equals 1 vegetable exchange plus 2½ fat exchanges and contains 145 calories.

# White, Yellow, or Red Onions

**Preparation:** Peel onions under cold running water. (Peeling them under running water should help prevent tears by washing the irritating vapors down the sink). Slice off the tops and root ends. Slice them if they are large and you wish to saute them.

**Conventional stove top cooking:** To boil onions, bring 3 to 4 inches of water and 1 teaspoon of salt to a boil in a saucepan. Add the onions, return the water to a boil, and simmer them for 15 to 20 minutes for small onions or 25 to 35 minutes for large onions, or until they are tender or done to your preference. You may also put them in a steamer over boiling water and steam for 10 to 20 minutes or until they are tender.

Sauteed or braised onions are great because they give you the onion flavor developed by oil without the damaged fats you get with deep-fat fried onion rings. To saute or braise onions, heat about 2 tablespoons of olive oil in a frying pan. Add the onions and heat and stir them. If you wish to saute them, cook them, stirring often, for 10 to 15 minutes or until they are tender or done to your preference.

Braising takes less "tending." To braise onions, after 2 to 3 minutes of cooking them in the oil, add 2 tablespoons of water, cover the pan, and cook them for an additional 10 to 12 minutes or until they are done to your preference.

**Oven cooking:** Onions are a good vegetable to have as part of an oven meal. See the "Oven Onions" recipes on page 211.

**Microwave cooking:** Put about 1½ pounds of small onions in a 2 to 3 quart casserole dish with ¼ cup water and ¼ teaspoon salt. Cover and microwave on high for 3 minutes. Stir the onions and microwave until tender, another 3 to 5 minutes. Let stand for 3 minutes. Drain and serve.

**Serving suggestions:** Serve with a little butter or oil and salt.

**Nutritional Analysis per serving:** About ½ medium raw onion or ¼ cup cooked chopped onion per serving

| | | |
|---|---|---|
| Calories: ...........................24 | Total fat: ...........................0 g | Calcium: ...........................12 mg |
| Protein: ..............................1 g | Saturated fat: ...............0 g | Magnesium: .....................6 mg |
| Carbohydrate: ..................5 g | Omega-3 fatty acids:...0 g | Potassium: .......................87 mg |
| Sugars:.............................3 g | Omega-6 fatty acids: ..0 g | Sodium: ............................2 mg |
| Fiber (total):.....................1 g | Cholesterol: .....................0 mg | Iron: ..................................0 mg |
| Vitamin C:.........................3 mg | Vitamin A: .........................0 RE | Zinc:..................................0 mg |

Diabetic exchanges: 1 serving equals 1 vegetable exchange

# Parsnips

*These look like yellow carrots but have a wonderful sweet and distinctive flavor all their own.*

**Preparation:** Peel parsnips like carrots, cut off the ends, and cut them into ¼ inch slices.

**Conventional cooking:** In a saucepan, heat one inch of water and ½ teaspoon of salt to the boiling point. Add sliced parsnips. Cover and bring the water back to a boil. Lower the heat and simmer about 30 minutes or until tender and done to your preference.

**Microwave cooking:** Put 1½ pounds of parsnips (about 6 to 8) which have been peeled and sliced in a 1 quart casserole dish with ¼ cup water and ¼ teaspoon salt. Cover and microwave on high for 4 minutes. Stir and microwave an additional 4 to 6 minutes or until they are tender. Let them stand one minute, drain and serve.

**Serving suggestions:** Serve plain or with a little butter or oil and salt.

**Nutritional Analysis per serving:** About ⅙ raw 9 inch parsnip or ⅓ cup cooked slices per serving

| | | |
|---|---|---|
| Calories: ...........................25 | Total fat: ..............................0 g | Calcium: ..............................12 mg |
| Protein:...............................0 g | Saturated fat: ................0 g | Magnesium:..........................9 mg |
| Carbohydrate:...................6 g | Omega-3 fatty acids:...0 g | Potassium:.........................115 mg |
| Sugars: ...............................2 g | Omega-6 fatty acids: ..0 g | Sodium: ..............................77 mg |
| Fiber (total): .....................1 g | Cholesterol: ......................0 mg | Iron: .....................................0 mg |
| Vitamin C: ..........................4 mg | Vitamin A: ..........................0 RE | Zinc:......................................0 mg |

Diabetic exchanges: 1 serving equals 1 vegetable exchange

# Pea Pods

**Preparation:** Wash the pea pods. Break off the tips and remove the strings from the sides of the pods. This is like "snapping" beans; as you break the tip, the string will be attached to the tip and you can pull it from the side of the pea pod.

**Conventional cooking:** Pea pods are most often cooked in Oriental stir-fries. Heat a few teaspoons of oil in a frying pan or wok over medium to high heat. Add the pea pods and cook, stirring constantly, for a few minutes until they are crisp-tender.

**Microwave cooking:** Put 1 pound of pea pods in a 1½ quart casserole dish with ¼ cup water and ¼ teaspoon salt. Cover and microwave on high for 3 minutes. Stir and then microwave them an additional 3 to 5 minutes or until they are crisp-tender. Let them stand 5 minutes, drain and serve.

**Serving suggestions:** Drizzle with a small amount of soy sauce or chill and add to salads.

**Nutritional Analysis per serving:** About 1 cup raw whole pea pods or ⅓ cup cooked pea pods per serving

| | | |
|---|---|---|
| Calories: ...........................25 | Total fat: ..............................0 g | Calcium:...............................27 mg |
| Protein: ...............................2 g | Saturated fat: ................0 g | Magnesium: ........................15 mg |
| Carbohydrate: ...................5 g | Omega-3 fatty acids:...0 g | Potassium: .......................126 mg |
| Sugars:................................3 g | Omega-6 fatty acids: ..0 g | Sodium: ................................3 mg |
| Fiber (total):.....................2 g | Cholesterol: ......................0 mg | Iron:......................................1 mg |
| Vitamin C: ..........................38 mg | Vitamin A:...........................9 RE | Zinc:......................................0 mg |

Diabetic exchanges: 1 serving equals 1 vegetable exchange

# Peas

**Preparation:** Wash and shuck peas just before cooking them. To shuck peas, squeeze the tip towards the body of the pea pod to pop the pod open. Then remove the peas by running your finger down the inside of the pod.

**Conventional stove top cooking:** In a saucepan, heat ½ inch of water and ¼ teaspoon of salt to the boiling point. Add the peas. Cover and bring the water back to a boil. Lower the heat and simmer for 8 to 12 minutes or until tender and done to your preference. Frozen peas are cooked by the same method, but they cook much more quickly, usually in 3 to 5 minutes. See package directions for the cooking time.

**Microwave cooking:** Put peas from 3 pounds of mature pea pods in a 1½ quart casserole dish with ½ cup water and ¼ teaspoon salt. Cover and microwave on high for 4 minutes. Stir and microwave an additional 4 to 6 minutes or until they are tender. Let them stand 3 minutes, drain and serve.

**Oven cooking:** Peas are a vegetable that is well-suited to being cooked in the oven as part of an oven meal. To do this, see the "Oven Peas or Beans" recipe on page 210.

**Serving suggestions:** Serve plain or with a little butter or oil and salt.

**Nutritional Analysis per serving:** About ½ cup cooked peas per serving

| | | |
|---|---|---|
| Calories: ...........................80 | Total fat: ...........................0 g | Calcium: ...........................26 mg |
| Protein: ...........................5 g | Saturated fat: ...............0 g | Magnesium: ....................37 mg |
| Carbohydrate: .................15 g | Omega-3 fatty acids:...0 g | Potassium: ....................260 mg |
| Sugars: ...........................5 g | Omega-6 fatty acids: ..0 g | Sodium: ...........................3 mg |
| Fiber (total): ...................5 g | Cholesterol: ...................0 mg | Iron: ...........................1 mg |
| Vitamin C: ........................14 mg | Vitamin A: .......................58 RE | Zinc: ...........................1 mg |

Diabetic exchanges: 1 serving equals 1 starch exchange

# Peppers – Bell

**Preparation:** Wash peppers. Cut in them half and remove the seeded core and stem.

**Conventional oven cooking:** See "Baked Stuffed Peppers," page 167, for baking directions.

**Pan fried:** Slice the peppers. Heat a few teaspoons of olive oil over medium heat in a frying pan and add the slices. Cook the peppers, stirring often, for 3 to 5 minutes or until crisp-tender and lightly browned, or cook them longer if you prefer them soft.

**Roasted:** Preheat your oven to 400°F. Put the peppers on a baking sheet and place them in the oven. Turn them about every 15 minutes while they are cooking. Bake the peppers until they are darkened and blistered on all sides, or for about 45 to 60 minutes total baking time. Remove them from the oven and put them in a paper bag to steam and cool for a few minutes. Rub the blackened skin off. Slice the cooked peppers from the core. Discard the seeds and stem and cut the flesh of the peppers into strips.

**Microwave cooking:** Slice two peppers. Put the slices in a 1½ quart casserole dish with 1 tablespoon of water. Cover and microwave on high for 2 minutes. Stir and microwave an additional 3 to 5 minutes or until the slices are crisp-tender. Let them stand one minute, drain, and serve.

**Serving suggestions:** Serve plain or with a little oil and salt.

**Nutritional Analysis per serving:** About ½ large green bell pepper per serving

| | | |
|---|---|---|
| Calories: ...................24 | Total fat: .........................0 g | Calcium: ............................7 mg |
| Protein: ............................1 g | Saturated fat: ..............0 g | Magnesium: ......................8 mg |
| Carbohydrate: .................5 g | Omega-3 fatty acids:...0 g | Potassium: .....................145 mg |
| Sugars: ...........................2 g | Omega-6 fatty acids: .0 g | Sodium: .............................2 mg |
| Fiber (total): ....................1 g | Cholesterol: ...................0 mg | Iron: ..................................0 mg |
| Vitamin C:........................73 mg | Vitamin A: .......................52 RE | Zinc:...................................0 mg |

Diabetic exchanges: 1 serving equals 1 vegetable exchange

# Potatoes – Sweet

Sweet potatoes are often called yams, although they are really in a different food family from true yams. They come in all colors, from pale yellow to orange to red. The yellow or "white" sweet potatoes are less sweet and more mealy.

**Preparation:** Scrub potatoes under running water. Pierce with a fork in several places to keep them from exploding in the oven or microwave oven.

**Conventional oven baking:** Bake in a 350°F to 400°F oven for 1 to 1½ hours until the potatoes "give" when squeezed. The baking time will depend on the size of the potatoes. Sweet potatoes are also delicious cooked as an oven vegetable casserole. See page 212 for this recipe.

**Microwave cooking:** Put a piece of paper towel on the turntable of your microwave oven. Arrange the sweet potatoes in a circle on the paper towel, spacing them at least two inches from each other. Microwave on high until tender when pierced with a fork. This will be about 5 minutes for one potato or about 12 minutes for 4 potatoes, with varying times between for two or three potatoes. Allow the potatoes to stand for 5 minutes before serving.

**Serving suggestions:** Serve with a little butter or oil and salt.

**Nutritional Analysis per serving:** 1 small (about 3 ounce) sweet potato per serving

| | | |
|---|---|---|
| Calories: ...................77 | Total fat: .........................0 g | Calcium: ............................21 mg |
| Protein: ............................1 g | Saturated fat: ..............0 g | Magnesium: ......................15 mg |
| Carbohydrate:.................18 g | Omega-3 fatty acids:...0 g | Potassium: .....................261 mg |
| Sugars:............................8 g | Omega-6 fatty acids: ..0 g | Sodium: .............................8 mg |
| Fiber (total):....................2 g | Cholesterol: ...................0 mg | Iron: ..................................0 mg |
| Vitamin C: .......................18 mg | Vitamin A:.......................1637 RE | Zinc:...................................0 mg |

Diabetic exchanges: 1 serving equals 1 starch exchange

# Potatoes – White

**Preparation:** Scrub potatoes under running water. Pierce with a fork in several places to keep them from exploding in the oven or microwave oven.

**Conventional oven baking:** Bake in a 350°F to 400°F oven for 1 to 1½ hours until the potatoes "give" when squeezed. The baking time will depend on the size of the potatoes. White potatoes are also delicious cooked as an oven vegetable casserole. See page 212 for this recipe. Also see the recipes for "Oven Fries," page 214, "Scalloped Potatoes," page 213, and "Mashed Potatoes," page 214.

**Microwave cooking:** Put a piece of paper towel on the turntable of your microwave oven. Arrange the potatoes in a circle on the paper towel, spacing them at least two inches from each other. Microwave on high until tender when pierced with a fork. This will be about 5 minutes for one potato or about 12 to 15 minutes for 4 potatoes, with varying times between for two or three potatoes. Allow the baked potatoes to stand for 5 minutes before serving. Mashed potatoes can also be made in the microwave oven. See the recipe on page 238.

**Serving suggestions:** Serve with a little butter or oil and salt.

**Nutritional Analysis per serving:** ½ large or 1 small (about 3 ounce) potato per serving

| | | |
|---|---|---|
| Calories: ...........................80 | Total fat: ...........................0 g | Calcium: ...........................7 mg |
| Protein: ...........................2 g | Saturated fat: ..............0 g | Magnesium: .................20 mg |
| Carbohydrate:.................19 g | Omega-3 fatty acids:...0 g | Potassium: .................308 mg |
| Sugars: ...........................1 g | Omega-6 fatty acids: ..0 g | Sodium: ...........................5 mg |
| Fiber (total):.....................2 g | Cholesterol: .....................0 mg | Iron:...........................1 mg |
| Vitamin C:.........................0 mg | Vitamin A: .........................0 RE | Zinc:...........................0 mg |

Diabetic exchanges: 1 serving equals 1 starch exchange

# Spinach

Spinach is one of the most nutritious vegetables we have. If you don't think you like spinach, try it raw in a salad. See page 133 for this recipe. To wash and/or cook spinach, see the instructions for preparing and cooking greens of all kinds on page 193.

# Squash – Spaghetti

**Preparation:** Rinse any dirt from the outside of the squash.

**Conventional cooking:** Cut the spaghetti squash in half and scoop out the seeds. Lay it cut side down on a baking sheet. Bake at 350°F for 35 to 45 minutes or until it just begins to give when you squeeze it. Be careful not to overbake spaghetti squash or it will be soft throughout rather than coming out in spaghetti "strands." Of course, it will still be delicious, just a little less fun to eat!

**Microwave cooking:** Pierce the squash with a knife in at least two places, going all the way into the center cavity, to allow steam to escape as it cooks. Place it on a paper towel in the microwave oven. For a 2½ pound medium-sized squash, microwave it on high for 8 minutes. Turn the squash over and microwave it for another 8 to 12 minutes or until it gives when squeezed. Allow it to stand for 10 minutes. Cut it in half and scoop out the seeds.

**Serving suggestions:** Use a fork to remove the inside of the squash in spaghetti-like strands. Serve with a little oil and salt, grated cheese, spaghetti sauce, or pesto.

**Nutritional Analysis per serving:** About ½ cup cooked spaghetti squash per serving

| | | |
|---|---|---|
| Calories: .........................25 | Total fat: .......................0 g | Calcium: ...........................19 mg |
| Protein: ...............................1 g | Saturated fat: ...............0 g | Magnesium: ......................10 mg |
| Carbohydrate: .................6 g | Omega-3 fatty acids:...0 g | Potassium: .....................107 mg |
| Sugars: ............................2 g | Omega-6 fatty acids: ..0 g | Sodium: .............................16 mg |
| Fiber (total): .....................1 g | Cholesterol: ....................0 mg | Iron: ...................................0 mg |
| Vitamin C: ........................3 mg | Vitamin A: ........................10 RE | Zinc: ...................................0 mg |

Diabetic exchanges: 1 serving equals 1 vegetable exchange

# Squash – Summer (Zucchini, Crookneck, etc.)

**Preparation:** Wash the squash and cut about ¼ inch off of each end. Cut it into ½ inch thick slices.

**Conventional cooking:** In a saucepan, heat one inch of water and ½ teaspoon of salt to the boiling point. Add the sliced squash. Cover the pan and bring the water back to a boil. Lower the heat and simmer for 8 to 12 minutes or until the squash is tender or done to your preference. Or put the squash slices in a steamer basket and steam for 8 to 12 minutes or until they are tender.

**Microwave cooking:** Put the squash slices in a 1½ quart casserole dish with ¼ cup of water and ¼ teaspoon of salt. Cover and microwave on high for 4 minutes. Stir, cover, and microwave until tender, another 3 to 7 minutes. Let stand for one minute, drain and serve.

**Serving suggestions:** Serve with a little butter or oil and salt.

**Nutritional Analysis per serving:** About ⅞ cup slices per serving

| | | |
|---|---|---|
| Calories: .........................25 | Total fat: .......................0 g | Calcium: ...........................20 mg |
| Protein: ...............................1 g | Saturated fat: ...............0 g | Magnesium: ......................35 mg |
| Carbohydrate: .................6 g | Omega-3 fatty acids:...0 g | Potassium: .....................398 mg |
| Sugars: ............................4 g | Omega-6 fatty acids: ..0 g | Sodium: .............................5 mg |
| Fiber (total): .....................2 g | Cholesterol: ....................0 mg | Iron: ...................................1 mg |
| Vitamin C: ........................7 mg | Vitamin A: ........................38 RE | Zinc: ...................................0 mg |

Diabetic exchanges: 1 serving equals 1 vegetable exchange

# Squash – Winter

**Preparation:** Cut small varieties of squash in half. Cut very large varieties such as Hubbard squash into serving-sized pieces. Remove the seeds and strings from the cavity of the squash.

**Conventional oven cooking:** Place halves of small squash cut-side down in a baking dish. Bake at 350°F to 400°F for 30 to 60 minutes, or until they are tender when pierced with a fork. For pieces of a large squash such as Hubbard squash, put them in the baking dish skin side down. Add water to the dish to a depth of about ¼ inch. Cover the dish with its lid or aluminum foil. Bake at 350°F to 400°F for 30 to 45 minutes, or until the squash is tender when pierced with a fork.

**Oven casserole cooking:** Butternut squash is firm enough to be well-suited to being cooked in the oven as part of an oven meal. To do this, see the "Oven Squash" recipe on page 211.

**Microwave cooking:** Pierce squash in at least two places, being sure to go all the way into the center cavity. Place whole small squash in the microwave oven. For 2 pounds of squash (about one medium squash), microwave on high for 6 minutes. Cut the squash in half and remove the seeds and strings. Arrange the halves cut-side down in a baking dish. Cover and microwave on high for 6 to 9 minutes more or until the squash is tender when pierced with a fork. Allow it to stand for 3 minutes before serving.

**Serving suggestions:** Serve with a little butter or oil and salt or honey.

**Nutritional Analysis per serving:** About ½ cup baked mashed squash per serving

| | | |
|---|---|---|
| Calories: ...........................75 | Total fat: ...........................0 g | Calcium: ...........................59 mg |
| Protein: ...........................2 g | Saturated fat: ...............0 g | Magnesium: ...................58 mg |
| Carbohydrate: ..................19 g | Omega-3 fatty acids: ...0 g | Potassium: ...................589 mg |
| Sugars: ...........................5 g | Omega-6 fatty acids: ..0 g | Sodium: ...........................5 mg |
| Fiber (total): ....................6 g | Cholesterol: ....................0 mg | Iron: ...........................1 mg |
| Vitamin C: ........................15 mg | Vitamin A: ......................58 RE | Zinc: ...........................0 mg |

Diabetic exchanges: 1 serving equals 1 starch exchange

# Turnips and Rutabagas

**Preparation:** Wash the turnips or rutabagas and peel them. Cut them into ½ inch slices or cubes, or leave small vegetables whole.

**Conventional stove top cooking:** In a saucepan, heat one inch of water and ½ teaspoon of salt to the boiling point. Add the prepared turnips or rutabagas. Cover the pan with its lid and bring the water back to a boil. Lower the heat and simmer. Cook turnips about 25 to 30 minutes for whole small vegetables or 15 to 25 minutes for cubes, or until they are tender when pierced with a fork or done to your preference. Cook rutabagas for 20 to 25 minutes for cubes or 30 to 35 minutes for slices. Or put turnip or rutabaga slices in a steamer basket and steam for 15 to 30 minutes or until they are tender.

**Oven cooking:** Turnips and rutabagas are vegetables that are well-suited to being cooked in the oven as part of an oven meal. To do this, see the "Oven Turnips or Rutabagas" recipe on page 212.

**Microwave cooking:** To cook turnips, put 1½ pounds sliced turnips in a 2 quart casserole dish with ¼ cup of water and ½ teaspoon of salt. Cover and microwave on high for 12 to 15 minutes, stirring every 4 minutes, or until they are tender. Let them stand for one minute. Drain and serve.

To cook rutabagas, put 1½ pounds sliced rutabagas in a 2 quart casserole dish with ½ cup of water and ½ teaspoon of salt. Cover and microwave on high for 15 to 20 minutes, stirring every 5 minutes, or until they are tender. Let them stand for one minute. Drain and serve.

**Serving suggestions:** Serve with a little butter or oil and salt.

## Turnips:

**Nutritional Analysis per serving:** About ¾ cup boiled cubes per serving

| | | |
|---|---|---|
| Calories: ............................25 | Total fat: ..............................0 g | Calcium:.............................26 mg |
| Protein: ...............................1 g | Saturated fat:.................0 g | Magnesium:........................9 mg |
| Carbohydrate:..................6 g | Omega-3 fatty acids:...0 g | Potassium:.....................158 mg |
| Sugars: ..............................2 g | Omega-6 fatty acids: ..0 g | Sodium: ............................59 mg |
| Fiber (total):.....................2 g | Cholesterol: ......................0 mg | Iron: ....................................0 mg |
| Vitamin C:.........................14 mg | Vitamin A: ..........................0 RE | Zinc:....................................0 mg |

Diabetic exchanges: 1 serving equals 1 vegetable exchange

## Rutabagas:

**Nutritional Analysis per serving:** About ⅜ cup boiled cubes per serving

| | | |
|---|---|---|
| Calories: ...........................25 | Total fat: ...........................0 g | Calcium: ...........................31 mg |
| Protein: ..............................1 g | Saturated fat:.................0 g | Magnesium: .....................15 mg |
| Carbohydrate:..................6 g | Omega-3 fatty acids:...0 g | Potassium:.....................208 mg |
| Sugars: ..............................2 g | Omega-6 fatty acids: ..0 g | Sodium:..............................13 mg |
| Fiber (total): .....................1 g | Cholesterol: ......................0 mg | Iron: ....................................0 mg |
| Vitamin C:.........................12 mg | Vitamin A:........................36 RE | Zinc:....................................0 mg |

Diabetic exchanges: 1 serving equals 1 vegetable exchange

Footnotes

1. The editors of *Cooking Light*, "The New Light," *Cooking Light*, March, 2001, p. 117.

# Side Dishes and Special Vegetables

This chapter contains the recipes that can turn an entree into a very special meal. It also includes timesaving ideas for oven meals. For an oven meal, choose a main dish which bakes in the oven. When you put your main dish into the oven, also put in an oven grain, an oven vegetable, and possibly even some baked apples or pears. Get a salad ready to go and slice some bread. Then just sit back and relax, study, or run errands, and in an hour or two, you will have a complete meal ready to eat.

## Oven Grains

*If you wish to cook less-common grains such as kamut, milo, rye, teff, spelt, or oat groats in the oven, see pages 93-94 of* The Ultimate Food Allergy Cookbook and Survival Guide *which is described on the last page of this book.*

**Brown rice:**
1 cup brown rice
2½ cups water
½ teaspoon salt, or to taste
1 tablespoon oil

**White rice:**
1 cup white rice
2½ cups water
½ teaspoon salt, or to taste
1 tablespoon oil

**Wild rice:**
1 cup wild rice
4 cups water
½ teaspoon salt, or to taste
1 tablespoon oil

**Pearled or hulless barley:**
1 cup pearled or hulless barley
3½ cups water
½ teaspoon salt, or to taste
1 tablespoon oil

## Quinoa:

1 cup quinoa
2½ cups water
½ teaspoon salt, or to taste
1 tablespoon oil

## Millet:

1 cup millet
3½ cups water
½ teaspoon salt, or to taste
1 tablespoon oil

## Buckwheat:

1 cup white or roasted buckwheat groats
3½ cups water
½ teaspoon salt, or to taste
1 tablespoon oil

Choose one set of ingredients from the list above. Put all of the ingredients in a 2 to 3 quart glass casserole dish with a lid. Cover the dish and bake at about 350°F until the grain is tender and all the water is absorbed. The baking time is flexible so these grains can be baked the same amount of time as the entree of an oven meal, but approximate baking times for each type of grain are 1 to 1½ hours for the brown or white rice, hulless barley, or buckwheat, 1½ to 2 hours for the wild rice, 2 to 2½ hours for the pearled barley, 1 hour for the quinoa, or 30 to 45 minutes for the millet. If you will be baking the grain for much longer than these times, you may need to add a little more water. Makes about 2 cups of cooked grain or four half-cup to nine ¼-cup servings.

**Nutritional Analysis per serving:** eight to nine ¼ cup servings per recipe.

| | | |
|---|---|---|
| Calories: .........................89 | Total fat:...........................2 g | Calcium:...............................5 mg |
| Protein: ...............................2 g | Saturated fat:................0 g | Magnesium: ......................29 mg |
| Carbohydrate:..................16 g | Omega-3 fatty acids:...0.15 g | Potassium: ........................46 mg |
| Sugars:................................0 g | Omega-6 fatty acids: ..0.51 g | Sodium: ............................132 mg |
| Fiber (total): .....................1 g | Cholesterol: ......................0 mg | Iron: ......................................0 mg |
| Vitamin C:............................0 mg | Vitamin A: ..........................0 RE | Zinc:......................................0 mg |

Diabetic exchanges: 1 serving equals 1 starch exchange, ¼ fat exchange

Note: A nutritional analysis was calculated for all the grains in this recipe and the results were very similar, so only one analysis (brown rice) is included here.

# Stove-top Grains

*If you wish to cook less-common grains such as kamut, amaranth, milo, rye, teff, spelt, or oat groats on the stove, see pages 90-92 of* The Ultimate Food Allergy Cookbook and Survival Guide *which is described on the last page of this book.*

### Brown rice – cooking time 45 to 50 minutes:
1 cup brown rice
2½ cups water
¼ teaspoon salt

### White rice – cooking time 20 minutes:
1 cup white rice
2 cups water
¼ teaspoon salt

### Wild rice – cooking time 60 minutes:
1 cup wild rice
4 cups water
¼ teaspoon salt

### Barley – cooking time 1½ hours for whole barley or 45 to 55 minutes for pearled barley:
1 cup barley
3 cups water
¼ teaspoon salt

### Quinoa – cooking time 20 minutes:
1 cup quinoa
2 cups water
¼ teaspoon salt

### Millet – cooking time 25 to 35 minutes:
1 cup millet
3 cups water
¼ teaspoon salt

### Buckwheat, raw or white – cooking time 20 to 25 minutes:
1 cup buckwheat
3 cups water
½ teaspoon salt

### Buckwheat, roasted – cooking time 20 to 30 minutes:
1 cup roasted buckwheat
2½ cups water
½ teaspoon salt

Choose one set of ingredients above. For fluffy grains, put the water into a saucepan and bring it to a boil. Add the grain and salt. Put the lid on the pan and return it to a boil. Then lower the heat and simmer it for the time specified above for the grain you are cooking. Remove the pan from the heat. Allow the grain to stand for a few minutes, fluff it with a fork, and serve.

For creamy rather than fluffy grains, combine the grain, water, and salt in a saucepan. Put the lid on the pan. Bring it to a boil; then lower the heat and simmer it for the time specified above. Remove the pan from the heat. Allow the grain to stand for a few minutes before serving. Makes about 2 cups of cooked grain or 4 half-cup to 9 quarter-cup servings.

**Nutritional Analysis per serving:** *8 to 9 quarter-cup servings per recipe*

| | | |
|---|---|---|
| Calories: ...........................80 | Total fat:...............................1 g | Calcium:................................5 mg |
| Protein: ................................2 g | Saturated fat:...............0 g | Magnesium: ...................331 mg |
| Carbohydrate: ..................17 g | Omega-3 fatty acids:...0.01 g | Potassium:.........................49 mg |
| Sugars:................................0 g | Omega-6 fatty acids: ..0.22 g | Sodium:.............................140 mg |
| Fiber (total):.....................1 g | Cholesterol: ...................0 mg | Iron:.......................................0 mg |
| Vitamin C:..........................0 mg | Vitamin A: ...........................0 RE | Zinc:.......................................0 mg |

Diabetic exchanges: 1 serving equals 1 starch exchange

Note: A nutritional analysis was calculated for all the grains in this recipe and the results were very similar, so only one analysis (brown rice) is included here.

# Savory Celery Grain Pilaf

2 cups sliced celery
¼ small onion, chopped (optional)
4 tablespoons oil
1 cup of any uncooked grain from the "Stove-top Grains" recipe, above
Water in the amount specified for the chosen grain in the "Stove-top Grains" recipe, above
½ to 1 teaspoon salt, to taste
¼ teaspoon black pepper
3 tablespoons finely chopped fresh parsley or 1 tablespoon dried parsley
1 tablespoon finely chopped fresh sweet basil or 1 teaspoon dried sweet basil

Combine the celery, onion, and oil in a saucepan. Place it on the stove over medium heat and cook it until the vegetables begin to brown. Add the grain and water to the pan. Bring the pan to a boil over medium to high heat. Reduce the heat and simmer it for the time specified for the grain you are using in the "Stove-top Grains" recipe, above. Stir the pepper, parsley, and sweet basil into the grain. Remove the pan from the heat and allow it to stand for a few minutes before serving. Makes 6 to 9 servings.

**Nutritional Analysis per serving:** *9 servings per recipe*

| | | |
|---|---|---|
| Calories: ...........................135 | Total fat:...............................7 g | Calcium:..............................23 mg |
| Protein: ................................2 g | Saturated fat:...............1 g | Magnesium: .....................33 mg |
| Carbohydrate: ..................17 g | Omega-3 fatty acids:...0.57 g | Potassium: .......................129 mg |
| Sugars:.............................0.4 g | Omega-6 fatty acids: ....1.45 g | Sodium:.............................156 mg |
| Fiber (total):.....................1 g | Cholesterol: ...................0 mg | Iron:.......................................1 mg |
| Vitamin C: ..........................2 mg | Vitamin A:...........................9 RE | Zinc:.......................................0 mg |

Diabetic exchanges: 1 serving equals 1 starch exchange, ¼ vegetable exchange, 1 fat exchange

# Spicy Carrot Grain Pilaf

1 cup of any uncooked grain from the "Stove-top Grains" recipe on page 206
Water in the amount specified for the chosen grain in the "Stove-top Grains" recipe,
    above, PLUS 1 additional cup of water
2½ cups shredded carrots
4 tablespoons oil
½ teaspoon salt, or to taste (optional)
1 teaspoon cinnamon
¼ teaspoon cloves (optional)

If you are using any grain except the whole barley or wild rice, combine the grain, carrots, and water in a saucepan. Bring them to a boil and simmer for the time specified for the grain you are using in the "Stove-top Grains" recipe, above.

If you are using whole barley or wild rice, combine just the grain and water in the saucepan. Place it on the stove over medium heat and bring it to a boil; reduce the heat and simmer it. Add the carrots to the pan after 45 minutes for the whole barley or 15 minutes for the wild rice. Return the pan to a boil over heat. Reduce the heat and simmer it for an additional 45 minutes.

At the end of the cooking time, stir the oil, salt, and spice(s) into the grain and carrots. Remove the pan from the heat and allow it to stand for a few minutes before serving. Makes 6 to 9 servings.

**Nutritional Analysis per serving:** 9 servings per recipe

| | | |
|---|---|---|
| Calories: ...................146 | Total fat: ...........................7 g | Calcium:..............................17 mg |
| Protein: .........................2 g | Saturated fat: ................1 g | Magnesium: ....................35 mg |
| Carbohydrate: .............20 g | Omega-3 fatty acids:...0.58 g | Potassium: ....................161 mg |
| Sugars: ........................2 g | Omega-6 fatty acids: ....1.46 g | Sodium: .........................144 mg |
| Fiber (total):.................2 g | Cholesterol: ....................0 mg | Iron:......................................1 mg |
| Vitamin C:....................3 mg | Vitamin A:...................1000 RE | Zinc:......................................0 mg |

Diabetic exchanges: 1 serving equals 1 starch exchange, ¾ vegetable exchange, 1 fat exchange

# Sweet and Spicy Rice

2 tablespoons oil
¼ cup chopped onion (optional)
¾ cup sliced celery
1 to 1½ teaspoons salt, to taste
¼ teaspoon pepper
¼ teaspoon cinnamon
⅛ teaspoon allspice
1 cup white rice
½ cup plus 1 tablespoon apple juice concentrate, thawed
2 to 2½ cups water
½ cup raisins
⅓ cup chopped or slivered almonds (optional)

Combine the oil and vegetables in a saucepan. Cook them over medium heat until they are just beginning to become tender. Add the salt, pepper, cinnamon, allspice, rice, apple juice concentrate, 2 cups of the water, and raisins. Put the cover on the pan. Bring it to a boil over medium to medium-high heat. Reduce the heat and simmer for 25 to 30 minutes or until all the liquid is absorbed and the rice is tender. Begin checking the rice every five minutes after it has been cooking for 20 minutes to see if the liquid has been absorbed. If the liquid is all absorbed early and the rice is not tender yet, you may have had extra-dry raisins. Add another ½ cup of water and cook the rice for another 5 to 10 minutes or until the liquid is all absorbed. When the rice is tender, remove it from the heat and let it stand 5 minutes. Fluff the rice with a fork and stir in the nuts. Let it stand a few more minutes before serving. Makes 6 to 9 servings.

**Nutritional Analysis per serving:** *9 servings per recipe*

| | | |
|---|---|---|
| Calories: ......................157 | Total fat:............................3 g | Calcium: .............................19 mg |
| Protein: ...............................2 g | Saturated fat:.................0 g | Magnesium:........................12 mg |
| Carbohydrate: ................30 g | Omega-3 fatty acids:...0.29 g | Potassium: .......................192 mg |
| Sugars: ...........................13 g | Omega-6 fatty acids: ..0.67 g | Sodium:............................276 mg |
| Fiber (total):.....................1 g | Cholesterol: ....................0 mg | Iron:.......................................1 mg |
| Vitamin C: ...........................1 mg | Vitamin A:............................1 RE | Zinc:.......................................0 mg |

Diabetic exchanges: 1 serving equals 1 starch exchange, 1 fruit exchange, ⅓ fat exchange

# Oven Cabbage

1 head of cabbage (about 1½ to 1¾ lbs.)
½ teaspoon salt
¼ teaspoon pepper (optional)
½ cup water
3 tablespoons oil

Coarsely chop or shred the cabbage and put it into a 3-quart glass casserole dish with a lid. Add the salt, pepper, and water to the dish and stir. Drizzle the oil over the top of the cabbage. Cover the dish with its lid and bake at 350°F for 1 to 2 hours. Makes 6 to 9 servings.

**Nutritional Analysis per serving:** *9 servings per recipe*

| | | |
|---|---|---|
| Calories: ........................65 | Total fat:............................5 g | Calcium:...............................48 mg |
| Protein: ...............................1 g | Saturated fat:.................0 g | Magnesium: .......................15 mg |
| Carbohydrate: ..................5 g | Omega-3 fatty acids:...0.49 g | Potassium:.......................248 mg |
| Sugars: .............................2 g | Omega-6 fatty acids: ..0.98 g | Sodium:............................148 mg |
| Fiber (total):.....................2 g | Cholesterol: ....................0 mg | Iron:.......................................1 mg |
| Vitamin C: .........................32 mg | Vitamin A:..........................13 RE | Zinc:.......................................0 mg |

Diabetic exchanges: 1 serving equals 1 vegetable exchange, 1 fat exchange

# Oven Carrots

*This dish will make you a cooked carrot lover. If you don't have time to peel and cut carrots, you can used pre-peeled mini-carrots instead.*

2 to 2½ pounds carrots
½ cup water with cut carrots or 2 tablespoons water with pre-peeled mini-carrots
½ teaspoon salt
2 to 3 tablespoons oil

Peel the carrots and cut them lengthwise into quarters or into eighths if they are very large. Lay the carrot sticks parallel to each other in a 2 to 3 quart glass casserole dish with a lid. Add the salt and water to the dish and drizzle the oil over the top of the carrots. Cover the dish with its lid and bake at 350°F for 1 to 1½ hrs. Makes 6 to 12 servings.

**Nutritional Analysis per serving:** 12 servings per recipe

| | | |
|---|---|---|
| Calories: ...................54 | Total fat: ..........................2 g | Calcium: ...........................19 mg |
| Protein: .......................1 g | Saturated fat: ...............0 g | Magnesium: .......................9 mg |
| Carbohydrate: ..............8 g | Omega-3 fatty acids:...0.21 g | Potassium: .......................271 mg |
| Sugars: .......................5 g | Omega-6 fatty acids: ..0.46 g | Sodium: ..........................137 mg |
| Fiber (total): ................2 g | Cholesterol: .....................0 mg | Iron: ..................................0 mg |
| Vitamin C: ...................6 mg | Vitamin A: ..................1308 RE | Zinc: .................................0 mg |

Diabetic exchanges: 1 serving equals 1⅓ vegetable exchanges, ½ fat exchange

# Oven Peas or Beans

1 10 ounce package frozen peas, cut green beans, or lima beans
⅓ cup water
⅛ teaspoon salt
1 tablespoon oil

Combine all of the ingredients in a 1 to 1½ quart glass casserole dish with a lid, cover it with the lid, and bake at 350°F for 1 to 1½ hours for the beans or 20 minutes to 1 hour for the peas. Makes 2 to 4 servings.

**Nutritional Analysis per serving:** 4 servings per recipe

**Peas:**

| | | |
|---|---|---|
| Calories: ...................85 | Total fat: ..........................4 g | Calcium: ...........................16 mg |
| Protein: .......................4 g | Saturated fat: ...............0 g | Magnesium: ......................18 mg |
| Carbohydrate: ............10 g | Omega-3 fatty acids:...0.34 g | Potassium: .......................106 mg |
| Sugars: .......................4 g | Omega-6 fatty acids: ..0.79 g | Sodium: ..........................153 mg |
| Fiber (total): ................3 g | Cholesterol: .....................0 mg | Iron: ..................................1 mg |
| Vitamin C: ...................13 mg | Vitamin A: ......................52 RE | Zinc: .................................1 mg |

Diabetic exchanges: 1 serving equals ⅔ starch exchange, ⅔ fat exchange

**Green Beans:**

| | | |
|---|---|---|
| Calories: ...................54 | Total fat: ..........................4 g | Calcium: ...........................30 mg |
| Protein: .......................1 g | Saturated fat: ...............0 g | Magnesium: ......................16 mg |
| Carbohydrate: ..............5 g | Omega-3 fatty acids:...0.36 g | Potassium: .......................132 mg |
| Sugars: .......................1 g | Omega-6 fatty acids: ..0.72 g | Sodium: ............................75 mg |
| Fiber (total): ................2 g | Cholesterol: .....................0 mg | Iron: ..................................1 mg |
| Vitamin C: ...................9 mg | Vitamin A: ......................34 RE | Zinc: .................................0 mg |

Diabetic exchanges: 1 serving equals 1 vegetable exchange, ⅔ fat exchange

**Lima beans:**

| | | |
|---|---|---|
| Calories: ...................112 | Total fat: ..........................4 g | Calcium: ...........................22 mg |
| Protein: .......................5 g | Saturated fat: ...............0 g | Magnesium: ......................44 mg |
| Carbohydrate: ............15 g | Omega-3 fatty acids:...0.35 g | Potassium: .......................320 mg |
| Sugars: .......................2 g | Omega-6 fatty acids: ..0.77 g | Sodium: ............................96 mg |
| Fiber (total): ................5 g | Cholesterol: .....................0 mg | Iron: ..................................2 mg |
| Vitamin C: ...................5 mg | Vitamin A: ......................13 RE | Zinc: .................................0 mg |

Diabetic exchanges: 1 serving equals 1 starch exchange, ⅔ fat exchange

# Oven Onions

1½ pounds of peeled onions
Water
Salt
1 tablespoon oil (optional)

Put the onions into a 3 quart casserole dish. Add water to ¼ inch depth and cover the dish with its lid or aluminum foil. Bake at 350°F for 40 to 50 minutes or up to 1½ hours until they are tender or done to your preference, or cook them until the rest of your oven meal is done. (For longer baking times, add water to ½ inch depth). Drain off the water. Season with salt and drizzle with a little oil before serving if desired. Makes 6 to 10 servings.

**Nutritional Analysis per serving:** 10 servings per recipe

| | | |
|---|---|---|
| Calories: 26 | Total fat: 0 g | Calcium: 14 mg |
| Protein: 1 g | Saturated fat: 0 g | Magnesium: 7 mg |
| Carbohydrate: 6 g | Omega-3 fatty acids: 0 g | Potassium: 107 mg |
| Sugars: 4 g | Omega-6 fatty acids: 0 g | Sodium: 26 mg |
| Fiber (total): 1 g | Cholesterol: 0 mg | Iron: 0 mg |
| Vitamin C: 4 mg | Vitamin A: 0 RE | Zinc: 0 mg |

Diabetic exchanges: 1 serving equals 1 vegetable exchange

# Oven Squash

2½ pounds butternut squash
¼ teaspoon salt
2 tablespoons oil

Peel the squash. Cut it in half lengthwise and remove the seeds. Slice it into ¼-inch slices. Put the slices into an 11 inch by 7 inch baking dish, sprinkle them with the salt, and drizzle them with the oil. Stir to coat all of the slices. Bake at 350°F for 1½ to 2 hours, turning the slices after the first hour. Makes 6 to 9 servings.

**Nutritional Analysis per serving:** 9 servings per recipe

| | | |
|---|---|---|
| Calories: 79 | Total fat: 3 g | Calcium: 56 mg |
| Protein: 1 g | Saturated fat: 0 g | Magnesium: 39 mg |
| Carbohydrate: 14 g | Omega-3 fatty acids: 0.03 g | Potassium: 408 mg |
| Sugars: 3 g | Omega-6 fatty acids: 0.02 g | Sodium: 70 mg |
| Fiber (total): 4 g | Cholesterol: 0 mg | Iron: 1 mg |
| Vitamin C: 24 mg | Vitamin A: 904 RE | Zinc: 0 mg |

Diabetic exchanges: 1 serving equals 2 vegetable exchanges, ⅔ fat exchange

# Oven Turnips or Rutabagas

2 pounds turnips or rutabagas
¼ teaspoon salt
2 tablespoons oil

Peel the turnips or rutabagas and cut them into ¼-inch slices. Put the slices into an 11 inch by 7 inch baking dish, sprinkle them with the salt, and drizzle them with the oil. Stir to coat all of the slices. Bake at 350°F for 1½ to 2 hours, turning the slices after the first hour. Makes 6 to 9 servings.

## Turnips:
**Nutritional Analysis per serving:** 9 servings per recipe

| | | |
|---|---|---|
| Calories: ...........................48 | Total fat:...........................3 g | Calcium: ...........................22 mg |
| Protein: ...........................1 g | Saturated fat:...............0 g | Magnesium:.......................8 mg |
| Carbohydrate: ..................5 g | Omega-3 fatty acids:...0.03 g | Potassium:....................136 mg |
| Sugars:...........................2 g | Omega-6 fatty acids: ..0.01 g | Sodium:..........................116 mg |
| Fiber (total):.....................2 g | Cholesterol: .....................0 mg | Iron: ...............................0 mg |
| Vitamin C:..........................12 mg | Vitamin C:..........................12 mg | Zinc:................................0 mg |

Diabetic exchanges: 1 serving equals 1 vegetable exchange, ½ fat exchange

## Rutabagas:
**Nutritional Analysis per serving:** 9 servings per recipe

| | | |
|---|---|---|
| Calories: ...........................63 | Total fat:...........................3 g | Calcium:...........................47 mg |
| Protein: ...........................1 g | Saturated fat:...............0 g | Magnesium: ....................23 mg |
| Carbohydrate:..................8 g | Omega-3 fatty acids:...0.05 g | Potassium:....................340 mg |
| Sugars:...........................6 g | Omega-6 fatty acids: ..0.04 g | Sodium: ..........................85 mg |
| Fiber (total):.....................3 g | Cholesterol: .....................0 mg | Iron:.................................1 mg |
| Vitamin C:..........................25 mg | Vitamin A:........................58 RE | Zinc:................................0 mg |

Diabetic exchanges: 1 serving equals 1⅔ vegetable exchanges, ½ fat exchange

# Oven Sweet Potatoes or White Potatoes

1½ pounds white potatoes or 2 pounds sweet potatoes
2 tablespoons oil
½ teaspoon salt
Pepper to taste (optional; it is great with the white potatoes)

Peel the potatoes and slice them into ¼-inch slices. Put the slices into an 11 inch by 7 inch baking dish, sprinkle them with the salt and optional pepper, and drizzle them with the oil. Stir to coat all of the slices. Bake at 350°F for 1½ to 2 hours, turning the slices after the first hour. Makes 4 to 8 servings.

## Sweet potatoes:
**Nutritional Analysis per serving:** 8 servings per recipe

| | | |
|---|---|---|
| Calories: ...........................149 | Total fat:...........................3 g | Calcium: ...........................25 mg |
| Protein: ...........................2 g | Saturated fat:...............0 g | Magnesium:.......................11 mg |
| Carbohydrate: ..................27 g | Omega-3 fatty acids:...0.34 g | Potassium: ....................231 mg |
| Sugars:...........................6 g | Omega-6 fatty acids: ..0.82 g | Sodium:..........................161 mg |
| Fiber (total):.....................3 g | Cholesterol: .....................0 mg | Iron:.................................1 mg |
| Vitamin C:..........................26 mg | Vitamin A:....................2275 RE | Zinc:................................0 mg |

Diabetic exchanges: 1 serving equals 1½ starch exchanges, ⅔ fat exchange

**White potatoes:**
**Nutritional Analysis per serving:** 6 servings per recipe

| | | |
|---|---|---|
| Calories: .........................117 | Total fat:...........................5 g | Calcium:...........................4 mg |
| Protein:.............................2 g | Saturated fat:.................0 g | Magnesium:....................21 mg |
| Carbohydrate:................18 g | Omega-3 fatty acids:...0.43 g | Potassium:....................324 mg |
| Sugars: ............................1 g | Omega-6 fatty acids: ..0.95 g | Sodium: .........................200 mg |
| Fiber (total):.....................1 g | Cholesterol: ....................0 mg | Iron: ..................................0 mg |
| Vitamin C:........................3 mg | Vitamin A: .........................0 RE | Zinc:...................................0 mg |

Diabetic exchanges: 1 serving equals 1 starch exchange, 1 fat exchange

# Scalloped Potatoes

3 to 4 medium or 2 to 3 large potatoes, weighing 1½ to 2 pounds
2 tablespoons butter, goat butter, or oil
2½ tablespoons all purpose, unbleached, or white spelt flour
1 teaspoon salt
⅛ teaspoon pepper
1½ cups skim, whole, or goat milk
2 tablespoons chopped onion (optional)

Peel the potatoes. Slice them in about ¼ inch slices. If the potatoes are large, cut the slices in half. Cover them with cold water to keep them from discoloring while you prepare the sauce.

In a saucepan, melt the butter or heat the oil for a minute or two over low heat. Stir in the flour, salt, and pepper. Cook and stir for one minute. Pour the milk into the pan all at once. Raise the heat to medium, and cook and stir the milk mixture until it thickens and just begins to boil.

Drain the water from the potatoes. Put about half of the potatoes into a 2 quart or larger casserole dish. Sprinkle with half of the onion and pour about half of the sauce evenly over the vegetables. Put the rest of the potatoes into the dish, sprinkle with the remaining onion, and pour the rest of the sauce evenly over the top of the vegetables. Cover the casserole dish with its lid or foil. Bake at 350°F for one hour. Remove the cover from the casserole dish and bake for another 30 minutes or until the top is beginning to brown. Makes 6 to 8 servings.

**Nutritional Analysis per serving:** 8 servings per recipe

| | | |
|---|---|---|
| Calories: .........................115 | Total fat:...........................4 g | Calcium:...........................58 mg |
| Protein:.............................3 g | Saturated fat:.................0 g | Magnesium:....................6 mg |
| Carbohydrate:................19 g | Omega-3 fatty acids:...0.32 g | Potassium:....................80 mg |
| Sugars: ............................2 g | Omega-6 fatty acids: ..0.70 g | Sodium: .........................347 mg |
| Fiber (total):.....................1 g | Cholesterol: ....................1 mg | Iron: ..................................0 mg |
| Vitamin C:........................3 mg | Vitamin A: .......................28 RE | Zinc:...................................0 mg |

Diabetic exchanges: 1 serving equals 1 starch exchange, 1/5 milk exchange, ½ fat exchange

# Mashed Potatoes

6 medium sized potatoes, or about 2 pounds of potatoes of any size
4 cups water
1 to 1½ teaspoons salt, divided, or to taste
3 tablespoons butter or goat butter
⅓ cup skim, whole, or goat milk

Wash and peel the potatoes. Cut them into quarters, or if you are in a hurry, into smaller slices or cubes. Put them in a saucepan with the water and ½ teaspoon of the salt and cover the pan. Bring them to a boil over medium heat. Reduce the heat and simmer them for 20 to 45 minutes, or until they are tender when pierced with a fork. Pour off the water. Add the butter, milk, and ½ teaspoon of salt to the pan and mash the potatoes with a potato masher. Taste them and add the remaining ½ teaspoon salt if needed. If they seem dry, add more milk. Mash in the additional salt and milk if you added them. If you are allergic to milk, including goat milk, substitute reserved potato cooking water for the milk and milk-free Earth Balance™ margarine or oil for the butter. Makes 6 to 8 servings.

**Nutritional Analysis per serving:** 8 servings per recipe

| | | |
|---|---|---|
| Calories: ..........122 | Total fat: ..........4 g | Calcium: ..........14 mg |
| Protein: ..........2 g | Saturated fat: ..........3 g | Magnesium: ..........1 mg |
| Carbohydrate: ..........21 g | Omega-3 fatty acids: ..0.06 g | Potassium: ..........18 mg |
| Sugars: ..........1 g | Omega-6 fatty acids: ..0.10 g | Sodium: ..........382 mg |
| Fiber (total): ..........1 g | Cholesterol: ..........12 mg | Iron: ..........0 mg |
| Vitamin C: ..........3 mg | Vitamin A: ..........46 RE | Zinc: ..........0 mg |

Diabetic exchanges: 1 serving equals 1 starch exchange, 1 fat exchange

# Oven Fries

1 pound of white potatoes
1 tablespoon oil, preferably olive oil
¼ to ½ teaspoon salt, or to taste

Preheat your oven to 400°F. Peel the potatoes and cut them into ⅜ to ½ inch slices. Cut the slices into ⅜ to ½ inch sticks or fries. Toss the sticks with the oil and salt. Spread them in a single layer on a baking sheet. Bake them for 15 to 20 minutes. Remove the baking sheet from the oven and turn the fries over with a spatula. Bake them for another 15 to 20 minutes or until they are nicely browned. Makes 2 to 4 servings.

**Nutritional Analysis per serving:** 4 servings per recipe

| | | |
|---|---|---|
| Calories: ..........87 | Total fat: ..........1 g | Calcium: ..........4 mg |
| Protein: ..........2 g | Saturated fat: ..........0 g | Magnesium: ..........21 mg |
| Carbohydrate: ..........18 g | Omega-3 fatty acids: ..0.01 g | Potassium: ..........324 mg |
| Sugars: ..........1 g | Omega-6 fatty acids: ..0.11 g | Sodium: ..........151 mg |
| Fiber (total): ..........1 g | Cholesterol: ..........0 mg | Iron: ..........0 mg |
| Vitamin C: ..........11 mg | Vitamin A: ..........0 RE | Zinc: ..........0 mg |

Diabetic exchanges: 1 serving equals 1 starch exchange, ¼ fat exchange

# Baked Beans

1 pound small white or small navy beans
Water
¾ cup apple juice concentrate, thawed
1 15 ounce can tomato sauce or 1½ teaspoons paprika (optional)
1 tablespoon finely chopped onion or 1 teaspoon dried onion flakes (optional)
1 teaspoon dry mustard powder (optional)
1 tablespoon finely chopped fresh sweet basil or 1 teaspoon dried sweet basil
1½ teaspoons salt
¼ teaspoon pepper
¼ pound bacon (optional)

The night before you plan to serve this dish, wash the beans by putting them in a strainer and running cold water over them. Remove and discard any shriveled beans. Put the beans in a 3 quart or larger pot and fill the pot with water until the volume of the water is two to three times the volume of the beans. The next day, pour the water off the beans and replace it with fresh water three times. (This rinsing removes indigestible carbohydrates that can cause "gas"). Pour off all the water after the last rinse. Add enough water to the pot to reach about an inch above the beans and put the lid on the pot. Put the beans on the stove and bring them to a boil over medium heat. Lower the heat and simmer the beans about 3 hours or until they are very tender. Check them during cooking and add more water if necessary. Drain all but about 2 cups of the cooking water from the beans. Add all of the rest of the ingredients to the pot and stir them into the beans thoroughly. Heat your oven to 250°F. If the pot you cooked the beans in is not oven-proof, transfer the beans to an oven-proof dish. Lay the bacon strips on top of the beans. Cover the dish with its lid and bake the beans for 6 to 9 hours. Check them every hour or two during the baking time and add water if the beans are drying out. Makes 10 to 18 servings. If you would like to make these beans with less tending, see "Crock Pot Baked Beans," page 226. Leftovers freeze well.

**Nutritional Analysis per serving:** 18 servings per recipe

| | | |
|---|---|---|
| Calories: .........................104 | Total fat: ...........................0 g | Calcium: ............................44 mg |
| Protein:................................6 g | Saturated fat:................0 g | Magnesium:......................46 mg |
| Carbohydrate: .................20 g | Omega-3 fatty acids:...0.07 g | Potassium:......................340 mg |
| Sugars:................................6 g | Omega-6 fatty acids: ..0.09 g | Sodium:..........................202 mg |
| Fiber (total): .....................6 g | Cholesterol: .......................0 mg | Iron:.......................................2 mg |
| Vitamin C: ..........................1 mg | Vitamin A: ...........................1 RE | Zinc: .....................................1 mg |

Diabetic exchanges: 1 serving equals 1 starch exchange, ⅓ fruit exchange

# Crock Pot Creations

A crock pot is an appliance that is very much worth owning. It can make a busy life easier and more pleasant. With a crock pot, you can start your dinner before you leave for work or school in the morning and have a delicious meal waiting for you when you get home. A crock pot will also save you money because less expensive cuts of meat are delicious and tender when cooked all day, and also because dried beans are easily prepared in a crock pot.

The recipes in this chapter are the right size for a three quart crock pot. Smaller crock pots are available, and the recipes in this book can be cut in half for the smaller size pot. However, one drawback of the smaller pots is that they are more expensive than three quart crock pots and usually must be ordered from a cooking catalogue. Three quart crock pots can be bought for a very good price (at the time if this writing, $20 or less) at a discount department store or even more cheaply at a thrift store. Take the plunge! Invest in a three quart crock pot. Make the three-quart sized batch of these recipes and freeze part of the batch for future quick dinners. You will be glad that you did.

## Crock Pot Roast Beef Dinner

*This recipe makes inexpensive, less-tender cuts of beef taste like gourmet fare! It's a great meal to cook for company and so easy that you can really enjoy your guests.*

    1 2 to 2½ pound chuck roast, rump roast, or pot roast
    2 large or 3 small potatoes, peeled and cut into chunks (optional)
    3 carrots, peeled and cut into 2-inch pieces
    1 onion, peeled and sliced (optional)
    ½ cup water, beef broth, or red wine
    1 tablespoon tomato paste or 2 to 3 tablespoons catsup
    Dash of salt
    Dash of pepper

Peel and cut up the vegetables and put them into the bottom of a three quart crock pot. Set the roast on top of the vegetables. Stir together the water, broth, or wine with the tomato paste or catsup. Pour the liquid over the roast. Sprinkle the roast with the salt and pepper. Cook on low heat for 10 to 12 hours or on high heat for 5 to 8 hours. You may use a baster to baste the roast with the cooking liquid once or twice during the cooking time if you are around to do so. This recipe is very tasty when made with red wine such as a sweet Marsala. The alcohol evaporates during cooking, just leaving the flavor. If you prefer more "juice" with your roast, increase the amount of water, broth or wine to 1 cup and double the amount of tomato paste or catsup. Makes 8 servings.

**Nutritional Analysis per serving:** *8 servings per recipe*

| | | |
|---|---|---|
| Calories: ...............332 | Total fat: ...............21 g | Calcium:...............16 mg |
| Protein:...............22 g | Saturated fat:...............8 g | Magnesium: ...............24 mg |
| Carbohydrate:...............13 g | Omega-3 fatty acids:...0.27 g | Potassium:...............471 mg |
| Sugars: ...............2 g | Omega-6 fatty acids: ..0.54 g | Sodium:...............133 mg |
| Fiber (total): ...............1 g | Cholesterol: ...............77 mg | Iron:...............2 mg |
| Vitamin C: ...............5 mg | Vitamin A:...............511 RE | Zinc:...............5 mg |

Diabetic exchanges: 1 serving equals 3 medium-fat meat exchanges, ½ starch exchange, ¾ vegetable exchange, 1 fat exchange

# Corned Beef Dinner

1 2 to 3 pound corned beef brisket
2 to 3 potatoes, peeled and cut into large chunks
3 to 4 carrots, peeled and cut into 2-inch pieces
Water
1 head of cabbage
½ teaspoon salt
Dash of pepper (optional)

Peel and cut up the carrots and potatoes and put them into the bottom of a three quart crock pot. Set the corned beef on top of the vegetables. If the corned beef spices come in a separate package, sprinkle them over the meat. Add water to the crock pot until it is almost up to the top of the meat. Cook on low heat for 10 to 12 hours or on high heat for 5 to 8 hours. About a half hour before dinner time, cut the cabbage into wedges. Fill a large saucepan about ⅔ full of water and bring it to a boil. Add the cabbage wedges, salt, and pepper and boil until the cabbage is cooked to your preference. Drain the cabbage. (If you will be home for an hour or two before dinner, "Oven Cabbage," page 209, is a very tasty accompaniment to this meal. Substitute it for the boiled cabbage). Remove the brisket from the crock pot and slice it against the grain. For company, arrange the meat and vegetables on a serving platter. Makes 6 to 8 servings.

**Nutritional Analysis per serving:** *8 servings per recipe*

| | | |
|---|---|---|
| Calories: ...............306 | Total fat:...............17 g | Calcium:...............69 mg |
| Protein: ...............19 g | Saturated fat: ...............5 g | Magnesium:...............33 mg |
| Carbohydrate:...............19 g | Omega-3 fatty acids:...0.25 g | Potassium:...............721 mg |
| Sugars:...............5 g | Omega-6 fatty acids: ..0.49 g | Sodium: ...............340 mg |
| Fiber (total):...............4 g | Cholesterol: ...............61 mg | Iron: ...............3 mg |
| Vitamin C: ...............71 mg | Vitamin A:...............521 RE | Zinc:...............3 mg |

Diabetic exchanges: 1 serving equals 2½ medium-fat meat exchanges, ½ starch exchange, 2 vegetable exchanges, ⅔ fat exchange

# Sauerbraten Dinner

1 2 to 3 pound rump roast
1¼ cups water, divided
1 cup vinegar
1 tablespoon salt
2 tablespoons Fruit Sweet™ or honey or ¼ cup apple juice concentrate, thawed
1 medium onion, sliced (optional)
1 unpeeled lemon, sliced
10 whole cloves
4 bay leaves
10 whole peppercorns
¼ cup all purpose, unbleached, or white spelt flour

A day or two before you plan to serve this, put the meat into a deep glass bowl or casserole dish. Stir together 1 cup of the water, the vinegar, salt, and sweetener. Pour them over the meat. Add the onion, lemon, cloves, bay leaves, and peppercorns to the liquid around the meat. Refrigerate for 24 to 36 hours, turning the meat once or twice during the marinating time. The morning of the day you plan to serve this, remove the meat from the liquid and put it in a 3 quart crock pot. Add 1 cup of the marinating liquid to the crock pot. Discard the rest of the marinating liquid. Cover the pot and cook it on low for 8 to 10 hours or on high for 5 to 8 hours. Remove the meat from the pot and put it on a serving platter. If you will make the gravy slowly in the crock pot, put the platter and meat into a 250°F oven to stay warm. Combine the flour thoroughly with the remaining ¼ cup of water until the lumps are gone. (A hand blender is good for this job). Add the flour-water mixture to the crock pot, turn the heat to high, and cook for 15 to 30 minutes until the gravy thickens. If you are in a hurry, you can transfer the juice from the meat to a saucepan, add the flour mixture, and cook it on the stove over medium heat for a few minutes until it comes to a boil and thickens. Serve the gravy with the meat. Makes 6 to 9 servings.

**Nutritional Analysis per serving:** 9 servings per recipe

| | | |
|---|---|---|
| Calories: 205 | Total fat: 10 g | Calcium: 14 mg |
| Protein: 21 g | Saturated fat: 4 g | Magnesium: 30 mg |
| Carbohydrate: 6 g | Omega-3 fatty acids: 0.10 g | Potassium: 378 mg |
| Sugars: 3 g | Omega-6 fatty acids: 0.30 g | Sodium: 318 mg |
| Fiber (total): 0 g | Cholesterol: 63 mg | Iron: 3 mg |
| Vitamin C: 0 mg | Vitamin A: 0 RE | Zinc: 3 mg |

Diabetic exchanges: 1 serving equals 3 lean meat exchanges, ¼ starch exchange, 1 fruit exchange

# Chicken Fricasee

1 2 to 3 pound chicken, skinned and cut into pieces, or skinless chicken breasts or
   other meaty chicken pieces
1 teaspoon salt
½ teaspoon paprika
1 small onion, sliced (optional)
3 stalks of celery, sliced
3 to 5 carrots, peeled and sliced (about 1 pound)
1 bay leaf
2 cups water or chicken broth
¼ cup water
¼ cup all purpose, unbleached, or white spelt flour, or cornstarch, tapioca starch,
   or arrowroot

Sprinkle the chicken pieces with the salt and paprika. Put the onion, celery, carrots,
and bay leaf in a 3 quart crock pot. Place the chicken pieces on top. Pour the 2 cups of
water or broth into the pot. Cover and cook on low for 8 to 12 hours or on high for 4
to 5 hours. Remove the chicken pieces. Turn the crock pot to high. Thoroughly combine
the ¼ cup water with the flour or starch and stir them into the vegetables and liquid in
the pot. Remove the chicken meat from the bones and skin. Discard the bones and skin.
When the liquid in the pot has thickened, return the chicken meat to the pot and cook
for a few minutes more to reheat the chicken. Add more boiling water to the pot of you
like your fricasee juicier. Serve over hot noodles or cooked rice. Makes 6 to 8 servings.

## Nutritional Analysis per serving: 8 servings per recipe

| | | |
|---|---|---|
| Calories: ......................173 | Total fat:.........................3 g | Calcium:.........................34 mg |
| Protein:............................26 g | Saturated fat: ................1 g | Magnesium: ....................32 mg |
| Carbohydrate:................10 g | Omega-3 fatty acids:...0.06 g | Potassium:....................529 mg |
| Sugars:...........................4 g | Omega-6 fatty acids: ..0.62 g | Sodium: .........................421 mg |
| Fiber (total):....................2 g | Cholesterol: ...................78 mg | Iron:..................................1 mg |
| Vitamin C:..........................8 mg | Vitamin A:....................1006 RE | Zinc:..................................2 mg |

Diabetic exchanges: 1 serving equals 1 lean meat exchange, 2 very lean meat
exchanges, ¼ starch exchange, 1 vegetable exchange

# Crock Pot Stew

2 pounds round or chuck steak or stew meat of any kind – beef, buffalo, lamb, or
      red game meat
5 carrots (about 1 pound)
3 stalks of celery
1 onion (optional)
1½ pounds of potatoes (about 3 or 4, optional)
½ cup quick-cooking granulated or "minute" tapioca
2 bay leaves (optional)
2 teaspoons salt
¼ teaspoon pepper
2¼ cups water or 1 28 ounce can peeled tomatoes

Trim the fat and gristle from the meat and cut it into one or two inch cubes. Peel
the carrots and potatoes. Cut the carrots into one inch pieces and cut the potatoes into
two inch chunks. Slice the celery into one inch slices. Put the meat, vegetables, tapioca,
seasonings, and water or tomatoes into a 3 quart crock pot. Stir the stew thoroughly to
evenly distribute the tapioca. Cook it on low for 8 to 12 hours or on high for 5 to 6
hours. If you like your stew juicy, check the stew about 1 hour before the end of the cooking time and add some boiling water if needed. Makes 6 to 12 servings. If made without
the potatoes, this stew freezes well. The potatoes may become mushy if they are frozen.

**Nutritional Analysis per serving:** 12 servings per recipe

| | | |
|---|---|---|
| Calories: ......................200 | Total fat:............................5 g | Calcium:............................20 mg |
| Protein: ........................28 g | Saturated fat: ...............2 g | Magnesium: ....................19 mg |
| Carbohydrate:..................10 g | Omega-3 fatty acids:...0.03 g | Potassium:...................430 mg |
| Sugars: ............................2 g | Omega-6 fatty acids: ..0.17 g | Sodium: ........................460 mg |
| Fiber (total):......................1 g | Cholesterol: ..................68 mg | Iron: ..................................3 mg |
| Vitamin C: ..........................4 mg | Vitamin A:.....................655 RE | Zinc:..................................3 mg |

Diabetic exchanges: 1 serving equals 1 lean meat exchange, 3 very lean meat
exchanges, 1 vegetable exchange, ⅙ starch exchange (without the potatoes). With
the potatoes, this stew contains ½ starch exchange, 19 grams of carbohydrate, and
238 calories per serving.

# Economy Chili for a Crowd

1 pound dry kidney beans
Water
1½ to 2 pounds of lean ground beef, ground buffalo, or other red game meat
1 12 ounce can tomato paste
1 16 ounce can tomato sauce
1 small onion, chopped (optional)
1 teaspoon salt
1 to 3 teaspoons of chili powder, to taste

The night before you plan to serve the chili, sort over and rinse the beans. In a 3
to 5 quart crock pot, cover the beans with cold water. Allow the beans to soak overnight.
In the morning, drain the water from the beans, add fresh water to the pot, and drain

the water again. Rinse the beans this way three times. (This soaking and rinsing process removes difficult-to-digest carbohydrates which can cause "gas"). Add enough water to the beans in the pot to cover them. Cook them on high for 4 to 6 hours. In a separate pan on the stove, brown the ground meat. Drain and discard the fat. Add the onion and cook for a few minutes more. When the beans are tender, drain the water until it is an inch or so below the level of the beans in the pot. Stir the tomato paste into the pot thoroughly. Add the cooked meat, tomato sauce, and seasonings. Cook the chili for another 1 to 2 hours on high. Makes 8 to 10 servings.

**Nutritional Analysis per serving:** 10 servings per recipe

| | | |
|---|---|---|
| Calories: ....................309 | Total fat: ...........................7 g | Calcium: ...........................90 mg |
| Protein: ...........................27 g | Saturated fat: ...............3 g | Magnesium: ...................106 mg |
| Carbohydrate: ...............37 g | Omega-3 fatty acids: ...0.13 g | Potassium: .................1355 mg |
| Sugars: .............................3 g | Omega-6 fatty acids: ..0.17 g | Sodium: .........................333 mg |
| Fiber (total): ................14 g | Cholesterol: .....................25 mg | Iron: ....................................6 mg |
| Vitamin C: .......................23 mg | Vitamin A: ......................140 RE | Zinc: .....................................5 mg |

Diabetic exchanges: 1 serving equals 2 lean meat exchanges, 2 starch exchanges, 1½ vegetable exchanges

# Crock Pot Vegetable Soup

1 pound beef or buffalo round steak, or other lean meat
6 cups water
1 14 ounce can of diced tomatoes
2 to 3 stalks of celery, diced
1 small onion, diced (optional)
1 large potato, peeled and cubed (optional)
½ of a 15 ounce can of red beans, drained, or ½ of a 10 ounce package of frozen
    lima beans
1 10 ounce box or ½ of a 16 ounce bag of frozen peas and carrots
¼ cup pearled barley (uncooked)
2 to 3 teaspoons of salt, or to taste
¼ teaspoon pepper
¼ small head of cabbage, coarsely chopped (optional)

If you want to start this recipe in your crock pot before leaving for school or work in the morning, prepare the meat the night before. Cut the round steak into small cubes, removing the fat. You may use the fat to rub the inside of your frying pan. Then discard the fat. Put the cubes of meat into the pan and cook them over medium heat, stirring them occasionally, until they are well browned. Allow the drippings in the bottom of the frying pan to dry out and become very well browned as well. Put the meat into the crock pot (if you are doing this in the morning) or into a container in which to refrigerate the meat overnight. Put one to two cups of the water into the frying pan and heat it over medium heat, stirring to remove the browned bits and coating from the pan. Pour this flavorful liquid into the crock pot or into the refrigerator container with the meat. If you are preparing the meat the day before you plan to serve the soup, in the morning put the meat and flavorful liquid into the crock pot. Add the remaining water and the tomatoes, celery, onion, potatoes, beans, peas and carrots, barley, salt, and pepper. Cook on low for 8 to 12 hours or on high for 4 to 5 hours. If you are at home an hour before serving time, add the optional cabbage to the crock pot. Makes 6 to 10 servings. Freeze any leftover soup for future quick, highly nutritious dinners or lunches. If you plan to freeze the soup, you may want to omit the potatoes, because their texture deteriorates with freezing.

**Nutritional Analysis per serving:** 10 servings per recipe

| | | |
|---|---|---|
| Calories: ..........................167 | Total fat:...............................3 g | Calcium: .............................29 mg |
| Protein: ..............................20 g | Saturated fat: .................1 g | Magnesium:....................36 mg |
| Carbohydrate:.................15 g | Omega-3 fatty acids:...0.06 g | Potassium:.....................362 mg |
| Sugars: ...............................2 g | Omega-6 fatty acids: ..0.23 g | Sodium:..........................577 mg |
| Fiber (total):........................5 g | Cholesterol: ....................41 mg | Iron:......................................2 mg |
| Vitamin C:............................8 mg | Vitamin A:.........................341 RE | Zinc:.....................................3 mg |

Diabetic exchanges: 1 serving equals 1 lean meat exchange, 1 very lean meat exchange, ⅔ starch exchange, 1 vegetable exchange

# Black Bean Soup

1 pound dry black beans
Water
2 bell peppers, preferably one red and one green, seeded and diced
1 small onion, diced (optional)
1 pound tomatoes, chopped
1 teaspoon ground cumin (optional)
2 teaspoons salt
½ teaspoon pepper or a 2 inch chili pepper, seeded and crumbled
2 tablespoons chopped fresh oregano or 2 teaspoons dry oregano

The night before you plan to serve this soup for dinner, sort through and rinse the beans, discarding any shriveled ones. Put them in a 3 quart crock pot and cover them with two or three times their volume of water. Soak them overnight. The next morning, pour off the water and replace it with fresh water three times. (This soaking and rinsing process removes indigestible carbohydrates which can cause "gas"). Drain off all the water after the last rinse. Add 4 cups of water to the crock pot, the peppers, onion, cumin, salt, pepper, and oregano. Cover the crock pot with its lid and cook the soup on high for 6 hours or on low for 8 to 10 hours. Add the chopped tomatoes an hour before the end of the cooking time. Check the soup near the end of the cooking time and add a little boiling water to the pot if the soup is thicker than you prefer. Makes about 2½ quarts of soup, or 6 to 10 servings. Leftover soup freezes well.

**Nutritional Analysis per serving:** 10 servings per recipe

| | | |
|---|---|---|
| Calories: ..........................162 | Total fat: ..............................1 g | Calcium:.............................40 mg |
| Protein: ..............................10 g | Saturated fat:................0 g | Magnesium:.....................85 mg |
| Carbohydrate: ................30 g | Omega-3 fatty acids:...0.13 g | Potassium:.....................548 mg |
| Sugars: ...............................4 g | Omega-6 fatty acids: ..0.23 g | Sodium: ..........................475 mg |
| Fiber (total):........................11 g | Cholesterol: .....................0 mg | Iron: .....................................3 mg |
| Vitamin C:............................38 mg | Vitamin A: ........................52 RE | Zinc: .......................................1 mg |

Diabetic exchanges: 1 serving equals 1¾ starch exchanges, ¼ very lean meat exchange, 1 vegetable exchange

# Navy Bean Soup

1 pound dry navy beans
Water
2 carrots, peeled and sliced
3 stalks celery, sliced
2 teaspoons salt
½ teaspoon pepper
3 tablespoons chopped fresh parsley or 1 tablespoon dry parsley
1 tablespoon chopped fresh sweet basil or 1 teaspoon dry sweet basil
1 potato, peeled and grated (optional)

The night before you plan to serve this soup for dinner, sort through and rinse the beans, discarding any shriveled ones. Put them in a 3 quart crock pot and cover them with two or three times their volume of water. Soak them overnight. The next morning, pour off the water and replace it with fresh water three times. (This soaking and rinsing process removes indigestible carbohydrates which can cause "gas"). Drain off all the water after the last rinse. Add 6 cups of water to the crock pot, the carrots, celery, salt, pepper, parsley, and sweet basil. Cover the crock pot with its lid and cook the soup on high for 6 hours or on low for 8 to 10 hours. Add the optional potatoes two hours before the end of the cooking time. Check the soup near the end of the cooking time and add a little boiling water to the pot if the soup is thicker than you prefer. Makes about 2½ quarts of soup, or 6 to 10 servings. Leftover soup freezes well.

**Nutritional Analysis per serving:** 10 servings per recipe

| | | |
|---|---|---|
| Calories: ......................163 | Total fat:.............................1 g | Calcium: ...........................86 mg |
| Protein:...............................11 g | Saturated fat:...............0 g | Magnesium:......................80 mg |
| Carbohydrate: ...............30 g | Omega-3 fatty acids:...0.12 g | Potassium: ....................636 mg |
| Sugars:...........................3 g | Omega-6 fatty acids: ..0.14 g | Sodium: ..........................499 mg |
| Fiber (total): ....................12 g | Cholesterol: .....................0 mg | Iron: ......................................3 mg |
| Vitamin C: ..........................4 mg | Vitamin A: .....................276 RE | Zinc: ......................................1 mg |

Diabetic exchanges: 1 serving equals 1¾ starch exchanges, ¼ very lean meat exchange, ⅓ vegetable exchange

# Split Pea Soup

1 pound split peas
Water
3 to 4 carrots, peeled and sliced
3 stalks celery, sliced
2 teaspoons salt
¼ teaspoon pepper
1 bay leaf
1 to 2 cups cubed cooked ham (optional)

The night before you plan to serve this soup for dinner, sort through and rinse the peas, discarding any shriveled ones. Put them in a 3 quart crock pot and cover them with two or three times their volume of water. Soak them overnight. The next morning, pour off the water and replace it with fresh water three times. (This soaking and rinsing process removes indigestible carbohydrates which can cause "gas"). Drain off all the water after the last rinse. Add 5 cups of water to the crock pot, the carrots, celery, salt, pepper, ham, and bay leaf. Cover the crock pot with its lid and cook the soup on high for 6 hours or on low for 8 to 10 hours. Check the soup near the end of the cooking time and add a little boiling water to the pot if the soup is thicker than you prefer. Remove the bay leaf before serving. Makes about 2½ quarts of soup, or 6 to 10 servings. Leftover soup freezes well.

**Nutritional Analysis per serving:** 10 servings per recipe

| | | |
|---|---|---|
| Calories: ..........................168 | Total fat: ...............................1 g | Calcium: ...............................38 mg |
| Protein: ...............................12 g | Saturated fat: ................0 g | Magnesium: .....................52 mg |
| Carbohydrate: ..................31 g | Omega-3 fatty acids: ...0.04 g | Potassium: ......................582 mg |
| Sugars: ..............................5 g | Omega-6 fatty acids: ..0.19 g | Sodium: ..........................503 mg |
| Fiber (total): ....................12 g | Cholesterol: ......................0 mg | Iron: .....................................52 mg |
| Vitamin C: ..........................4 mg | Vitamin A: .......................414 RE | Zinc: .........................................1 mg |

Diabetic exchanges: 1 serving equals 1¾ starch exchanges, ½ very lean meat exchange, ½ vegetable exchange

# Basic Lentil Soup

*Because lentils are among the least allergenic legumes, this recipe is very "hypoallergenic" if the optional ingredients are not used. For another lentil soup recipe, see "Lentil-Barley Soup" on page 148.*

1 pound dry lentils
Water
3 to 5 carrots, peeled and sliced
3 stalks celery, sliced
2 teaspoons salt
¼ teaspoon pepper (optional)
1 14 ounce can diced tomatoes (optional)

The night before you plan to serve this soup for dinner, sort through and rinse the lentils, discarding any shriveled ones. Put them in a 3 quart crock pot and cover them with two or three times their volume of water. Soak them overnight. The next morning, pour off the water and replace it with fresh water three times. (This soaking and rinsing process removes indigestible carbohydrates which can cause "gas"). Drain off all the water after the last rinse. Add 5 cups of water to the crock pot, the carrots, celery, salt, and pepper. Cover the crock pot with its lid and cook the soup on high for 6 hours or on low for 8 to 10 hours. Add the optional tomatoes an hour before the end of the cooking time. Check the soup near the end of the cooking time and add a little boiling water to the pot if the soup is thicker than you prefer. Makes about 2½ quarts of soup, or 6 to 10 servings. Leftover soup freezes well.

**Nutritional Analysis per serving:** 10 servings per recipe

| | | |
|---|---|---|
| Calories: ..........................167 | Total fat: ..............................0.4 g | Calcium: ...............................36 mg |
| Protein: ...............................13 g | Saturated fat: ................0 g | Magnesium: .....................49 mg |
| Carbohydrate: ..................29 g | Omega-3 fatty acids: ...0.04 g | Potassium: ......................548 mg |
| Sugars: ..............................4 g | Omega-6 fatty acids: ..0.16 g | Sodium: ..........................501 mg |
| Fiber (total): ....................15 g | Cholesterol: ......................0 mg | Iron: .......................................4 mg |
| Vitamin C: ..........................6 mg | Vitamin A: .......................408 RE | Zinc: .........................................2 mg |

Diabetic exchanges: 1 serving equals 1¾ starch exchanges, ½ very lean meat exchange, ½ vegetable exchange

# Multi-Bean Soup

1 pound dry mixed beans, or 2 ounces each of 8 of the following kinds of beans:
  Black beans
  Lentils
  Yellow split peas
  Green split peas
  Navy beans
  Medium lima beans
  Black-eyed peas
  Small red beans
  Pinto beans
  Kidney beans
Water
3 carrots, peeled and sliced
3 stalks celery, sliced
1 small onion, chopped (optional)
2 teaspoons salt
¼ teaspoon pepper (optional)
1 14 ounce can diced tomatoes (optional)

The night before you plan to serve this soup for dinner, sort through and rinse the beans, discarding any shriveled ones. Put them in a 3 quart crock pot and cover them with two or three times their volume of water. Soak them overnight. The next morning, pour off the water and replace it with fresh water three times. (This soaking and rinsing process removes indigestible carbohydrates which can cause "gas"). Drain off all the water after the last rinse. Add 6 cups of water to the crock pot, the carrots, celery, onion, salt, and pepper. Cover the crock pot with its lid and cook the soup on high for 6 hours or on low for 8 to 10 hours. Add the optional tomatoes an hour before the end of the cooking time. Check the soup near the end of the cooking time and add a little boiling water to the pot if the soup is thicker than you prefer. Makes about 2½ quarts of soup, or 6 to 10 servings. Leftover soup freezes well.

**Nutritional Analysis per serving:** 10 servings per recipe

| | | |
|---|---|---|
| Calories: ......................167 | Total fat: ..........................0.5 g | Calcium:............................63 mg |
| Protein:.............................11 g | Saturated fat:................0 g | Magnesium: ......................66 mg |
| Carbohydrate:.................31 g | Omega-3 fatty acids:...0.10 g | Potassium:......................727 mg |
| Sugars: .............................5 g | Omega-6 fatty acids: ..0.12 g | Sodium:..........................502 mg |
| Fiber (total):....................11 g | Cholesterol: ....................0 mg | Iron: ....................................3 mg |
| Vitamin C: .........................5 mg | Vitamin A:.....................409 RE | Zinc: ....................................1 mg |

Diabetic exchanges: 1 serving equals 1¾ starch exchanges, ½ very lean meat exchange, ½ vegetable exchange

# *White Bean and Escarole Soup*

1 pound dry small white beans or navy beans
Water
½ small head of cabbage, chopped (about ¾ pound)
2 teaspoons salt
¼ teaspoon pepper (optional)
1 tablespoon chopped fresh sweet basil or 1 teaspoon dry sweet basil
1 head of escarole weighing about ¾ pound, washed and chopped into large pieces
2 medium potatoes, peeled and diced (optional)

The night before you plan to serve this soup for dinner, sort through and rinse the beans, discarding any shriveled ones. Put them in a 3 quart crock pot and cover them with two or three times their volume of water. Soak them overnight. The next morning, pour off the water and replace it with fresh water three times. (This soaking and rinsing process removes indigestible carbohydrates which can cause "gas"). Drain off all the water after the last rinse. Add 5½ cups of water to the crock pot, the cabbage, salt, pepper, and sweet basil. Cover the crock pot with its lid and cook the soup on high for 6 hours or on low for 8 to 10 hours. Add the escarole and optional potatoes two hours before the end of the cooking time. Check the soup near the end of the cooking time and add a little boiling water to the pot if the soup is thicker than you prefer. Makes about 2½ quarts of soup, or 6 to 10 servings. Leftover soup freezes well if the potatoes are not used.

**Nutritional Analysis per serving:** 10 servings per recipe

| | | |
|---|---|---|
| Calories: ...................170 | Total fat: ..........................1 g | Calcium: ...........................113 mg |
| Protein: .........................11 g | Saturated fat: ...............0 g | Magnesium: ....................91 mg |
| Carbohydrate: ..................31 g | Omega-3 fatty acids: ...0.15 g | Potassium: ......................741 mg |
| Sugars: ...........................4 g | Omega-6 fatty acids: ..0.19 g | Sodium: ..........................491 mg |
| Fiber (total): ....................13 g | Cholesterol: .......................0 mg | Iron: ..................................4 mg |
| Vitamin C: ........................18 mg | Vitamin A: .........................77 RE | Zinc: .................................2 mg |

Diabetic exchanges: 1 serving equals 1¾ starch exchanges, ½ very lean meat exchange, ¾ vegetable exchange

# *Crock Pot Baked Beans*

1 pound small white or small navy beans
Water
¾ cup apple juice concentrate, thawed
1 6 ounce can tomato paste or 1½ teaspoons paprika (optional)
1 tablespoon finely chopped onion or 1 teaspoon dried onion flakes (optional)
1 teaspoon dry mustard powder (optional)
1 tablespoon finely chopped fresh sweet basil or 1 teaspoon dried sweet basil
1½ teaspoons salt
¼ teaspoon pepper

The night before you plan to serve this dish, wash the beans by putting them in a strainer and running cold water over them. Remove and discard any shriveled beans. Put the beans in a 3 quart crock pot and fill the pot almost to the top with water. The volume of the water should be two to three times the volume of the beans. The next morning, pour the water off the beans and replace it with fresh water two or three times. (This soaking and rinsing process removes indigestible carbohydrates that can cause "gas"). Pour off all the water after the last rinse. Add 4 cups of water to the crock pot and put the lid on the pot. Cook the beans 4 to 6 hours on "high" or until they are very tender. Check them during cooking and add more water if necessary. It is all right if the level of the water goes a little lower than the level of the beans in the pot.

If you are using the tomato paste, stir it into the apple juice until the mixture is smooth. Add this mixture (or just the apple juice if you're not using the tomato paste) and the seasonings to the crock pot. Stir these ingredients into the beans thoroughly. Cover the pot and cook the beans on high another 3 to 10 hours. Check them during cooking and add more water if necessary. If you like a thick sauce, smash a few beans against the side of the pot an hour or so before the end of the cooking time. If the sauce still isn't thick enough, set the lid ajar so some of the liquid can evaporate. For very thick, oven-style baked beans, start cooking the beans in the middle of the day. Add the seasonings and apple juice in the evening and then cook the beans overnight. Refrigerate or freeze the beans until you want to use them, or eat them for breakfast! Makes 8 to 10 servings. Leftovers freeze well.

**Nutritional Analysis per serving:** 10 servings per recipe

| | | |
|---|---|---|
| Calories: ...............188 | Total fat: ...........................1 g | Calcium: .......................78 mg |
| Protein: ...................10 g | Saturated fat: ..............0 g | Magnesium:......................83 mg |
| Carbohydrate: ................36 g | Omega-3 fatty acids:...0.12 g | Potassium: ......................617 mg |
| Sugars:...........................11 g | Omega-6 fatty acids: ..0.16 g | Sodium: ..........................364 mg |
| Fiber (total):.................11 g | Cholesterol: .....................0 mg | Iron: ...............................3 mg |
| Vitamin C: .........................2 mg | Vitamin A:.........................2 RE | Zinc: ...............................1 mg |

Diabetic exchanges: 1 serving equals 1¾ starch exchanges, ¼ very lean meat exchange, ⅔ fruit exchange

# Microwave Marvels

This chapter can stave off starvation for college students who have a small microwave oven in their dormitory room. All of the recipes can be cooked in a small microwave and require little or no refrigerator space for the ingredients used. They also require a minimum of utensils and cookware. See "Equipping your Dormitory Room," pages 69 to 72 for a list of the equipment you may need.

Some of these recipes, like "Bacon" and "Hot Breakfast Beverages," are recipes that people with full kitchens will want to use because it is easier to make these foods in a microwave oven than by conventional methods. However, since microwave ovens are really better for reheating foods than for cooking them the first time, the criteria by which the recipes in this chapter are judged is different than for the rest of the recipes in this book. When we decided whether or not to include a recipe in this chapter, the questions asked were not, "Is this really delicious?" or "Is this as healthy as it can be?" but rather, "Is this tastier and healthier than what is served in the average college dormitory cafeteria?" One has to make compromises at times, so the "standards" for this chapter are a little lower than for the rest of the book, both in the finished quality of the food and in the health aspects of the ingredients used.

Because the recipes were judged by comparing them to "dorm food," and also to meet the limitations of time, space, and money that most college students have, some of the recipes in this chapter use ingredients, such as processed cheese, that I'd rather avoid if possible. However, fresh natural cheese cannot be stored in an under-bed pantry, and your dorm-room-made macaroni and cheese will probably be better than what you'd eat in the cafeteria, even if it isn't ideally healthy. If you have more room for fresh ingredients and equipment, some of the recipes in the other chapters can also be made in your dormitory room. See the end of this chapter for a list of other recipes in this book that you should check out.

Most of these recipes make one or two servings. If you have friends you would like to feed, the recipes can be doubled, but the cooking time will have to be adjusted. With microwave cooking, it can be hard to predict how much to change the cooking time, and you will have to taste-test to see when your food is done when you double a recipe. A general rule of thumb is that for most recipes, you should increase the cooking time by 50% when you double the recipe. If you're not very hungry and want to halve a recipe, reduce the cooking time by one third.

The cooking times given in the recipes in this chapter are not absolutes. You may need to adjust the cooking times given if your microwave is older or varies in strength from the 600 to 700 watt small ovens on the market today. A 500 watt oven may require ⅓ to ½ more cooking time than indicated in the recipes. If you are using a large 900 watt microwave oven, your food may be cooked in a shorter time than the recipe says. Check the food a few minutes before it should be done if you are using a high-power oven.

Cooking times will also vary with altitude. Students at the University of Wyoming (altitude 7,500 feet) will have to cook their meals a few minutes longer than those at the University of California-San Diego (sea level) because the boiling point of water decreases as altitude increases. Taste your food when it should be cooked, and if it is not done, just cook it some more. Write down how long you cooked it in the margin of this book so you'll know how long to cook it the next time you make it.

When it's time to eat a meal, if at all possible, put your books away for a few minutes. Sit down at your desk and look out the window or talk to a friend while you eat. Enjoy, rather than ignore, your food. Nourish your spirit while you nourish your body. The break will do you good, and you can go back to your studies refreshed.

# Hot Breakfast Beverages

Water
Tea bags, Dacopa™, cocoa mix, or instant coffee

Fill a mug with water. Microwave on high for two to three minutes or until the water boils. Stir the water to prevent vigorous boiling when you add your tea bag or powdered beverage. Add a tea bag and steep or add a teaspoon (the kind you eat with is O.K. – you don't have to measure this one) of instant coffee or Dacopa™ or an envelope of cocoa mix and stir. If you'd like to have healthier and cheaper cocoa, or if you want to make it with carob or goat milk and no sugar, see "Pantry Microwave Cocoa" on page 295.

**Tea and coffee:** 0 calories, 0 diabetic exchanges

**Dacopa:** Nutritional information is not available.

**Cocoa, 1 envelope of fat-free mix:** (Read the nutrition facts on the mix you use for more information).

**Nutritional Analysis per serving:** 1 serving per recipe

| | | |
|---|---|---|
| Calories: ...................70 | Total fat: ......................0 g | Calcium: .......................250 mg |
| Protein:.............................6 g | Saturated fat:................0 g | Magnesium: ....................24 mg |
| Carbohydrate:................10 g | Omega-3 fatty acids:...0 g | Potassium:...................395 mg |
| Sugars: ............................7 g | Omega-6 fatty acids: ..0 g | Sodium: ..........................160 mg |
| Fiber (total): .................0 g | Cholesterol: .................0 mg | Iron: ....................................0 mg |
| Vitamin C:.......................0 mg | Vitamin A: .....................86 RE | Zinc:....................................0 mg |

Diabetic exchanges: 1 serving equals ¾ skim milk exchange

# Hard-Cooked Egg

1 egg (nutritional analysis is based on a large egg)
About ¼ teaspoon butter, goat butter, ghee, or milk-free Earth Balance™ margarine
Salt and pepper (optional)

Throughly butter a small glass custard cup or bowl. Break the egg into the bowl. Pierce the yolk with a wooden toothpick or the tine of a fork. Tightly cover the bowl with plastic wrap. Microwave on medium (50%) for 1½ to 2 minutes, or until the white is set and the yolk is almost set. Allow the egg to stand with the plastic cover still on the bowl for an additional minute to complete cooking. Sprinkle the egg with salt and/or pepper and enjoy it or chill it and use it in an egg salad sandwich, page 125.

**Nutritional Analysis per serving:** 1 serving per recipe

| | | |
|---|---|---|
| Calories: ...86 | Total fat: ...6 g | Calcium: ...25 mg |
| Protein: ...6 g | Saturated fat: ...2 g | Magnesium: ...5 mg |
| Carbohydrate: ...1 g | Omega-3 fatty acids: ...0.05 g | Potassium: ...63 mg |
| Sugars: ...0 g | Omega-6 fatty acids: ...0.69 g | Sodium: ...72 mg |
| Fiber (total): ...0 g | Cholesterol: ...214 mg | Iron: ...1 mg |
| Vitamin C: ...0 mg | Vitamin A: ...93 RE | Zinc: ...1 mg |

Diabetic exchanges: 1 serving equals 1 medium-fat meat exchange, ¼ fat exchange

# Microwave Cooked Oatmeal

*If you are in a real hurry, you can have instant oatmeal ready even faster than this "from scratch" oatmeal. Just put some water in a bowl or cup, bring it to a boil in the microwave, stir in a package of instant oatmeal or other instant cereal, let it stand a minute, and eat!*

1 cup water or milk
½ cup of quick-cooking oatmeal or regular oatmeal (not instant)
Dash of salt

Combine the water or milk, oatmeal, and salt in a glass bowl or two cup measuring cup. Microwave on high for 1½ to 2 minutes for quick-cooking oatmeal or microwave on medium (50%) power for 5 to 6 minutes for regular oatmeal. Let it stand for a minute and then taste it. If it is not sufficiently cooked, microwave it longer. (Cooking time may vary due to differences in the microwave oven or the altitude). Record the cooking time for future use. Makes one serving.

**Nutritional Analysis per serving:** 1 serving per recipe

| | | |
|---|---|---|
| Calories: ...156 | Total fat: ...3 g | Calcium: ...21 mg |
| Protein: ...6 g | Saturated fat: ...0 g | Magnesium: ...60 mg |
| Carbohydrate: ...27 g | Omega-3 fatty acids: ...0.04 g | Potassium: ...142 mg |
| Sugars: ...1 g | Omega-6 fatty acids: ...0.89 g | Sodium: ...236 mg |
| Fiber (total): ...4 g | Cholesterol: ...0 mg | Iron: ...2 mg |
| Vitamin C: ...0 mg | Vitamin A: ...4 RE | Zinc: ...1 mg |

Diabetic exchanges: 1 serving equals 2 starch exchanges. The recipe may be halved if you want only 1 starch exchange.

# Microwave Pasta

*Not all shapes of pasta hold up equally well when microwaved. Use this recipe with the sturdy types of pasta listed below rather than with spaghetti if you want pasta that is worlds better than dorm mush pasta!*

¼ to ½ pound mostaccioli, penne rigate, ziti, or rigatoni (R & F brand if possible) or Purity Foods whole spelt or white spelt macaroni
Water – 3 cups for ¼ pound of pasta; 5-6 cups for ½ pound of pasta
Salt – ¼ teaspoon for ¼ pound of pasta; ½ teaspoon for ½ pound of pasta
Pasta sauce of your choice – from Mom's freezer, or bottled sauce from the grocery store
Grated Romano or Parmesan cheese (optional)

Warm the sauce you intend to use in its jar or in a glass bowl or measuring cup. Set it aside.

Put the water in a 2½ to 3 quart casserole dish and microwave on high until it comes to a boil. (This will take a while – probably at least 15 minutes). Add the salt and pasta and cook on high. For wheat pasta, cook ¼ pound of pasta for 7 to 10 minutes or ½ pound of pasta for 10 to 15 minutes, or until it is *al dente*. For spelt pasta, cook ¼ pound for 5 to 8 minutes and ½ pound for 7 to 11 minutes, or until it is *al dente*. (*Al dente* means it is cooked but not mushy; it should offer some resistance to the tooth). Check your pasta by biting a piece every minute or two beginning after 3 minutes for ¼ pound of spelt pasta, 5 minutes for a ¼ pound of wheat pasta or ½ pound of spelt pasta, or 8 minutes for a ½ pound of wheat pasta. When it is cooked to *al dente*, pour it through a colander to drain the water from the pasta. Return the pasta to the casserole dish. Rewarm the sauce if necessary and put some on the pasta. Serve more sauce and grated cheese on the side. Makes one to four servings. ¼ pound of pasta will serve one college student who is not extremely hungry; cook ½ pound if you are really starved or want to share with your roommate. ½ pound of pasta makes four servings for the students' parents.

**Nutritional Analysis per serving:** 4 servings per recipe if ½ pound of pasta is used

| | | | | | |
|---|---|---|---|---|---|
| Calories: | 203 | Total fat: | 1 g | Calcium: | 12 mg |
| Protein: | 8 g | Saturated fat: | 0 g | Magnesium: | 27 mg |
| Carbohydrate: | 41 g | Omega-3 fatty acids: | 0 g | Potassium: | 106 mg |
| Sugars: | 2 g | Omega-6 fatty acids: | 0 g | Sodium: | 120 mg |
| Fiber (total): | 2 g | Cholesterol: | 0 mg | Iron: | 2 mg |
| Vitamin C: | 0 mg | Vitamin A: | 0 RE | Zinc: | 1 mg |

Diabetic exchanges: 1 serving equals 2½ starch exchanges

# Pantry Macaroni and Cheese

*See page 170 for another easy microwave macaroni and cheese recipe that uses healthier natural cheese from your refrigerator rather than room-temperature-stable processed cheese.*

4 cups water
8 ounces macaroni (R & F brand if possible) or Purity Foods whole spelt or white spelt macaroni
8 ounces pasteurized processed cheese, such as Velveeta™ brand
1 5 ounce can evaporated milk

Put the water in a large casserole dish and bring it to a boil. (This will take a while – probably at least 15 minutes). Add the macaroni and then microwave, uncovered, on high for 5 minutes for wheat pasta or 3 minutes for spelt pasta. While the macaroni is cooking, cut the cheese into cubes about ½-inch in size. Drain the water from the macaroni when it has finished cooking. Combine the drained pasta, cheese, and milk in the casserole dish. Cover the dish with its lid or plastic wrap. Microwave it on high for 3 to 9 minutes, stirring every 2 to 3 minutes, or until the cheese is melted, the sauce is bubbly and thickened, and the pasta is cooked. (Smaller, lower-power microwaves will require a longer cooking time). Makes 3 to 6 servings.

**Nutritional Analysis per serving:** 6 servings per recipe

| | | |
|---|---|---|
| Calories: .......................299 | Total fat: ............................10 g | Calcium: ...........................302 mg |
| Protein: ...........................19 g | Saturated fat: ...............6 g | Magnesium: ....................40 mg |
| Carbohydrate: ..................31 g | Omega-3 fatty acids: ...0.04 g | Potassium: ....................269 mg |
| Sugars: .............................7 g | Omega-6 fatty acids: ..0.34 g | Sodium: ...........................559 mg |
| Fiber (total): ......................1 g | Cholesterol: ....................32 mg | Iron: ..................................2 mg |
| Vitamin C: ..........................0 mg | Vitamin A: .....................256 RE | Zinc: ..................................2 mg |

Diabetic exchanges: 1 serving equals 1¾ starch exchanges, 1⅞ medium-fat meat exchanges, ⅕ skim milk exchange

# Italian Macaroni and Cheese

*When I was in college, my friend Barb Tarantola used to complain bitterly every time we had "that awful orange macaroni and cheese" for lunch in the dormitory cafeteria. Her mother had immigrated from Italy, so she was a little closer to her roots than I, a second generation Italian-American, was. This version of macaroni and cheese is dedicated her. If you want to keep all of the ingredients for this recipe at room temperature in your dorm room, you can. For the cream you can use and store at room temperature small aseptic packages of half-and-half such as are used in restaurants for coffee.*

> 8 ounces macaroni, R & F brand if possible, or Purity Foods whole spelt or white spelt macaroni
> 4 cups water
> ¼ teaspoon salt
> 3 tablespoons butter or ghee (Ghee can be stored at room temperature).
> 4 tablespoons half-and-half or cream
> ¼ cup grated Romano or Parmesan cheese
> Pepper to taste (optional)

Put the water in a 2½ to 3 quart casserole dish and microwave on high until it comes to a boil. (This will take a while – probably at least 15 minutes). Add the salt and pasta and cook wheat pasta on high for 10 to 15 minutes or spelt pasta for 7 to 11 minutes, or until it is *al dente*. (*Al dente* is cooked but not mushy; it should offer some resistance to the tooth). Check and taste your macaroni every minute or two beginning at about 8 minutes for wheat pasta or 5 minutes for spelt pasta. When it is cooked, pour it through a colander to drain the water from the pasta. Return the pasta to the casserole dish. Cut the butter into pieces, add it to the pasta, and toss it until it is melted. Add the cream and toss. Sprinkle it with the cheese and pepper and toss. Makes 2 to 3 main course servings for hungry college students or 4 to 6 servings for their parents.

**Nutritional Analysis per serving:** 6 servings per recipe

| | | |
|---|---|---|
| Calories: ....................222 | Total fat: .........................9 g | Calcium: .........................71 mg |
| Protein: ............................10 g | Saturated fat: ...............5 g | Magnesium: .....................26 mg |
| Carbohydrate: ................25 g | Omega-3 fatty acids:...0.13 g | Potassium: ......................96 mg |
| Sugars: ............................2 g | Omega-6 fatty acids: ..0.48 g | Sodium: ..........................156 mg |
| Fiber (total): ......................1 g | Cholesterol: ...................25 mg | Iron: ..................................2 mg |
| Vitamin C: ........................0 mg | Vitamin A: ......................59 RE | Zinc: ....................................1 mg |

Diabetic exchanges: 1 serving equals 1¾ starch exchanges, ¼ medium-fat meat exchange, 1½ fat exchanges

# *Microwave Pantry Pasta Casserole*

8 ounces of pasta, such as penne, medium sized sea shells, or white spelt macaroni
4 cups water
¼ teaspoon salt
1 14.5 ounce can diced tomatoes or 1 14.5 ounce can Italian-flavor
    diced tomatoes
¼ teaspoon dry sweet basil (omit if you use the flavored diced tomatoes)
¼ teaspoon dry oregano (omit if you use the flavored diced tomatoes)
1 15 ounce can plain corn, drained
1 15 ounce can french cut green beans, drained
1½ cups water plus one chicken bouillon cube or 1½ cups chicken broth*
¼ cup all purpose, unbleached, or white spelt flour*
2 to 3 cups, or about 8 ounces, shredded Monterey jack cheese or goat cheese

Bring the water to a boil in a 2½ to 3 quart casserole dish. (This will take a while – probably at least 15 minutes). Add the salt and pasta and cook on high for 4 to 8 minutes. (The pasta should be underdone). Drain the water from the pasta with a colander. Set the pasta aside while you use the casserole dish to cook the sauce if you are making it rather than using soup.

Make a sauce of the chicken broth and flour as below. *(Or you can substitute a 10.5 ounce can of cream of celery, cream of chicken, or cream of mushroom soup for the broth and flour in this step. The soup contains some strange chemicals and is not as healthy but is quicker). Thoroughly combine ¼ cup of the broth (or water you will use to make the broth) with the flour in your casserole dish. Add the remaining broth or water and the bouillon cube (if you are using it) and stir thoroughly. Heat the sauce in the microwave oven for 5 to 8 minutes, stirring it every 1 to 2 minutes, until it thickens and boils. Stir vigorously or blend it with a hand blender if lumps form in the sauce.

Add the cooked pasta to the sauce or soup in the casserole dish. Also add the tomatoes, spices, corn, and beans and stir everything together. Microwave the casserole for 10 to 20 minutes, stirring it every 3 minutes, until the pasta is tender and it is hot throughout. Stir in the cheese until it is melted. Makes 4 servings for hungry college students or 8 servings for their parents. Store leftovers in the refrigerator.

**Nutritional Analysis per serving:** 8 servings per recipe

| | | |
|---|---|---|
| Calories: ....................292 | Total fat: .........................10 g | Calcium: .........................271 mg |
| Protein: ............................13 g | Saturated fat: ...............5 g | Magnesium: .....................43 mg |
| Carbohydrate: ................39 g | Omega-3 fatty acids:...0.10 g | Potassium: ......................246 mg |
| Sugars: ............................7 g | Omega-6 fatty acids: ..0.62 g | Sodium: ..........................644 mg |
| Fiber (total): ......................4 g | Cholesterol: ...................25 mg | Iron: ..................................3 mg |
| Vitamin C: ........................16 mg | Vitamin A: ......................114 RE | Zinc: ....................................1 mg |

Diabetic exchanges: 1 serving equals 2 starch exchanges, 1 lean meat exchange, 1⅓ vegetable exchanges, 1 fat exchange

# Microwave Pizza

**Sauce:**
>1 8 ounce can tomato sauce
>1 6 ounce can tomato paste
>1 teaspoon oil (Olive oil is best, or your can omit the oil completely if necessary).
>1 teaspoon dried oregano
>½ teaspoon dried sweet basil
>½ teaspoon dried thyme

**Dough:**
>1 4 ounce can of crescent roll dough for one pizza, or half of an 8 ounce can

**Toppings:**
>1 ounce part-skim or low fat grated mozzarella cheese, about ¼ to ⅓ cup
>1 to 2 teaspoons grated Romano or Parmesan cheese
>About 12 slices of pepperoni (optional)
>Assorted chopped vegetables – green peppers, black olives, etc. (optional)

Combine the tomato sauce, tomato paste, oil and spices in a 2-cup glass measuring cup or a glass bowl. Cover with plastic wrap. Microwave on high for 10 to 15 minutes, stirring every 4 to 5 minutes, or until the sauce is very thick. This makes enough sauce for 3 or 4 pizzas. Refrigerate or freeze ¾ of the sauce if you are making only one pizza.

Cut two pieces of wax or parchment paper about the size of a paper plate. Put one on a paper plate. Open the crescent roll dough can and spread the rolls out on the wax or parchment paper on the plate, pressing together the holes and, if you want a round pizza, pressing the dough into a more circular shape. Microwave the dough at 50% power for 4 minutes. Remove the paper and dough from the plate. Line the plate with the second piece of paper. Flip the first piece of paper and dough over onto the second piece of paper on the plate. Peel off and discard the first piece of paper. Microwave the dough at 50% power for another 2 to 4 minutes. Watch it carefully after two minutes – it should not brown! Remove it from the microwave immediately if it begins to brown .

Top the pizza with the sauce, cheeses, pepperoni, and optional vegetables. Microwave the pizza at 50% power for another 2 to 3 minutes, or until the cheese is melted. Makes two servings.

**Nutritional Analysis per serving:** 2 servings per recipe

| | | |
|---|---|---|
| Calories: ........289 | Total fat: ........15 g | Calcium: ........114 mg |
| Protein: ........9 g | Saturated fat: ........5 g | Magnesium: ........20 mg |
| Carbohydrate: ........29 g | Omega-3 fatty acids: ...0.02 g | Potassium: ........317 mg |
| Sugars: ........5 g | Omega-6 fatty acids: ..0.10 g | Sodium: ........546 mg |
| Fiber (total): ........1 g | Cholesterol: ........9 mg | Iron: ........2 mg |
| Vitamin C: ........13 mg | Vitamin A: ........106 RE | Zinc: ........1 mg |

Diabetic exchanges: 1 serving equals 1½ starch exchanges, ½ medium-fat meat exchange, ¾ vegetable exchange, 2½ fat exchanges

# Cooked Ground Meat

*Use this in recipes such as Easy Microwave "Chili," page 236, or "Sea Shell Casserole," below.*

Crumble ¼ pound to 1 pound of lean ground beef, ground turkey, or other meat into a hard plastic colander. Place the colander in a glass casserole or bowl. Place it in the microwave oven and microwave on high for 4 to 8 minutes, stirring every two minutes, until the meat no longer has any pink spots. (You will need the longer cooking time for the larger amount of meat). Drain the grease (see note below), put the colander back into the bowl or casserole, and microwave another two minutes on high. Use in the recipes below as directed.

Note: Pour the grease into an empty milk carton or can, let it solidify, and throw it out in the trash. Never pour grease down the sink unless you want a clogged drain!

### Ground beef:
**Nutritional Analysis per serving:** 1 serving using ¼ pound of ground meat per recipe

| | | |
|---|---|---|
| Calories: ...................192 | Total fat: ...................10 g | Calcium: ...................9 mg |
| Protein: ...................23 g | Saturated fat: ...............4 g | Magnesium: ...................25 mg |
| Carbohydrate: ...................0 g | Omega-3 fatty acids:...0.04 g | Potassium: ...................354 mg |
| Sugars: ...................0 g | Omega-6 fatty acids: ..0.22 g | Sodium: ...................82 mg |
| Fiber (total): ...................0 g | Cholesterol: ...................81 mg | Iron: ...................2 mg |
| Vitamin C: ...................0 mg | Vitamin A: ...................0 RE | Zinc: ...................5 mg |

Diabetic exchanges: 1 serving equals 2 lean meat exchanges, 1 medium-fat meat exchange

### Ground turkey:
**Nutritional Analysis per serving:** 1 serving using ¼ pound of ground meat per recipe

| | | |
|---|---|---|
| Calories: ...................178 | Total fat: ...................8 g | Calcium: ...................15 mg |
| Protein: ...................25 g | Saturated fat: ...............2 g | Magnesium: ...................27 mg |
| Carbohydrate: ...................0 g | Omega-3 fatty acids:...0.11 g | Potassium: ...................312 mg |
| Sugars: ...................0 g | Omega-6 fatty acids: ....1.70 g | Sodium: ...................67 mg |
| Fiber (total): ...................0 g | Cholesterol: ...................74 mg | Iron: ...................1 mg |
| Vitamin C: ...................0 mg | Vitamin A: ...................2 RE | Zinc: ...................2 mg |

Diabetic exchanges: 1 serving equals 3¼ lean meat exchanges

# Sea Shell Casserole

½ pound medium sized sea shell pasta (the dried sea shells should be about
    ¾ inch long)
4 cups water
½ teaspoon salt
1 pound ground beef
1 16 ounce can of tomato sauce
8 ounces grated cheddar cheese or goat cheese or cubed pasteurized process cheese

Bring the water to a boil in a 2½ to 3 quart casserole dish. (This will take a while – probably at least 15 minutes). Add the salt and pasta and cook on high for 5 minutes. (The pasta will be underdone). Drain the water from the pasta with a colander. Rinse the pasta with cold water to stop the cooking process. Set the pasta aside in a storage container while you use the casserole and colander to cook the meat.

Cook the beef for 5 to 8 minutes as in "Cooked Ground Meat," above. Drain the fat from the casserole dish and then return the meat to the casserole dish. Add the tomato sauce, cover the casserole dish with its lid or plastic wrap, and microwave it on high for 10 minutes, stirring every 3 minutes. Stir the cooked pasta and cheese into the meat mixture. You may refrigerate this casserole until right before serving time at this point in the recipe if desired. Microwave the casserole on high until it is hot and bubbly through-out, stirring the food near the outside of the dish to the center and the food in the center of the dish to the outside every 5 minutes. The final microwaving time will be 5 to 10 minutes if it was not refrigerated and 10 to 15 minutes if it was refrigerated. Makes 4 servings for hungry college students or 8 servings for their parents.

**Nutritional Analysis per serving:** 8 servings per recipe

| | | |
|---|---|---|
| Calories: ......................337 | Total fat: ...........................15 g | Calcium: ...........................226 mg |
| Protein: ...........................24 g | Saturated fat: ...............8 g | Magnesium: ...................50 mg |
| Carbohydrate: .................27 g | Omega-3 fatty acids:...0.11 g | Potassium: ...................568 mg |
| Sugars: ............................4 g | Omega-6 fatty acids: ..0.22 g | Sodium: ...........................600 mg |
| Fiber (total): ....................2 g | Cholesterol: ....................50 mg | Iron: ...................................3 mg |
| Vitamin C: .........................12 mg | Vitamin A: .......................160 RE | Zinc: ...................................4 mg |

Diabetic exchanges: 1 serving equals 1⅓ starch exchanges, 3 lean meat exchanges, 1 vegetable exchange, 1 fat exchange

# Easy Microwave Chili

1 pound lean ground beef
3 8 ounce cans tomato sauce
3 15 ounce cans kidney beans
¼ teaspoon salt
½ to 1 teaspoon chili powder, or to taste

Crumble the ground beef into a hard plastic colander set in a large glass casserole dish. Microwave on high for 5 to 8 minutes, stirring and breaking up the meat every 2 minutes, until the meat no longer has any pink spots. Drain the grease from the casse-role dish. Add the cooked meat and tomato sauce to the casserole, cover it with the lid or plastic wrap, and microwave on high for 5 minutes. Drain the liquid in the can from the beans and add them to the casserole dish. Add the seasonings and microwave on high for another 5 to 7 minutes, stirring every 2 to 3 minutes. Makes 3 to 8 servings. To make one large or two servings, use ⅓ pound ground beef, 1 can of tomato sauce, 1 can of beans, and a dash of salt and chili powder. Microwave the meat for 3 to 5 minutes, the meat and tomato sauce for 5 minutes, and all of the ingredients together for another 5 minutes.

**Nutritional Analysis per serving:** 8 servings per recipe

| | | |
|---|---|---|
| Calories: ......................250 | Total fat: ...........................6 g | Calcium: ...........................18 mg |
| Protein: ...........................21 g | Saturated fat: ...............2 g | Magnesium: ...................72 mg |
| Carbohydrate: .................30 g | Omega-3 fatty acids:...0.17 g | Potassium: ...................524 mg |
| Sugars: ............................2 g | Omega-6 fatty acids: ..0.13 g | Sodium: ...........................128 mg |
| Fiber (total): ....................11 g | Cholesterol: ....................21 mg | Iron: ...................................2 mg |
| Vitamin C: .........................12 mg | Vitamin A: .......................101 RE | Zinc: ...................................4 mg |

Diabetic exchanges: 1 serving equals 1½ starch exchanges, 1⅔ lean meat exchanges, ¼ vegetable exchange

# Microwave Burritos

    1 pound lean ground beef
    1 16 ounce can of tomato sauce
    8 to 10 burrito-sized flour tortillas
    1 15 ounce can refried beans
    1 cup grated cheddar cheese, goat cheese, or processed cheese.

Cook the beef for 5 to 8 minutes as in "Cooked Ground Meat," page 235. Drain the fat from the casserole dish and then return the meat to the casserole dish. Add the tomato sauce, cover the casserole dish with its lid or plastic wrap, and microwave it on high for 10 minutes, stirring every 3 minutes.

Down the middle of each burrito, spread about ⅛ to ⅒ of the refried beans. Top the beans with ⅛ to ⅒ of the beef-tomato mixture, and sprinkle with 2 tablespoons of cheese. Fold over one side of the burrito, fold the ends in, and roll it up over the other side of the burrito. Use a toothpick to hold each burrito closed or put them on a dish seam-side down. You may wrap the burritos in plastic wrap and refrigerate or freeze them at this point. When you are ready to eat them, microwave each burrito for 2 to 3 minutes or until it is hot throughout. Makes 8 to 10 servings.

**Nutritional Analysis per serving:** 10 servings per recipe

| | | |
|---|---|---|
| Calories: ...................411 | Total fat: .....................14 g | Calcium: ...................197 mg |
| Protein:...........................21 g | Saturated fat: ..............5 g | Magnesium: ...................55 mg |
| Carbohydrate: ...............50 g | Omega-3 fatty acids:...0.09 g | Potassium: ...................542 mg |
| Sugars: ...........................2 g | Omega-6 fatty acids: ..0.85 g | Sodium: ...................580 mg |
| Fiber (total):...................5 g | Cholesterol: ...................32 mg | Iron: ...................5 mg |
| Vitamin C: ...................9 mg | Vitamin A: ...................79 RE | Zinc:...................4 mg |

Diabetic exchanges: 1 serving equals 3¼ starch exchanges, 2 medium-fat meat exchanges

# Microwave Rice

*I usually avoid instant rice, but for microwave cooking instant rice is the best kind to use for good results.*

    1 cup instant rice, uncooked
    1 cup water
    1 teaspoon oil, butter, ghee, or milk-free Earth Balance™ margarine
    ¼ teaspoon salt

Mix all the ingredients in a 1 quart or larger glass casserole dish. Cover it with its lid and microwave on high until the rice is tender, about 5 to 7 minutes, or for the time directed on the rice box. Let it stand for two to four minutes until the water is all absorbed, fluff it with a fork, and serve it. The oil or butter keeps it from boiling all over your microwave as it cooks. Makes 2 to 4 servings. For one large serving, cut all the amounts in half and cook the rice for 3 to 5 minutes.

**Nutritional Analysis per serving:** 4 servings per recipe

| | | |
|---|---|---|
| Calories: ...................92 | Total fat:.....................1 g | Calcium: ...................7 mg |
| Protein:...........................2 g | Saturated fat:..............0 g | Magnesium:...................4 mg |
| Carbohydrate:...............18 g | Omega-3 fatty acids:...0.11 g | Potassium: ...................3 mg |
| Sugars: ...........................0 g | Omega-6 fatty acids: ..0.26 g | Sodium:...................149 mg |
| Fiber (total): ...................1 g | Cholesterol: ...................0 mg | Iron:...................1 mg |
| Vitamin C:...................0 mg | Vitamin A: ...................0 RE | Zinc:...................0 mg |

Diabetic exchanges: 1 serving equals 1 starch exchange, ¼ fat exchange

# Microwave Mashed Potatoes

2 potatoes (about ¾ of a pound)
⅓ cup water
½ teaspoon salt, divided
1 tablespoon butter, ghee, milk-free Earth Balance™ margarine, or oil
2 tablespoons milk (optional)

Peel the potatoes and cut them into ½ inch cubes. Put them in a glass casserole dish with the water and ¼ teaspoon of the salt. Cover the casserole with its lid or plastic wrap and microwave on high for 4 minutes. Stir the potatoes, re-cover the dish, and microwave another 2 to 5 minutes, or until the potatoes are tender when pierced with a fork. Drain the water, reserving 2 tablespoons if you do not wish to use the milk. Add the remaining ¼ teaspoon of salt, the butter, ghee, margarine or oil, and the milk or reserved potato water and mash the potatoes using a potato masher. Makes 2 to 3 servings.

**Nutritional Analysis per serving:** 3 servings per recipe

| | | | | | |
|---|---|---|---|---|---|
| Calories: ...111 | Total fat: ...4 g | Calcium: ...6 mg |
| Protein: ...2 g | Saturated fat: ...2 g | Magnesium: ...21 mg |
| Carbohydrate: ...18 g | Omega-3 fatty acids: ...0.06 g | Potassium: ...326 mg |
| Sugars: ...1 g | Omega-6 fatty acids: ...0.11 g | Sodium: ...278 mg |
| Fiber (total): ...1 g | Cholesterol: ...10 mg | Iron: ...0 mg |
| Vitamin C: ...11 mg | Vitamin A: ...36 RE | Zinc: ...0 mg |

Diabetic exchanges: 1 serving equals 1 starch exchange, ⅔ fat exchange

# Pantry Microwave Pudding

¼ cup cocoa or carob powder
3 tablespoons cornstarch or 5 tablespoons arrowroot
1 cup non-fat dried milk powder or goat milk powder
½ cup Fruit Sweet™ or honey
2 cups water, divided
1 teaspoon vanilla flavoring (optional)

Stir together the cocoa or carob, arrowroot or cornstarch, and powered milk in a glass casserole. Add about ½ cup of the water and stir it to make a lump-free paste. Add the honey or Fruit Sweet™ and the remaining water and stir. Microwave on high for 7 to 10 minutes, stirring every 2 minutes, or until the pudding is bubbly and thickened. Stir in the vanilla. Pour the pudding into paper cups and refrigerate the servings you will not eat immediately or share them with your friends. Makes 4 to 6 servings.

**Vanilla pudding variation:** Omit the cocoa or carob powder and increase the amount of vanilla to 1 tablespoon.

**Nutritional Analysis per serving:** 6 servings per recipe

| | | | | | |
|---|---|---|---|---|---|
| Calories: ...213 | Total fat: ...1 g | Calcium: ...543 mg |
| Protein: ...15 g | Saturated fat: ...0 g | Magnesium: ...44 mg |
| Carbohydrate: ...36 g | Omega-3 fatty acids: ...0.01 g | Potassium: ...777 mg |
| Sugars: ...30 g | Omega-6 fatty acids: ...0.02 g | Sodium: ...218 mg |
| Fiber (total): ...2 g | Cholesterol: ...8 mg | Iron: ...1 mg |
| Vitamin C: ...3 mg | Vitamin A: ...264 RE | Zinc: ...2 mg |

Diabetic exchanges: 1 serving equals 1 starch/other carbohydrate exchange, 1½ skim milk exchanges

# Microwave "Baked" Apples

1 apple
Dash of cinnamon
2 tablespoons apple juice concentrate, thawed, or 1 tablespoon Fruit Sweet™ or honey

Core the apple while it is still whole using an apple corer or large apple peeler. If you have neither of these utensils, cut the apple in quarters and core it. Sprinkle the cinnamon down the hole in the center of the whole apple or on the cut surfaces of the apple if you quartered it. Put the apple in a glass bowl and drizzle the sweetener over it. Cover it with plastic wrap and microwave it on high for 3 to 4 minutes or until it is tender. Makes one serving.

**Nutritional Analysis per serving:** 1 serving per recipe

| | | |
|---|---|---|
| Calories: 118 | Total fat: 0.1 g | Calcium: 11 mg |
| Protein: 1 g | Saturated fat: 0 g | Magnesium: 12 mg |
| Carbohydrate: 31 g | Omega-3 fatty acids: 0.01 g | Potassium: 261 mg |
| Sugars: 28 g | Omega-6 fatty acids: 0.03 g | Sodium: 12 mg |
| Fiber (total): 3 g | Cholesterol: 0 mg | Iron: 1 mg |
| Vitamin C: 8 mg | Vitamin A: 4 RE | Zinc: 0 mg |

Diabetic exchanges: 1 serving equals 2 fruit exchanges

# Microwave Marshmallow Crisp Rice Cookies

*This recipe probably does not belong in a "healthy" cookbook. However, there is that old saying, "Kids will be kids," and I know you dorm dwellers will want to whip up something like this occasionally! It's better than some other things you might be eating.*

¼ cup butter or ghee from your under-bed pantry
1 10 ounce bag of marshmallows
5 cups crisp rice cereal
Additional butter or ghee

Grease a 13 inch by 9 inch pan or a large sheet of waxed or parchment paper, foil, or (in a pinch) plastic wrap with butter or ghee. Put the ¼ cup butter or ghee in a large 2½ quart or larger bowl or casserole dish and microwave it on high for 1 to 2 minutes or until it is melted. Add the marshmallows to the bowl and microwave on high for 1 to 3 minutes, stirring every minute, until the marshmallows are melted. Stir the rice cereal into the marshmallows until completely mixed. Thoroughly grease your hands with butter or ghee. Use your hands to spread and press the cereal mixture in the prepared pan or on the prepared paper, foil, or plastic wrap. Refrigerate the cereal mixture until chilled. Then cut it into squares with a buttered knife. Makes about 24 cookies.

**Nutritional Analysis per serving:** 24 1-cookie servings per recipe

| | | |
|---|---|---|
| Calories: 78 | Total fat: 2 g | Calcium: 2 mg |
| Protein: 1 g | Saturated fat: 1 g | Magnesium: 3 mg |
| Carbohydrate: 15 g | Omega-3 fatty acids: 0.03 g | Potassium: 6 mg |
| Sugars: 7 g | Omega-6 fatty acids: 0.05 g | Sodium: 76 mg |
| Fiber (total): 0 g | Cholesterol: 5 mg | Iron: 0 mg |
| Vitamin C: 3 mg | Vitamin A: 95 RE | Zinc: 0 mg |

Diabetic exchanges: 1 serving equals ¾ starch/other carbohydrate exchange, ⅓ fat exchange

# Other Dorm-Room Compatible Recipes

## Breakfast ideas:

**Banana Breakfast Smoothie**, page 108 or **Berry-Orange Breakfast Smoothie**, page 109. These are great if you have some yogurt and frozen fruit in your fridge. You will also need a hand blender.

**On the Go Smoothie**, page 108. All you need for this one is a straw and a fridge to store yogurt. Just shake or stir a carton of yogurt until it's liquid, put in a straw, and sip it on the way to class.

**Microwave-method Bacon**, page 122. Be sure you have lots of paper towel on hand for this.

Healthy varieties of cold breakfast cereal or **Homemade Granola**, page 109. Make this granola when you have access to an oven, or if you ask, maybe your mom will make you a batch and send it to you.

## Lunch and Dinner ideas:

**Macaroni and Cheese** made with natural cheese, page 170

**Sandwiches** of many kinds. Make them with nut butters and jelly, deli meats, cheese, and vegetables.

**Vegetables** of all kinds can be cooked in a microwave oven. See the chapter called "A Vegetable Primer," pages 182 to 203.

## Snacks and Beverages:

**Pantry Microwave Cocoa**, page 295

**Coffee Without the Pot**, page 293

GORP, page 291.

**Cottage Cheese Dip**, page 292, with fresh vegetables. You will need a hand blender for this recipe.

# Breads

Bread is the staff of life, the most basic of all foods. We pray, "Give us this day our daily bread." Without bread, a meal or a day does not seem complete. The aroma of muffins or yeast bread baking will make your house or apartment seem like a home. Because wheat allergies are common, bread is a food that people with food allergies may find challenging to replace in their diets. Some white spelt recipes, which make very "normal" appearing and tasting baked goods, are found among the recipes in this chapter. If you want more recipes, such as for crackers, tortillas, or non-yeast breads, or need recipes made with other grains such as kamut, rye, barley, oats, rice, millet, milo, teff, amaranth, quinoa, or buckwheat, see *The Ultimate Food Allergy Cookbook and Survival Guide* as described on the last page of this book.

Grains are an important part of a nutritious diet. They supply complex carbohydrates, vitamins, and minerals. Whole grains also supply fiber which is important for maintaining regularity. The "kids" in our family are not that fond of whole grains, so only some of the recipes in this chapter include whole grains.

This chapter contains recipes for both yeast and non-yeast breads. Non-yeast breads are called "quick breads" because they are quick and easy to make. The "quick breads" category also includes muffins and biscuits. The procedure to use to make quick breads, cookies, and the cakes in this book is this: first stir the dry ingredients together in a large bowl. Mix the liquid ingredients in another bowl or in the cup you used to measure them. Before the oil and water or other liquids can separate, quickly stir them into the dry ingredients until they are just mixed. It is better to undermix than overmix. If you undermix, small floury spots will moisten up in baking. If you overmix, you will "use up" the leavening power of the baking powder or baking soda and acid ingredient during mixing rather than having this power act in the oven where the leavening should cause your bread to rise.

As soon as the ingredients are mixed, quickly put the batter into a prepared pan and slide it into a preheated oven. Bake your bread for the shortest time specified in the recipe. Then look at it. Is it beginning to brown? Is the bread beginning to pull away from the sides of the pans slightly? If you think your bread might be done, stick a toothpick into the center of the loaf or the center of a muffin. If the toothpick comes out dry, the bread is done. If there is moist batter (not dry crumbs) on the toothpick, bake the bread for another five to ten minutes and then test it with a toothpick again. When the bread, muffins, or biscuits are done, remove them from the pan immediately and put them on a cooling rack. Some cookies, cakes, and sweet breads should be cooled in the pan for the time directed in the recipe before removing them to a cooking rack. If you can stand to wait, cool bread completely before slicing it.

Making yeast breads by hand is a very rewarding experience. As you knead the dough, your frustrations and anxieties will melt away. Try it. You'll like it! Making yeast bread is not that hard to do nor is it especially time consuming. You will have to be home for a few hours to tend the bread intermittently, but the actual total amount of time you spend working on the bread will be less than an hour.

Making homemade bread is like yeast farming. (Here is another lesson in microbiology!) To make good bread, you must keep the yeast happy so it will produce the gas that causes the bread to rise, and you must develop the dough so it can trap this gas. The yeast needs be fed just a little food (the sweetener in most recipes) and must be kept at the right temperature to grow and reproduce optimally. Use the right temperature of liquid to dissolve the yeast. For active dry yeast or quick-rise yeast dissolved directly into liquid, the temperature of your liquid ingredients should be between 105°F and 115°F. After the dough is made, keep the yeast happy by holding the dough at a temperature of 85°F to 90°F while it is rising. It is worthwhile to invest in a yeast thermometer so you can check these temperatures.

The procedure for making yeast breads is this: warm your liquid ingredients to between 105°F and 115°F. In a large bowl, stir togther the water or milk and the sweetener. Sprinkle the yeast over the surface of the liquid. Let it sit for a minute, and then stir the yeast in. Allow the liquid and yeast to stand for about 10 minutes; the liquid should start to become bubbly. (This is called "proofing" the yeast because it proves that it is still alive). Stir in the salt, oil, and other ingredients which the recipe specifies adding at this point. Then, using a spoon, beat in about half of the flour. Add the remaining flour, mixing with a spoon and then your hands, until a soft dough forms. Turn the dough out onto a floured surface and knead in enough of the remaining flour to produce a smooth, non-sticky, elastic dough. The amount of flour needed is given as a range in the recipe. How much you need may vary each time depending on the weather (in damp weather the flour will have absorbed moisture), the batch of flour, and other factors. Just learn what the right texture of the dough is, maybe from your mom, and try to get that "feel" each time.

To properly trap the gas produced by the yeast, you must develop the gluten in the flour. Gluten is a protein in wheat and some of the other grain flours that forms long strands and sheets when the dough is kneaded. These elastic sheets then trap the gas produced by the yeast and cause the bread to rise. Adequate kneading is important in developing the gluten. Knead the bread by pushing on it with the heels of your hands.

Then fold it over, turn it, and push on it again. Repeat this process over and over for at least 10 minutes, or until the dough becomes smooth and elastic. When you poke it with your finger, it should spring back again rather than leaving a finger hole.

After kneading the bread dough, let it rise once in a warm place, about 85°F to 90°F. After the dough has risen to about double its original size, punch it down by plunging your fist into the middle of it. Shape the loaf of bread or buns and put them in an oiled pan or on an oiled baking sheet to rise again in a warm place. If you have a gas oven, the pilot light will keep the inside of the oven at the right temperature for yeast bread to rise. If you have an electric oven, turn it on to 350°F while you are kneading your dough. After it has heated, turn it off and open the door for 8 to 10 minutes. Put a yeast thermometer in the oven, close the door, and check the temperature after a few minutes. If it's too hot, open the oven for another minute or two. The oven should hold its cozy temperature long enough for your bread dough to rise both initially and after being shaped into a loaf or rolls.

Remove the bread from its rising place in the oven when it has almost doubled in volume and is ready to bake. Preheat your oven, put the bread back in, and bake it for the time specified in the recipe. To tell when your yeast bread is done, see if it is nicely browned, has pulled away from the sides of the pan, and sounds hollow when tapped on the bottom of the loaf. When it is done, remove it from the pan immediately and put it on a wire rack to cool. If you can stand to wait to eat your bread, it's best to let it cool completely before slicing it.

In this book, the kitchen equipment lists stick to the bare essentials, and a bread machine may seem like quite a luxury for an apartment kitchen. However, with a bread machine you can make all of your own bread with about 5 minutes worth of work for each loaf. You can make your own pizza dough with the same minimal effort. This is a good appliance to ask Santa to bring you! To make the recipes in this book with a bread machine, just add the ingredients to your machine in the amounts listed (using the smaller amount for the flour) and start the machine. After about 5 or 10 minutes of kneading, adjust the consistency of the dough by adding more flour, 1 tablespoon at a time, or more water one teaspoon at a time. Read the instruction booklet for your machine before starting to use it and add the ingredients to the bread pan in the order it specifies. For more about baking with a bread machine, see page 252. For more bread recipes, see *Easy Breadmaking for Special Diets* as described on the last page of this book.

Baking bread is the crowning touch to becoming a good cook. You can do it! Here are the recipes you need.

# Quick Breads

These are quick, easy and a great addition to any meal. Some of the recipes found here, such as the banana bread and date nut bread, are great for breakfast but can even double as desserts.

## Basic Muffins

2¼ cups all purpose or unbleached flour
3 teaspoons baking powder
¼ teaspoon salt (optional)
1 cup apple juice concentrate, thawed
⅓ cup oil
Optional additional ingredients (choose one):
    1 cup fresh or solidly frozen blueberries
    ⅔ cup peeled diced apple or pear
    ⅔ cup diced dried fruit, such as apricots, dates, apples, peaches, or papaya
    ⅔ cups raisins
    ⅔ cup chopped nuts
    ⅓ cup nuts plus ⅓ cup diced dried fruit or raisins
    2 tablespoons grated lemon or orange peel (Use just the outer colored zest).

Preheat your oven to 350°F. Oil 12 to 15 muffin cups or line them with paper liners. In a large bowl, mix together the flour, baking powder, and salt. In a separate bowl or cup, combine the apple juice and oil. Stir the liquid ingredients into the dry ingredients until just mixed. Gently fold in the optional additional ingredients. Fill the muffin cups about ⅔ full with the batter. Bake for 18 to 22 minutes. Remove the muffins from the pan and allow them to cool on a wire rack. Makes 12 to 15 muffins.

**Nutritional Analysis per serving:** 14 servings per recipe

| | | |
|---|---|---|
| Calories: 161 | Total fat: 5 g | Calcium: 80 mg |
| Protein: 2 g | Saturated fat: 0 g | Magnesium: 9 mg |
| Carbohydrate: 26 g | Omega-3 fatty acids: 0.49 g | Potassium: 114 mg |
| Sugars: 8 g | Omega-6 fatty acids: 1.16 g | Sodium: 125 mg |
| Fiber (total): 1 g | Cholesterol: 0 mg | Iron: 1 mg |
| Vitamin C: 0 mg | Vitamin A: 0 RE | Zinc: 0 mg |

Diabetic exchanges: 1 serving equals 1 starch exchange, ½ fruit exchange, 1 fat exchange

# Basic Whole Wheat Muffins

2¼ cups whole wheat flour or white whole wheat flour (See "Sources," page 323).
3 teaspoons baking powder
¼ teaspoon salt (optional)
1 cup apple juice concentrate, thawed
⅓ cup oil
Optional additional ingredients (choose one):
    1 cup fresh or solidly frozen blueberries
    ⅔ cup peeled diced apple or pear
    ⅔ cup diced dried fruit, such as apricots, dates, apples, peaches, or papaya
    ⅔ cups raisins
    ⅔ cup chopped nuts
    ⅓ cup nuts plus ⅓ cup diced dried fruit or raisins
    2 tablespoons grated lemon or orange peel (Use just the outer colored zest).

Preheat your oven to 350°F. Oil 10 to 14 muffin cups or line them with paper liners. In a large bowl, mix together the flour, baking powder, and salt. In a separate bowl or cup, combine the apple juice and oil. Stir the liquid ingredients into the dry ingredients until just mixed. Gently fold in the optional additional ingredients. Fill the muffin cups about ⅔ full with the batter. Bake for 20 to 24 minutes. Remove the muffins from the pan and allow them to cool on a wire rack. Makes 10 to 14 muffins.

**Nutritional Analysis per serving:** 14 servings per recipe

| | | |
|---|---|---|
| Calories: 165 | Total fat: 6 g | Calcium: 77 mg |
| Protein: 4 g | Saturated fat: 0 g | Magnesium: 4 mg |
| Carbohydrate: 24 g | Omega-3 fatty acids: 0.49 g | Potassium: 90 mg |
| Sugars: 9 g | Omega-6 fatty acids: 1.07 g | Sodium: 125 mg |
| Fiber (total): 3 g | Cholesterol: 0 mg | Iron: 1 mg |
| Vitamin C: 0 mg | Vitamin A: 0 RE | Zinc: 0 mg |

Diabetic exchanges: 1 serving equals 1 starch exchange, ½ fruit exchange, 1 fat exchange

# Basic White Spelt Muffins

*These muffins are so close to "normal" that your guests will never realize they aren't eating wheat.*

2¾ cups white spelt flour
3 teaspoons baking powder*
¼ teaspoon salt (optional)
⅓ cup oil
1 cup apple juice concentrate, thawed
Optional additional ingredients (choose one):
    1 cup fresh or solidly frozen blueberries
    ⅔ cup peeled diced apple or pear
    ⅔ cup diced dried fruit, such as apricots, dates, apples, peaches, or papaya
    ⅔ cups raisins
    ⅔ cup chopped nuts
    ⅓ cup nuts plus ⅓ cup diced dried fruit or raisins
    2 tablespoons grated lemon or orange peel (Use just the outer colored zest).

Preheat the oven to 350°F. Oil 13 to 15 muffin cups or line them with paper liners. In a large bowl, mix together the flour, baking powder, and salt. In a separate bowl or cup, combine the apple juice and oil. Stir the liquid ingredients into the dry ingredients until just mixed. Gently fold in the optional additional ingredients. Fill the muffin cups about ⅔ full with the batter. Bake for 20 to 24 minutes. Remove the muffins from the pan and allow them to cool on a wire rack. Makes 13 to 15 muffins.

    * Note on baking powder: Use Featherweight™ brand baking powder if you are allergic to corn. It contains potato starch instead of cornstarch.

**Nutritional Analysis per serving:** 14 servings per recipe

| | | |
|---|---|---|
| Calories: .......................158 | Total fat: ...........................6 g | Calcium: ...............................77 mg |
| Protein: ...........................3 g | Saturated fat: ...............0 g | Magnesium: ......................4 mg |
| Carbohydrate: ..............25 g | Omega-3 fatty acids: ....0.49 g | Potassium: ......................90 mg |
| Sugars: ..........................9 g | Omega-6 fatty acids: ......1.07 g | Sodium: ...........................125 mg |
| Fiber (total): ...................1 g | Cholesterol: ......................0 mg | Iron: ...........................................1 mg |
| Vitamin C: ....................0 mg | Vitamin A: ........................0 RE | Zinc: ............................................0 mg |

Diabetic exchanges: 1 serving equals 1 starch exchange, ½ fruit exchange, 1 fat exchange

# Basic Whole Spelt Muffins

*If you'd like to make wheat-free muffins using any of fourteen additional non-wheat flours besides spelt, see pages 159 to 164 of* The Ultimate Food Allergy Cookbook and Survival Guide, *which is described on the last page of this book.*

2½ cups whole spelt flour
3 teaspoons baking powder*
¼ teaspoon salt (optional)
⅓ cup oil
1 cup apple juice concentrate, thawed
Optional additional ingredients (choose one):
    1 cup fresh or solidly frozen blueberries
    ⅔ cup peeled diced apple or pear

⅔ cup diced dried fruit, such as apricots, dates, apples, peaches, or papaya
⅔ cups raisins
⅔ cup chopped nuts
⅓ cup nuts plus ⅓ cup diced dried fruit or raisins
2 tablespoons grated lemon or orange peel (Use just the outer colored zest).

Preheat the oven to 350°F. Oil 11 to 14 muffin cups or line them with paper liners. In a large bowl, mix together the flour, baking powder, and salt. In a separate bowl or cup, combine the apple juice and oil. Stir the liquid ingredients into the dry ingredients until just mixed. Gently fold in the optional additional ingredients. Fill the muffin cups about ⅔ full with the batter. Bake for 20 to 25 minutes. Remove the muffins from the pan and allow them to cool on a wire rack. Makes 11 to 14 muffins.

\* Note on baking powder: Use Featherweight™ brand baking powder if you are allergic to corn. It contains potato starch instead of cornstarch.

**Nutritional Analysis per serving:** 14 servings per recipe

| | | |
|---|---|---|
| Calories: 151 | Total fat: 6 g | Calcium: 77 mg |
| Protein: 3 g | Saturated fat: 0 g | Magnesium: 4 mg |
| Carbohydrate: 26 g | Omega-3 fatty acids: 0.49 g | Potassium: 197 mg |
| Sugars: 8 g | Omega-6 fatty acids: 1.07 g | Sodium: 125 mg |
| Fiber (total): 4 g | Cholesterol: 0 mg | Iron: 1 mg |
| Vitamin C: 0 mg | Vitamin A: 0 RE | Zinc: 0 mg |

Diabetic exchanges: 1 serving equals 1 starch exchange, ½ fruit exchange, 1 fat exchange

# Buttermilk Biscuits

2 cups all purpose or unbleached flour
2 teaspoons baking powder
½ teaspoon baking soda
½ teaspoon salt
5 tablespoons unsalted butter
¾ cup buttermilk

Preheat your oven to 450°F. In a large bowl, stir together the flour, baking powder, baking soda, and salt. Cut the butter into chunks. (It should be cold or just slightly warmer than refrigerator temperature). Put the butter into the bowl with the flour mixture and combine it with the flour by pressing a pastry cutter through it repeatedly. Keep working with the pastry cutter until the flour and butter are combined into very coarse crumbs. Stir in the buttermilk until the dough forms a ball. Turn the dough out onto a lightly floured board and knead it several times. Pat or roll it to ½ inch thickness. Cut it into rounds with a floured biscuit cutter or drinking glass. Put the biscuits on an ungreased baking sheet and bake them for 10 to 15 minutes or until they begin to turn brown. Makes 10 to 12 biscuits.

**Nutritional Analysis per serving:** 12 servings per recipe

| | | |
|---|---|---|
| Calories: 125 | Total fat: 5 g | Calcium: 114 mg |
| Protein: 3 g | Saturated fat: 3 g | Magnesium: 7 mg |
| Carbohydrate: 17 g | Omega-3 fatty acids: 0.08 g | Potassium: 47 mg |
| Sugars: 1 g | Omega-6 fatty acids: 0.19 g | Sodium: 266 mg |
| Fiber (total): 1 g | Cholesterol: 13 mg | Iron: 1 mg |
| Vitamin C: 0 mg | Vitamin A: 46 RE | Zinc: 0 mg |

Diabetic exchanges: 1 serving equals 1 starch exchange, 1 fat exchange

# Basic Biscuits

2½ cups all purpose or unbleached flour
3 teaspoons baking powder
½ teaspoon salt
⅓ cup oil
⅔ cup water, skim milk, or buttermilk

Preheat your oven to 450°F. In a large bowl, stir together the flour, baking powder, and salt. Mix the oil with the water, milk, or buttermilk and stir these liquid ingredients into the flour mixture until the dough forms a ball. Turn the dough out onto a lightly floured board and knead it several times. Pat or roll it to ½ inch thickness. Cut it into rounds with a floured biscuit cutter or drinking glass. Put the biscuits on an ungreased baking sheet and bake them for 10 to 15 minutes or until they begin to turn brown. Makes 10 to 14 biscuits.

**Nutritional Analysis per serving:** 14 servings per recipe

| | | |
|---|---|---|
| Calories: ........................128 | Total fat: ...........................5 g | Calcium: ...........................76 mg |
| Protein: ................................2 g | Saturated fat: ...............0 g | Magnesium: .......................5 mg |
| Carbohydrate: ..................17 g | Omega-3 fatty acids:...0.49 g | Potassium: .......................24 mg |
| Sugars: .................................0 g | Omega-6 fatty acids:....1.14 g | Sodium: ...........................162 mg |
| Fiber (total): .......................1 g | Cholesterol: ....................0 mg | Iron: .....................................1 mg |
| Vitamin C: .......................0 mg | Vitamin A: .......................0 RE | Zinc: .....................................0 mg |

Diabetic exchanges: 1 serving equals 1 starch exchange, 1 fat exchange

# Wheat-free Biscuits

*If you want recipes for wheat-free biscuits made with a variety of flours, see* The Ultimate Food Allergy Cookbook and Survival Guide *as described on the last page of this book.*

3 cups white spelt flour
3 teaspoons baking powder*
½ teaspoon salt
⅓ cup oil
⅔ cup water, skim milk, or buttermilk

Preheat your oven to 450°F. In a large bowl, stir together the flour, baking powder, and salt. Mix the oil with the water, milk, or buttermilk and stir these liquid ingredients into the flour mixture until the dough forms a ball. Turn the dough out onto a lightly floured board and knead it several times. Pat or roll it to ½ inch thickness. Cut it into rounds with a floured biscuit cutter or drinking glass. Put the biscuits on an ungreased baking sheet and bake them for 10 to 15 minutes or until they begin to turn brown. Makes 10 to 15 biscuits.

* Note on baking powder: Use Featherweight™ brand baking powder if you are allergic to corn. It contains potato starch instead of cornstarch.

**Nutritional Analysis per serving:** 15 servings per recipe

| | | |
|---|---|---|
| Calories: ........................123 | Total fat: ...........................5 g | Calcium: ...........................68 mg |
| Protein: ................................3 g | Saturated fat: ...............0 g | Magnesium: .......................1 mg |
| Carbohydrate: ..................17 g | Omega-3 fatty acids:...0.45 g | Potassium: .........................1 mg |
| Sugars: .................................1 g | Omega-6 fatty acids:....0.98 g | Sodium: ...........................151 mg |
| Fiber (total): .......................1 g | Cholesterol: ....................0 mg | Iron: .....................................1 mg |
| Vitamin C: .......................0 mg | Vitamin A: .......................0 RE | Zinc: .....................................0 mg |

Diabetic exchanges: 1 serving equals 1 starch exchange, 1 fat exchange

# Corn Bread

1 cup all purpose or unbleached flour or 1¼ cups white spelt flour
¾ cup yellow cornmeal
2 teaspoons baking powder
½ teaspoon salt
1 large egg, slightly beaten
¼ cup oil
¼ cup water or milk
¾ cup Fruit Sweet™ or honey

Preheat your oven to 425°F. Oil and flour an 8 inch by 8 inch baking pan. (Use white spelt flour both to flour the pan and to make the batter for wheat-free corn bread). Stir together the flour, corn meal, baking powder, and salt in a large bowl. Mix the water or milk with the sweetener until thoroughly mixed; stir in the oil and slightly beaten egg. Add the liquid ingredients to the dry ingredients and stir until the dry ingredients are just moistened. (Don't worry if there are still a few lumps or floury spots in the batter). Pour the batter into the pan and pop it into the oven. Bake it for 20 to 27 minutes or until it is golden brown and a toothpick inserted in the center of the pan comes out dry. Test the cornbread with the toothpick at the minimum baking time or when it is just beginning to brown. Overcooking the cornbread may make it dry. When it is done, remove it from the oven. Cut it into 9 to 12 squares and serve it from the pan. Makes 9 to 12 servings.

**Nutritional Analysis per serving:** 12 servings per recipe

| | | |
|---|---|---|
| Calories: ...........................76 | Total fat:...............................1 g | Calcium:............................90 mg |
| Protein: ...............................2 g | Saturated fat: ...............0 g | Magnesium:......................3 mg |
| Carbohydrate:..................16 g | Omega-3 fatty acids:...0.01 g | Potassium: .......................17 mg |
| Sugars: ............................7 g | Omega-6 fatty acids: ..0.12 g | Sodium: ...........................166 mg |
| Fiber (total):......................1 g | Cholesterol: .....................18 mg | Iron:..................................1 mg |
| Vitamin C:.......................0 mg | Vitamin A: ..........................7 RE | Zinc:..................................0 mg |

Diabetic exchanges: 1 serving equals 1 starch/other carbohydrate exchange

# Banana Bread

*For banana bread made with other flours, such as kamut, barley, amaranth, milo, mil-let, and whole spelt, see* The Ultimate Food Allergy Cookbook and Survival Guide *which is described on the last page of this book.*

2 cups all purpose or unbleached flour or 2¼ cups white spelt flour
½ cup date sugar
2½ teaspoons baking powder*
½ teaspoon salt
1½ teaspoons cinnamon
¼ teaspoon cloves
¼ teaspoon allspice
¼ cup oil
2 cups pureed or thoroughly mashed ripe bananas
½ teaspoon vanilla extract (optional)

Preheat your oven to 350°F. Oil and flour an 8 inch by 4 inch loaf pan. (Flour the pan with white spelt flour if you are making wheat-free spelt banana bread). In a large bowl, stir together the flour, date sugar, baking powder, salt and spices. Throughly mash or puree the bananas with a hand blender and stir the bananas together with the oil and vanilla. Stir the banana mixture into the flour mixture until they are just combined. Spread the batter into the prepared pan and bake the bread for 50 to 60 minutes or until it is brown. Insert a toothpick into the center of the loaf. If it comes out dry, the bread is done. Cool the bread in the pan for 10 minutes; then turn it out onto a cooling rack. Let it cool completely before slicing it. If you wish to, you can slice this bread and freeze the slices. When you want to eat it, toast the frozen slices. Makes 10 to 12 servings.

* Note on baking powder: Use Featherweight™ brand baking powder if you are allergic to corn. It contains potato starch instead of cornstarch.

**Nutritional Analysis per serving:** 12 servings per recipe

| | | |
|---|---|---|
| Calories: ...164 | Total fat:...5 g | Calcium: ...78 mg |
| Protein:...3 g | Saturated fat:...0 g | Magnesium:...17 mg |
| Carbohydrate: ...28 g | Omega-3 fatty acids:...0.44 g | Potassium: ...202 mg |
| Sugars: ...10 g | Omega-6 fatty acids: ...1.03 g | Sodium:...174 mg |
| Fiber (total):...2 g | Cholesterol: ...0 mg | Iron:...1 mg |
| Vitamin C:...3 mg | Vitamin A:...3 RE | Zinc:...0 mg |

Diabetic exchanges: 1 serving equals 1 starch exchange, ⅔ fruit exchange, 1 fat exchange

# Applesauce Bread

2 cups all purpose or unbleached or 2⅜ cups (2¼ cups plus 2 tablespoons) white spelt flour
1 teaspoon baking powder*
½ teaspoon baking soda
½ teaspoon salt
1 teaspoon cinnamon
¼ cup oil
½ apple juice concentrate, thawed
¾ cup unsweetened applesauce
½ cup raisins (optional)

Preheat your oven to 350°F. Oil and flour an 8 inch by 4 inch loaf pan. (Flour the pan with white spelt flour if you are making wheat-free spelt bread). In a large bowl, stir together the flour, baking powder, baking soda, salt, and cinnamon. Stir together the oil, apple juice, and applesauce in a separate bowl of the measuring cup with which you measured them. Stir the apple mixture into the flour mixture until they are just combined. Gently fold in the raisins. Spread the batter into the prepared pan and bake the bread for 50 to 60 minutes or until it is brown. Insert a toothpick into the center of the loaf. If it comes out dry, the bread is done. Cool the bread in the pan for 10 minutes; then turn it out onto a cooling rack. Let it cool completely before slicing it. Makes 10 to 12 servings.

* Note on baking powder: Use Featherweight™ brand baking powder if you are allergic to corn. It contains potato starch instead of cornstarch.

**Nutritional Analysis per serving:** 12 servings per recipe

| | | |
|---|---|---|
| Calories: ...142 | Total fat:...5 g | Calcium: ...34 mg |
| Protein:...2 g | Saturated fat:...0 g | Magnesium:...7 mg |
| Carbohydrate:...23 g | Omega-3 fatty acids:...0.43 g | Potassium: ...86 mg |
| Sugars:...6 g | Omega-6 fatty acids: ...1.02 g | Sodium:...184 mg |
| Fiber (total):...1 g | Cholesterol: ...0 mg | Iron:...1 mg |
| Vitamin C: ...3 mg | Vitamin A: ...0 RE | Zinc:...0 mg |

Diabetic exchanges: 1 serving equals 1 starch exchange, ⅓ fruit exchange, 1 fat exchange

# Date Nut Bread

2 cups all purpose or unbleached or 2¼ cups whole spelt or white spelt flour
½ cup date sugar
3 teaspoons baking powder*
½ teaspoon salt
⅜ cup oil
¾ cup apple juice concentrate, thawed
¾ cup chopped dates
¾ cup chopped walnuts or other nuts

Preheat your oven to 350°F. Oil and flour an 8 inch by 4 inch loaf pan. (Flour the pan with spelt flour if you are making wheat-free spelt bread). In a large bowl, stir together the flour, date sugar, baking powder, and salt. Combine the apple juice concentrate with the oil and stir them into the flour mixture until they are just combined. Gently fold in the dates and nuts. Pour the batter into the prepared pan and bake the bread for 50 to 60 minutes or until it is brown. Insert a toothpick into the center of the loaf. If it comes out dry, the bread is done. Cool the bread in the pan for 10 minutes; then turn it out onto a cooling rack. Let it cool completely before slicing it. Makes 10 to 12 servings.

* Note on baking powder: Use Featherweight™ brand baking powder if you are allergic to corn. It contains potato starch instead of cornstarch.

**Nutritional Analysis per serving:** 12 servings per recipe

| | | |
|---|---|---|
| Calories: ........................258 | Total fat: ...........................12 g | Calcium: ............................104 mg |
| Protein: .................................4 g | Saturated fat: ..................1 g | Magnesium: .....................25 mg |
| Carbohydrate: ................36 g | Omega-3 fatty acids: ....1.32 g | Potassium: ....................237 mg |
| Sugars: ...........................18 g | Omega-6 fatty acids:...4.34 g | Sodium:...........................193 mg |
| Fiber (total):.......................2 g | Cholesterol: ......................0 mg | Iron:.......................................2 mg |
| Vitamin C:..........................0 mg | Vitamin A: ...........................1 RE | Zinc:......................................0 mg |

Diabetic exchanges: 1 serving equals 1 starch exchange, ¼ lean meat exchange, 1¼ fruit exchanges, 2 fat exchanges

# Yeast Breads

Beginning cooks usually don't have all the latest in kitchen appliances, but at our house a bread machine is something we can't live without! The recipes that follow can be made with a bread machine more easily than by hand. Read your machine's instruction booklet and add the ingredients to the pan in the order listed in the booklet. For most machines that order is first water or milk, followed by salt, oil or other fat, spices, flour and yeast. For some older machines, the ingredients are added in reverse order. Add the smaller amount listed for the flour in the recipes below. After 5 to 10 minutes of kneading, reach into the machine and touch the dough. It should be soft and somewhat tacky but not sticky. Adjust the consistency of the dough by adding more flour, 1 tablespoon at a time, or more water one teaspoon at a time. For more about baking with a bread machine and more bread recipes made with a wide variety of grains, see *Easy Breadmaking for Special Diets* as described on the last page of this book. For more about making yeast breads by hand, see pages 242 to 243 at the beginning of this chapter.

## White Bread

      1 cup water or skim or whole milk
      2 tablespoons Fruit Sweet™ or honey
      1¾ teaspoons active dry or quick-rise yeast
      1 tablespoon oil
      ½ tablespoon liquid lecithin or additional oil
      1 teapoon salt
      3 to 3¼ cups bread flour

Heat the milk or water to between 105°F and 115°F. (Use a yeast thermometer to check the temperature). Stir in the Fruit Sweet™ or honey thoroughly. Sprinkle the yeast over the surface of the liquid and let it sit to dissolve for a minute or two; then stir it into the liquid. Let the yeast mixture stand for 10 to 15 minutes. (It should be starting to bubble after that amount of time). Stir in the oil, lecithin, and salt. Stir in about half of the flour, then stir in as much of the rest of the flour as you can adding about a half cup at a time. Turn the dough out onto a floured board and knead in enough of the remaining flour to form a smooth elastic dough. Knead the dough for 10 minutes. Wash out the mixing bowl and dry it. Rub the inside of the bowl with oil. Put the ball of dough into the bowl and turn it over so the top side of the dough is oiled. Cover it with plastic wrap and a towel and let it rise in a warm place until it is doubled in volume, which should take about 45 minutes to one hour. (See page 243 for how to make your oven into a cozy rising spot for bread dough). Punch down the dough by plunging your fist into it. Oil the inside of a loaf pan. Form the bread dough into a log shape and put it into the pan. Let it rise in a warm place again until it has doubled in volume, or for about 40 to 45 minutes. If it is rising in your oven, remove it from the oven. Preheat the oven to 375°F. Bake the bread for 40 to 45 minutes or until it is nicely browned, has pulled away from the sides of the pan, and sounds hollow when tapped on the bottom of the loaf. Remove the bread from the pan immediately after taking it from the oven. Allow it to cool on a wire rack before slicing it. Makes 15 to 18 servings.

**Nutritional Analysis per serving:** 18 servings per recipe

| | | | | | |
|---|---|---|---|---|---|
| Calories: | 90 | Total fat: | 1 g | Calcium: | 7 mg |
| Protein: | 2 g | Saturated fat: | 0 g | Magnesium: | 5 mg |
| Carbohydrate: | 17 g | Omega-3 fatty acids: | 0.11 g | Potassium: | 30 mg |
| Sugars: | 1 g | Omega-6 fatty acids: | 0.31 g | Sodium: | 131 mg |
| Fiber (total): | 1 g | Cholesterol: | 0 mg | Iron: | 1 mg |
| Vitamin C: | 0 mg | Vitamin A: | 0 RE | Zinc: | 0 mg |

Diabetic exchanges: 1 serving equals 1 starch exchange, ¼ fat exchange

# White Spelt Bread

¾ cup water
3 tablespoons apple juice concentrate, thawed
1¾ teaspoons active dry or quick-rise yeast
2½ teaspoons oil
1 teaspoon liquid lecithin or additional oil
¾ teaspoon salt
2⅞ to 3⅛ cups Purity Foods™ white spelt flour

Combine the water and apple juice concentrate and heat them to between 105°F and 115°F. (Use a yeast thermometer to check the temperature). Sprinkle the yeast over the surface of the liquid and let it sit to dissolve for a minute or two; then stir it into the liquid. Let the yeast mixture stand for 10 to 15 minutes. (It should be starting to bubble after that amount of time). Stir in the oil, lecithin, and salt. Stir in about half of the flour, then stir in as much of the rest of the flour as you can adding about a half cup at a time. Turn the dough out onto a floured board and knead in enough of the remaining flour to form a smooth elastic dough. Knead the dough for 10 minutes. Wash out the mixing bowl and dry it. Rub the inside of the bowl with oil. Put the ball of dough into the bowl and turn it over so the top side of the dough is oiled. Cover it with plastic wrap and a towel and let it rise in a warm place until it is doubled in volume, which should take about 45 minutes to one hour. (See page 243 for how to make your oven into a cozy rising spot for bread dough). Punch down the dough by plunging your fist into it. Oil the inside of a loaf pan. Spelt bread tends to stick to the pan, so you may also wish to line the pan with waxed or parchment paper. Form the bread dough into a log shape and put it into the pan. Let it rise in a warm place again until it has doubled in volume, or for about 40 to 45 minutes. If it is rising in your oven, remove it from the oven. Preheat the oven to 375°F. Bake the bread for 40 to 45 minutes or until it is nicely browned, has pulled away from the sides of the pan, and sounds hollow when tapped on the bottom of the loaf. Remove the bread from the pan immediately after taking it from the oven. Allow it to cool on a wire rack before slicing it. Makes 15 to 16 servings.

**Nutritional Analysis per serving:** 16 servings per recipe

| | | | | | |
|---|---|---|---|---|---|
| Calories: | 91 | Total fat: | 2 g | Calcium: | 1 mg |
| Protein: | 3 g | Saturated fat: | 0 g | Magnesium: | 1 mg |
| Carbohydrate: | 17 g | Omega-3 fatty acids: | 0.09 g | Potassium: | 24 mg |
| Sugars: | 2 g | Omega-6 fatty acids: | 0.20 g | Sodium: | 112 mg |
| Fiber (total): | 1 g | Cholesterol: | 0 mg | Iron: | 1 mg |
| Vitamin C: | 0 mg | Vitamin A: | 0 RE | Zinc: | 0 mg |

Diabetic exchanges: 1 serving equals 1 starch exchange, ¼ fat exchange

# Traditional Whole Wheat Bread

1 cup water
¼ cup apple juice concentrate, thawed
2 teaspoons active dry or quick-rise yeast
1½ tablespoons oil
½ tablespoon liquid lecithin or additional oil
1 teaspoon salt
1½ cups whole wheat flour
1¾ to 2 cups bread flour
1 tablespoon vital wheat gluten (optional)

Combine the water and apple juice concentrate and heat them to between 105°F and 115°F. (Use a yeast thermometer to check the temperature). Sprinkle the yeast over the surface of the liquid and let it sit to dissolve for a minute or two; then stir it into the liquid. Let the yeast mixture stand for 10 to 15 minutes. (It should be starting to bubble after that amount of time). Stir in the oil, lecithin, and salt. Stir together the whole wheat flour and vital wheat gluten and stir them into the liquid ingredients. Then stir in as much of the bread flour as you can adding about a half cup at a time. Turn the dough out onto a floured board and knead in enough of the remaining flour to form a smooth elastic dough. Knead the dough for 10 minutes. Wash out the mixing bowl and dry it. Rub the inside of the bowl with oil. Put the ball of dough into the bowl and turn it over so the top side of the dough is oiled. Cover it with plastic wrap and a towel and let it rise in a warm place until it is doubled in volume, which should take about 45 minutes to one hour. (See page 243 for how to make your oven into a cozy rising spot for bread dough). Punch down the dough by plunging your fist into it. Oil the inside of a loaf pan. Form the bread dough into a log shape and put it into the pan. Let it rise in a warm place again until it has doubled in volume, or for about 40 to 45 minutes. If it is rising in your oven, remove it from the oven. Preheat the oven to 375°F. Bake the bread for 40 to 45 minutes or until it is nicely browned, has pulled away from the sides of the pan, and sounds hollow when tapped on the bottom of the loaf. Remove the bread from the pan immediately after taking it from the oven. Allow it to cool on a wire rack before slicing it. Makes 15 to 20 servings.

**Nutritional Analysis per serving:** 20 servings per recipe

| | | |
|---|---|---|
| Calories: ...95 | Total fat: ...2 g | Calcium: ...3 mg |
| Protein: ...3 g | Saturated fat: ...0 g | Magnesium: ...3 mg |
| Carbohydrate: ...17 g | Omega-3 fatty acids: ...0.13 g | Potassium: ...36 mg |
| Sugars: ...2 g | Omega-6 fatty acids: ...0.32 g | Sodium: ...119 mg |
| Fiber (total): ...2 g | Cholesterol: ...0 mg | Iron: ...1 mg |
| Vitamin C: ...0 mg | Vitamin A: ...0 RE | Zinc: ...0 mg |

Diabetic exchanges: 1 serving equals 1 starch exchange, ⅓ fat exchange

# 100% Whole Wheat Bread

*This bread can be very dense. It is best made with a high-quality whole wheat flour such as Arrowhead Mills™ brand. For a lighter color and flavor without skimping on any whole-grain nutrients, use white whole wheat flour from the King Arthur Flour Company. (See "Sources," page 323).*

1⅛ cups (1 cup plus 2 tablespoons) water or skim or whole milk
2 tablespoons Fruit Sweet™ or honey
2 teaspoons active dry or quick-rise yeast
1 large egg at room temperature
1½ tablespoons oil
½ tablespoon liquid lecithin or additional oil
1¼ teaspoons salt
3½ to 3¾ cups whole wheat flour or white whole wheat flour
1½ tablespoons vital wheat gluten

Heat the water or milk to between 105°F and 115°F. (Use a yeast thermometer to check the temperature). Stir in the sweetener thoroughly. Sprinkle the yeast over the surface of the liquid and let it sit to dissolve for a minute or two; then stir it into the liquid. Let the yeast mixture stand for 10 to 15 minutes. (It should be starting to bubble after that amount of time). If you forgot to take the egg out of the refrigerator early, put it in a bowl of warm water while the yeast is "proofing." Then stir the egg, oil, lecithin, and salt into the yeast mixture. Stir together the gluten and about half of the flour and stir them into the liquid ingredients. Then stir in as much of the remaining flour as you can adding about a half cup at a time. Turn the dough out onto a floured board and knead in enough of the remaining flour to form a smooth elastic dough. Knead the dough for 10 minutes. Wash out the mixing bowl and dry it. Rub the inside of the bowl with oil. Put the ball of dough into the bowl and turn it over so the top side of the dough is oiled. Cover it with plastic wrap and a towel and let it rise in a warm place until it is doubled in volume, which should take about 45 minutes to one hour. (See page 243 for how to make your oven into a cozy rising spot for bread dough). Punch down the dough by plunging your fist into it. Oil the inside of a loaf pan. Form the bread dough into a log shape and put it into the pan. Let it rise in a warm place again until it has doubled in volume, or for about 45 to 55 minutes. If it is rising in your oven, remove it from the oven. Preheat the oven to 375°F. Bake the bread for 40 to 45 minutes or until it is nicely browned, has pulled away from the sides of the pan, and sounds hollow when tapped on the bottom of the loaf. Remove the bread from the pan immediately after taking it from the oven. Allow it to cool on a wire rack before slicing it. Makes 15 to 18 servings.

**Nutritional Analysis per serving:** 18 servings per recipe

| | | |
|---|---|---|
| Calories: ......................167 | Total fat:............................3 g | Calcium: ............................55 mg |
| Protein:...............................6 g | Saturated fat:...............0 g | Magnesium: .........................1 mg |
| Carbohydrate:..................31 g | Omega-3 fatty acids:...0.14 g | Potassium:.........................13 mg |
| Sugars: ...........................13 g | Omega-6 fatty acids: ..0.34 g | Sodium:............................171 mg |
| Fiber (total):.....................4 g | Cholesterol: ........................0 mg | Iron: .....................................3 mg |
| Vitamin C:........................0 mg | Vitamin A:..........................5 RE | Zinc:....................................0 mg |

Diabetic exchanges: 1 serving equals 2 starch exchanges, ¼ fat exchange. (Note: Because this bread is so dense, each slice is two starch exchanges).

# Whole Spelt Bread

1 cup water
¼ cup apple juice concentrate, thawed
2¼ teaspoons active dry or quick-rise yeast
1 tablespoon oil
½ tablespoon liquid lecithin or additional oil
¾ teaspoon salt
3⅓ to 3½ cups Purity Foods™ whole spelt flour

Combine the water and apple juice concentrate and heat them to between 105°F and 115°F. (Use a yeast thermometer to check the temperature). Sprinkle the yeast over the surface of the liquid and let it sit to dissolve for a minute or two; then stir it into the liquid. Let the yeast mixture stand for 10 to 15 minutes. (It should be starting to bubble after that amount of time). Stir in the oil, lecithin, and salt. Stir in about half of the flour, then stir in as much of the rest of the flour as you can adding about a half cup at a time. Turn the dough out onto a floured board and knead in enough of the remaining flour to form a smooth elastic dough. Knead the dough for 10 minutes. Wash out the mixing bowl and dry it. Rub the inside of the bowl with oil. Put the ball of dough into the bowl and turn it over so the top side of the dough is oiled. Cover it with plastic wrap and a towel and let it rise in a warm place until it is doubled in volume, which should take about 45 minutes to one hour. (See page 243 for how to make your oven into a cozy rising spot for bread dough). Punch down the dough by plunging your fist into it. Oil the inside of a loaf pan. Spelt bread tends to stick to the pan, so you may also wish to line the pan with waxed or parchment paper. Form the bread dough into a log shape and put it into the pan. Let it rise in a warm place again until it has doubled in volume, or for about 40 to 45 minutes. If it is rising in your oven, remove it from the oven. Preheat the oven to 375°F. Bake the bread for 40 to 45 minutes or until it is nicely browned, has pulled away from the sides of the pan, and sounds hollow when tapped on the bottom of the loaf. Remove the bread from the pan immediately after taking it from the oven. Allow it to cool on a wire rack before slicing it. Makes 15 to 18 servings.

**Nutritional Analysis per serving:** 18 servings per recipe

| | | |
|---|---|---|
| Calories: ...........................92 | Saturated fat:................0 g | Magnesium: ........................1 mg |
| Protein:.............................3 g | Omega-3 fatty acids:...0.11 g | Potassium:.....................139 mg |
| Carbohydrate: ................20 g | Omega-6 fatty acids: ..0.23 g | Sodium: ............................99 mg |
| Sugars:............................2 g | Cholesterol: ......................0 mg | Iron:.....................................1 mg |
| Fiber (total):.....................4 g | Vitamin A: ........................0 RE | Zinc:....................................0 mg |
| Vitamin C:.........................0 mg | Calcium: ..............................1 mg | |

Diabetic exchanges: 1 serving equals 1 starch exchange, ¼ fat exchange

# Oat Bran Bread

*When you make oat bran bread or wheat-free oat bran bread on the next page, you can enjoy the heart-health benefits of soluble fiber from oats in an especially tasty way.*

1 cup water
¼ cup apple juice concentrate, thawed
1¾ teaspoons active dry or quick-rise yeast
2 teaspoons oil
1 teaspoon liquid lecithin or additional oil
1 teaspoon salt
¾ cup oat bran
2⅔ to 3 cups bread flour

Combine the water and apple juice concentrate and heat them to between 105°F and 115°F. (Use a yeast thermometer to check the temperature). Sprinkle the yeast over the surface of the liquid and let it sit to dissolve for a minute or two; then stir it into the liquid. Let the yeast mixture stand for 10 to 15 minutes. (It should be starting to bubble after that amount of time). Stir in the oil, lecithin, and salt. Stir in the oat bran. Stir in about half of the flour, then stir in as much of the rest of the flour as you can adding about a half cup at a time. Turn the dough out onto a floured board and knead in enough of the remaining flour to form a smooth elastic dough. Knead the dough for 10 minutes. Wash out the mixing bowl and dry it. Rub the inside of the bowl with oil. Put the ball of dough into the bowl and turn it over so the top side of the dough is oiled. Cover it with plastic wrap and a towel and let it rise in a warm place until it is doubled in volume, which should take about 45 minutes to one hour. (See page 243 for how to make your oven into a cozy rising spot for bread dough). Punch down the dough by plunging your fist into it. Oil the inside of a loaf pan. Form the bread dough into a log shape and put it into the pan. Let it rise in a warm place again until it has doubled in volume, or for about 40 to 45 minutes. If it is rising in your oven, remove it from the oven. Preheat the oven to 375°F. Bake the bread for 40 to 45 minutes or until it is nicely browned, has pulled away from the sides of the pan, and sounds hollow when tapped on the bottom of the loaf. Remove the bread from the pan immediately after taking it from the oven. Allow it to cool on a wire rack before slicing it. Makes 15 to 18 servings.

**Nutritional Analysis per serving:** 18 servings per recipe

| | | |
|---|---|---|
| Calories: 91 | Total fat: 1 g | Calcium: 6 mg |
| Protein: 3 g | Saturated fat: 0 g | Magnesium: 14 mg |
| Carbohydrate: 18 g | Omega-3 fatty acids: 0.08 g | Potassium: 67 mg |
| Sugars: 2 g | Omega-6 fatty acids: 0.33 g | Sodium: 132 mg |
| Fiber (total): 1 g | Cholesterol: 0 mg | Iron: 1 mg |
| Vitamin C: 0 mg | Vitamin A: 0 RE | Zinc: 0 mg |

Diabetic exchanges: 1 serving equals 1 starch exchange, ¼ fat exchange

# Wheat-free Oat Bran Bread

1 cup water
¼ cup apple juice concentrate, thawed
2¼ teaspoons active dry or quick-rise yeast
1 tablespoon oil
½ tablespoon liquid lecithin or additional oil
¾ teaspoon salt
¾ cup oat bran
3 to 3¼ cups white spelt flour

Combine the water and apple juice concentrate and heat them to between 105°F and 115°F. (Use a yeast thermometer to check the temperature). Sprinkle the yeast over the surface of the liquid and let it sit to dissolve for a minute or two; then stir it into the liquid. Let the yeast mixture stand for 10 to 15 minutes. (It should be starting to bubble after that amount of time). Stir in the oil, lecithin, and salt. Stir in the oat bran. Stir in about half of the flour, then stir in as much of the rest of the flour as you can adding about a half cup at a time. Turn the dough out onto a floured board and knead in enough of the remaining flour to form a smooth elastic dough. Knead the dough for 10 minutes. Wash out the mixing bowl and dry it. Rub the inside of the bowl with oil. Put the ball of dough into the bowl and turn it over so the top side of the dough is oiled. Cover it with plastic wrap and a towel and let it rise in a warm place until it is doubled in volume, which should take about 45 minutes to one hour. (See page 243 for how to make your oven into a cozy rising spot for bread dough). Punch down the dough by plunging your fist into it. Oil the inside of a loaf pan. Spelt bread tends to stick to the pan, so you may also wish to line the pan with waxed or parchment paper. Form the bread dough into a log shape and put it into the pan. Let it rise in a warm place again until it has doubled in volume, or for about 40 to 45 minutes. If it is rising in your oven, remove it from the oven. Preheat the oven to 375°F. Bake the bread for 40 to 45 minutes or until it is nicely browned, has pulled away from the sides of the pan, and sounds hollow when tapped on the bottom of the loaf. Remove the bread from the pan immediately after taking it from the oven. Allow it to cool on a wire rack before slicing it. Makes 15 to 18 servings.

**Nutritional Analysis per serving:** 18 servings per recipe

| | | |
|---|---|---|
| Calories: ...........................94 | Total fat: ..............................2 g | Calcium: ...............................3 |
| Protein: .............................4 g | Saturated fat: ................0 g | Magnesium: .....................10 mg |
| Carbohydrate: ...................18 g | Omega-3 fatty acids: ...0.11 g | Potassium: .......................50 mg |
| Sugars: ............................2 g | Omega-6 fatty acids: ..0.34 g | Sodium: ...........................100 mg |
| Fiber (total): ......................1 g | Cholesterol: ......................0 mg | Iron: ..................................1 mg |
| Vitamin C: ..........................0 mg | Vitamin A: ........................0 RE | Zinc: ..................................0 mg |

Diabetic exchanges: 1 serving equals 1 starch exchange, ¼ fat exchange

# Light Rye Bread

1⅛ cups (1 cup plus 2 tablespoons) water
¼ cup apple juice concentrate, thawed
2 teaspoons active dry or quick-rise yeast
1 tablespoon oil
½ tablespoon liquid lecithin or additional oil
1 teaspoon salt
1 tablespoon caraway seed
1 cup rye flour
2½ to 2¾ cups bread flour

Combine the water and apple juice concentrate and heat them to between 105°F and 115°F. (Use a yeast thermometer to check the temperature). Sprinkle the yeast over the surface of the liquid and let it sit to dissolve for a minute or two; then stir it into the liquid. Let the yeast mixture stand for 10 to 15 minutes. (It should be starting to bubble after that amount of time). Stir in the oil, lecithin, and salt. Stir in the rye flour. Stir in about a cup of the bread flour, then stir in as much of the rest of the flour as you can adding about a half cup at a time. Turn the dough out onto a floured board and knead in enough of the remaining flour to form a smooth elastic dough. Knead the dough for 10 minutes. Wash out the mixing bowl and dry it. Rub the inside of the bowl with oil. Put the ball of dough into the bowl and turn it over so the top side of the dough is oiled. Cover it with plastic wrap and a towel and let it rise in a warm place until it is doubled in volume, which should take about 45 minutes to one hour. (See page 243 for how to make your oven into a cozy rising spot for bread dough). Punch down the dough by plunging your fist into it. Oil the inside of a loaf pan. Form the bread dough into a log shape and put it into the pan. Let it rise in a warm place again until it has doubled in volume, or for about 40 to 45 minutes. If it is rising in your oven, remove it from the oven. Preheat the oven to 375°F. Bake the bread for 40 to 45 minutes or until it is nicely browned, has pulled away from the sides of the pan, and sounds hollow when tapped on the bottom of the loaf. Remove the bread from the pan immediately after taking it from the oven. Allow it to cool on a wire rack before slicing it. Makes 15 to 20 servings.

**Nutritional Analysis per serving:** 20 servings per recipe

| | | |
|---|---|---|
| Calories: ...........................91 | Total fat: ...............................1 g | Calcium: ...............................5 mg |
| Protein: ................................2 g | Saturated fat: ................0 g | Magnesium: .........................8 mg |
| Carbohydrate: ..................17 g | Omega-3 fatty acids:...0.10 g | Potassium: .....................58 mg |
| Sugars: ...........................2 g | Omega-6 fatty acids: ..0.31 g | Sodium: ...........................119 mg |
| Fiber (total): .....................1 g | Cholesterol: ......................0 mg | Iron: .......................................1 mg |
| Vitamin C: .......................0 mg | Vitamin A: ........................0 RE | Zinc: ......................................0 mg |

Diabetic exchanges: 1 serving equals 1 starch exchange, ¼ fat exchange

# Wheat-free Light Rye Bread

1 cup water
¼ cup apple juice concentrate, thawed
2 teaspoons active dry or quick-rise yeast
1 tablespoon oil
½ tablespoon liquid lecithin or additional oil
1 teaspoon salt
1 tablespoon caraway seed
1 cup rye flour
3 to 3¼ cups white spelt flour

Combine the water and apple juice concentrate and heat them to between 105°F and 115°F. (Use a yeast thermometer to check the temperature). Sprinkle the yeast over the surface of the liquid and let it sit to dissolve for a minute or two; then stir it into the liquid. Let the yeast mixture stand for 10 to 15 minutes. (It should be starting to bubble after that amount of time). Stir in the oil, lecithin, and salt. Stir in the rye flour. Stir in about a cup of the white spelt flour, then stir in as much of the rest of the flour as you can adding about a half cup at a time. Turn the dough out onto a floured board and knead in enough of the remaining flour to form a smooth elastic dough. Knead the dough for 10 minutes. Wash out the mixing bowl and dry it. Rub the inside of the bowl with oil. Put the ball of dough into the bowl and turn it over so the top side of the dough is oiled. Cover it with plastic wrap and a towel and let it rise in a warm place until it is doubled in volume, which should take about 45 minutes to one hour. (See page 243 for how to make your oven into a cozy rising spot for bread dough). Punch down the dough by plunging your fist into it. Oil the inside of a loaf pan. Spelt bread tends to stick to the pan, so you may also wish to line the pan with waxed or parchment paper. Form the bread dough into a log shape and put it into the pan. Let it rise in a warm place again until it has doubled in volume, or for about 40 to 45 minutes. If it is rising in your oven, remove it from the oven. Preheat the oven to 375°F. Bake the bread for 40 to 45 minutes or until it is nicely browned, has pulled away from the sides of the pan, and sounds hollow when tapped on the bottom of the loaf. Remove the bread from the pan immediately after taking it from the oven. Allow it to cool on a wire rack before slicing it. Makes 15 to 20 servings.

**Nutritional Analysis per serving:** 20 servings per recipe

| | | |
|---|---|---|
| Calories: ..........................94 | Total fat: ..............................1 g | Calcium: ..............................2 mg |
| Protein: ...........................3 g | Saturated fat: ...............0 g | Magnesium: ........................5 mg |
| Carbohydrate: ...................18 g | Omega-3 fatty acids:...0.10 g | Potassium: ........................41 mg |
| Sugars: ...........................2 g | Omega-6 fatty acids: ..0.24 g | Sodium: ..........................119 mg |
| Fiber (total): ......................1 g | Cholesterol: ....................0 mg | Iron:........................................1 mg |
| Vitamin C: .........................0 mg | Vitamin A: .........................0 RE | Zinc:.......................................0 mg |

Diabetic exchanges: 1 serving equals 1 starch exchange, ¼ fat exchange

# Dinner, Hamburger, or Hot Dog Buns

1 batch of bread dough from any of the preceeding yeast bread recipes
Oil

Make the dough for any of the yeast bread recipes as directed and follow the recipe through the first rise. Punch down the dough by plunging your fist into it. If you are making the dough in a bread machine, put all the ingredients in the machine in the order specified in your machine's instruction manual, select the "dough" cycle, adjust the consistency of the dough, and let the cycle run to completion. After the first rise or the completion of the dough cycle, divide the dough into 12 pieces for large dinner buns, hot-dog rolls, or hamburger buns, or into more pieces to give you smaller dinner buns of the size you desire. Oil a very large (14 inch by 16 or 17 inch) baking sheet or a normal-sized baking sheet plus another small pan, such as a toaster oven sized pan. For hamburger or dinner buns, form each piece of dough into a ball and put it on the baking sheet. Let the buns rise in a warm place until they have doubled in volume, which will take about 45 minutes for most of the kinds of dough and a little longer for 100% whole wheat dough. (See page 243 for how to make your oven into a cozy rising spot for bread dough). If they are rising in your oven, remove them from the oven. Preheat the oven to 375°F. Bake the buns for 20 to 25 minutes or until they are nicely browned. Remove them from the pan immediately after taking them from the oven and allow them to cool on a wire rack. Makes 12 or more buns.

For hot dog buns, oil three 8 inch by 8 inch baking pans. (Or you may wish to make 4 hot dog buns in one square baking pan and 8 dinner or hamburger buns on a baking sheet). Form each piece of dough into a thin 8-inch long roll. Put the buns parallel to each other in the square baking pan. Let the buns rise in a warm place until they have filled the pan, which will take about 30 to 45 minutes. (See page 243 for how to make your oven into a cozy rising spot for bread dough). If they are rising in your oven, remove them from the oven. Preheat the oven to 375°F. Bake the buns for 25 to 30 minutes or until they are nicely browned. Remove them from the pan immediately after taking them from the oven and allow them to cool on a wire rack. Makes 12 buns.

**Nutritional Analysis per serving (if made with white bread dough):** 12 servings per recipe

| | | |
|---|---|---|
| Calories: ....................136 | Total fat:............................2 g | Calcium: ............................10 mg |
| Protein:.............................3 g | Saturated fat:................0 g | Magnesium: ........................7 mg |
| Carbohydrate:................25 g | Omega-3 fatty acids:...0.17 g | Potassium:........................45 mg |
| Sugars: ............................2 g | Omega-6 fatty acids: ..0.47 g | Sodium: ..........................197 mg |
| Fiber (total):.......................1 g | Cholesterol: .........................0 mg | Iron:....................................2 mg |
| Vitamin C:.......................0 mg | Vitamin A: ..........................0 RE | Zinc:....................................0 mg |

Diabetic exchanges: 1 serving equals 1½ starch exchanges, ⅓ fat exchange

# Dinner Rolls

1 batch of bread dough from any of the preceeding yeast bread recipes
Oil

Make the dough for any of the yeast bread recipes as directed and follow the recipe through the first rise. Punch down the dough by plunging your fist into it. If you are making the dough in a bread machine, put all the ingredients in the machine in the order specified in your machine's instruction manual, select the "dough" cycle, adjust the consistency of the dough, and let the cycle run to completion. After the first rise or the completion of the dough cycle, divide the dough into 14 to 18 pieces. Oil the wells of muffin tins. Form each piece of dough into a ball and put it into one well of the tin. Let the rolls rise in a warm place until they have doubled in volume, which will take about 45 minutes for most of the kinds of dough and a little longer for 100% whole wheat dough. (See page 243 for how to make your oven into a cozy rising spot for bread dough). If they are rising in your oven, remove them from the oven. Preheat the oven to 375°F. Bake the buns for 15 to 20 minutes or until they are nicely browned. Remove them from the pan immediately after taking them from the oven and allow them to cool on a wire rack. Makes 14 to 18 rolls.

**Cloverleaf rolls variation:** If you wish to make cloverleaf rolls, divide each ball of dough into three smaller balls. Put three small balls into each oiled well of the muffin tin. Let the dough rise as above. Bake and cool the rolls as in the paragraph above. Makes 14 to 18 cloverleaf rolls.

**Nutritional Analysis per serving (if made with white bread dough):** 18 servings per recipe

| | | |
|---|---|---|
| Calories: ..........................90 | Total fat: ...............................1 g | Calcium: ................................7 mg |
| Protein: ...........................2 g | Saturated fat: ...............0 g | Magnesium: .......................5 mg |
| Carbohydrate: .................17 g | Omega-3 fatty acids:...0.11 g | Potassium: .......................30 mg |
| Sugars: .............................1 g | Omega-6 fatty acids: ..0.31 g | Sodium: ............................131 mg |
| Fiber (total): .......................1 g | Cholesterol: ......................0 mg | Iron: ........................................1 mg |
| Vitamin C: ..........................0 mg | Vitamin A: ..........................0 RE | Zinc: .......................................0 mg |

Diabetic exchanges: 1 serving equals 1 starch exchange, ¼ fat exchange

# Pan Dinner Rolls

1 batch of bread dough from any of the preceeding yeast bread recipes
Oil

Make the dough for any of the yeast bread recipes as directed and follow the recipe through the first rise. Punch down the dough by plunging your fist into it. If you are making the dough in a bread machine, put all the ingredients in the machine in the order specified in your machine's instruction manual, select the "dough" cycle, adjust the consistency of the dough, and let the cycle run to completion. After the first rise or the completion of the dough cycle, divide the dough into 15 pieces. Oil a 13 inch by 9 inch cake pan. Form each piece of dough into a ball and brush it lightly with oil. (Or if you're not counting calories, dip each ball in oil). Put five rows of three balls each into the pan. Let the rolls rise in a warm place until they have doubled in volume and filled the pan, which will take about 30 to 40 minutes for most of the kinds of dough and a little longer for 100% whole wheat dough. (See page 243 for how to make your oven into a cozy rising spot for bread dough). If they are rising in your oven, remove them from the oven. Preheat the oven to 375°F. Bake the rolls for 25 to 35 minutes or until they are nicely browned. Remove them from the pan immediately after taking them from the oven and allow them to cool on a wire rack. For a soft top crust, brush the tops of the rolls with oil after removing them from the pan. Makes 15 rolls.

**Nutritional Analysis per serving (if made with white bread dough):** 15 servings per recipe

| | | |
|---|---|---|
| Calories: ...............108 | Total fat:............................2 g | Calcium:.............................8 mg |
| Protein:.............................3 g | Saturated fat:...............0 g | Magnesium: .......................6 mg |
| Carbohydrate: ...............20 g | Omega-3 fatty acids:...0.13 g | Potassium: .......................36 mg |
| Sugars: ...........................1 g | Omega-6 fatty acids: ..0.37 g | Sodium: ..........................157 mg |
| Fiber (total):.....................1 g | Cholesterol: ....................0 mg | Iron:......................................1 mg |
| Vitamin C:.........................0 mg | Vitamin A: ..........................0 RE | Zinc:......................................0 mg |

Diabetic exchanges: 1 serving equals 1¼ starch exchanges, ¼ fat exchange

# Desserts

Sweet treats are a part of some of the most enjoyable occasions in life. It is unrealistic to expect anyone, let alone anyone young, to go completely without them. Desserts do not have to be unhealthy. In this chapter you will find recipes for sweet treats made with healthy fats and without sugar which can be a part of a good, nutritious diet. Many of them are so quick and easy to make that you won't be tempted to go out and buy a less-healthy treat instead. For more fruit-sweetened dessert recipes, see the new dessert cookbook by this author (anticipated publication date: 2004).

The cakes and cookies in this book do not require an electric mixer; you can mix them with a spoon. The procedure to follow is the same as for quick breads. See page 241 to 242 for instructions on how to mix these cookie and cake recipes.

Some of the recipes in this chapter do require a hand blender. See page 68 for more about hand blenders. If you have a standard blender or food processor, you can use it instead.

## Pineapple Sorbet

One 20 ounce can of pineapple chunks or tidbits packed in their own juice

Put the can of pineapple in the freezer and let it freeze for several hours or overnight, or you may store it in the freezer for an extended period of time if you wish to have it ready for sorbet whenever the mood strikes. When you are ready to have the sorbet, remove the can of pineapple from the freezer and let it stand at room temperature for 10 to 20 minutes. Open the can on both ends and push the pineapple out. Put about half of the can into the cup that came with your hand blender and blend it with the hand blender until smooth. Do the same with the other half-can of pineapple. (If you use a food processor or standard blender, you can puree the whole can at one time). Serve immediately for a smooth, creamy dessert. Freeze leftovers. Remove the leftovers from the freezer about 20 minutes before serving them. Makes 3 to 6 servings.

**Nutritional Analysis per serving:** 6 servings per recipe

| | | |
|---|---|---|
| Calories: ...........................57 | Total fat: .............................0 g | Calcium: ...............................13 mg |
| Protein:...............................0 g | Saturated fat: ................0 g | Magnesium: ......................13 mg |
| Carbohydrate:..................15 g | Omega-3 fatty acids:....0 g | Potassium:........................115 mg |
| Sugars: ..............................12 g | Omega-6 fatty acids:....0 g | Sodium:...................................1 mg |
| Fiber (total):......................1 g | Cholesterol: .......................0 mg | Iron: .........................................0 mg |
| Vitamin C: ..........................9 mg | Vitamin A:..........................4 RE | Zinc:.........................................0 mg |

Diabetic exchanges: 1 serving equals 1 fruit exchange

# Banana Sorbet

2 large bananas
2 to 3 tablespoons Fruit Sweet™ or honey, to taste (optional)

Cut the bananas into chunks, put the chunks into a plastic bag and freeze them for several hours or overnight, or you may store them in the freezer for an extended period of time if you wish. When you are ready to have the sorbet, remove them from the freezer and let them stand at room temperature for 10 minutes. Put them into the cup that came with your hand blender and blend it with the hand blender until smooth or puree them with a food processor or standard blender. Taste the sorbet and blend in the sweetener if desired. Serve immediately for a smooth, creamy dessert. Freeze leftovers. Remove the leftovers from the freezer about 20 minutes before serving them. Makes 2 to 4 servings. This sorbet is especially good with fruit sauce. There are recipes for several varieties of fruit sauce on pages 114 to 115.

**Nutritional Analysis per serving:** 4 servings per recipe

| | | |
|---|---|---|
| Calories: .........................63 | Total fat: ..........................0 g | Calcium:...............................4 mg |
| Protein: ...............................1 g | Saturated fat:...............0 g | Magnesium:.....................20 mg |
| Carbohydrate:................16 g | Omega-3 fatty acids:...0 g | Potassium:....................269 mg |
| Sugars: ............................13 g | Omega-6 fatty acids: ..0 g | Sodium:...............................1 mg |
| Fiber (total):.....................2 g | Cholesterol: ....................0 mg | Iron: ....................................0 mg |
| Vitamin C:.........................6 mg | Vitamin A:..........................5 RE | Zinc:....................................0 mg |

Diabetic exchanges: 1 serving equals 1 fruit exchange

# Easy Fruit Tapioca

1 16 to 20 ounce can of fruit, such as juice packed sliced peaches, pears, or pineapple chunks, not drained, or water-packed pie cherries, drained
¼ cup minute tapioca
1 cup water or fruit juice for the peaches, pears, or pineapple, or 1 cup apple juice concentrate plus ½ cup water for the cherries

In a 1½-quart casserole dish, combine all of the ingredients. Bake at 350°F for 40 to 60 minutes, or until the tapioca is clear. Makes 4 servings.

**Nutritional Analysis per serving:** 4 servings per recipe

| | | |
|---|---|---|
| Calories: .........................89 | Total fat: ..........................0 g | Calcium:...............................9 mg |
| Protein: ...............................1 g | Saturated fat:...............0 g | Magnesium:.......................9 mg |
| Carbohydrate:................23 g | Omega-3 fatty acids:...0 g | Potassium:....................160 mg |
| Sugars: ............................13 g | Omega-6 fatty acids: ..0 g | Sodium: ..............................5 mg |
| Fiber (total):.....................2 g | Cholesterol: ....................0 mg | Iron: ....................................0 mg |
| Vitamin C: ........................4 mg | Vitamin A: ......................47 RE | Zinc:....................................0 mg |

Diabetic exchanges: 1 serving equals 1 fruit exchange, ½ other carbohydrate exchange

# Baked Apples or Pears

4 large baking apples* or pears
½ cup thawed apple juice concentrate, apple juice, pear juice, or water or ¼ cup
    Fruit Sweet™ or honey plus ¼ cup water
½ teaspoon cinnamon (optional)
¼ cup raisins (optional)

Core the apples or pears and put them in a 2½ quart glass casserole dish with a lid. Pour in the juice, sweetener, and/or water and sprinkle the cinnamon down the centers of the fruit. Stuff the fruit with raisins, if desired. Bake at 350°F for 40 to 50 minutes for the apples or 1 to 1½ hours for the pears or until the fruit is tender when pierced with a fork. Makes 4 servings.

*Note on baking apples: Some varieties of apples hold their shape well when they are baked, such as Rome, Pink Lady, and Granny Smith. If you're planning to make this dessert for guests and will be buying the apples especially for baking, chose a baking apple. However, if you have old apples in your refrigerator that you want to use up, any kind will be fine to use in this recipe.

## Apples baked with apple juice concentrate:
**Nutritional Analysis per serving:** 4 servings per recipe

| | | |
|---|---|---|
| Calories: 109 | Total fat: 0 g | Calcium: 4 mg |
| Protein: 0 g | Saturated fat: 0 g | Magnesium: 3 mg |
| Carbohydrate: 29 g | Omega-3 fatty acids: 0 g | Potassium: 249 mg |
| Sugars: 23 g | Omega-6 fatty acids: 0 g | Sodium: 4 mg |
| Fiber (total): 5 g | Cholesterol: 0 mg | Iron: 1 mg |
| Vitamin C: 5 mg | Vitamin A: 10 RE | Zinc: 0 mg |

Diabetic exchanges: 1 serving equals 1¾ fruit exchanges

## Pears baked with water:
**Nutritional Analysis per serving:** 4 servings per recipe

| | | |
|---|---|---|
| Calories: 100 | Total fat: 1 g | Calcium: 20 mg |
| Protein: 1 g | Saturated fat: 0 g | Magnesium: 6 mg |
| Carbohydrate: 25 g | Omega-3 fatty acids: 0 g | Potassium: 210 mg |
| Sugars: 17 g | Omega-6 fatty acids: 0 g | Sodium: 0 mg |
| Fiber (total): 4 g | Cholesterol: 0 mg | Iron: 0 mg |
| Vitamin C: 6 mg | Vitamin A: 0 RE | Zinc: 0 mg |

Diabetic exchanges: 1 serving equals 1⅔ fruit exchanges

# Easy Apple Crisp

*You can make this dessert quickly with water-packed canned sliced apples, such as Mussleman's™ brand. For variety, use fresh seasonal fruits such as peaches or blueberries instead.*

## Filling ingredients:
2 20 ounce cans of sliced apples canned in water, drained
1 tablespoon plus 1 teaspoon cornstarch, arrowroot, or tapioca starch
1½ teaspoons cinnamon
⅓ cup apple juice concentrate, thawed

## Topping ingredients:

¾ cup oatmeal, quick cooking or regular (not instant)
¾ cup all purpose, unbleached, or white spelt flour
½ teaspoon baking soda
¼ cup oil
¼ cup Fruit Sweet™ or 3 tablespoons honey plus 1 tablespoon water
1 teaspoon vanilla extract

Drain the canned apples. Put the slices in a 2½ to 3 quart glass casserole dish. Add the starch and cinnamon and toss with the apple slices to coat the slices thoroughly. Drizzle the apple juice concentrate over the apple slices.

Preheat your oven to 350°F. In a mixing bowl, stir together the oatmeal, flour, and baking soda. If you are using the honey, warm it slightly and mix it well with the water. In a cup, combine the sweetener, oil, and vanilla. Stir them into the dry ingredients until just mixed. Drop and spread the topping over the apples in the casserole dish. Bake the dish for 35 to 40 minutes or until the apples are tender and bubbling and the topping is browned. Check the apple crisp after 30 minutes; if the topping is already getting quite brown but the fruit is not done, cover it with foil for the rest of the baking time. Makes 6 to 8 servings.

**Fresh Peach Crisp Variation:** Substitute 10 to 12 peaches weighing about 3 pounds, peeled, cored, and sliced, for the canned apples and increase the amount of apple juice concentrate you use in the filling to ½ cup.

**Blueberry Crisp Variation:** Substitute 2 pounds of blueberries for the canned apples and omit the cinnamon.

**Fresh Apple Crisp Variation:** Substitute 8 large apples, weighing about 3 pounds, for the canned apples. Peel, core and slice the apples and put them in a saucepan with 1½ cups of water. Cover the pan and bring the apple slices to a boil. Reduce the heat to medium, and simmer them for 5 to 10 minutes or until they just begin to soften. Drain the apple slices and use them in the recipe above.

**Nutritional Analysis per serving:** *8 servings per recipe*

| | | |
|---|---|---|
| Calories: ......................242 | Total fat: ..............................7 g | Calcium: ............................23 mg |
| Protein: ...............................2 g | Saturated fat: ..................1 g | Magnesium: ......................16 mg |
| Carbohydrate: ..................41 g | Omega-3 fatty acids:...0.65 g | Potassium: ..........................91 mg |
| Sugars: ..........................23 g | Omega-6 fatty acids: ....1.61 g | Sodium: ...........................83 mg |
| Fiber (total):.....................3 g | Cholesterol: .....................0 mg | Iron:......................................2 mg |
| Vitamin C: ..........................0 mg | Vitamin A: ...........................1 RE | Zinc:......................................0 mg |

Diabetic exchanges: 1 serving equals 1 starch exchange, 1½ fruit exchanges, 1½ fat exchanges

# Mix and Match Fruit Cobbler

*Chose your fruit, choose your topping, and you have a great dessert! If you would like to make this with other types of flour, such as kamut, teff, amaranth, buckwheat, barley, quinoa, or rice, see* The Ultimate Food Allergy Cookbook and Survival Guide *as described on the last page of this book.*

## Filling ingredients:

Fruit: choose one:
> Apples – 4 to 5, peeled, cored and sliced to make 3½ to 4 cups of slices
> Blueberries – 4 cups fresh or a 1 pound bag of frozen unsweetened blueberries
> Strawberries – 1 pound of fresh or a 1 pound bag of frozen unsweetened strawberries
> Peaches – 4 cups fresh or a 1 pound bag of frozen unsweetened peaches
> Black (sweet) cherries – 4 cups fresh or a 1 pound bag of frozen unsweetened sweet cherries
> Pie (tart) cherries – 4 cups fresh or 2 1 pound cans of pitted water-packed pie cherries, drained

Starch – 5 teaspoons cornstarch, arrowroot, or tapioca starch with any of the fruits except strawberries; 3 tablespoons with the strawberries
Sweetener – ½ cup apple juice concentrate with any of the fruits except the tart cherries; ¾ cup Fruit Sweet™ or honey with the cherries
½ teaspoon cinnamon with the apples only

## Topping ingredients:

⅞ cup (¾ cup plus 2 tablespoons) all purpose flour, unbleached flour, or whole spelt flour or 1 cup white spelt flour
1 teaspoon baking powder*
¼ teaspoon baking soda
⅜ cup (¼ cup plus 2 tablespoons) apple juice concentrate, thawed
2 tablespoons oil

In a saucepan, stir together the fruit, starch, sweetener, and cinnamon (for the apples only). Heat them to a boil over low to medium heat, stirring frequently, until the mixture begins to boil and thickens.

While the fruit is cooking, preheat your oven to 350°F. In a mixing bowl, stir together the flour, baking powder, and baking soda. In a separate bowl or cup stir together the apple juice concentrate and oil.

When the fruit mixture boils and thickens, put it into a 2½ to 3 quart glass casserole dish. Mix the apple juice and oil for the topping into the flour mixture until they are just mixed. Spoon the topping batter over the hot fruit. Immediately put the cobbler into the oven. Bake for 25 to 35 minutes or until the topping is slightly browned. Makes 8 servings.

* Note on baking powder: Use Featherweight™ brand baking powder if you are allergic to corn. It contains potato starch instead of cornstarch.

**Made with apples (most other fruits similar):**
**Nutritional Analysis per serving:** 8 servings per recipe

| | | |
|---|---|---|
| Calories: ...........178 | Total fat:............4 g | Calcium: ............51 mg |
| Protein: ............2 g | Saturated fat:.....0 g | Magnesium:..........9 mg |
| Carbohydrate: ......36 g | Omega-3 fatty acids:...0.33 g | Potassium:.........238 mg |
| Sugars: ............20 g | Omega-6 fatty acids: ..0.77 g | Sodium: ............93 mg |
| Fiber (total):......3 g | Cholesterol: ......0 mg | Iron:..............1 mg |
| Vitamin C:..........3 mg | Vitamin A:.........5 RE | Zinc:..............0 mg |

Diabetic exchanges: 1 serving equals ¾ starch exchange, 1½ fruit exchanges, ⅔ fat exchange

Made with cherries (more concentrated sweetener required):

**Nutritional Analysis per serving:** *8 servings per recipe*

| | | |
|---|---|---|
| Calories: ............194 | Total fat: .............4 g | Calcium: ............105 mg |
| Protein: ............2 g | Saturated fat: ............0 g | Magnesium: ............12 mg |
| Carbohydrate: ............39 g | Omega-3 fatty acids: ...0.33 g | Potassium: ............185 mg |
| Sugars: ............25 g | Omega-6 fatty acids: ..0.77 g | Sodium: ............100 mg |
| Fiber (total): ............2 g | Cholesterol: ............0 mg | Iron: ............3 mg |
| Vitamin C: ............3 mg | Vitamin A: ............85 RE | Zinc: ............0 mg |

Diabetic exchanges: 1 serving equals 1¼ starch/other carbohydrate exchanges, 1 fruit exchange, ⅔ fat exchange

# Strawberry Shortcake

2 cups all purpose or unbleached flour or 2¼ cups white spelt flour
2 teaspoons baking powder*
½ teaspoon baking soda
½ teaspoon salt
¾ cup apple juice concentrate, thawed
⅓ cup oil
1 large egg, slightly beaten
4 cups sliced strawberries, peaches, or other fruit
Whipped cream, recipe on page 281 (optional)

Preheat your oven to 375°F. Oil and flour an 8 or 9 inch square or round cake pan, or for a romantic occasion, use a heart-shaped cake pan of a similar size. Line the bottom of the pan with waxed or parchment paper. In a large bowl, stir together the flour, baking powder, baking soda, and salt. In a cup, thoroughly stir together the juice, oil, and egg. Pour the liquid ingredients into the dry ingredients and stir until just mixed. Put the batter into the prepared pan and bake for 25 to 30 minutes for the wheat shortcake or 30 to 35 minutes for the spelt shortcake, or until the shortcake is nicely browned and a toothpick stuck into the center comes out dry. Cool the shortcake in the pan for about 10 minutes. Then remove it from the pan and allow it to cool completely. Using a serrated knife, slice each piece horizontally. Serve with fruit and whipped cream between the two layers and on the top of the shortcake. Makes 6 to 12 servings.

\* Note on baking powder: Use Featherweight™ brand baking powder if you are allergic to corn. It contains potato starch instead of cornstarch.

**Nutritional Analysis per serving:** *12 servings per recipe*

| | | |
|---|---|---|
| Calories: ............211 | Total fat: .............7 g | Calcium: ............77 mg |
| Protein: ............3 g | Saturated fat: ............1 g | Magnesium: ............17 mg |
| Carbohydrate: ............34 g | Omega-3 fatty acids: ...0.62 g | Potassium: ............277 mg |
| Sugars: ............17 g | Omega-6 fatty acids: ....1.45 g | Sodium: ............226 mg |
| Fiber (total): ............2 g | Cholesterol: ............0 mg | Iron: ............2 mg |
| Vitamin C: ............32 mg | Vitamin A: ............9 RE | Zinc: ............0 mg |

Diabetic exchanges: 1 serving equals 1 starch exchange, 1¼ fruit exchanges, 1¼ fat exchanges

# Apple Pie

6 to 7 apples, peeled, cored and sliced to make about 5 cups of slices or 1½ 20 ounce cans of water-packed apple slices, such as Mussleman's™ brand, drained
⅝ cup (½ cup plus 2 tablespoons) apple juice concentrate, thawed
1 teaspoon cinnamon
An additional ¼ cup of apple juice concentrate, thawed
2 tablespoons cornstarch, arrowroot, or tapioca starch OR 3 tablespoons of quick-cooking ("minute") tapioca
Pastry for a two crust pie, recipes below on pages 274 to 276

If you are using the canned apples, thoroughly drain the water from the cans. Combine the apple slices, ⅝ cup apple juice concentrate, and cinnamon in a saucepan. Bring them to a boil and reduce the heat to a simmer. For fresh apples, simmer for about 15 to 20 minutes. If you are using canned apples, simmer for just a few minutes to heat them. While they are cooking, in a separate cup stir together the additional ¼ cup apple juice concentrate with the starch or tapioca. If you are using minute tapioca, let it stand for 5 minutes in the juice. Stir the starch mixture into the saucepan at the end of the simmering time for the apples. Continue to simmer until the fruit mixture returns to a boil and thickens.

Preheat your oven to 400°F. Put the filling into the prepared bottom pie crust. Cover it with the top crust and crimp the edges together. Prick the top crust to allow steam to escape. Bake the pie at 400°F for 10 minutes; then reduce the heat to 350°F and continue to bake it for another 40 to 50 minutes or until the top and bottom crusts are golden brown. Makes 6 to 8 servings.

**Nutritional Analysis per serving, pie filling only:** *8 servings per recipe*

| | | |
|---|---|---|
| Calories: 119 | Total fat: 0 g | Calcium: 6 mg |
| Protein: 0 g | Saturated fat: 0 g | Magnesium: 5 mg |
| Carbohydrate: 31 g | Omega-3 fatty acids: 0 g | Potassium: 265 mg |
| Sugars: 24 g | Omega-6 fatty acids: 0 g | Sodium: 8 mg |
| Fiber (total): 4 g | Cholesterol: 0 mg | Iron: 1 mg |
| Vitamin C: 4 mg | Vitamin A: 8 RE | Zinc: 0 mg |

Diabetic exchanges: 1 serving equals ⅙ starch exchange, 1¾ fruit exchanges. Add the exchanges for the crust recipe you use to these exchanges for the filling.

# Blueberry Pie

1½ pounds fresh or frozen unsweetened blueberries
1 cup of apple juice concentrate, thawed
3 tablespoons cornstarch, arrowroot, or tapioca starch OR 5 tablespoons quick-cooking ("minute") tapioca
Pastry for a two crust pie, recipes below on pages 274 to 276

Combine the apple juice concentrate and thickener in a saucepan. If you are using the minute tapioca, let it stand for 5 minutes before you begin cooking it. Add the blueberries to the pan and stir. Heat the fruit mixture over low to medium heat, stirring frequently, until it comes to a boil and thickens.

Preheat your oven to 400°F. Put the filling into the prepared bottom pie crust. Cover it with the top crust and crimp the edges together. Prick the top crust to allow steam to escape. Bake the pie at 400°F for 10 minutes; then reduce the heat to 350°F and continue to bake it for another 40 to 50 minutes or until the top and bottom crusts are golden brown. Makes 6 to 8 servings.

**Nutritional Analysis per serving, pie filling only:** 8 servings per recipe

| | | |
|---|---|---|
| Calories: ...........................117 | Total fat: ...........................0 g | Calcium: ...........................12 mg |
| Protein: ...............................1 g | Saturated fat:...............0 g | Magnesium: ......................10 mg |
| Carbohydrate:................29 g | Omega-3 fatty acids:...0 g | Potassium: ....................233 mg |
| Sugars: ...........................23 g | Omega-6 fatty acids: ..0 g | Sodium:...............................14 mg |
| Fiber (total):......................2 g | Cholesterol: .....................0 mg | Iron: ......................................0 mg |
| Vitamin C:........................12 mg | Vitamin A:..........................9 RE | Zinc:.....................................0 mg |

Diabetic exchanges: 1 serving equals ¼ starch exchange, 1⅔ fruit exchanges. Add the exchanges for the crust recipe you use to these exchanges for the filling.

# Cherry Pie

2 16 ounce cans water-packed tart pie cherries, drained
¾ cup Fruit Sweet™ or ⅝ cup (½ cup plus 2 tablespoons) honey plus ¼ cup water
3 tablespoons cornstarch, arrowroot, or tapioca starch OR ¼ cup quick-cooking ("minute") tapioca
Pastry for a two crust pie, recipes below on pages 274 to 276

Thoroughly drain the liquid from the cherries in the can. Combine the Fruit Sweet™ or water and thickener in a saucepan. If you are using the minute tapioca, let it stand for 5 minutes before you begin cooking it. Add the cherries and, if you are using the honey, add it to the pan and stir. Heat the fruit mixture over low to medium heat, stirring frequently, until it comes to a boil and thickens.

Preheat your oven to 400°F. Put the filling into the prepared bottom pie crust. Cover it with the top crust and crimp the edges together. Prick the top crust to allow steam to escape. Bake the pie at 400°F for 10 minutes; then reduce the heat to 350°F and continue to bake it for another 40 to 50 minutes or until the top and bottom crusts are golden brown. Makes 6 to 8 servings.

**Nutritional Analysis per serving, pie filling only:** 8 servings per recipe

| | | |
|---|---|---|
| Calories: ...........................97 | Total fat: ...........................0 g | Calcium:...........................58 mg |
| Protein: ...............................1 g | Saturated fat:...............0 g | Magnesium: ........................7 mg |
| Carbohydrate:................24 g | Omega-3 fatty acids:...0 g | Potassium: ....................111 mg |
| Sugars: ...........................19 g | Omega-6 fatty acids: ..0 g | Sodium:...............................12 mg |
| Fiber (total):......................2 g | Cholesterol: .....................0 mg | Iron: ......................................3 mg |
| Vitamin C:..........................2 mg | Vitamin A:........................85 RE | Zinc:.....................................0 mg |

Diabetic exchanges: 1 serving equals ½ starch/other carbohydrate exchange, 1 fruit exchange. Add the exchanges for the crust recipe you use to these exchanges for the filling.

# Peach Pie

5 cups of peeled, pitted, and sliced fresh peaches or 1½ pounds of frozen unsweet-
    ened sliced peaches or 5 cups drained water-packed canned sliced peaches
⅞ cup (¾ cup plus 2 tablespoons) of apple juice concentrate, thawed
3 tablespoons cornstarch, arrowroot, or tapioca starch
¼ teaspoon cinnamon or nutmeg (optional)
Pastry for a two crust pie, recipes below on pages 274 to 276

Stir together the apple juice concentrate and starch in a saucepan. Add the sliced
peaches and spice to the pan and stir. Heat the fruit mixture over low to medium heat,
stirring frequently, until it comes to a boil and thickens.

Preheat your oven to 400°F. Put the filling into the prepared bottom pie crust.
Cover it with the top crust and crimp the edges together. Prick the top crust to allow
steam to escape. Bake the pie at 400°F for 10 minutes; then reduce the heat to 350°F and
continue to bake it for another 40 to 50 minutes or until the top and bottom crusts are
golden brown. Makes 6 to 8 servings.

**Nutritional Analysis per serving, pie filling only:** 8 servings per recipe

| | | |
|---|---|---|
| Calories: ...........108 | Total fat: .............0 g | Calcium: ...............12 mg |
| Protein: ................1 g | Saturated fat: .........0 g | Magnesium: ..........13 mg |
| Carbohydrate: .......27 g | Omega-3 fatty acids:...0 g | Potassium: ...........347 mg |
| Sugars: ................21 g | Omega-6 fatty acids: ..0 g | Sodium: ................8 mg |
| Fiber (total): ...........2 g | Cholesterol: ............0 mg | Iron: .....................0 mg |
| Vitamin C: ..............8 mg | Vitamin A: ...........57 RE | Zinc: .....................0 mg |

Diabetic exchanges: 1 serving equals ¼ starch exchange, 1½ fruit exchanges. Add
the exchanges for the crust recipe you use to these exchanges for the filling.

# No-Bake Strawberry Pie

6 cups (about 1½ quarts) fresh strawberries
½ cup Fruit Sweet™ or honey
4 tablespoons cornstarch or 6 tablespoons Quick Thick™
1 baked single-crust pie shell, recipes below on pages 274 to 276

Wash and hull the strawberries. If they are very large, cut them in half. Set aside
about 4½ cups of the strawberries. Mash the remaining 1½ cups thoroughly with a fork
to yield 1 cup of mashed strawberries. If the yield is less than 1 cup, add some more whole
strawberries and mash them to bring the volume of mashed strawberries up to 1 cup. If
you are using the cornstarch, combine the mashed strawberries, sweetener, and cornstarch
in a saucepan. Cook the mixture over medium heat, stirring it frequently at first and then
constantly as it gets quite warm, until it thickens and boils. Then cook it another minute
or two until the color becomes darker and clearer. Remove the pan from the heat and
allow the strawberry mixture to cool until it is just warm. Then stir in the whole or halved
strawberries and put the filling into the pie shell. Chill the pie at least three hours or until
it is set before you serve it.

If you are using the Quick Thick™, prepare the whole or halved strawberries and
1 cup of mashed strawberries as above. Add the Quick Thick™ to the mashed strawberries and sweetner and stir until the mixture begins to thicken. Immediately stir in the
whole or halved strawberries and put the mixture into the pie shell. Chill the pie at least
one hour or until it is set before you serve it. Makes 6 to 8 servings.

**Corn-free variation:** Substitute 4 tablespoons of tapioca starch or arrowroot for the cornstarch. The glaze for this pie will be a little gooey, but it is still good and better than not having strawberry pie if you are allergic to corn.

**Nutritional Analysis per serving, pie filling only:** *8 servings per recipe*

| | | |
|---|---|---|
| Calories: ...................79 | Total fat: ..........................0 g | Calcium:...........................46 mg |
| Protein: ..............................1 g | Saturated fat:................0 g | Magnesium:......................12 mg |
| Carbohydrate:................19 g | Omega-3 fatty acids:...0 g | Potassium:......................189 mg |
| Sugars:............................12 g | Omega-6 fatty acids: ..0 g | Sodium: ...............................4 mg |
| Fiber (total):......................3 g | Cholesterol: ....................0 mg | Iron:.......................................1 mg |
| Vitamin C: ......................65 mg | Vitamin A:..........................3 RE | Zinc:......................................0 mg |

Diabetic exchanges: 1 serving equals ¼ starch exchange, 1 fruit exchange. Add the exchanges for the crust recipe you use to these exchanges for the filling.

# No Bake Pumpkin Pie

1 16 ounce can of plain pumpkin
1 cup water
1 envelope unflavored gelatin
1 cup date sugar
1 teaspoon cinnamon
1 teaspoon nutmeg
¼ teaspoon cloves
¼ teaspoon allspice
¼ teaspoon ginger
1 baked single-crust pie shell, recipes below on pages 274 to 276

Prepare and bake the pie shell. Put the water in a saucepan and sprinkle the gelatin over the surface of the water. Heat the water over medium heat, stirring occasionally, until it comes to a boil and the gelatin dissolves. Stir in the rest of the ingredients. Put the pumpkin mixture into the pie shell and refrigerate it for several hours until it is thoroughly chilled. Serve with whipped cream. (A recipe for whipped cream is on page 281). Makes 6 to 8 servings.

**Nutritional Analysis per serving, pie filling only:** *8 servings per recipe*

| | | |
|---|---|---|
| Calories: .........................83 | Total fat: ..........................0 g | Calcium: .........................22 mg |
| Protein: ..............................2 g | Saturated fat:................0 g | Magnesium:......................21 mg |
| Carbohydrate:................21 g | Omega-3 fatty acids:...0 g | Potassium:......................262 mg |
| Sugars:............................16 g | Omega-6 fatty acids: ..0 g | Sodium: ...............................5 mg |
| Fiber (total):......................3 g | Cholesterol: ....................0 mg | Iron:.......................................1 mg |
| Vitamin C: ..........................2 mg | Vitamin A: ..................1252 RE | Zinc:......................................0 mg |

Diabetic exchanges: 1 serving equals ¼ starch exchange, 1 fruit exchange. Add the exchanges for the crust recipe you use to these exchanges for the filling.

# Cream Pies

*Use this recipe to make chocolate, carob, vanilla, or coconut cream pie.*

1 baked pie shell, recipes below on pages 274 to 276
1 batch of any pudding, recipes on page 282

Prepare and bake a single crust pie shell. Allow it to cool thoroughly. Make the pudding according to the recipe. Cover the surface of the pudding with waxed or parchment paper or with plastic wrap to prevent a "skin" from forming and allow it to cool slightly. Put it into the pie shell and refrigerate it for several hours or until it is thoroughly chilled. Serve with whipped cream. (A recipe for whipped cream is on page 281). Makes 6 to 8 servings.

**Nutritional analysis per serving:** Add the values for the pudding recipe you use and the pie crust recipe you use.

Diabetic exchanges: Add the exchanges for the pudding recipe you use to the exchanges for the pie crust recipe you use.

# Oil Pastry

*The pastry recipes in this book create a pastry that is a little more difficult to handle than pastry made with shortening, but they avoid the trans fats contained in shortening. Spare your body the unhealthy fats! Use some waxed or parchment paper or a pasty cloth to roll your pastry out, or just press half of the dough into the pie plate for the bottom crust and crumble the remaining half of the dough to sprinkle over your fruit filling.*

2¼ cups all purpose or unbleached flour or 2½ cups white spelt flour
½ teaspoon salt
⅜ cup (¼ cup plus 2 tablespoons) oil
5 to 6 tablespoons water

In a large mixing bowl, stir together the flour and salt. Stir in the oil. Blend the oil into the flour by cutting the mixture repeatedly with a pastry cutter until it forms crumbs. Using a spoon, stir in 4 tablespoons of the water. Then add enough of the remaining water, 1 tablespoon at a time, until the dough forms a ball when you press it together with your hands. Divide the dough in half.

To make two one-crust pie shells, flour your fingers and press each half of the dough into a glass pie dish, or use a pastry cloth to roll out the dough and put it in the pie plate as in the following recipe. You may also roll each half of the dough out between two floured sheets of waxed or parchment paper. Remove the top sheet of paper and flip the other sheet of the paper, with the dough still attached to it, into the pie plate. Peel off the second piece of paper from the dough. Fit the dough into the pie plate, prick it all over with a fork, fold the edge under, and crimp or flute the edge. Preheat your oven to 400°F. Bake the crusts for 18 to 22 minutes or until they are lightly browned on the bottom. Cool the crusts completely before filling them.

For a two-crust pie, prepare your pie filling according to the recipes on pages 270 to 274. Preheat your oven to the temperature directed in the filling recipe. Flour your fingers and press half of the dough into the pie plate. If you don't mind working just a little harder, roll one piece of the dough out into a 12-inch round on a floured pastry cloth or use two pieces of waxed or parchment paper as directed above. Fit the dough into a 9-inch glass pie plate and trim the edge even with the plate. Fill the crust with the filling. Crumble the remaining pie crust over the filling or roll out the other piece of dough into a 12-inch round as directed above and put it on the top of the pie. Turn the edge of the top crust under the edge of the bottom crust and crimp it or press together with the tines of a fork. Prick the top crust with a fork or knife to allow steam to escape from the pie as it bakes. Bake as directed in the filling recipe.

Makes enough pastry for two single crusts or one double crust pie.

**Double crust pie, crust only:**
**Nutritional Analysis per serving:** *8 servings per recipe*

| | | |
|---|---|---|
| Calories: ...............218 | Total fat: ................11 g | Calcium: ................5 mg |
| Protein: ..................4 g | Saturated fat: .............1 g | Magnesium: ................8 mg |
| Carbohydrate: ...........27 g | Omega-3 fatty acids: ...0.96 g | Potassium: ...............38 mg |
| Sugars: ..................1 g | Omega-6 fatty acids: ...2.21 g | Sodium: ................147 mg |
| Fiber (total): ...........1 g | Cholesterol: ............0 mg | Iron: ....................2 mg |
| Vitamin C: ..............0 mg | Vitamin A: ..............0 RE | Zinc: ...................0 mg |

Diabetic exchanges: 1 serving equals 1⅔ starch exchanges, 2 fat exchanges. Add the exchanges for the crust to the exchanges for the filling you use.

**Single crust pie, crust only:**
**Nutritional Analysis per serving:** *16 servings per recipe*

| | | |
|---|---|---|
| Calories: ...............109 | Total fat: .................5 g | Calcium: ................3 mg |
| Protein: ..................2 g | Saturated fat: .............0 g | Magnesium: ................4 mg |
| Carbohydrate: ...........13 g | Omega-3 fatty acids: ...0.48 g | Potassium: ...............19 mg |
| Sugars: ..................0 g | Omega-6 fatty acids: ...1.11 g | Sodium: .................74 mg |
| Fiber (total): ...........0 g | Cholesterol: ............0 mg | Iron: ....................1 mg |
| Vitamin C: ..............0 mg | Vitamin A: ..............0 RE | Zinc: ...................0 mg |

Diabetic exchanges: 1 serving equals ⅚ starch exchange, 1 fat exchange. Add the exchanges for the crust to the exchanges for the filling you use.

# Butter Pastry

*While not especially easy to handle, this is the most delicious, flaky pie crust you will ever eat. You will avoid the unhealthy trans fats contained in shortening if you use butter to make your pastry.*

2½ cups all purpose or unbleached flour
½ teaspoon salt
1 cup plus 2 tablespoons chilled unsalted butter or goat butter
8 to 10 tablespoons very cold water

In a large mixing bowl, stir together the flour and salt. Cut the butter into small pieces by cutting the stick down the middle and then slicing it. Blend the butter into the flour using a pastry cutter until the mixture resembles coarse meal; it is all right if there are still a few pea-sized pieces of butter left. Sprinkle in the water, stirring while you add it, until the dough begins to hold together. Press the dough into a ball. Divide the ball in half and flatten each half into a disk. Wrap the disks in plastic wrap and refrigerate them for one hour. If you are pressed for time, rather than refrigerating the dough at this point and rolling it out, you can press it into the pie plate and crumble it over the top of the pie as directed in the "Oil Pastry" recipe, above.

To make two one-crust pie shells, preheat the oven to 400°F. Allow the dough to sit at room temperature for a few minutes before rolling it out. Using one half of the dough at a time, place each piece of dough on a floured pastry cloth. Sprinkle flour on the top of the dough and roll it out into a 12-inch round. Fold the pastry cloth, with the dough on it, in half. Then peel back the top of the pastry cloth, leaving the dough folded in half. Lift the folded dough into a 9-inch glass pie plate and unfold it. Fit each piece of the pastry into a pie plate, prick all over with a fork, fold the edge under, and crimp or flute the edge. Bake the crusts for 15 to 20 minutes or until they are lightly browned on the bottom. Cool the crusts completely before filling them.

For a two-crust pie, prepare your pie filling according to the recipes on pages 270 to 274. Allow the dough to sit at room temperature for a few minutes before rolling it out. Preheat your oven to the temperature directed in the filling recipe. Roll one piece of the dough out into a 12-inch round on a floured pastry cloth as directed above. Fit it into a 9-inch glass pie plate and trim the edge even with the plate. Fill the crust with the filling. Roll out the other piece of dough into a 12-inch round and place it on the top of the pie. Turn the edge of the top crust under the edge of the bottom crust and crimp it or press together with the tines of a fork. Prick the top crust with a fork or knife to allow steam to escape from the pie as it bakes. Bake as directed in the filling recipe.

Makes enough crust for one two crust pie or two single pie crusts.

### Double crust pie, crust only:
**Nutritional Analysis per serving:** 8 servings per recipe

| | | |
|---|---|---|
| Calories: ........................371 | Total fat:..........................26 g | Calcium: ............................14 mg |
| Protein:................................4 g | Saturated fat: ..............16 g | Magnesium:........................9 mg |
| Carbohydrate:................30 g | Omega-3 fatty acids:...0.39 g | Potassium: ......................50 mg |
| Sugars: ..............................1 g | Omega-6 fatty acids: ..0.74 g | Sodium: ..........................151 mg |
| Fiber (total):......................1 g | Cholesterol: ....................70 mg | Iron:......................................2 mg |
| Vitamin C:......................0 mg | Vitamin A:......................241 RE | Zinc:......................................0 mg |

Diabetic exchanges: 1 serving equals 1⅞ starch exchanges, 5 fat exchanges. Add the exchanges for the crust to the exchanges for the filling you use.

### Single crust pie, crust only:
**Nutritional Analysis per serving:** 16 servings per recipe

| | | |
|---|---|---|
| Calories: ........................186 | Total fat:..........................13 g | Calcium: ..............................7 mg |
| Protein:................................2 g | Saturated fat:................8 g | Magnesium:........................5 mg |
| Carbohydrate:................15 g | Omega-3 fatty acids:...0.19 g | Potassium: ......................25 mg |
| Sugars:................................0 g | Omega-6 fatty acids: ..0.37 g | Sodium: ............................75 mg |
| Fiber (total):......................1 g | Cholesterol: ....................35 mg | Iron:......................................1 mg |
| Vitamin C:......................0 mg | Vitamin A: ....................120 RE | Zinc:......................................0 mg |

Diabetic exchanges: 1 serving equals 1 starch exchange, 2½ fat exchanges. Add the exchanges for the crust to the exchanges for the filling you use.

# Spice Cake

*Try this topped with warm peach or apple fruit sauce, page 114, instead of frosting.*

3 cups all purpose, unbleached, or barley flour or 3⅜ cups (3¼ cups plus
    2 tablespoons) white spelt flour
¾ cups date sugar
3¾ teaspoons baking powder*
½ teaspoon salt
2 teaspoons cinnamon
½ teaspoon cloves
¼ teaspoon allspice
3 cups pureed or throughly mashed bananas
½ cup plus 1 tablespoon oil
1 teaspoon vanilla extract (optional)

Preheat your oven to 375°F. Oil and flour an 8 or 9 inch square cake pan. (Flour the pan with white spelt or barley flour if you are making a wheat-free cake). In a large bowl, stir together the flour, date sugar, baking powder, salt and spices. Throughly mash or puree the bananas with a hand blender and stir the bananas together with the oil and vanilla. Stir the banana mixture into the flour mixture until they are just combined. Spread the batter in the prepared pan (it will be thick) and bake the cake for 45 to 50 minutes or until it is brown. Insert a toothpick into the center of the pan. If it comes out dry, the cake is done. Place the cake on a cooling rack and allow it to cool completely. If desired, frost it with the date frosting below. Cut it into squares and serve it from the pan. Makes 9 to 12 servings.

* Note on baking powder: Use Featherweight™ brand baking powder if you are allergic to corn. It contains potato starch instead of cornstarch.

**Date frosting:** Combine ⅔ cup water and 1½ tablespoons all purpose, unbleached, white spelt, or barley flour in a saucepan. Heat it over medium heat, stirring frequently, until it thickens and boils. Stir 1 cup of date sugar into the flour mixture until it is smooth. Immediately use it to frost the top of the spice cake. Allow it to cool before serving the cake.

**Nutritional Analysis per serving:** 12 servings per recipe
**Cake only:**

| | | |
|---|---|---|
| Calories: ............276 | Total fat: ............11 g | Calcium: ............116 mg |
| Protein: ............4 g | Saturated fat: ............1 g | Magnesium: ............26 mg |
| Carbohydrate: ............43 g | Omega-3 fatty acids: ....0.98 g | Potassium: ............302 mg |
| Sugars: ............15 g | Omega-6 fatty acids: ....2.23 g | Sodium: ............213 mg |
| Fiber (total): ............3 g | Cholesterol: ............0 mg | Iron: ............2 mg |
| Vitamin C: ............5 mg | Vitamin A: ............5 RE | Zinc: ............0 mg |

Diabetic exchanges: 1 serving equals 1⅓ starch exchanges, 1¼ fruit exchanges, 2 fat exchanges. Add the exchanges of any frosting you use to the cake exchanges.

**Frosting only:**

| | | |
|---|---|---|
| Calories: ............44 | Total fat: ............0 g | Calcium: ............5 mg |
| Protein: ............0 g | Saturated fat: ............0 g | Magnesium: ............5 mg |
| Carbohydrate: ............12 g | Omega-3 fatty acids: ....0 g | Potassium: ............98 mg |
| Sugars: ............10 g | Omega-6 fatty acids: ....0 g | Sodium: ............0 mg |
| Fiber (total): ............1 g | Cholesterol: ............0 mg | Iron: ............0 mg |
| Vitamin C: ............0 mg | Vitamin A: ............1 RE | Zinc: ............0 mg |

Diabetic exchanges: 1 serving equals ¾ fruit exchange. Add these frosting exchanges to the cake exchanges.

# Chocolate or Carob Cake

*This is great served with cherry fruit sauce, page 115, instead of frosting.*

2⅓ cups all purpose, unbleached, or white spelt flour
¼ cup cocoa or carob powder
1¼ teaspoons baking soda
½ teaspoon salt
1⅛ cups (1 cup plus 2 tablespoons) apple juice concentrate, thawed
3¾ teaspoons lemon juice
3 tablespoons oil
1 teaspoon vanilla extract (optional)

Preheat your oven to 350°F. Oil and flour an 8 inch square cake pan. (Flour the pan with white spelt flour if you are making a wheat-free cake). In a large bowl, stir together the flour, baking soda, and salt. In a cup combine the apple juice concentrate, lemon juice, oil and vanilla. Stir the liquid mixture into the flour mixture until they are just combined. Pour the batter into the prepared pan and bake the cake for 25 to 40 minutes or until a toothpick inserted into the center of the pan comes out dry. Do not overbake chocolate or carob cakes since extra baking time tends to make them dry. Place the cake on a cooling rack and allow it to cool completely. If desired, top it with chocolate or carob drizzle or coconut topping, below, or frost it with cream cheese frosting, page 280. Cut it into squares and serve it from the pan. Makes 9 to 12 servings.

## Chocolate or carob drizzle:

6 ounces (about 1 cup) chocolate or carob chips (See note below).
¼ to ½ cup heavy cream

Combine the chocolate or carob chips and ¼ cup of the cream in the top of a double boiler over simmering water. Heat and stir them until the chips are melted and they are thoroughly mixed with the cream. Alternately, to make this topping in a microwave oven, put the chips and cream into a glass bowl. Heat them together in a microwave oven on 50% power, stirring every 30 seconds, until the chips are melted and uniformly mixed into the cream. Drizzle and spread the chocolate or carob mixture over the cake.

Note: Sugar-sweetened chocolate chips produce the most creamy, smooth cake topping and "take" ¼ cup of cream. If you use grain-sweetened chocolate chips or carob chips, the topping may be grainy, and you may have to add up to ¼ cup more cream to produce a creamy topping. Just keep melting, stirring, and adding more cream until the desired consistency is reached.

## Coconut spread for chocolate or carob cake:

½ cup Fruit Sweet™ or honey
½ cup water
2½ tablespoons cornstarch, 3 tablespoons arrowroot, or 2½ tablespoons of
    tapioca flour
2 to 3 cups of unsweetened coconut – 2 cups if it is very finely shredded or up to
    3 cups for "regular" shredded unsweetened coconut

Combine the sweetener, water, and starch in a saucepan. Cook it over medium heat, stirring frequently, until it thickens and boils. Immediately stir in enough of the coconut to make a thick, yet spreadable, paste. Spread it on the cake immediately before it cools.

**Nutritional Analysis per serving:** 12 servings per recipe

**Cake only:**

| | | |
|---|---|---|
| Calories: ...................168 | Total fat:...........................4 g | Calcium:................................9 mg |
| Protein:................................3 g | Saturated fat:...............0 g | Magnesium: .......................10 mg |
| Carbohydrate: ................30 g | Omega-3 fatty acids:...0.33 g | Potassium:........................175 mg |
| Sugars:..............................11 g | Omega-6 fatty acids: ..0.82 g | Sodium: ..........................236 mg |
| Fiber (total): ......................1 g | Cholesterol: ......................0 mg | Iron:.........................................1 mg |
| Vitamin C: ..........................1 mg | Vitamin A: .........................0 RE | Zinc:........................................0 mg |

Diabetic exchanges: 1 serving equals 1¼ starch exchanges, ¾ fruit exchange, ½ fat exchange. Add the exchanges of any frosting you use to the cake exchanges.

**Chocolate drizzle only:**

| | | |
|---|---|---|
| Calories: ...................85 | Total fat: ...........................6 g | Calcium:................................8 mg |
| Protein: ..............................1 g | Saturated fat: ...............4 g | Magnesium:........................17 mg |
| Carbohydrate: ..................9 g | Omega-3 fatty acids:...0.04 g | Potassium:..........................55 mg |
| Sugars:................................8 g | Omega-6 fatty acids: ..0.17 g | Sodium: ................................3 mg |
| Fiber (total):......................1 g | Cholesterol: ......................0 mg | Iron: .......................................0 mg |
| Vitamin C:..........................0 mg | Vitamin A: .........................21 RE | Zinc:........................................0 mg |

Diabetic exchanges: 1 serving equals ½ other carbohydrate exchange, 1 fat exchange. Add these frosting exchanges to the cake exchanges.

**Coconut spread only:**

| | | |
|---|---|---|
| Calories: ...................112 | Total fat: ...........................8 g | Calcium: .............................23 mg |
| Protein: ..............................1 g | Saturated fat:...............7 g | Magnesium:........................12 mg |
| Carbohydrate:.................10 g | Omega-3 fatty acids:...0 g | Potassium:..........................70 mg |
| Sugars:................................6 g | Omega-6 fatty acids: ..0.09 g | Sodium:.................................7 mg |
| Fiber (total):......................2 g | Cholesterol: ......................0 mg | Iron:.........................................1 mg |
| Vitamin C:..........................0 mg | Vitamin A: .........................0 RE | Zinc:........................................0 mg |

Diabetic exchanges: 1 serving equals ⅓ other carbohydrate exchange, ¼ fruit exchange, 1½ fat exchanges. Add these frosting exchanges to the cake exchanges.

# *Extra Nutrition Carrot Cake*

*With all the color and flavor in this cake, you can probably get away with feeding your family or guests whole grain flour!*

2½ cup whole wheat flour or 2¼ cups Purity Foods whole spelt flour
1¾ teaspoons baking soda
1½ teaspoon cinnamon
¼ teaspoon cloves
1 cup raisins (optional)
1½ cups grated carrots
1 cup pineapple juice concentrate, thawed
1 cup water
¼ cup oil

Peel the carrots and grate them on a cheese grater using the largest holes. Oil and flour an 8 inch square cake pan. Preheat your oven to 375°F. In a large bowl, stir together the flour, baking soda, and spices. Stir in the raisins. In a separate bowl or cup combine the pineapple juice concentrate, water, oil, and carrots. Stir the liquid ingredients into the dry ingredients until just mixed. Pour the batter into the prepared pan. Bake the cake for 45 to 55 minutes or until it is browned and a toothpick inserted into the center of the cake comes out dry. Cool completely on a wire rack before frosting the cake with cream cheese frosting. If this frosting is too high-fat for you, serve the cake alone or with whipped cream, page 281. Makes 9 to 12 servings.

## Cream cheese frosting:

    1 8 ounce package cream cheese (preferably low fat) at room temperature
    ½ cup (1 stick) butter at room temperature
    3 to 4 tablespoons Fruit Sweet™ or honey, to taste
    1 teaspoon vanilla extract

Using an electric mixer, if you have one, or otherwise using a hand blender, mix together and "cream" (beat until fluffy) the cream cheese and butter. Mix in the vanilla extract. Add the Fruit Sweet™ or honey one tablespoon at a time, to taste. Spread on the top of the carrot cake. This frosting will be very soft but it gets firmer when chilled. Store any cake frosted with this frosting in the refrigerator.

**Nutritional Analysis per serving:** 12 servings per recipe

### Cake only:

| | | |
|---|---|---|
| Calories: .........................189 | Total fat:...........................5 g | Calcium: ..............................13 mg |
| Protein: .............................5 g | Saturated fat: ................0 g | Magnesium: ......................10 mg |
| Carbohydrate: ...............30 g | Omega-3 fatty acids:...0.43 g | Potassium: .......................158 mg |
| Sugars:...........................12 g | Omega-6 fatty acids: ..0.94 g | Sodium:.............................189 mg |
| Fiber (total):......................4 g | Cholesterol: .....................0 mg | Iron:.........................................1 mg |
| Vitamin C: ........................11 mg | Vitamin A:....................388 RE | Zinc:........................................0 mg |

Diabetic exchanges: 1 serving equals 1¼ starch exchanges, ⅔ fruit exchange, ¼ vegetable exchange, 1 fat exchange. Add the exchanges of any frosting you use to the cake exchanges.

### Frosting only:

| | | |
|---|---|---|
| Calories: .........................119 | Total fat:...........................11 g | Calcium: ..............................31 mg |
| Protein: .............................2 g | Saturated fat: ................7 g | Magnesium: ........................2 mg |
| Carbohydrate: .................3 g | Omega-3 fatty acids:...0.16 g | Potassium:.........................34 mg |
| Sugars:.............................3 g | Omega-6 fatty acids: ..0.25 g | Sodium:.............................135 mg |
| Fiber (total): ....................0 g | Cholesterol: ...................31 mg | Iron:........................................1 mg |
| Vitamin C: ........................0 mg | Vitamin A:....................113 RE | Zinc:........................................0 mg |

Diabetic exchanges: 1 serving equals ¼ other carbohydrate exchange, ¼ lean meat exchange, 2 fat exchanges. Add these frosting exchanges to the cake exchanges.

# *Extra Nutrition Gingerbread*

*This dessert is another place to give some whole grains to your loved ones. It is great served with whipped cream.*

    2 cups whole wheat or 2⅜ cups (2¼ cups plus 2 tablespoons) Purity Foods whole
        spelt flour
    2 teaspoons baking powder
    1 teaspoon cinnamon

¾ teaspoon ginger
½ cup molasses
½ cup water
¼ cup oil

Oil and flour an 8 inch square or 9 inch square cake pan. Preheat your oven to 350°F. In a large bowl, stir together the flour, baking powder, and spices. In a separate bowl or cup combine the molasses, water, and oil. Stir the liquid ingredients into the dry ingredients until just mixed. Pour the batter into the prepared pan. Bake the cake for 30 to 40 minutes or until it is browned and a toothpick inserted into the center of the cake comes out dry. Cool on a wire rack. Makes 9 to 12 servings.

# Whipped Cream:

1 cup heavy or "whipping" cream
2 to 4 teaspoons of Fruit Sweet™ or honey, to taste.

If you have an electric mixer, this is the time to use it! Pour the whipped cream into the narrow bowl and beat it at the "whipped cream" setting. Whip it until soft peaks form. Add sweetener to your taste and continue to whip it until the peaks become firm. This will happen quickly with an electric mixer, so watch it closely.

If you do not have an electric mixer, pour the whipped cream into the narrow cup that came with your hand blender. Blend it, letting the cup go around while moving the blender up and down, until soft peaks form. This may take 10 to 15 minutes and your thumb may become tired of holding down the button. Add the sweetener to taste and whip it a few minutes more until the peaks become firm. Makes 8 to 12 servings.

**Nutritional Analysis per serving:** 12 servings per recipe
**Cake only:**

| | | |
|---|---|---|
| Calories: ...................157 | Total fat:....................5 g | Calcium:....................85 mg |
| Protein: ......................3 g | Saturated fat:..............0 g | Magnesium:................33 mg |
| Carbohydrate:............24 g | Omega-3 fatty acids:...0.42 g | Potassium:................200 mg |
| Sugars:.......................9 g | Omega-6 fatty acids: ..0.93 g | Sodium:.....................66 mg |
| Fiber (total):...............3 g | Cholesterol: ................0 mg | Iron:..............................2 mg |
| Vitamin C:..................0 mg | Vitamin A: ..................0 RE | Zinc:.............................0 mg |

Diabetic exchanges: 1 serving equals 1 starch exchange, ½ other carbohydrate exchange, 1 fat exchange. Add the exchanges of any frosting you use to the cake exchanges.

**Whipped cream only:**

| | | |
|---|---|---|
| Calories: ....................70 | Total fat:....................7 g | Calcium: ...................14 mg |
| Protein:......................0 g | Saturated fat:..............5 g | Magnesium: ..................1 mg |
| Carbohydrate:..............1 g | Omega-3 fatty acids:...0.11 g | Potassium: .................15 mg |
| Sugars: ......................1 g | Omega-6 fatty acids: ..0.17 g | Sodium:.......................8 mg |
| Fiber (total): ..............0 g | Cholesterol: ..............27 mg | Iron: ............................0 mg |
| Vitamin C:..................0 mg | Vitamin A:.................84 RE | Zinc:.............................0 mg |

Diabetic exchanges: 1 serving equals 1½ fat exchanges. Add these whipped cream exchanges to the gingerbread exchanges or the exchanges for whatever you use it on.

# Chocolate or Carob Pudding

2 cups milk of any kind – skim, whole, goat, soy, or coconut
½ cup Fruit Sweet™ or honey
¼ cup cocoa or carob powder
3 tablespoons cornstarch or 5 tablespoons arrowroot or tapioca starch
2 teaspoons vanilla extract

Stir together the cocoa or carob and starch in a saucepan. Stir in about a half cup of the milk to form a smooth paste. Stir in the rest of the milk and the sweetener. Cook the pudding over medium heat, stirring frequently until it thickens and just begins to boil. Stir in the vanilla. Makes 4 to 8 servings.

**Nutritional Analysis per serving:** 8 servings per recipe

| | | |
|---|---|---|
| Calories: ...70 | Total fat: ...0 g | Calcium: ...106 mg |
| Protein: ...3 g | Saturated fat: ...0 g | Magnesium: ...7 mg |
| Carbohydrate: ...15 g | Omega-3 fatty acids:...0 g | Potassium: ...145 mg |
| Sugars: ...10 g | Omega-6 fatty acids: ..0 g | Sodium: ...34 mg |
| Fiber (total): ...2 g | Cholesterol: ...1 mg | Iron: ...1 mg |
| Vitamin C: ...1 mg | Vitamin A: ...37 RE | Zinc: ...0 mg |

Diabetic exchanges: 1 serving equals ⅔ starch/other carbohydrate exchange, ¼ skim milk exchange

# Vanilla Pudding

2 cups milk of any kind – skim, whole, goat, soy, or coconut
⅓ cup Fruit Sweet™ or honey
3 tablespoons cornstarch or 5 tablespoons arrowroot or tapioca starch
2 teaspoons vanilla extract

In a saucepan stir together about ⅓ cup of the milk and the starch to form a smooth paste. Stir in the rest of the milk and the sweetener. Cook the pudding over medium heat, stirring frequently until it thickens and just begins to boil. Stir in the vanilla. Makes 4 to 8 servings.

**Coconut pudding variation:** Use 1 teaspoon coconut flavoring instead of the vanilla. Sprinkle the pudding with grated coconut if desired.

**Nutritional Analysis per serving:** 8 servings per recipe

| | | |
|---|---|---|
| Calories: ...53 | Total fat: ...0 g | Calcium: ...95 mg |
| Protein: ...2 g | Saturated fat: ...0 g | Magnesium: ...7 mg |
| Carbohydrate: ...11 g | Omega-3 fatty acids:...0 g | Potassium: ...102 mg |
| Sugars: ...8 g | Omega-6 fatty acids: ..0 g | Sodium: ...33 mg |
| Fiber (total): ...0 g | Cholesterol: ...0 mg | Iron: ...1 mg |
| Vitamin C: ...1 mg | Vitamin A: ...37 RE | Zinc: ...0 mg |

Diabetic exchanges: 1 serving equals ⅖ starch/other carbohydrate exchange, ¼ skim milk exchange

# Fruit Tapioca Pudding

3 to 4 pounds of apples, peaches, or nectarines
1 cup apple juice concentrate, thawed
3 tablespoons quick-cooking ("minute") tapioca
1½ teaspoons cinnamon with the apples or ¼ teaspoon nutmeg with the peaches
    or nectarines

Peel, core, and slice the fruit to produce about 9 or 10 cups of slices. Combine ½ cup of the apple juice concentrate, the fruit, and the spice in a large saucepan. Bring them to a boil over medium heat, reduce the heat, and simmer until the fruit is tender, about 15 to 25 minutes. Near the end of the cooking time, combine the tapioca with the remaining ½ cup apple juice concentrate and allow it to stand for at least 5 minutes. Stir the tapioca mixture into the fruit when it is tender. Return the pan to a boil, and simmer the pudding for an additional 5 minutes. Let the pudding stand for at least 20 minutes before serving it. Makes 8 to 10 servings.

**Nutritional Analysis per serving:** 10 servings per recipe

| | | | | | |
|---|---|---|---|---|---|
| Calories: | 128 | Total fat: | 0 g | Calcium: | 6 mg |
| Protein: | 0 g | Saturated fat: | 0 g | Magnesium: | 5 mg |
| Carbohydrate: | 33 g | Omega-3 fatty acids: | 0 g | Potassium: | 277 mg |
| Sugars: | 25 g | Omega-6 fatty acids: | 0 g | Sodium: | 7 mg |
| Fiber (total): | 5 g | Cholesterol: | 0 mg | Iron: | 1 mg |
| Vitamin C: | 5 mg | Vitamin A: | 9 RE | Zinc: | 0 mg |

Diabetic exchanges: 1 serving equals 2 fruit exchanges

# Chocolate Chip or Carob Chip Cookies

3 cups all purpose or unbleached flour
1 teaspoon baking powder
½ teaspoon baking soda
¼ teaspoon salt
1 cup Fruit Sweet™ or honey
¾ cup oil
2 eggs
2 teaspoons vanilla extract
1 cup chocolate or carob chips

Preheat your oven to 375°F. In a large bowl stir together the flour, baking powder, baking soda, and salt. In a separate bowl thoroughly combine the sweetener, oil, eggs, and vanilla extract. Stir the liquid ingredients into the dry ingredients until they are just mixed. Fold in the chocolate or carob chips. Drop the batter by heaping teaspoonfuls 2 to 3 inches apart on an ungreased baking sheet. Bake the cookies for 10 to 13 minutes or until they are golden brown. Remove them from the baking sheets and put them on paper towels to cool. Makes 3 to 4 dozen cookies.

**Lower-fat variation:** Substitute ½ cup oil plus ¼ cup water for the ¾ cup oil in the recipe above.

**Nutritional Analysis per serving:** 48 1-cookie servings per recipe

| | | | | | |
|---|---|---|---|---|---|
| Calories: | 89 | Total fat: | 5 g | Calcium: | 20 mg |
| Protein: | 1 g | Saturated fat: | 1 g | Magnesium: | 6 mg |
| Carbohydrate: | 11 g | Omega-3 fatty acids: | 0.32 g | Potassium: | 24 mg |
| Sugars: | 5 g | Omega-6 fatty acids: | 0.78 g | Sodium: | 37 mg |
| Fiber (total): | 1 g | Cholesterol: | 9 mg | Iron: | 1 mg |
| Vitamin C: | 0 mg | Vitamin A: | 4 RE | Zinc: | 0 mg |

Diabetic exchanges: 1 serving equals ¾ starch/other carbohydrate exchange, ¾ fat exchange

**Lower fat variation:**

| | | |
|---|---|---|
| Calories: ....................79 | Total fat:...................4 g | Calcium:......................20 mg |
| Protein: .......................1 g | Saturated fat: ...............1 g | Magnesium: ...................6 mg |
| Carbohydrate: ................11 g | Omega-3 fatty acids:...0.22 g | Potassium:....................24 mg |
| Sugars:..........................5 g | Omega-6 fatty acids: ..0.55 g | Sodium:.........................37 mg |
| Fiber (total):..................1 g | Cholesterol: .................9 mg | Iron:..............................1 mg |
| Vitamin C:....................0 mg | Vitamin A:....................4 RE | Zinc:.............................0 mg |

Diabetic exchanges: 1 serving equals ¾ starch/other carbohydrate exchange, ½ fat exchange

# Wheat-free Egg-free Chocolate Chip or Carob Chip Cookies

3½ cups white spelt flour
1 teaspoon baking powder*
½ teaspoon baking soda
¼ teaspoon salt
1 cup Fruit Sweet™ or honey
1 cup oil
2 teaspoons vanilla extract (optional)
1 cup chocolate or carob chips

Preheat your oven to 375°F. In a large bowl stir together the flour, baking powder, baking soda, and salt. In a separate bowl thoroughly combine the sweetener, oil, and vanilla extract. Stir the liquid ingredients into the dry ingredients until they are just mixed. Fold in the chocolate or carob chips. Drop the batter by heaping teaspoonfuls 2 to 3 inches apart on an ungreased baking sheet. Bake the cookies for 9 to 13 minutes or until they are golden brown. Remove them from the baking sheets and put them on paper towels to cool. Makes 3 to 4 dozen cookies.

**Lower-fat variation:** Substitute ⅔ cup oil plus ⅓ cup water for the 1 cup oil in the recipe above.

*Note on baking powder: Use Featherweight™ brand baking powder if you are allergic to corn. It contains potato starch instead of cornstarch.

**Nutritional Analysis per serving:** 48 1-cookie servings per recipe

| | | |
|---|---|---|
| Calories: ....................96 | Total fat: ....................6 g | Calcium:......................18 mg |
| Protein: .......................1 g | Saturated fat: ...............1 g | Magnesium:...................4 mg |
| Carbohydrate: ................11 g | Omega-3 fatty acids:...0.42 g | Potassium:....................13 mg |
| Sugars:..........................5 g | Omega-6 fatty acids: ..0.95 g | Sodium: ........................34 mg |
| Fiber (total):..................1 g | Cholesterol: .................0 mg | Iron:..............................1 mg |
| Vitamin C:....................0 mg | Vitamin A: ...................0 RE | Zinc:.............................0 mg |

Diabetic exchanges: 1 serving equals ¾ starch/other carbohydrate exchange, ¾ fat exchange

**Lower fat variation:**

| | | |
|---|---|---|
| Calories: ....................82 | Total fat:...................4 g | Calcium:......................18 mg |
| Protein: .......................1 g | Saturated fat: ...............1 g | Magnesium:...................4 mg |
| Carbohydrate: ................11 g | Omega-3 fatty acids:...0.28 g | Potassium:....................13 mg |
| Sugars:..........................5 g | Omega-6 fatty acids: ..0.64 g | Sodium: ........................34 mg |
| Fiber (total):..................1 g | Cholesterol: .................0 mg | Iron:..............................1 mg |
| Vitamin C:....................0 mg | Vitamin A: ...................0 RE | Zinc:.............................0 mg |

Diabetic exchanges: 1 serving equals ¾ starch/other carbohydrate exchange, ½ fat exchange

# Peanut Butter Oatmeal Cookies

1¼ cups all purpose or unbleached flour or 1½ cups white spelt flour
1 cups oatmeal, regular or quick-cooking (not instant)
1 teaspoon baking soda
½ cup natural peanut butter
¼ cup oil
1 cup Fruit Sweet™ or ¾ cup honey plus ¼ cup water
1 teaspoon vanilla (optional)

Preheat your oven to 375°F. In a large bowl, combine the flour, oatmeal, and baking soda. Thoroughly stir the oil which is at the top of the peanut butter jar into the peanut butter at the bottom before measuring the peanut butter. In another bowl or cup, mix together the peanut butter, oil, Fruit Sweet™ or honey plus water and vanilla. (If you have a hand blender, use it to mix the liquid ingredients). Stir them into the dry ingredients until they are just mixed. Drop the dough by heaping teaspoonfuls 2 to 3 inches apart on an ungreased baking sheet. Bake for 7 to 11 minutes. Cool the cookies for about five minutes on the baking sheet. Then use a spatula to transfer them to paper towels to cool. Makes about 3½ dozen cookies.

**Nutritional Analysis per serving:** 42 1-cookie servings per recipe

| | | |
|---|---|---|
| Calories: ....................62 | Total fat:.....................3 g | Calcium: .....................15 mg |
| Protein: ......................1 g | Saturated fat:.............0 g | Magnesium:....................9 mg |
| Carbohydrate:................8 g | Omega-3 fatty acids:...0.12 g | Potassium: ...................31 mg |
| Sugars:.......................3 g | Omega-6 fatty acids: ..0.80 g | Sodium: .......................39 mg |
| Fiber (total):................1 g | Cholesterol: ...............0 mg | Iron:...........................1 mg |
| Vitamin C:....................0 mg | Vitamin A: ...................0 RE | Zinc:...........................0 mg |

Diabetic exchanges: 1 serving equals ½ starch/other carbohydrate exchange, ½ fat exchange

# Tropical Delights

2 cups all purpose or unbleached flour or 2⅛ cups white spelt flour
½ teaspoon baking soda
¼ teaspoon salt
1 cup unsweetened shredded coconut
1 cup pineapple canned in its own juice with the juice (crushed, chunks, or
    tidbits work well)
¾ cup pineapple juice concentrate, thawed
½ cup oil

Preheat your oven to 375°F. Lightly oil your baking sheets. Put the pineapple in the narrow cup of your hand blender and puree it, or puree it with a food processor or standard blender. In a large bowl stir together the flour, baking soda, salt, and coconut. In a separate bowl thoroughly combine the pineapple juice concentrate, pureed pineapple, and oil. Stir the liquid ingredients into the dry ingredients until they are just mixed. Drop the batter by heaping teaspoonfuls 2 to 3 inches apart on the prepared baking sheets. Bake the cookies for 15 to 19 minutes or until they are golden brown on the bottom and just beginning to brown on the top. Remove them from the baking sheets and put them on paper towels to cool. Makes 2½ to 3 dozen cookies.

**Nutritional Analysis per serving:** 36 1-cookie servings per recipe

| | | |
|---|---|---|
| Calories: ...........................81 | Total fat:...........................5 g | Calcium:...............................5 mg |
| Protein: .............................1 g | Saturated fat: ................1 g | Magnesium: ........................7 mg |
| Carbohydrate:..................10 g | Omega-3 fatty acids:...0.28 g | Potassium: .....................56 mg |
| Sugars:............................4 g | Omega-6 fatty acids: ..0.66 g | Sodium: ..........................35 mg |
| Fiber (total):.......................1 g | Cholesterol: .....................0 mg | Iron: ......................................0 mg |
| Vitamin C:...........................3 mg | Vitamin A: ...........................1 RE | Zinc:.......................................0 mg |

Diabetic exchanges: 1 serving equals ¼ starch exchange, ¼ fruit exchange, 1 fat exchange

# Oatmeal Treasures

2 cups all purpose, unbleached, or 2½ cups white spelt flour
2 cups oatmeal, regular or quick-cooking (not instant)
1 teaspoon baking soda
½ teaspoon salt
1 teaspoon cinnamon
1¼ cups Fruit Sweet™ or 1 cup honey plus ¼ cup water
½ cup oil
2 teaspoons lemon juice
1 teaspoon vanilla extract (optional)
1 cup raisins or ½ cup raisins plus ½ cup chocolate or carob chips

Preheat your oven to 375°F. Lightly oil your baking sheets. In a large bowl stir together the flour, oatmeal, baking soda, cinnamon, and salt. In a separate bowl thoroughly combine the Fruit Sweet™ or honey plus water, oil, lemon juice, and vanilla extract. Stir the liquid ingredients into the dry ingredients until they are just mixed. Fold in the raisins and chocolate or carob chips. Drop the batter by heaping teaspoonfuls 2 to 3 inches apart on the prepared baking sheets. Bake the cookies for 8 to 13 minutes or until they are golden brown. Let them cool on the baking sheets for about five minutes after you take them out of the oven. Remove them from the baking sheets and put them on paper towels to cool. Makes 3½ to 4 dozen cookies.

**Nutritional Analysis per serving:** 48 1-cookie servings per recipe

| | | |
|---|---|---|
| Calories: ...........................74 | Total fat:...........................3 g | Calcium:...............................17 mg |
| Protein: .............................1 g | Saturated fat:................0 g | Magnesium: ........................7 mg |
| Carbohydrate:..................12 g | Omega-3 fatty acids:...0.22 g | Potassium: .....................40 mg |
| Sugars:............................5 g | Omega-6 fatty acids: ..0.56 g | Sodium: ..........................39 mg |
| Fiber (total):.......................1 g | Cholesterol: .....................0 mg | Iron:.......................................1 mg |
| Vitamin C:...........................0 mg | Vitamin A: ...........................0 RE | Zinc:.......................................0 mg |

Diabetic exchanges: 1 serving equals ½ starch/other carbohydrate exchange, ⅙ fruit exchange, ½ fat exchange

# Good and Easy Shortbread

1¼ cups all-purpose flour or 1½ cups white spelt flour
1 cup cornstarch, tapioca starch, or arrowroot
½ teaspoon baking soda
¼ teaspoon salt
½ cup oil
⅜ cup Fruit Sweet™ or slightly warmed honey

Preheat your oven to 350°F. Lightly oil a baking sheet. In a large bowl, stir together the flour, starch, salt, and baking soda. In a measuring cup or small bowl, thoroughly stir together the oil and sweetener. The mixture of the liquids should look opaque and somewhat granular. Immediately (before the oil and sweetener have time to separate) stir them into the dry ingredients. Put the dough on the prepared baking sheet and roll it out to ¼ inch thickness. Cut it into rectangles which are about 1 inch wide and 2 inches long. Bake for 12 to 18 minutes, or until the shortbread is golden brown. Take the baking sheet from the oven and re-cut the shortbread on the lines where it was previously cut. Remove the shortbread to a piece of paper towel to cool. Makes about 3 dozen pieces of shortbread.

**Nutritional Analysis per serving:** 36 1-cookie servings per recipe

| | | |
|---|---|---|
| Calories: ...........................61 | Total fat:.........................3 g | Calcium: ...............................6 mg |
| Protein: ...........................2 g | Saturated fat:................0 g | Magnesium: ..........................1 mg |
| Carbohydrate: ..................8 g | Omega-3 fatty acids:...0.28 g | Potassium: ...........................5 mg |
| Sugars: ............................1 g | Omega-6 fatty acids: ..0.63 g | Sodium: .............................35 mg |
| Fiber (total): .....................0 g | Cholesterol: ...................0 mg | Iron: ....................................0 mg |
| Vitamin C:........................0 mg | Vitamin A: .........................0 RE | Zinc:....................................0 mg |

Diabetic exchanges: 1 serving equals ½ starch/other carbohydrate exchange, ½ fat exchange

# Oatmeal Bars

2½ cups unbleached or all-purpose flour or 2¾ cups white spelt flour
1 cup oatmeal, regular or quick-cooking
1 teaspoon baking soda
¼ teaspoon salt
1¼ cups Fruit Sweet™ or 1 cup honey plus ¼ cup water
½ cup oil
1 cup raisins, chopped nuts, carob chips, or chocolate chips, or any combination
    of these ingredients (optional)

Preheat your oven to 350°F. Oil and flour a 13-inch by 9-inch baking pan. In a large bowl, combine the flour, oatmeal, baking soda, and salt. In a separate bowl or cup, stir together the oil with the Fruit Sweet™ or honey plus water until thoroughly combined. (The mixture will look granular). Stir the liquid ingredients into the dry ingredients until just mixed. Quickly fold in the raisins, nuts, or chips, if you are using them. Spread the batter in the prepared pan. Bake for 20 to 28 minutes, or until the cookies are golden brown. Do not overcook them or they will become dry! Cool the cookies for 15 minutes in the pan; then cut them into 1½ to 2-inch squares. If your cake pan has a lid, you can store the cookies in the pan, or remove them from the pan at this point if desired. Makes 2 to 3 dozen cookies. If you want 12 to 16 cookies, make a half batch and bake it in an 8 inch square cake pan.

**Nutritional Analysis per serving:** 36 1-bar servings per recipe

| | | |
|---|---|---|
| Calories: ...........................84 | Total fat:.........................3 g | Calcium: .............................19 mg |
| Protein: ...........................1 g | Saturated fat:................0 g | Magnesium:..........................5 mg |
| Carbohydrate: ................12 g | Omega-3 fatty acids:...0.29 g | Potassium: .........................17 mg |
| Sugars: ............................4 g | Omega-6 fatty acids: ..0.70 g | Sodium: .............................53 mg |
| Fiber (total): .....................1 g | Cholesterol: ...................0 mg | Iron:.....................................1 mg |
| Vitamin C:........................0 mg | Vitamin A: .........................0 RE | Zinc:....................................0 mg |

Diabetic exchanges: 1 serving equals ¾ starch/other carbohydrate exchange, ⅔ fat exchange

# Brownies

2 ounces unsweetened baking chocolate
⅓ cup oil
2 eggs
1½ cups granular Fruit Source™
¾ cup all purpose, unbleached, or white spelt flour
½ teaspoon baking powder*
½ teaspoon salt

Preheat your oven to 350°F. Oil the bottom only of an 8 inch square cake pan. In the top of a double boiler over simmering water, melt the chocolate. (If you don't have a double boiler, melt it very carefully in a saucepan over very low heat or in a microwave oven on 50% power stirring every minute). Remove the chocolate from the heat and stir in the oil and eggs. Then stir in the Fruit Source™. In a bowl, mix together the flour, baking powder, and salt. Stir the flour mixture into the chocolate mixture. Spread the batter in the prepared pan. Bake the brownies for 30 minutes. Cool them in the pan, and then cut into 16 squares. Makes 16 brownies. If you're cooking for a crowd, you can double this recipe and bake it in a 13 inch by 9 inch cake pan.
* Note on baking powder: Use Featherweight™ brand baking powder if you are allergic to corn. It contains potato starch instead of cornstarch.

## Nutritional Analysis per serving: 16 1-brownie servings per recipe

| | | |
|---|---|---|
| Calories: ................113 | Total fat: ......................7 g | Calcium: ......................19 mg |
| Protein: ....................2 g | Saturated fat: ..............2 g | Magnesium: ..................13 mg |
| Carbohydrate: ..........12 g | Omega-3 fatty acids:...0.42 g | Potassium: ..................44 mg |
| Sugars: ....................6 g | Omega-6 fatty acids: ....1.08 g | Sodium: ......................93 mg |
| Fiber (total): ............1 g | Cholesterol: ................27 mg | Iron: ..........................1 mg |
| Vitamin C: ................0 mg | Vitamin A: ....................11 RE | Zinc: ..........................0 mg |

Diabetic exchanges: 1 serving equals ¾ starch/other carbohydrate exchange, 1¼ fat exchanges

# Date Squares

**Filling ingredients:**

2 cups pitted natural (unsweetened) dates
½ cup water
2 tablespoons lemon juice

## Crust ingredients:

1¼ cups all purpose, unbleached, or white spelt flour
1½ cups oatmeal, regular or quick-cooking (not instant)
½ teaspoon baking soda
Dash of salt
¼ cup Fruit Sweet™ or slightly warmed honey
⅜ cup (¼ cup plus 2 tablespoons) oil
2 teaspoons vanilla extract

For the filling, cut the dates into halves or quarters. Combine the dates, water, and lemon juice in a small saucepan. Cook them over medium heat, stirring often, until the dates form a smooth, very thick paste. If they dry out, add more water as necessary while they are cooking.

Preheat your oven to 350°F. In an 8 inch square cake pan, stir together the flour, oatmeal, baking soda, and salt. Mix together the oil, sweetener, and vanilla in a cup or bowl. Stir the liquids into the flour mixture in the pan. Remove about one third of the crumbs from the pan. Press the remaining crumbs into a thin layer of dough which covers the whole bottom of the pan. Bake for five minutes. Let the dough cool on a wire rack until it is at least lukewarm; being cooler is all right also. Spread the date mixture on top of the crust in the pan. Crumble the remaining dough over the date mixture. Bake for 20 to 25 minutes or until lightly browned. Put the pan on a wire rack to cool. Cut the cookies in the pan into 16 squares. Makes 16 cookies.

**Nutritional Analysis per serving:** 16 1-bar servings per recipe

| | | |
|---|---|---|
| Calories: ......................179 | Total fat: ...........................6 g | Calcium:............................20 mg |
| Protein:..............................3 g | Saturated fat: ................1 g | Magnesium:.......................21 mg |
| Carbohydrate:..................31 g | Omega-3 fatty acids:...0.49 g | Potassium: ......................184 mg |
| Sugars: ...........................16 g | Omega-6 fatty acids: ....1.25 g | Sodium: .............................56 mg |
| Fiber (total):......................3 g | Cholesterol: ......................0 mg | Iron:.......................................1 mg |
| Vitamin C: ........................1 mg | Vitamin A:..........................2 RE | Zinc:......................................0 mg |

Diabetic exchanges: 1 serving equals 1 starch/other carbohydrate exchange, 1 fruit exchange, 1 fat exchange

# Snacks and Beverages

Snacks are the place where almost everyone's diet falls short nutritionally. Usually a snack is something you grab when you're hungry without giving thought or preparation to your selection. It doesn't have to be this way! Make some of the healthy snacks below to keep on hand and you'll be much less tempted to grab something loaded with sugar or trans fats when the hungries hit!

## Sweet 'n Nutty Popcorn

2 to 2½ quarts air-popped popcorn or one batch of "Good and Healthy Popcorn," page 291
1 cup slivered almonds or chopped nuts of any kind
¼ cup (½ stick) of butter, ghee, goat butter, or Earth Balance™ margarine
½ cup honey or Fruit Sweet™
½ teaspoon salt (optional – use only if you use unsalted butter or ghee)
1 teaspoon vanilla extract, almond flavoring, orange flavoring, or flavoring of your choice
¼ teaspoon baking soda

Pop the popcorn and put it in a large bowl with the nuts. In a saucepan, combine the butter or margarine, sweetener, and salt. Use the salt only if you use unsalted butter or ghee. Heat the mixture over medium heat until it begins to bubble. Reduce the heat to low and let it simmer for 5 minutes. While it is cooking, preheat your oven to 250°F. Remove the pan from the stove when the simmering time is completed. Stir in the flavoring thoroughly. Then stir in the baking soda thoroughly. The liquid will become a very fine foam. Pour the liquid over the popcorn and nuts and stir thoroughly to coat the popcorn and nuts uniformly. Put the popcorn mixture in a 13 inch by 9 inch cake pan, a jelly roll pan, two 8 or 9 inch cake pans or whatever pans you have. Bake the popcorn for 30 minutes, stirring it every 10 minutes. Remove it from the oven and allow it to cool. Stir it a couple of times while it is cooling to break it up. When it is completely cooled, store it in a tightly covered container or plastic bag. Makes 4 to 8 servings.

**Nutritional Analysis per serving:** 8 servings per recipe

| | | |
|---|---|---|
| Calories: 248 | Total fat: 15 g | Calcium: 46 mg |
| Protein: 5 g | Saturated fat: 4 g | Magnesium: 62 mg |
| Carbohydrate: 27 g | Omega-3 fatty acids: 0.09 g | Potassium: 143 mg |
| Sugars: 17 g | Omega-6 fatty acids: 2.12 g | Sodium: 101 mg |
| Fiber (total): 3 g | Cholesterol: 15 mg | Iron: 1 mg |
| Vitamin C: 0 mg | Vitamin A: 55 RE | Zinc: 1 mg |

Diabetic exchanges: 1 serving equals ½ starch exchange, ¾ other carbohydrate exchange, ½ lean meat exchange, 3 fat exchanges

# Good and Healthy Popcorn

*This is the way popcorn used to be when I was a kid. If you make your own popcorn using this recipe, you can control the amount and type of fat you consume. Even organic and "natural" microwave popcorn is loaded with trans fats. This popcorn is also very economical and delicious.*

2 tablespoons olive oil
⅓ cup unpopped popcorn
⅛ teaspoon salt, or to taste

Put the oil in a 3 quart or slightly larger saucepan. Add three kernels of popcorn to the pan and heat it over medium heat on your stove. For safety's sake, stay close by and watch the pan carefully! (The only kitchen fire I ever had occurred while making popcorn this way). In a few minutes, you will hear the three kernels of popcorn pop. Immediately add the rest of the popcorn to the pan. Move the pan back and forth on the burner while it is heating. In a few minutes, you will hear the corn beginning to pop. Keep moving the pan, and when the popping slows down and nearly stops, remove the pan from the stove and turn the burner off. Pour the popcorn into a bowl. Sprinkle it with a high-quality iodadized sea salt which does not contain aluminum as an anti-caking agent. Now you have a great, nutritious, very healthy snack! Makes 2 to 2½ quarts of popcorn, or 3 servings.

**Nutritional Analysis per serving:** 3 servings per recipe

| | | |
|---|---|---|
| Calories: ...........................159 | Total fat:............................10 g | Calcium:................................0 mg |
| Protein: ...............................3 g | Saturated fat: ................1 g | Magnesium:.........................0 mg |
| Carbohydrate:..................16 g | Omega-3 fatty acids:...0.05 g | Potassium:.........................62 mg |
| Sugars: ...............................0 g | Omega-6 fatty acids: ..0.70 g | Sodium: .............................98 mg |
| Fiber (total):.......................3 g | Cholesterol: .......................0 mg | Iron:......................................0 mg |
| Vitamin C:..........................0 mg | Vitamin A: .........................0 RE | Zinc:.....................................0 mg |

Diabetic exchanges: 1 serving equals 1 starch exchange, 1¾ fat exchanges

# GORP

*This is a take-off on Good Old Raisins and Peanuts. Make it with almonds, pumpkin seeds, and sunflower seeds for a good helping of omega-6 and omega-3 fatty acids.*

2 cups of nuts and seeds of two or three different kinds (i.e. peanuts and sunflower seeds, almonds and cashews, or pumpkin seeds, sunflower seeds and almonds)
1½ cups of raisins or other small or diced dried fruit
1 cup of carob chips or grain-sweetened chocolate chips

Mix all of the ingredients together in a plastic bag. Take the bag along with you for a healthy snack wherever you go. Makes about 3½ cups of snack mix or 14 ¼ cup servings.

**Nutritional Analysis per serving:** 14 servings per recipe

| | | |
|---|---|---|
| Calories: ...........................192 | Total fat: .............................9 g | Calcium: ............................94 mg |
| Protein:...............................6 g | Saturated fat: ................3 g | Magnesium: ......................13 mg |
| Carbohydrate:..................23 g | Omega-3 fatty acids:...0.01 g | Potassium:.......................200 mg |
| Sugars: .............................23 g | Omega-6 fatty acids: ....1.07 g | Sodium: .............................57 mg |
| Fiber (total):......................2 g | Cholesterol: .......................0 mg | Iron:......................................1 mg |
| Vitamin C: ..........................1 mg | Vitamin A:..........................2 RE | Zinc:.....................................0 mg |

Diabetic exchanges: 1 serving equals ½ starch/other carbohydrate exchange, ½ lean meat exchange, ¾ fruit exchange, 1¾ fat exchanges

# Guacamole

*If you have unbuffered vitamin C around but no lemon juice, you can still make this guacamole dip and it will have an extra nutritional advantage.*

1 large ripe avocado, weighing about ½ pound
1½ teaspoons lemon juice or ⅛ teaspoon unbuffered vitamin C powder
1 tablespoon finely chopped onion (optional)
1 green chili pepper, finely chopped (optional)
1 small tomato, peeled and finely chopped (optional)
¼ teaspoon salt, or to taste
⅛ to ¼ teaspoon pepper, to taste

Peel and seed the avocado. Put it in a bowl with the lemon juice or vitamin C, onion, chili pepper, salt, and pepper. Mash all of the ingredients together thoroughly with a fork or blend them with a hand blender. Gently fold in the tomato. Serve the dip immediately with vegetable dippers, such as celery or carrot sticks, or with healthy chips such as baked corn chips. This sauce may darken if it stands very long. Makes about ⅔ to 1 cup of dip or 6 servings.

**Nutritional Analysis per serving:** 6 servings per recipe

| | | |
|---|---|---|
| Calories: ............................46 | Total fat:............................4 g | Calcium:...............................0 mg |
| Protein: ..............................1 g | Saturated fat: ................1 g | Magnesium:.......................0 mg |
| Carbohydrate: ...................3 g | Omega-3 fatty acids:...0 g | Potassium: .....................143 mg |
| Sugars:............................0 g | Omega-6 fatty acids: ..0 g | Sodium: ...........................98 mg |
| Fiber (total):....................3 g | Cholesterol: .....................0 mg | Iron: .....................................0 mg |
| Vitamin C:.........................3 mg | Vitamin A: .........................0 RE | Zinc:.....................................0 mg |

Diabetic exchanges: 1 serving equals 1 fat exchange

# Cottage Cheese Dip

1 carrot
3 large radishes
1 cup low-fat cottage cheese
¼ cup plain low-fat yogurt, sour cream, or mayonnaise
½ teaspoon salt
¼ teaspoon pepper
2 teaspoons caraway seeds (optional)

Peel the carrot and grate it by rubbing it over the largest holes of a cheese grater. Finely chop the radishes. Put the cottage cheese in a bowl and puree it with your hand blender until it is smooth, or you can use a food processor or standard blender to puree it. Add the yogurt, sour cream or mayonnaise, salt, and pepper and puree the dip with again briefly. Stir in the caraway seeds, carrot, and radishes. Refrigerate until serving time. Serve this dip with vegetable dippers, such as broccoli florets, celery, or carrot sticks, or with healthy chips such as baked potato or corn chips. Makes about 1¾ cups of dip or 7 servings.

**Nutritional Analysis per serving:** 7 servings per recipe

| | | |
|---|---|---|
| Calories: .........................28 | Total fat: ..........................0 g | Calcium: ..........................32 mg |
| Protein: ..............................4 g | Saturated fat: ...............0 g | Magnesium: ......................0 mg |
| Carbohydrate: .................2 g | Omega-3 fatty acids:...0 g | Potassium: .......................82 mg |
| Sugars: ..........................2 g | Omega-6 fatty acids: ..0 g | Sodium: ..........................282 mg |
| Fiber (total): ....................0 g | Cholesterol: .......................4 mg | Iron: ....................................0 mg |
| Vitamin C: ..........................1 mg | Vitamin A: ......................193 RE | Zinc: ....................................0 mg |

Diabetic exchanges: 1 serving equals ⅔ very lean meat exchange ¼ vegetable exchange

# Coffee Without the Pot

*This is for those times when instant coffee just isn't good enough. If you find yourself making coffee this way often or if you're a real coffee fan, ask for a drip coffee maker for Christmas.*

## Flavorful Microwave Method:

¼ cup finely ground coffee, regular or decaffeinated
2 cups water

Combine the coffee and water in a 4-cup measuring cup or a glass bowl, making sure that the coffee is all moistened. Put the cup or bowl in the microwave oven and heat it on high for 8 minutes. Flatten out a large coffee filter, fold it in quarters, and open it up to form a cone shape. Put the cone in a funnel. (Does this remind you of chemistry lab?) Put the funnel into a 2-cup container of any kind or into your coffee mug, with a spare mug standing by. Pour the coffee into the funnel. Do the dishes, shave or put on your makeup while the coffee is running through the funnel. (This will go more quickly if you try not to pour the coffee grounds into the funnel. They will settle as the coffee-water mixture stands after cooking). If you're using two mugs, transfer the funnel to the second mug when the first mug is full. Makes 1½ to 2 servings, depending on how big your mugs are. If you have large mugs and want enough coffee to share with a friend, use ⅜ cup coffee and 3 cups water, and heat it on high for 10 minutes. The coffee may have cooled by the time you've filtered the entire batch of coffee. Reheat it very briefly in the microwave if necessary.

## Drip Method (stovetop or microwave):

For each serving use:
2 tablespoons finely ground coffee, regular or decaffeinated
¾ to 1 cup water (Use the smaller amount of water if you like your coffee strong).

Flatten out a large coffee filter, fold it in quarters, and open it up to form a cone shape. Put the cone in a funnel. Put the funnel into a serving container of any kind, such as a carafe or teapot, or into your coffee mug if you are only making one serving. Pour the coffee into the funnel. Draw cold, fresh water and measure it. Bring the water to a boil in a saucepan on your stove or in a glass measuring cup or bowl in your microwave oven. Pour the boiling water into the filter, a little at a time if necessary. As soon as the coffee has finished dripping into your serving container or mug, serve the coffee.

**Nutritional Analysis per serving:** 1 serving

| | | |
|---|---|---|
| Calories: .........................4 | Magnesium: ..................9 mg | Sodium: ..........................4 mg |
| Calcium: ..........................4 mg | Potassium: ..............96 mg | Caffeine ..........................103 mg |

# Drip Brewed Coffee

*This is how to make coffee with a drip coffee maker. To make really good coffee, keep your coffee maker clean, always use freshly drawn cold water and use high quality coffee.*

For each serving use:
   2 tablespoons finely ground coffee, regular or decaffeinated
   ¾ cup water

Put the proper filter for your coffee maker in the basket. Put the coffee into the filter basket. Draw fresh cold water, measure the right amount, and put it into the water reservoir of your coffee maker. (If possible, use naturally soft water. Do not use "softened" water). Start the coffee maker cycle and allow it to run its course. Serve the coffee immediately at the end of the cycle.

**Nutritional Analysis per serving:** 1 serving

| | | |
|---|---|---|
| Calories: ...........................4 | Magnesium: ................9 mg | Sodium: ...............................4 mg |
| Calcium:.............................4 mg | Potassium: .............96 mg | Caffeine...........................103 mg |

# Tea

For each serving use:
   ¾ cup water
   1 teaspoon tea leaves (any kind) or one tea bag

Draw fresh cold water. Bring it to a full boil, either on your stove or in a microwave oven, but do not allow it to boil for very long. Rinse the teapot out with boiling water. Put the tea leaves or tea bag into the teapot or into a mug if you are just making one serving. Pour the right amount of boiling water over the tea. Steep the tea for 3 to 5 minutes. Remove the tea bags or pour the tea through a strainer to remove the tea leaves. If you have loose tea but want to avoid the straining process, use a tea ball to make your tea.

**Nutritional Analysis per serving:** 1 serving, black tea

| | | |
|---|---|---|
| Calories: ...........................2 | Magnesium:.....................5 mg | Sodium: ...............................5 mg |
| Folate:................................9 mcg | Potassium:.................... 66 mg | Caffeine ...........................36 mg |

**Nutritional Analysis per serving:** 1 serving, herbal tea (chamomile):

| | | |
|---|---|---|
| Calories: ...........................2 | Magnesium:.....................2 mg | Sodium: ...............................2 mg |
| Calcium:.............................4 mg | Potassium: .................... 16 mg | Caffeine ............................0 mg |

# Old Fashioned Cocoa

1½ cups skim, whole, or goat milk
2 tablespoons cocoa
Dash of salt
½ cup boiling water
2 to 4 tablespoons Fruit Sweet™ or honey

Heat the milk in a saucepan until it is steaming and just under the boiling point. Remove it from the heat. While the milk is heating, stir together the cocoa and salt in a second saucepan. Stir in enough of the boiling water to make a smooth, lumpless paste. Stir in the scalded milk and sweetener. Heat the cocoa over low to medium heat, stirring often, until it is steaming and has tiny bubbles around the edge of the pan. Watch it carefully and do not allow it to boil. Makes 2 servings.

**Nutritional Analysis per serving:** 2 servings per recipe

| | | |
|---|---|---|
| Calories: .....................109 | Total fat:..........................1 g | Calcium:..........................257 mg |
| Protein: ...............................7 g | Saturated fat:...............0 g | Magnesium:.......................21 mg |
| Carbohydrate:.................19 g | Omega-3 fatty acids:...0 g | Potassium:.......................391 mg |
| Sugars: .........................16 g | Omega-6 fatty acids: ..0.03 g | Sodium: ..........................214 mg |
| Fiber (total):....................3 g | Cholesterol: .......................3 mg | Iron:........................................1 mg |
| Vitamin C: .........................2 mg | Vitamin A: .........................8 RE | Zinc: .......................................1 mg |

Diabetic exchanges: 1 serving equals ¾ other carbohydrate exchange, ¾ skim milk exchange

# Pantry Microwave Cocoa

*This is cheaper and healthier than commercial cocoa mixes.*

1½ tablespoons cocoa or carob powder
⅓ cup non-fat dry milk powder or goat milk powder
2½ tablespoons Fruit Sweet™ or honey
1 cup water

Stir together the cocoa or carob and powered milk in a mug. Add about ¼ cup of the water and stir it to make a lump-free paste. Add the honey or Fruit Sweet™ and the remaining water and stir. Microwave on high for 2 minutes or until hot. If you have fresh milk on hand, you can substitute 1 cup of milk for the dry milk powder and water. Makes one serving.

**Nutritional Analysis per serving:** 1 serving per recipe

| | | |
|---|---|---|
| Calories: .....................181 | Total fat:..........................1 g | Calcium:..........................360 mg |
| Protein: ...............................9 g | Saturated fat:...............0 g | Magnesium: .......................29 mg |
| Carbohydrate: ...............35 g | Omega-3 fatty acids:...0 g | Potassium: .......................519 mg |
| Sugars: .........................29 g | Omega-6 fatty acids: ..0 g | Sodium:..........................138 mg |
| Fiber (total):....................4 g | Cholesterol: .......................5 mg | Iron:........................................2 mg |
| Vitamin C: .........................1 mg | Vitamin A: .....................164 RE | Zinc: .......................................1 mg |

Diabetic exchanges: 1 serving equals 1 skim milk exchange, 1½ other carbohydrate exchanges

# Fruit Juice Soda

*This drink recipe avoids the sugar or corn syrup, phosphates, and caffeine found in most soft drinks.*

¼ cup of any sugar-free frozen fruit juice concentrate, thawed (Try apple, pineapple, grape, white grape, or fruit blends).
¾ cup chilled carbonated water
2 or 3 ice cubes.

Stir together all of the ingredients in a tall glass. Add a straw and enjoy. Makes one serving.

**Nutritional Analysis per serving:** 1 serving per recipe

| | | |
|---|---|---|
| Calories: ...........................117 | Total fat: .............................0 g | Calcium: .............................14 mg |
| Protein:..............................0 g | Saturated fat:................0 g | Magnesium:......................12 mg |
| Carbohydrate:.................29 g | Omega-3 fatty acids:...0.01 g | Potassium: ....................315 mg |
| Sugars:...........................27 g | Omega-6 fatty acids: ..0.06 g | Sodium:.............................18 mg |
| Fiber (total): .....................0 g | Cholesterol: .....................0 mg | Iron:......................................1 mg |
| Vitamin C: ...........................1 mg | Vitamin A: ..........................0 RE | Zinc:.....................................0 mg |

Diabetic exchanges: 1 serving equals 2 fruit exchanges

# Recipes to Impress

Food is meant to be shared. When you have guests for dinner, you want to put your most delicious dishes before them. Although the recipes in this chapter are very impressive, most of them are also easy to make. Some of them lend themselves well to being prepared ahead of time so you will be able to relax and enjoy the company of your guests.

There are many other recipes in this book that are good to serve to guests. Some of them are listed at the end of this chapter, but this is by no means an exhaustive list. Be creative when you entertain! Read "Entertaining 205" on pages 96 to 103 for sample menus and to get ideas of other foods you might want to serve when you have company.

## Baked Ham

*This recipe is so easy that it's great to have when you first begin entertaining. To really have time to enjoy your guests, make this ham part of an oven meal! See page 99 for a menu.*

A whole or half boneless pre-cooked ham, preferably a lean variety
Canned pineapple rings in their own juice – a 20 ounce can for a whole ham or 8
    ounce can for a half ham
Whole cloves

Score the ham diagonally across the top of the ham in two directions, perpendicular to each other, to form a diamond cut pattern. Place a whole clove in the center of each diamond. Lay slices of pineapple on the top of the ham and secure them with toothpicks. Place the ham in a covered casserole dish or in a baking pan. Cover it with the dish's lid or with aluminum foil. Bake it at 350°F for 15 minutes per pound or until it is heated through. If the ham is small, bake it at least one hour. Remove the ham from the oven and let it stand for a few minutes before slicing it. If desired, serve the ham with cherry sauce. (The recipe is on page 115). This sauce tastes best if the flavors blend overnight, so make it the day before your party and re-warm it right before serving time. You may wish to bake the ham without the pineapple if you will be serving it with cherry sauce.

**Nutritional Analysis per serving:** 1 serving = 3 ounces of ham and 1 slice of pineapple

| | | |
|---|---|---|
| Calories: ...........................139 | Total fat:.............................5 g | Calcium: ..............................13 mg |
| Protein: ...............................18 g | Saturated fat: ................2 g | Magnesium:.....................20 mg |
| Carbohydrate: ....................5 g | Omega-3 fatty acids:...0.06 g | Potassium:.......................304 mg |
| Sugars:............................5 g | Omega-6 fatty acids: ..0.42 g | Sodium: .........................1024 mg |
| Fiber (total): .....................0 g | Cholesterol: ....................45 mg | Iron:........................................1 mg |
| Vitamin C: .........................4 mg | Vitamin A: ..........................1 RE | Zinc:........................................3 mg |

Diabetic exchanges: 1 serving equals 2¼ lean meat exchanges, ¼ fruit exchange

# Roasted Turkey or Other Poultry

*A roasted turkey is a very impressive bird and almost a "must" for Thanksgiving, but for other occasions, try roasting a duck or a chicken.*

One turkey, duck, goose, or chicken
Salt

If you are using frozen poultry, be sure to buy it far enough in advance to thaw it. The best way to thaw poultry is by putting it in the refrigerator. Never just set it out at room temperature to thaw! However, a large turkey can take several days to thaw in the refrigerator, so I usually end up thawing mine by putting it, while still in its wrapping, in the sink with cool water to cover it. Change the water every half-hour to hour. When the breast feels spongy, take the turkey from the sink. I usually cut the wrapping open, remove the giblets, and clean out the turkey at this point (the day before the party) and put it into a plastic bag to go in the refrigerator. Refrigerate it until you are ready to cook it.

For any kind of bird, cut off excess skin and fat. This includes the "tail" at the lower end of the body cavity. If you are going to stuff the neck cavity, leave all the skin at the neck end of the bird. Use your fingers to scrape out any excess tissue in the body cavity. Then rinse out the neck cavity and body cavity with cool water.

For an unstuffed bird, right before cooking it, rub the body cavity with salt. Put it on a rack in the roasting pan. For a turkey, preheat your oven to 450°F. Put the turkey in and immediately lower the heat to 350°F. For all of the other birds listed above, you may turn the oven on to 350°F when you put them in the oven. Do not cover them. The approximate roasting times for unstuffed birds are:

Turkey: 20 minutes per pound for birds up to 6 pounds; 15 minutes per pound for larger birds
Duck or goose: 2½ to 3½ hours, or about 20 minutes per pound
Chicken: 1½ to 2½ hours.

For a stuffed bird, make the "Bread Stuffing" recipe on page 300. You can make the stuffing the day before your party, but don't put it into the bird until right before you are going to cook it. Stuff the body and neck cavities and close them with skewers. You can lace shut the body cavity of the turkey by sticking several skewers through both sides of the hole and then using string to lace them as you would a shoe. The approximate roasting times for stuffed birds are:

Turkey: 25 minutes per pound for birds up to 6 pounds; 20 minutes per pound for larger birds
Duck or goose: 3 to 4 hours
Chicken: 2 to 3 hours.

Baste the bird with the pan drippings occasionally during the roasting time. Watch it, and when it becomes nicely browned and the end of the roasting time is approaching, use your meat thermometer to check the temperature in the deepest part of the breast. If the turkey breast seems to be getting too brown, cover it loosely with a tent of aluminum foil. The temperature in the deepest part of the breast should reach 185°F. Smaller birds such as ducks, geese, or chickens are not as likely to dry out, so don't worry about overcooking them. If you don't have a meat thermometer, just cook the smaller birds until they are very brown and the leg joints are quite loose.

For a large turkey, you may also want to check the center of the stuffing in the body cavity, which should be 165°F. Remove the bird from the oven when these temperatures have been reached or exceeded. For safety reasons, it is much better to overcook than undercook your bird!

When the bird is cooked, remove it from the pan and put it on a cutting board. Let a large bird such as turkey stand for 10 to 15 minutes before carving it. During this time you can make gravy as directed in the following recipe. Smaller birds can be cut apart into breasts, legs, and wings immediately if you wish.

**Nutritional Analysis per serving:** 1 serving = 3 ounces of roasted turkey, chicken, duck, or goose without the skin

## Turkey:

| | | |
|---|---|---|
| Calories: ........................161 | Total fat: ..........................6 g | Calcium: .............................18 mg |
| Protein: ............................24 g | Saturated fat: ...............2 g | Magnesium: .....................23 mg |
| Carbohydrate: ..................0 g | Omega-3 fatty acids:...0.09 g | Potassium: ......................245 mg |
| Sugars:...........................0 g | Omega-6 fatty acids: ....1.37 g | Sodium:............................54 mg |
| Fiber (total): ....................0 g | Cholesterol: ..................63 mg | Iron:........................................1 mg |
| Vitamin C:.......................0 mg | Vitamin A: .......................0 RE | Zinc:.......................................2 mg |

Diabetic exchanges: 1 serving equals 2 lean meat exchanges, 1½ very lean meat exchanges

## Chicken:

| | | |
|---|---|---|
| Calories: ........................140 | Total fat:..........................3 g | Calcium: .............................13 mg |
| Protein: ............................26 g | Saturated fat: ...............1 g | Magnesium: .....................25 mg |
| Carbohydrate: ..................0 g | Omega-3 fatty acids:...0.05 g | Potassium:........................217 mg |
| Sugars:...........................0 g | Omega-6 fatty acids: ..0.55 g | Sodium: ...........................63 mg |
| Fiber (total): ....................0 g | Cholesterol: ..................72 mg | Iron:........................................1 mg |
| Vitamin C:.......................0 mg | Vitamin A:.......................5 RE | Zinc:.......................................1 mg |

Diabetic exchanges: 1 serving equals 1 lean meat exchange, 2½ very lean meat exchanges

## Duck:

| | | |
|---|---|---|
| Calories: ........................171 | Total fat:..........................10 g | Calcium: .............................10 mg |
| Protein: ............................20 g | Saturated fat: ...............4 g | Magnesium:......................17 mg |
| Carbohydrate: ..................0 g | Omega-3 fatty acids:...0.12 g | Potassium: ......................214 mg |
| Sugars:...........................0 g | Omega-6 fatty acids: ....1.10 g | Sodium: ...........................55 mg |
| Fiber (total): ....................0 g | Cholesterol: ..................76 mg | Iron:........................................2 mg |
| Vitamin C:.......................0 mg | Vitamin A:.......................20 RE | Zinc:.......................................2 mg |

Diabetic exchanges: 1 serving of duck or goose equals 3 lean meat exchanges. The nutritional values for goose are very similar to those for duck.

# Pan Gravy

*For the healthiest gravy, purchase a fat separator cup\* to remove the fat from your drippings.*

4 tablespoons pan drippings from a turkey, roast, or other meat which has been roasted\*\*
2 to 4 tablespoons all purpose, unbleached, or white spelt flour
About 2 cups water
Salt (about ½ to 1 teaspoon) and/or pepper to taste

Remove the meat or poultry from the roasting pan. Pour off all but about 4 tablespoons of the pan drippings. Try to pour off almost all of the fat\* (see note below) and retain mostly the brown meat juices. Put the pan over a burner, or two burners if it is a large turkey roaster, on your stove. Turn the heat on to low. Heat the drippings slightly and sprinkle the flour into the pan. Add enough flour to make a thick, creamy mixture, but not so much that it is like paste. Stir and cook the flour in the drippings until the mixture is smooth and begins to bubble. Then continue to cook and stir for at least one or two minutes longer. Gradually add the water a little at a time, stirring continually. Add enough water to bring the gravy to the desired thickness. Boil and stir the gravy for a few minutes. Season it to taste with salt and/or pepper. If your gravy has lumps, blend it with a hand blender to remove the lumps. Makes about 2¼ cups of gravy, or 9 quarter cup servings.

*Note on fat separator cups: A fat separator cup is a great kitchen tool for making gravy. It is a special cup with a spout which comes from the bottom of the cup. Pour all of the drippings into the cup, and then pour the brown juice from the bottom of the cup back into your roaster, leaving the fat behind. With a fat separator cup, you can easily and quickly separate the fat from the tasty brown juice. You can find these cups in cooking or home stores, or you can order one from the King Arthur Flour Baker's Catalogue. (See "Sources," page 323).

**Note on drippings: If you have more than 4 tablespoons of drippings and want to make a lot of gravy, or if you have less than 4 tablespoons, just scale the amount of flour and water up or down proportionately.

**Approximate Nutritional Analysis per serving:** 9 quarter-cup servings per recipe

| | | |
|---|---|---|
| Calories: ...........................35-45 | Total fat: .............................2-3 g | Calcium: ............................2 mg |
| Protein: ...................................1 g | Saturated fat: ................1-2 g | Magnesium: .......................1 mg |
| Carbohydrate: ....................3 g | Omega-3 fatty acids:...0 g | Potassium: ....................5-15 mg |
| Sugars:.................................0 g | Omega-6 fatty acids: ..0 g | Sodium: ....................200-300 mg |
| Fiber (total): ......................0 g | Cholesterol: .....................7-10 mg | Iron:....................................0 mg |
| Vitamin C:..........................0 mg | Vitamin A:........................25-45 RE | Zinc: ...................................0 mg |

# Bread Stuffing

12 to 14 cups of bread cubes or about ¾ loaf of bread
3 to 4 stalks of celery
1 small onion (optional)
3 to 4 tablespoons butter or oil
½ teaspoon salt (optional – Use this only if you use water rather than broth).
⅛ to ¼ teaspoon pepper, or to taste
⅛ teaspoon sage (optional)
¾ to 1 cup water or chicken broth

The day before you plan to make this stuffing, lay the bread slices out on your table or kitchen counter to dry. Turn them over in the evening so that the side of the slices that was down can dry overnight. The next morning break the bread into small pieces and put the pieces in a large bowl. Finely dice the celery and onion. Melt the butter or put the oil in a saucepan; add the celery and onion. Cook over medium heat until the vegetables just begin to brown. Pour them over the bread cubes. Sprinkle the bread cubes with the salt, pepper, and sage and mix thoroughly. While stirring the dressing, add enough of the water or chicken broth to just moisten the dressing. Put the dressing into a large casserole dish. Cover the dish with foil or its lid. Bake at 350°F for one hour or until it is nicely browned on top. You can refrigerate the dressing overnight before baking it if desired. If you would like to cook this dressing inside your bird, do not stuff the bird until immediately before you plan to cook it. Increase the cooking time for the bird as directed in the "Roasted Turkey or Other Poultry" recipe on page 298. Makes about 3 quarts of stuffing or 10 to 18 servings.

**Nutritional Analysis per serving:** 18 servings per recipe

| | | |
|---|---|---|
| Calories: ........................100 | Total fat:..........................3 g | Calcium: ............................19 mg |
| Protein:.............................2 g | Saturated fat: ...............1 g | Magnesium: ......................6 mg |
| Carbohydrate:.................15 g | Omega-3 fatty acids:...0.04 g | Potassium:.......................55 mg |
| Sugars: ...........................1 g | Omega-6 fatty acids: ..0.28 g | Sodium:..........................233 mg |
| Fiber (total):.....................1 g | Cholesterol: ....................5 mg | Iron:...................................1 mg |
| Vitamin C: .......................1 mg | Vitamin A: ......................19 RE | Zinc:..................................0 mg |

Diabetic exchanges: 1 serving equals 1 starch exchange, ½ fat exchange

# Cranberry Sauce

1 12 ounce package of fresh cranberries, about 4 cups of berries
1 cup Fruit Sweet™ or honey or 2 cups apple juice concentrate

Wash and pick over the berries, discarding any shriveled or soft berries. If you are using the apple juice concentrate, put it into a saucepan and bring it to a boil over medium-high to high heat. Reduce the heat to medium and boil it down until it reaches 1 cup in volume. Add the berries to the boiled-down apple juice concentrate or the Fruit Sweet™ or honey in a saucepan. Bring them to a boil over medium heat; then reduce the heat and simmer, stirring often, for 15 to 20 minutes or until all of the cranberries have popped. Pour the cranberry sauce into the serving bowl you plan to use, cover the bowl with plastic wrap, and refrigerate it until your party. (This is a good thing to make a day or two ahead of the party). If you are making this just for yourself, pour it into a glass jar to store it in the refrigerator. Makes about 2 cups of cranberry sauce or 12 servings.

**Nutritional Analysis per serving:** 12 servings per recipe

| | | |
|---|---|---|
| Calories: ........................56 | Total fat: ..........................0 g | Calcium: ............................42 mg |
| Protein:.............................0 g | Saturated fat: ...............0 g | Magnesium: ......................1 mg |
| Carbohydrate:.................14 g | Omega-3 fatty acids:...0 g | Potassium:.......................25 mg |
| Sugars: ...........................13 g | Omega-6 fatty acids: ..0 g | Sodium: .............................5 mg |
| Fiber (total):.....................1 g | Cholesterol: ....................0 mg | Iron:..................................10 mg |
| Vitamin C: .......................4 mg | Vitamin A:......................3 RE | Zinc:..................................0 mg |

Diabetic exchanges: 1 serving equals 1 fruit exchange

# Lemon Chicken

*This is an easy yet delicious recipe to make for guests.*

About 2 pounds of chicken pieces – breasts, thighs or legs – or a 2 pound chicken, cut up
3 to 4 potatoes, or about 1 to 1½ pounds of potatoes
2 tablespoons lemon juice
1½ tablespoons vegetable oil, divided
¼ teaspoon salt
Dash of pepper if you are not using lemon pepper
Dash of paprika
Dash of lemon pepper, optional

Lightly oil a 13 inch by 9 inch baking dish. Cut the potatoes in half lengthwise and then cut each half into three lengthwise wedges. Lay the potato wedges skin side down on one half of the dish. Brush the potatoes with ½ tablespoon of oil and sprinkle them with the paprika, about half of the salt, and pepper if desired. Remove the skin from the chicken and lay the chicken pieces on the other end of the dish. In a small bowl, mix together the remaining 1 tablespoon of the oil and the lemon juice. Brush the chicken pieces with the lemon-oil mixture. Sprinkle the chicken with the remaining salt and pepper or lemon pepper. Bake the dish at 400°F for 1½ hours, brushing the chicken with the remaining lemon-oil mixture every half hour. Makes 4 to 8 servings.

**Nutritional Analysis per serving:** 8 servings per recipe

| | | |
|---|---|---|
| Calories: ....................204 | Total fat: .........................4 g | Calcium: ............................18 mg |
| Protein: ...........................25 g | Saturated fat: .................1 g | Magnesium:...................46 mg |
| Carbohydrate:................16 g | Omega-3 fatty acids:...0.27 g | Potassium:...................526 mg |
| Sugars: .............................1 g | Omega-6 fatty acids: ..0.75 g | Sodium:........................130 mg |
| Fiber (total):.....................2 g | Cholesterol: ...................59 mg | Iron:....................................2 mg |
| Vitamin C:..........................11 mg | Vitamin A: .........................6 RE | Zinc:.....................................1 mg |

Diabetic exchanges: 1 serving equals 1 starch exchange, 1 lean meat exchange, 2 very lean meat exchanges

# Stuffed Cornish Hens

4 Cornish hens
1 4 ounce can sliced mushrooms
4 slices of bread (preferably whole grain day-old bread)
1 small carrot, peeled and grated
½ teaspoon dried or 2 teaspoons fresh parsley
½ teaspoon dried or 2 teaspoons fresh chopped onion, optional
Dash of salt
Dash of pepper
2 teaspoons melted butter or Earth Balance™ margarine
Strips of bacon, optional

Drain the mushrooms, reserving the juice. Peel the carrot and grate it using the large holes of a grater or a vegetable peeler. Cut the bread into cubes and put the cubes in a bowl. Add to the bowl the mushrooms, carrot, parsley, onion, salt, and pepper and mix. Add the butter or margarine and mix. Add enough of the reserved mushroom juice to barely moisten the stuffing and then mix it again. Put ¼ of the stuffing into each Cornish hen and close the cavity with a toothpick. Put the Cornish hens into a baking dish; lay bacon slices on the breasts if desired. Bake uncovered at 350°F for 1 to 1½ hours or until the birds are very brown. Makes 4 servings.

**Nutritional Analysis per serving:** 4 servings per recipe

| | | |
|---|---|---|
| Calories: ....................436 | Total fat: .........................13 g | Calcium:............................62 mg |
| Protein:............................62 g | Saturated fat: ...............4 g | Magnesium: ...................76 mg |
| Carbohydrate:................17 g | Omega-3 fatty acids:...0.34 g | Potassium: ...................804 mg |
| Sugars:..............................3 g | Omega-6 fatty acids:..4.00 g | Sodium:........................455 mg |
| Fiber (total): ...................0 g | Cholesterol: ...................269 mg | Iron:....................................3 mg |
| Vitamin C:..........................3 mg | Vitamin A:...................405 RE | Zinc:.....................................5 mg |

Diabetic exchanges: 1 serving equals 1 starch exchange, 3 lean meat exchanges, 5 very lean meat exchanges, ½ vegetable exchange

# Pesto alla Genovese

*This recipe requires the use of either a food processor or blender or a mortar and pestle similar to what you may have used in chemistry lab. Those who are allergic to tomatoes will have something to put on their pasta and pizza if they use this recipe.*

¼ pound sweet basil leaves, about 3½ cups
1 to 2 cloves of garlic, optional
½ cup pine nuts or other nuts
½ cup olive oil or other oil
½ to ¾ teaspoon salt (Use the smaller amount if you use the cheese).
2 tablespoons grated Romano or Parmesan cheese, optional

Wash the sweet basil and remove the leaves from the stems. Spread the leaves out on paper towels to dry. Blot the basil with a paper towel if it is not dry when you are ready to make the pesto. It does not have to be completely dry.

To make the pesto using a food processor or blender, put the garlic in the food processor or blender and pulse it to chop it. Add the sweet basil and pulse. Add the nuts and process continually until they are ground up. Add the oil in a thin stream while the food processor or blender is running. Add the salt and cheese and blend again briefly.

To make the pesto in the traditional way with a mortar and pestle, put the basil and garlic on a cutting board and chop them finely. Crush the pine nuts by rolling them with a rolling pin or pounding them with a meat pounder. Add them to the pile of basil and garlic. Sprinkle with the salt and continue to chop the pile. Then transfer the mixture to a large mortar. Pound and grind the mixture with the pestle until it forms a paste. Add the cheese and pound and grind some more. Add the olive oil one tablespoon at a time, working it with the pestle, until the pesto has absorbed as much of the oil as it can. If it begins to separate, stop adding oil even if you haven't added the full amount.

Serve the pesto over freshly cooked hot pasta or use about ¾ cup of pesto instead of tomato sauce to top one pizza. Freeze any leftover pesto. Makes about 1 to 1¼ cups of pesto, enough for 1 to 2 pounds of pasta, or about 8 to 10 servings.

**Nutritional Analysis per serving:** 10 servings per recipe

| | | |
|---|---|---|
| Calories: 137 | Total fat: 14 g | Calcium: 19 mg |
| Protein: 2 g | Saturated fat: 2 g | Magnesium: 25 mg |
| Carbohydrate: 1 g | Omega-3 fatty acids: 0.14 g | Potassium: 93 mg |
| Sugars: 0 g | Omega-6 fatty acids: 2.26 g | Sodium: 118 mg |
| Fiber (total): 1 g | Cholesterol: 0 mg | Iron: 1 mg |
| Vitamin C: 2 mg | Vitamin A: 44 RE | Zinc: 0 mg |

Diabetic exchanges: 1 serving equals ⅓ medium-fat meat exchange, 2½ fat exchanges

# Authentic Homemade
# Pasta Sauce with Meatballs

*This is "the real thing," a family recipe passed down from generation to generation on my mother's side of my family. This sauce gets its flavor from long cooking rather than from the addition of many seasonings.*

### Meatball ingredients:

2½ pounds of lean ground beef, buffalo, or other meat
1 tablespoon chopped fresh or 1 teaspoon dry parsley (optional)
½ teaspoon salt
¼ teaspoon pepper
1 clove of garlic, peeled (optional)

### Sauce ingredients:

1 28 ounce can tomato puree
3 6 ounce cans tomato paste (or 1 12 ounce can plus 1 6 ounce can)
1 cup water
1 teaspoon salt
¼ teaspoon pepper

To make the meatballs, put the meat, parsley, ½ teaspoon salt, and ¼ teaspoon pepper in a large bowl. Use your hands to mix the ingredients together thoroughly. Form the meat into 10 to 12 meatballs, pressing the meatballs together firmly. Put them in a skillet and cook them over medium heat, uncovered, turning them as they cook until all of the sides are well browned. If you wish to use the garlic, add the whole peeled clove of garlic to the rendered fat in the pan and cook it along with the meatballs. Remove and discard the garlic when the meatballs are cooked. Take the meatballs out of the pan and set them aside. Pour off all of the fat into a can. Discard it after it has cooled and solidified.

Add one 6 ounce can of tomato paste to the browned bits in the skillet you used to cook the meatballs. Heat the pan over medium heat and stir the tomato paste around to loosen and absorb all the browned bits and flavor from the meatballs. Scrape this tomato paste out into a large stockpot. Add about half of the water to the skillet and stir it around to remove the remaining tomato paste and browned bits; pour this into the stockpot as well.

Add the tomato puree, remaining tomato paste, remaining water, 1 teaspoon salt, and ¼ teaspoon pepper to the stockpot. (If you're of southern Italian persuasion, you may also add 1 teaspoon chopped fresh or ¼ teaspoon dry oregano and 1 teaspoon chopped fresh or ¼ teaspoon dry sweet basil to the sauce at this point). Stir the sauce ingredients together thoroughly. Then add the meatballs to the stockpot and cover the pot with its lid. Bring the sauce to a boil over medium heat, lower the heat, and simmer the sauce for one hour, stirring it at least every 10 minutes. Remove the meatballs from the sauce with a large slotted spoon. Return the sauce to a simmer and cook it, covered, for another hour. If you are planning to serve the sauce immediately, add as many meatballs as you will need for your meal back to the sauce and cook the sauce long enough to heat them through. Freeze the leftover meatballs and sauce. This recipe makes about 6 cups of sauce and 10 to 12 meatballs, enough sauce for 2 to 3 pounds of pasta or for two or three meals, or about 12 servings. If you have enough freezer space and a large enough pan, double or triple this recipe, and you'll have sauce for many meals. Pasta sauce in the freezer is like money in the bank. You're always ready for a rainy day or a special celebration.

**Nutritional Analysis per serving:** 12 servings per recipe

| | | |
|---|---|---|
| Calories: ......................194 | Total fat: ...........................9 g | Calcium: ...........................22 mg |
| Protein:...........................21 g | Saturated fat: ...............3 g | Magnesium: ....................42 mg |
| Carbohydrate:..................8 g | Omega-3 fatty acids:...0 g | Potassium: ....................672 mg |
| Sugars:............................5 g | Omega-6 fatty acids: ..0.06 g | Sodium: .........................659 mg |
| Fiber (total):....................2 g | Cholesterol: ...................34 mg | Iron: .................................3 mg |
| Vitamin C: .....................11 mg | Vitamin A: .....................111 RE | Zinc:..................................5 mg |

Diabetic exchanges: 1 serving equals 2¾ lean meat exchanges, 1¾ vegetable exchanges

Note: Many years ago my grandmother and mother used other meats in their sauce in addition to meatballs. Although we all "scaled down" to just meatballs, to be really authentic you may also add:

## Brugiolo:

1½ pounds beef round or shoulder steak
1 clove of garlic, very finely chopped
½ dry chili pepper, crumbled
½ teaspoon dry parsley or 1½ teaspoons chopped fresh parsley
Dash of salt
Dash of pepper

## Pork:

1½ to 2 pounds sweet Italian sausage or pork chops

To prepare the brugiolo, sprinkle the steak with the chopped garlic, chili pepper, parsley, salt, and pepper. Roll it up like a jelly roll and tie it into a bundle with cotton kitchen string. Brown it with the meatballs

To prepare the pork, brown the pork chops for 8 to 10 minutes on each side as in the pork chops recipe on page 159. If you are using the sausage, cut it into pieces about two inches long. Prick each piece in several places with a pin to keep it from bursting while it cooks. Put the sausage pieces in a frying pan and cook them over medium heat, turning them often, until they are well browned on all sides. Remove the sausage or pork chops from the pan and drain and discard the grease. Add one of the cans of the tomato paste called for in the recipe to the frying pan. Cook and stir it over medium heat for a few minutes to absorb all the browned bits and flavor from the pork. Add this tomato paste to the sauce.

Add the brugiolo and pork to the pot of sauce when you add the meatballs. Simmer them for one hour and remove them with the meatballs. Before serving, remove the string from the brugiolo and slice it.

# Authentic Pasta Sauce Made With Fresh Tomatoes

*This is a slightly different sauce from a different part of Italy. This is the way pasta sauce was made on my father's side of the family.*

6 pounds of ripe Italian plum tomatoes (Roma tomatoes)
Water
¼ cup olive oil
1 to 2 cloves of garlic, chopped (optional)
1 to 1½ teaspoons salt, or to taste
¼ teaspoon pepper
1 tablespoon chopped fresh or 1 teaspoon dry sweet basil, or to taste (optional)

Bring a large pan of water to a boil. Add the tomatoes to the pan several at a time. Return the water to a boil after adding each batch of tomatoes and boil them for 1 to 2 minutes. Remove the tomatoes from the pan with a slotted spoon, return the water to a boil, and add another batch of several tomatoes to the boiling water. Keep doing this until all of the tomatoes have been scalded.

While the tomatoes are being processed, peel the garlic and chop it. Put it into a large stockpot with the olive oil and cook it over medium heat until it is brown. Remove the garlic from the oil if you are not a real garlic fan.

After the tomatoes have all been scalded and have cooled slightly, slip the skins off the tomatoes with your fingers. Puree the tomatoes in a food processor or blender or blend them a few at a time with your hand blender until they are smooth. Add the tomato puree to the olive oil in the stockpot. Add the seasonings to the pot. Bring the sauce to a boil, reduce the heat and simmer it, covered, for one to two hours or until it is very thick. Stir it frequently, at least every 10 minutes, while it is simmering. Makes about 4 cups of sauce, enough for 1 to 2 pounds of pasta or 1 to 2 meals, or 6 to 10 servings.

**Fresh tomato sauce with meatballs variation:** Make meatballs as in the preceeding recipe from 1½ pounds of lean ground beef or other red meat, ½ teaspoon salt, and a dash of pepper. Brown them as in the preceeding recipe and add them to the sauce during its simmering time.

**Fresh tomato pizza sauce variation:** Make the sauce as directed above with one exception. In addition to the sweet basil, also add 1 tablespoon chopped fresh or 1 teaspoon dry oregano and 1 teaspoon chopped fresh or ½ teaspoon dry thyme. Makes enough sauce for three or four pizzas.

**Nutritional Analysis per serving:** 10 servings per recipe
**Sauce only, including pizza sauce variation:**

| | | |
|---|---|---|
| Calories: 105 | Total fat: 6 g | Calcium: 14 mg |
| Protein: 57 g | Saturated fat: 1 g | Magnesium: 30 mg |
| Carbohydrate: 13 g | Omega-3 fatty acids: 0.05 g | Potassium: 605 mg |
| Sugars: 8 g | Omega-6 fatty acids: 0.78 g | Sodium: 259 mg |
| Fiber (total): 3 g | Cholesterol: 0 mg | Iron: 1 mg |
| Vitamin C: 52 mg | Vitamin A: 169 RE | Zinc: 0 mg |

Diabetic exchanges: 1 serving equals 2½ vegetable exchanges, 1 fat exchange

**Sauce with meatballs variation:**

| | | |
|---|---|---|
| Calories: .....................220 | Total fat: .........................12 g | Calcium: ...........................19 mg |
| Protein: ...................16 g | Saturated fat: ..............3 g | Magnesium: ...................45 mg |
| Carbohydrate:..................13 g | Omega-3 fatty acids:...0.05 g | Potassium: ...................817 mg |
| Sugars:...........................8 g | Omega-6 fatty acids: ..0.78 g | Sodium:........................425 mg |
| Fiber (total):....................3 g | Cholesterol: ..................25 mg | Iron: ...................................3 mg |
| Vitamin C:.....................52 mg | Vitamin A: .....................169 RE | Zinc:....................................3 mg |

Diabetic exchanges: 1 serving equals 2 lean meat exchanges, 2½ vegetable exchanges, 1 fat exchange

# Pasta Dinner

*With homemade pasta sauce in your freezer and dry pasta in your pantry, you will always be ready to put on quite a spread for guests at a moment's notice.*

½ to 1 pound R & F thin spaghetti, vermicelli, mostaccioli, or other shape of pasta
   or a 10 ounce box of Purity Foods spelt pasta such as white spelt spaghetti
Water
½ teaspoon salt
About ⅓ to ½ batch of "Authentic Pasta Sauce" with at least 4 meatballs, page 304,
   ½ to 1 batch of "Pasta Sauce Made With Fresh Tomatoes, page 306, or ½ to
   1 batch of "Pesto alla Genovese," page 303
Grated Romano or Parmesan cheese

Fill a very large stockpot to within an inch or two from the top with water. Add the salt and bring it to a boil over high heat. The pot should be large enough for the pasta to move around freely while it is cooking. An Italian grandma would say that an 8 quart pot is about the minimum size for a pound of pasta, but you can probably "make do" with a 4½ quart pot.

Begin warming your sauce. Warm it in a saucepan over low heat and stir it about every 5 minutes to keep it from sticking and burning at the bottom of the pan. When it is ready and the pasta is nearly cooked, turn the heat off under the sauce so you don't forget to stir the sauce while you are intently involved with the pasta.

When the water comes to a full rolling boil, remove the lid and add the pasta. If your spaghetti is too long for the pan, don't break it! Just hold one end of the whole pound of spaghetti with your hand, stick the other end in the pot, and let it soften for a minute or so. Then push the end you are holding into the pot. Stir the pasta well. Strands of spaghetti or vermicelli may stick together if they end up cooking right next to the other strands especially if you are using a pot that is on the small side. Cover the pan and return it to a boil over high heat. As soon as it comes to a rolling boil again, lower the heat to medium, set the lid of the pot slightly ajar to help prevent boil overs, and begin timing the cooking time. (Don't panic if you have a boil over. A couple of boil overs are to be expected any time you cook pasta. The traditional process actually is not complete without a boil over and an "Oooooh!" from the cook!) Read the pasta package for the approximate cooking time. While the pasta is cooking, set a colander in the kitchen sink. At a minute or so before the recommended cooking time has elapsed, remove one piece of pasta from the pot and taste it. Is it *al dente?* This means does it still offer some resistance "to the tooth" although it is no longer hard? If not, keep cooking it for about two more minutes and then taste it again. When it is done, immediately pour the contents of the pot through the colander in the sink. Shake the colander to remove excess water and pour the pasta into your serving dish. Top it with some of the sauce and stir the sauce into the pasta thoroughly to coat all of the pieces. Serve the pasta with the remaining sauce, meatballs, and cheese. One pound of pasta serves 4 hungry college students or 8 of their parents. One-half pound of pasta serves 4 parents.

**Nutritional Analysis per serving:** 4 servings per recipe
(analysis based on ½ pound of pasta and ⅓ batch of Authentic Homemade Pasta Sauce with Meatballs).

| | | |
|---|---|---|
| Calories: .......................405 | Total fat: ...........................10 g | Calcium: ...........................33 mg |
| Protein: ..............................28 g | Saturated fat: ...............4 g | Magnesium: ....................69 mg |
| Carbohydrate: ................50 g | Omega-3 fatty acids: ...0.03 g | Potassium: ....................764 mg |
| Sugars: ..............................7 g | Omega-6 fatty acids: ..0.39 g | Sodium: ..........................663 mg |
| Fiber (total): ....................3 g | Cholesterol: ...................34 mg | Iron: .....................................5 mg |
| Vitamin C: ..........................11 mg | Vitamin A: .......................111 RE | Zinc: .....................................5 mg |

Diabetic exchanges: 1 serving equals 2½ starch exchanges, 2¾ lean meat exchanges, 1¾ vegetable exchanges

# Lasagne

*This is the perfect Italian dish for guests because it is very impressive but can be made ahead. Make it the day before your party and refrigerate it or make it a month ahead and freeze it if you wish.*

2 pounds lean ground beef, buffalo, or other meat
2 12 ounce cans tomato paste
1 28 ounce can tomato puree
3 cups water
1 teaspoon salt
⅛ teaspoon pepper
1 16 ounce box of R & F no-boil lasagne noodles
2 15 to 16 ounce containers of ricotta cheese (fat-free, part skim, or whole milk)
⅓ cup grated Romano or Parmesan cheese
1 24 ounce package of mozzarella cheese (fat-free, low fat, or part skim)
1 tablespoon chopped fresh or dried parsley (optional)

Put the meat in a large stockpot and cook it over medium heat, breaking it up and stirring it often, until it is well browned. Pour off the fat into a can. (Discard it after it has cooled and solidified). Add to the meat the tomato paste, tomato puree, water, salt, and pepper and stir thoroughly. Bring the sauce to a boil over medium heat, reduce the heat to low and simmer the sauce for 1½ to 2 hours, stirring it about every 10 minutes to keep it from sticking to the bottom of the pan and burning. When the sauce has thickened and tastes great, remove it from the stove.

In a bowl, combine the ricotta cheese, Romano or Parmesan cheese, and parsley. Mash them together with a potato masher. Slice the mozzarella cheese very thinly.

Spread about 1 cup of the sauce over the bottom of a 13 inch by 9 inch cake pan. Lay dry lasagne pasta in a single layer over the sauce. Spread the pasta with about 2 to 2½ cups of the sauce. Layer about half of the mozzarella cheese over the sauce. Spread about half of the ricotta mixture over the mozzarella. Add another layer of pasta to the dish, followed by another 2 to 2½ cups of sauce, the rest of the mozzarella, and the rest of the ricotta mixture. Add a third layer of pasta to the dish and top it with about 2 cups of sauce. Save any remaining sauce to serve on the side with the lasagne. If you wish to, you may refrigerate or freeze the lasagne at this point. Cover the dish with plastic wrap to refrigerate or freeze it, or cover it with aluminum foil if you are going to bake it immediately. Put the lasagne into your oven and turn it on to 350°F. Bake the lasagne for about 1½ hours or until it is hot throughout and bubbly at the edges. If you refrigerated the lasagne before baking it, allow at least an extra ½ hour of baking time. If you froze it, be sure it is thoroughly thawed before baking it, or it will take even longer to cook. Reheat the leftover lasagne sauce right before dinner time to serve with the lasagne. Serves 8 to 12 hungry college students or up to 20 of their parents.

**Wheat-free variation:** You can make this recipe with wheat-free lasagne pasta such as spelt or rice pasta. However, these types of pasta are not no-boil. Parboil the lasagne pasta as directed on the package before layering it in the pan with the sauce and cheese. See the "Manicotti" recipe on page 310 for instructions on how to parboil pasta.

**Nutritional Analysis per serving:** *20 servings per recipe*

| | | |
|---|---|---|
| Calories: 311 | Total fat: 9 g | Calcium: 646 mg |
| Protein: 29 g | Saturated fat: 4 g | Magnesium: 54 mg |
| Carbohydrate: 29 g | Omega-3 fatty acids: 0.05 g | Potassium: 718 mg |
| Sugars: 6 g | Omega-6 fatty acids: 0.32 g | Sodium: 695 mg |
| Fiber (total): 3 g | Cholesterol: 35 mg | Iron: 3 mg |
| Vitamin C: 19 mg | Vitamin A: 143 RE | Zinc: 3 mg |

Diabetic exchanges: 1 serving equals 1 starch exchange, 3¼ lean meat exchanges, 2 vegetable exchanges

# Manicotti

½ pound of manicotti pasta (1 box, or 14 to 16 manicotti)
Water
½ teaspoon salt
2 pounds ricotta cheese, preferably part skim or low fat
¾ cup grated Romano or Parmesan cheese
2 eggs
1 tablespoon fresh chopped or dried parsley
¼ teaspoon salt
⅛ teaspoon pepper
About ¾ batch of fresh tomato sauce, page 306, or ½ batch of pasta sauce with
    meatballs, page 304
Additional grated cheese

Bring at least 6 quarts of water to a rolling boil. Add the ½ teaspoon salt. Add the manicotti to the water, return it to a boil, lower the heat to medium, set the lid slightly ajar, and boil the manicotti for 6 minutes. Time this carefully and do not overcook them. They will not be *al dente* but only parboiled (partially cooked) after 6 minutes.

While they are boiling, put the ricotta, ½ cup of the grated cheese, eggs, parsley, ¼ teaspoon salt, and pepper in a bowl and mash them together with a potato masher.

When the 6 minutes of cooking time for the manicotti is up, pour off about half of the water. Put the pan in the sink and gently add cold water. Pour off about half of the water and add more cold water again until the water is fairly cool and the manicotti are easy to handle.

Put about 1 cup of sauce into the bottom of a 13 inch by 9 inch baking dish. (Use a glass baking dish if possible). Remove the manicotti from the water one at a time and, using a spoon, stuff them with the cheese mixture. Arrange the stuffed manicotti in a single layer in the baking dish. Top them with approximately another 1 cup of sauce. Cover the dish tightly with aluminum foil. You may refrigerate or freeze the manicotti at this point if you wish. Bake at 350°F for 30 minutes if freshly made or 45 minutes if refrigerated or frozen and thawed. Uncover the dish and sprinkle the manicotti with the remaining ¼ cup of grated cheese. Cover the dish with the foil again and bake the manicotti for 10 minutes more or until they are very hot throughout and bubbly. Warm the remaining sauce in a saucepan. Serve the manicotti with the remaining sauce and additional cheese. Makes about 5 to 10 servings. This dish freezes well. If you are cooking for two or three people, divide the manicotti into two 8 or 9 inch square baking dishes and freeze one of them for a future meal.

## Nutritional Analysis per serving: 10 servings per recipe

| | | |
|---|---|---|
| Calories: 302 | Total fat: 14 g | Calcium: 343 mg |
| Protein: 18 g | Saturated fat: 7 g | Magnesium: 43 mg |
| Carbohydrate: 28 g | Omega-3 fatty acids: 0.12 g | Potassium: 476 mg |
| Sugars: 6 g | Omega-6 fatty acids: 0.70 g | Sodium: 532 mg |
| Fiber (total): 2 g | Cholesterol: 73 mg | Iron: 2 mg |
| Vitamin C: 26 mg | Vitamin A: 212 RE | Zinc: 2 mg |

Diabetic exchanges: 1 serving equals 1 starch exchange, 2 lean meat exchanges, 1 vegetable exchange, 2 fat exchanges

# Make Ahead Tossed Salad

*This is an easy salad that you can make ahead of time when you have a large crowd of guests. For a small party, cut the recipe in half.*

½ cup oil, preferably walnut, canola, or another oil high in essential fatty acids
1 clove of garlic, crushed (optional)
2 teaspoons finely chopped fresh oregano, sweet basil or parsley or ½ teaspoon dried oregano, sweet basil or parsley (optional)
½ teaspoon salt
Dash of pepper
⅓ cup vinegar or lemon juice
½ to 1 cup sliced carrots, cucumbers, and/or radishes
2 to 3 medium tomatoes, each cut into eight pieces
12 cups of leaf lettuce or other greens, any variety or combination, torn into bite-sized pieces
Optional additions to make the salad more substantial:
    1 cup croutons or ¾ cup crumbled crackers
    ⅓ cup chopped nuts
    ⅓ cup crumbled or grated cheese
    ¾ cup cooked beans, such as garbanzo beans, drained

If you wish to use the garlic, crush it and put it and the oil in a glass jar. Refrigerate at least overnight. Remove the garlic from the oil and discard the garlic. Combine the oil with the rest of the seasonings and vinegar or lemon juice in a large salad bowl or 4-quart mixing bowl. Stir the dressing thoroughly. Add the carrots, cucumbers, radishes, and tomatoes to the dressing in the bowl. (They will prevent the lettuce from being immersed in the dressing before serving time). Put the lettuce and other greens on top of the cut vegetables. Cover the bowl with plastic wrap and refrigerate it until serving time. At serving time, toss the salad. Sprinkle the top of the salad with the croutons or crackers, nuts, cheese, and/or beans. Makes 8 to 10 servings. For a small party, cut the recipe in half.

## Nutritional Analysis per serving: 10 servings per recipe

| | | |
|---|---|---|
| Calories: ...........................119 | Total fat:................................11 g | Calcium: .............................49 mg |
| Protein: ...............................1 g | Saturated fat: .................1 g | Magnesium: ......................13 mg |
| Carbohydrate: ..................5 g | Omega-3 fatty acids: ....1.21 g | Potassium:....................274 mg |
| Sugars:.............................3 g | Omega-6 fatty acids:...5.84 g | Sodium: .........................128 mg |
| Fiber (total):.....................2 g | Cholesterol: ....................0 mg | Iron:.......................................1 mg |
| Vitamin C: ........................18 mg | Vitamin A:.....................317 RE | Zinc:......................................0 mg |

Diabetic exchanges: 1 serving equals 1 vegetable exchange, 2 fat exchanges

# Caesar Salad

*Although this salad is impressive, it isn't hard to make. If you can get pasteurized eggs and want to make Caesar salad in the original way, double the amounts of all the ingredients and used a pasteurized egg instead of the egg substitute. Never use a raw unpasteurized egg in this salad because of the risk of <u>Salmonella</u>.*

2 tablespoons (for weight watchers) to 4 tablespoons (for purists) olive oil
1½ tablespoons wine vinegar
2 tablespoons lemon juice, freshly squeezed if possible
½ teaspoon salt
⅛ teaspoon dry mustard
Dash of black pepper
2 tablespoons egg substitute, such as EggBeaters™ or ½ of a raw pasteurized egg
5 to 6 cups of bite-sized pieces of romaine lettuce, or about 7 ounces (or use 10
    ounces of lettuce to serve three rather than two)
1 tablespoon grated Romano cheese
2 to 3 anchovy fillets, chopped into small pieces (optional)
⅓ cup croutons

In a measuring cup or small jar, combine the oil, vinegar, lemon juice, salt, mustard, pepper, and egg substitute. Stir or shake the dressing ingredients together thoroughly. (If you're making this salad for just one person, make the dressing in a jar, use half or a third of it, and refrigerate the rest of the dressing in the jar). Put the romaine lettuce in a bowl. Sprinkle the Romano cheese over the lettuce and add the anchovies. Pour the dressing over the salad and toss the salad thoroughly. Top it with the croutons. Makes two servings, just enough for a romantic dinner for you and that special girl or guy. If you're watching your weight, you can use about 10 ounces of romaine lettuce and stretch the amount of dressing and toppings to make three servings.

**Nutritional Analysis per serving:** 3 servings per recipe

| | | |
|---|---|---|
| Calories: ...........................133 | Total fat:...............................11 g | Calcium: ...........................67 mg |
| Protein: .................................4 g | Saturated fat: ................2 g | Magnesium: ....................10 mg |
| Carbohydrate:....................6 g | Omega-3 fatty acids:...0.16 g | Potassium: ....................331 mg |
| Sugars: .............................1 g | Omega-6 fatty acids: ..0.98 g | Sodium: ..........................497 mg |
| Fiber (total):......................2 g | Cholesterol: .......................3 mg | Iron:........................................1 mg |
| Vitamin C:........................27 mg | Vitamin A: .....................272 RE | Zinc:........................................0 mg |

Diabetic exchanges: 1 serving equals ¼ starch exchange, ¼ lean meat exchange, ½ vegetable exchange, 2 fat exchanges

# *Yogurt Pie*

*This is a dessert you can whip up for guests in no time at all. However, it does contain sugar, some strange ingredients in the Cool Whip™, and probably partially hydrogenated fats if you use a store-bought graham cracker crust. I am including this less-healthy recipe in this book because I recently made it for guests when I mis-measured and my "healthy" dessert flopped!*

1 baked "Oil Pasty" pie shell (page 274) or graham cracker pie crust
2 8 ounce containers low fat fruit yogurt, any flavor
1 thawed 8 ounce container of Cool Whip™ or other whipped topping, preferably
    a "light" variety

Empty the yogurt into a large bowl and stir it until it is smooth. Add the Cool Whip™ to the bowl. Gently fold the Cool Whip™ into the yogurt, taking care not to stir the air out of the Cool Whip™. Put the mixture into the pie shell and refrigerate the pie until it is thoroughly chilled and set. Makes 6 to 8 servings.

## Made with oil pastry:
**Nutritional Analysis per serving:** 8 servings per recipe

| | | |
|---|---|---|
| Calories: 210 | Total fat: 9 g | Calcium: 45 mg |
| Protein: 3 g | Saturated fat: 4 g | Magnesium: 8 mg |
| Carbohydrate: 26 g | Omega-3 fatty acids: 0.48 g | Potassium: 91 mg |
| Sugars: 10 g | Omega-6 fatty acids: 1.11 g | Sodium: 90 mg |
| Fiber (total): 0 g | Cholesterol: 1 mg | Iron: 1 mg |
| Vitamin C: 0 mg | Vitamin A: 4 RE | Zinc: 0 mg |

Diabetic exchanges: 1 serving equals ¾ starch exchange, ¾ other carbohydrate exchange, 1¾ fat exchanges

## Made with a commercial graham cracker crust:
**Nutritional Analysis per serving:** 8 servings per recipe

| | | |
|---|---|---|
| Calories: 279 | Total fat: 12 g | Calcium: 91 mg |
| Protein: 4 g | Saturated fat: 6 g | Magnesium: 14 mg |
| Carbohydrate: 38 g | Omega-3 fatty acids: 0.10 g | Potassium: 152 mg |
| Sugars: 29 g | Omega-6 fatty acids: 1.99 g | Sodium: 203 mg |
| Fiber (total): 0 g | Cholesterol: 3 mg | Iron: 1 mg |
| Vitamin C: 0 mg | Vitamin A: 67 RE | Zinc: 1 mg |

Diabetic exchanges: 1 serving equals 2⅓ other carbohydrate exchanges, 2 fat exchanges

# *Wickedly Rich Cheesecake*

## Crust ingredients:

1 cup graham cracker crumbs, preferably made from natural fruit-sweetened graham crackers such as Hain™ brand

2 tablespoons date sugar (optional)

¼ cup (½ stick) butter, melted

## Filling ingredients:

2  8 ounce packages fat-free, low fat, or regular cream cheese

⅔ cup Fruit Sweet™ or honey

4 eggs

2 tablespoons lemon juice

¼ teaspoon salt

¼ teaspoon vanilla extract

## Topping:

2 cups fresh blueberries, raspberries, or sliced strawberries

Take the cream cheese out of the refrigerator an hour or two before you want to make this cheesecake and let it come to room temperature. Preheat your oven to 300°F.

Make crumbs out of the graham crackers by putting them in a plastic bag and rolling them with a rolling pin or drinking glass. In a 9 inch or 10 inch pie plate, stir together the graham cracker crumbs, date sugar, and melted butter. Press the crumbs firmly into the bottom and up the sides of the pie dish. If you have another pie plate of the same size, put it into the first pie plate and press it down to make a nice, firm crust. Bake the crust for 15 minutes or until it is nicely browned. Cool the crust completely before filling it. If you must, you can substitute a commercial graham cracker crust for this crust. However, it will probably contain sugar and partially hydrogenated fats.

Preheat your oven to 450°F. In a bowl, combine the cream cheese, sweetener, eggs, lemon juice, salt, and vanilla. Blend them with your hand blender until they are thoroughly mixed. Pour the filling into the crust. Bake the cheesecake for 10 minutes. Then turn the oven temperature down to 300°F. Bake the cheesecake for another 40 to 50 minutes or until it is set in the center. (This means that the filling doesn't jiggle in the center of the cheesecake when you move the pan). Allow the cheesecake to cool on a cooling rack for about a half hour. Then refrigerate it. At serving time, top it with fresh fruit. Makes 8 to 12 servings.

**Made with fat-free cream cheese:**
**Nutritional Analysis per serving:** 12 servings per recipe

| | | |
|---|---|---|
| Calories: .........................176 | Total fat: ...........................7 g | Calcium: ..........................109 mg |
| Protein:................................8 g | Saturated fat: ...............3 g | Magnesium:......................11 mg |
| Carbohydrate: ................20 g | Omega-3 fatty acids:...0.11 g | Potassium: .....................119 mg |
| Sugars:...............................11 g | Omega-6 fatty acids: ..0.68 g | Sodium:..........................376 mg |
| Fiber (total):......................1 g | Cholesterol: ...................76 mg | Iron:........................................1 mg |
| Vitamin C: ..........................4 mg | Vitamin A:...........................5 RE | Zinc: .....................................1 mg |

Diabetic exchanges: 1 serving equals 1 starch/other carbohydrate exchange, 1 lean meat exchange, ¼ fruit exchange, ⅔ fat exchange

**Made with low fat cream cheese:**
**Nutritional Analysis per serving:** 12 servings per recipe

| | | |
|---|---|---|
| Calories: .........................227 | Total fat: ...........................13 g | Calcium: ............................81 mg |
| Protein: ..............................7 g | Saturated fat:................7 g | Magnesium:........................9 mg |
| Carbohydrate:................21 g | Omega-3 fatty acids:...0.20 g | Potassium:......................121 mg |
| Sugars: ...............................13 g | Omega-6 fatty acids: ..0.81 g | Sodium:..........................282 mg |
| Fiber (total):......................1 g | Cholesterol: ...................94 mg | Iron:........................................2 mg |
| Vitamin C: ..........................4 mg | Vitamin A: .....................146 RE | Zinc: .....................................1 mg |

Diabetic exchanges: 1 serving equals 1 starch/other carbohydrate exchange, 1 lean meat exchange, ¼ fruit exchange, 1¾ fat exchanges

# Other recipes in this book that are well suited for entertaining:

Crock Pot Roast Beef Dinner, page 216
Corned Beef and Cabbage, page 217
Crock Pot Stew, page 220
Soups, pages 148 to 154 and 221 to 225
Crock Pot Baked Beans, page 226, served with hamburgers, hot dogs, or steak
Pizza, page 178
Homemade bread, rolls, or biscuits, pages 244 to 263

# For Further Reading

Crook, William G. M.D., *Detecting Your Hidden Allergies.* Professional Books, Inc., Box 3246, Jackson, TN 38303, 1988.

Crook, William G. M.D., *Tired – So Tired!* Professional Books, Inc., Box 3246, Jackson, TN 38303, 2001. (Note the "Vitamin/Mineral Supplements'" chapter).

Crook, William G. M.D. and Marjorie Hurt Jones, R.N., *The Yeast Connection Cookbook.* Professional Books, Inc., Box 3246, Jackson, TN 38303, 1995.

Dumke, Nicolette M. *Allergy Cooking with Ease,* Revised Edition. Adapt Books, Allergy Adapt, Inc., 1877 Polk Avenue, Louisville, CO 80027, 2007.

Dumke, Nicolette M. *Easy Breadmaking for Special Diets.* Adapt Books, Allergy Adapt, Inc., 1877 Polk Avenue, Louisville, CO 80027, 1995; Revised edition, 2007.

Dumke, Nicolette M. *The Ultimate Food Allergy Cookbook and Survival Guide: How to Cook with Ease for a Food Allergy Diet and Recover Good Health.* Adapt Books, Allergy Adapt, Inc., 1877 Polk Avenue, Louisville, CO 80027, 2007.

Fredericks, Carlton, Ph.D. and Herman Goodman, M.D., *Low Blood Sugar and You,* Grosset & Dunlap, New York, 1969.

Fredericks, Carlton, Ph.D., *The New Low Blood Sugar and You.* Perigee Books, The Berkely Publishing Group, 375 Hudson Street, New York, NY 10014, 1985.

Galland, Leo, M.D., *The Four Pillars of Healing.* Random House, New York, NY, 1997.

Hausman, Patricia, M.S. *The Right Dose: How to Take Vitamins and Minerals Safely.* Ballantine Books, New York, NY, 1987.

Holford, Patrick. *The Optimum Nutrition Bible.* Judy Piakus Publishers Ltd., London, 1997.

Jones, Marjorie Hurt, R.N., *The Allergy Self-Help Cookbook.* Rodale Press, Emmaus, PA, 1984, revised 2001.

Lewis, Sondra with Lonette Dietrich Blakely, *Allergy and Candida Cooking Made Easy.* Canary Connect Publications, P.O. Box 5317, Coralville, IA 52241, 1996.

Rombauer, Irma S. and Marion Rombauer Becker, *The Joy of Cooking.* The Bobbs-Merrill Company, Inc., Indianapolis, IN, 1931.

# Table of Measurements
## (Appendix A)

Measuring is extremely important to your success in cooking. There will be times when you want to make a half batch of a recipe or when you are having guests and want to double or triple a recipe. This table will help you with converting the measurements when you want to double or halve a recipe as well as helping you with "unusual" measurements such as ⅜ cup, ⅞ cup, or ⅛ teaspoon. Because measuring is so important, how to measure is also reviewed at the end of this table for easy reference.

⅛ teaspoon* = ½ of your ¼ teaspoon measure
⅜ teaspoon = ¼ teaspoon + ⅛ teaspoon
⅝ teaspoon = ½ teaspoon + ⅛ teaspoon
¾ teaspoon = ½ teaspoon + ¼ teaspoon
⅞ teaspoon = ½ teaspoon + ¼ teaspoon + ⅛ teaspoon
1 teaspoon = ⅓ tablespoon = ⅙ fluid ounce
1½ teaspoons = ½ tablespoon = ¼ fluid ounce
3 teaspoons = 1 tablespoon = ½ fluid ounce
½ tablespoon = 1½ teaspoons = ¼ fluid ounce
1 tablespoon = 3 teaspoons = ½ fluid ounce
2 tablespoons** = ⅛ cup = 1 fluid ounce
4 tablespoons = ¼ cup = 2 fluid ounces
5⅓ tablespoons = ⅓ cup = 2⅔ fluid ounces
8 tablespoons = ½ cup = 4 fluid ounces
16 tablespoons = 1 cup = 8 fluid ounces
⅛ cup = 2 tablespoons** = 1 fluid ounce
¼ cup = 4 tablespoons = 2 fluid ounces
⅜ cup = ¼ cup + 2 tablespoons** = 3 fluid ounces
⅝ cup = ½ cup + 2 tablespoons** = 5 fluid ounces
¾ cup = ½ cup + ¼ cup= 6 fluid ounces
⅞ cup = ¾ cup + 2 tablespoons** = 7 fluid ounces
   or ½ cup + ¼ cup + 2 tablespoons**
1 cup = ½ pint = 8 fluid ounces
1 pint = 2 cups = 16 fluid ounces
1 quart = 4 cups or 2 pints = 32 fluid ounces
1 gallon = 4 quarts = 128 fluid ounces

* To measure ⅛ teaspoon of a dry ingredient, you can measure ¼ teaspoon and then use a table knife to divide the amount down the middle of the spoon and push half of it out. However, the most accurate way to measure ⅛ teaspoon is to purchase a set of measuring spoons with a ⅛ teaspoon measure. Such sets may be found at cooking or department stores, or see the "Sources" section, page 323, to order such a set from the King Arthur Flour Baker's Catalogue.

**In my experience, measuring tablespoons are all a little scanty of ¹⁄₁₆ cup (The ones from King Arthur come the closest to the correct volume), so 2 tablespoons is a little short of ⅛ cup. Therefore, if you need to measure, for example, ⅜ cup of liquid, it will probably be more accurate to "eyeball" an amount halfway between ¼ cup and ½ cup than to use ¼ cup plus two tablespoons. The best way to measure ⅜ cup is to fill your measuring cup to the third ⅛-cup line if it is marked in ⅛-cup intervals or to the 3 ounce line if it is marked in ounces.

## *How to measure:*

Measure liquids in a glass or see-through plastic measuring cup designed for measuring liquids. On such cups, the top measurement line will be a little below the top of the cup. These cups usually have a spout for pouring liquids. Buy a cup that has ⅛-cup markings; two-cup capacity is most useful. To read the amount of liquid in a measuring cup, have your eyes down at the level of the cup. Fill the cup until the bottom of the meniscus (the curve that the surface of the liquid makes in the cup) lines up with the measurement you want to use. If you want fewer dirty dishes to wash, you can measure several liquid ingredients in the measuring cup at one time and then mix them together in the cup. For example, if your recipe calls for ½ cup water and ¼ cup oil, fill the cup with water to the ½ cup line. Then add oil until the level of the liquids reaches ¾ cup.

To measure dry ingredients such as flour, use a set of nested plastic or metal measuring cups. On these cups, the maximum capacity measurement is at the very top edge of the cup. Use the cup of the capacity that your recipe calls for. You may have to use more than one cup if, for example, your recipe calls for ¾ cup of flour. In this case, measure ½ cup of flour and add it to your mixing bowl, and then measure ¼ cup of flour and add it to the bowl. You do not need to sift flour before you measure it for the recipes in this book. Instead, get a large spoon, stir the flour to fluff it up, lightly spoon it into a measuring cup for dry ingredients, and then level it off with a straight-edged knife. Do not tap the cup or pack the flour into it.

Measuring spoons are used for both liquid and dry ingredients. It is helpful to have a set which includes an ⅛ teaspoon. To measure liquids, fill the spoon with the liquid, making sure that it does not round up over the top of the spoon. To measure dry ingredients, stir up the ingredient with the spoon to fluff it up, dip the spoon in, and level it off with a straight-edged knife. When measuring spices from their canisters, you can level off the spoon against the straight edge of the opening in the top of the canister.

# Sources
(Appendix B)

**BAKING POWDER, sodium- and corn-free:**

Distributor:
Featherweight™ Baking Powder
Hain Celestial Group
16007 Camino de la Cantera
Irwindale, CA 91706-7811
(800) 434-4246

Mail-Order source for Featherweight™ Baking Powder:
TED Enterprises
(800) 438-6153

**BEANS canned without sugar, corn syrup, or chemicals:**

Westbrae Natural Organic Cooked Beans (black beans, kidney beans, great northern beans, red beans, pinto beans, garbanzo beans, soybeans, lentils, split peas):

Westbrae Natural Foods
264 S. La Cienaga Boulevard Drive, Suite 508
Beverly Hills, CA 90211
(562) 948-2872
http://www.novelco.com/westbrae/

**DACOPA coffee substitute:**

California Natural Products
P.O. Box 1219
Lathrop, CA 95330
(209) 858-2525

Abundant Health
7737 Harlan Street
Arvada, CO 80003
(303) 422-3175

## DAIRY PRODUCTS:

Eggs, pasteurized:

Davidson's Pasteurized Eggs
Pasteurized Eggs Corporation
  1921 Paradise Road
  Laconia, NH 03246-1517
  (800) 410-7619
  www.davidsonseggs.com

Ghee (clarified butter):

Purity Farms, Inc.
  14635 Westcreek Road
  Sedalia, CO 80135
  (800) LOV-GHEE or (800) 568-4433
  http://www.purityfarms.org

Goat butter:

Mt. Sterling Cheese Corporation
Southwestern Wisconsin Dairy Goat Products Co-op
  310 Diagonal Street
  Mt. Sterling, WI 54645
  (608) 734-3151

Goat milk, powdered, canned or fresh:

Meyenberg Goat Milk
Jackson-Mitchell
  P.O. Box 5425
  Santa Barbara, CA 93150
  (800) 343-1185
  http://www.meyenberg.com

Goat yogurt:

> Redwood Hill Farm
>   5480 Thomas Road
>   Sebastopol, CA 95472
>   (707) 823-8250
>   http://www.redwoodhill.com

Margarine, trans fat and milk-free:

> Earth Balance™ 100% Vegan Natural Buttery Spread —
> no hydrogenated oils, but contains soy and grain derivatives.
> Ingredients: Expeller-pressed natural oil blend (soy, palm, canola,
> and olive), filtered water, pure salt, natural flavor (derived from
> grains), soy protein, soy lecithin, lactic acid (non-dairy, derived
> from sugar beets), vitamin A palmitate and beta carotene color.

> Earth Balance
> GFA Brands Inc.
>   P.O. Box 397
>   Cresskill, NJ 07626-0397
>   (201) 568-9300

Sheep yogurt and cheese:

> Old Chatham Sheepherding Company
>   P.O. Box 94
>   Old Chatham, NY 12136
>   (888) SHEEP60 or (518) 794-7333
>   http://www.blacksheepcheese.com

## FLOUR, SPELT:

Purity Foods™ white spelt and whole spelt flour:

> Purity Foods, Inc.
>   2871 W. Jolly Road
>   Okemos, MI 48864
>   (517) 351-9231
>   http://www.purityfoods.com

## KITCHEN EQUIPMENT, WHITE WHOLE WHEAT FLOUR:

General baking supplies, perforated plastic bags, measuring spoon sets with an ⅛ teaspoon, flour, etc.:

King Arthur Flour Baker's Catalogue
    P.O. Box 876
    Norwich, VT 05055-0876
    (800) 827-6836
    http://www.kingarthurflour.com

## MICROWAVE BACON COOKER:

Bacon Wave™ Microwave Bacon Cooker

Miles Kimball
    41 West Eighth Avenue
    Oshkosh, WI 54902
    (702) 617-3500
        Order Item #H434993; the price is about $10 or less.

## PASTA:

High quality wheat pasta of most kinds, except they no longer make manicotti:

R & F (Ravarino and Freschi) Pasta
    American Italian Pasta Company
    4100 North Mulberry Drive, Suite 200
    Kansas City, MO 64114
    (877) EAT PASTA or (877) 328-7278

Manicotti:

Da Vinci Pasta
Distributed by World Finer Foods, Inc.
    300 Broadacres Drive
    Bloomfield, NJ 07003
    (973) 338-0300
    http://www.worldfiner.com

Purity Foods' spelt pasta:

Purity Foods, Inc.
2871 W. Jolly Road
Okemos, MI 48864
(517) 351-9231
http://www.purityfoods.com

Rice pasta:

Ener-G Foods, Inc.
P.O. Box 84487
Seattle, WA 98124
(800) 331-5222; in Washington, (800) 325-9788

## QUICK THICK™:

Mountain Magic
P.O. Box 745248
Arvada, CO 80006
http://www.mtn-magic.com

## SALT:

Iodized sea salt, aluminum and dextrose-free:

Baliene™ Iodized Sea Salt
Gypsy Kitchen
1241 Hancock Street
Quincy, MA 02169
http://www.drhot.net

## SPREADS:

All-fruit jams and jellies:

R. W. Knudsen Company
P.O. Box 369
Speedway Avenue
Chico, CA 95927
(530) 899-5000
http://www.knudsenjuices.com

Butter and margarine: See "Dairy Products," above

Mayonnaise:

Spectrum Naturals™ Eggless Lite Canola Mayonnaise
Ingredients: Water, pure pressed canola oil, modified food starch
(corn), grain vinegar, cultured skim milk, whey protein concentrate,
sea salt, cider vinegar, natural spices, citric acid, onion, oil of
mustard, tumeric, and paprika.

Spectrum Organic Products, Inc.
1304 South Point Boulevard, Suite 280
Petaluma, CA 94954
(707) 778-8900
http://www.spectrumnaturals.com

## SUPPLEMENTS, NUTRIBIOTIC™ etc.:

Abundant Health
7737 Harlan Street
Arvada, CO 80003
(303) 422-3175

N.E.E.D.S
6666 Manlius Center Road
East Syracuse, NY 13057
1-800-634-1380
www.needs.com

**SWEETENERS:**

Date sugar:

NOW Natural Foods
550 W. Mitchell
Glendale Heights, IL 60139
(800) 283-3500
Have your health food store order date sugar from them for you.

Fruit Source™:

Fruit Source
1803 Mission Street, Suite 404
Santa Cruz, CA 95060
(408) 457-1136

Fruit Sweet™, Pear Sweet™, Grape Sweet™, and other all-fruit products such as syrups, jams, chutneys, and fudge toppings:

Wax Orchards
22744 Wax Orchards Road SW
Vashon, WA 98070
(800) 634-6231
www.waxorchards.com

**WATER-PACKED CANNED FRUITS AND VEGETABLES:**

S & W Fine Foods, Inc.
3160 Crow Canyon Road
San Ramon, CA 94538
(510) 866-4500

# YEAST:

SAF Yeast:

Mountain Magic
P.O. Box 745248
Arvada, CO 80006
http://www.mtn-magic.com

King Arthur Flour Baker's Catalogue
P.O. Box 876
Norwich, VT 05055-0876
(800) 827-6836
http://www.kingarthurflour.com

# Finding Help With Assessing Your Nutritional Needs

(Appendix C)

You are a unique individual possessing a unique biochemical makeup and nutritional needs. In addition, because you are an adult, you are not starting with a clean nutritional slate. Even if your mom was nutritionally aware when you were a child, chances are she learned things along the way and probably regrets some of the things she then let you eat! (If you are an older person, you may regret some of your own past food choices!) Now that you're busy, independent, and possibly a dorm-dwelling student, you probably have eaten a fair amount of refined sugar, hydrogenated fat, and processed foods — all stripped of many nutrients.

Because you are an individual, the diet best for your health is an individual matter. Many people feel better if they do not follow some of the USDA's dietary advice, such as the "food pyramid" recommendation that everyone eat eleven servings of complex carbohydrate foods each day. Although many conservative conventional doctors assert that hypoglycemia is a very rare condition caused by pancreatic tumors, in reality, reactive hypoglycemia leaves many people obese and feeling miserable. This condition easily can be controlled with a diet free of refined sugar and higher in protein and lower in carbohydrates than the USDA's recommended diet. See pages 43 to 45 of this book for more information about low blood sugar and the proper diet. *The New Low Blood Sugar and You* is an excellent resource about hypoglycemia.

Conservative conventional medicine also asserts that very few adults have food allergies. They define "allergy" as an immediate reaction mediated by IgE antibodies. They deny that the problem is allergy if any other type of antibodies or immune mechanism is involved. However, it is all a matter of semantics. In reality, many adults have "food intolerances" which are often delayed reactions and may be mediated by IgG antibodies, immune complexes, or cell-mediated immunity. If you suspect that you have food allergies or intolerances, refer to *The Ultimate Food Allergy Cookbook and Survival Guide* (described on the last page of this book) for more information about the diagnosis and treatment of food allergies and how you can help yourself with diet. In some cases, if you avoid your problem foods for six months to a year, you may be able to reintroduce them into your diet in moderation – possibly "rotating" you foods and eating them every few days – without a return of your symptoms. If you are searching for a doctor who "believes in" food allergies, contact the American Academy of Environmental Medicine for a referral. Their phone number is (215) 862-4544. A listing of doctors who are members of the American Academy of Environmental Medicine can be found on the Internet at http://www.aaem.com

If we all ate only minimally processed, nutrient-dense foods raised on soil that has not been depleted of essential minerals, most of us would probably not need nutritional supplements.[1] However, very few people have optimal nutrition and optimal health, so we can benefit from supplements. The "trick" is to determine which supplements you personally need. If you take supplements out of a proper balance with your needs and with each other, especially in high doses, you can worsen rather than help any nutritional deficits you have. You may wish to consult a medical nutritionist. To get a referral, send $3 to the International Academy of Preventive Medicine, 34 Corporate Woods, Suite 469, 10950 Grandview, Overland Park, KS 66210. Be sure the nutritionist you consult does testing in addition to taking a detailed history before prescribing a diet or supplements for you. Any nutritional counsel should be customized for you. Avoid "one size fits all, everybody needs more of this nutrient" types of advice. Be cautious about taking single-nutrient supplements in very high doses because each supplement should be balanced with the correct complementary nutrients and "fit" your individual needs and biochemical profile.

Many young adults are "strapped" financially. You are also well educated, intelligent, and able to manage your own body and affairs. If you need help with diagnosing food allergies or determining which supplements to take and do not have the resources to consult an environmental allergist or nutritionist, or even if you have consulted the professionals, you may wish to pursue some resources for self-help. York Nutritional Laboratories offers a self-administered blood test for food allergies. The price of the test includes dietary advice from the M.D.'s on their staff. You can contact them at (888) 751-3388 or http://www.yorkallergyusa.com. Analytical Research Laboratories offers self-administered hair tests for nutritional imbalances and deficiencies, especially mineral imbalances. Your test results will include a list of supplements and dietary advice that may be of benefit to you. Although I am not sure about some of their reasoning on the significance of particular ratios of minerals, I have seen many people with serious and long-standing health problems helped by following an individualized supplement protocol recommended by Analytical Research Laboratories. Contact them at (602) 995-1580.

A final word of advice is to listen to your own body. Follow the diet that makes you feel best. Take supplements that make you feel better. Seek testing or professional advice, read everything you can, and then make your own decisions. A much-needed change in the world of health in recent years is that people think for themselves rather than just following the doctor's advice blindly. You are an self-sufficient adult. Gather information, listen to your body, and then make your own well-educated decisions.

Footnotes

1. Crook, William G. M.D., *Tired – So Tired!* Professional Books, Inc., Box 3246, Jackson, TN 38303, 2001, pp. 86-91.

# Special Recipe Finder

## Recipes for diabetic diets:

Any recipe in this book may be eaten on a diabetic diet by using the exchanges given at the end of the nutritional analysis for the recipe to fit an appropriately-sized serving into your allotted exchanges for a meal or snack. Diabetics may wish to avoid large portions of desserts even though the desserts in this book are fruit-sweetened.

## Recipes for heart healthy low-fat diets:

Almost all of the recipes in this book are made with vegetable oils rather than saturated fats and so are good for a heart healthy diet. An exception is "Butter Pastry" on page 275. Instead of making your pastry with butter, use the "Oil Pastry" recipe on page 274. You may also use the nutritional analysis at the end of each recipe to choose the recipes which are lowest in fat. If you have been advised to limit your cholesterol intake, you may use an egg substitute such as EggBeaters™ in place of the eggs in any recipe.

## Recipes for weight loss and/or blood sugar control diets:

If you are following a conventional calorie-counting diet to lose weight, you may use the nutritional analysis at the end of each recipe to count calories. If you are following a blood sugar control diet, which will "reprogram" your hunger and is more likely to result in permanent weight loss, choose foods that are high in protein and slow-releasing complex carbohydrates. You may wish to avoid eating large portions of the desserts in this book even though they are fruit-sweetened.

## Recipes for food allergy diets:

The recipes in this book which can be used on food allergy diets are listed below. To find recipes that you can use on your diet, look at the recipe list(s) for the categories that "fit" your allergies. For example, if you are allergic to wheat and eggs, use recipes from the "Wheat- and Egg-free" list as well as the "Wheat-, Milk-, and Egg-free" list. If you are allergic to milk only, use recipes from the "Milk-free" list, the "Wheat- and Milk-free" list, the "Milk- and Egg-free" list, and the "Wheat-, Milk-, and Egg-free" list.

Some of the recipes have comments in italics after the recipe name. These comments indicate which optional ingredients should be used to make the recipe free of a certain food. If there are no comments after the recipe name, the recipe will be free of the allergen(s) without using any optional ingredients or omitting any ingredients.

Some people have food allergies that are very complex and they may find the recipes on this list are not quite restricted enough to meet their needs. If this is your situation, please refer to *The Ultimate Food Allergy Cookbook and Survival Guide* as described on the last page of this book.

# Wheat-, Milk-, and Egg-free Recipes:

# General Index

Recipes appear in italics. Informational material appears in standard type.

# Books to Help You With Your Special Diet

*Easy Cooking for Special Diets: How to Cook for Weight Loss/Blood Sugar Control, Food Allergy, Heart Healthy, Diabetic and "Just Healthy" Diets – Even if You've Never Cooked Before.* This book contains everything you need to know to stay on your diet plus 265 recipes complete with nutritional analyses and diabetic exchanges. It also includes basics such as how to grocery shop, equipping your kitchen, how to handle food safely, time management, information on nutrition, and sources of special foods.

ISBN 1-887624-09-0 or 978-1-887624-09-1 . . . . . . . . . . . . . . $24.95

*Easy Breadmaking for Special Diets* contains over 200 recipes for allergy, heart healthy, low fat, low sodium, yeast-free, controlled carbohydrate, diabetic, celiac, and low calorie diets. It includes recipes for breads of all kinds, bread and tortilla based main dishes, and desserts. Use your bread machine, food processor, mixer, or electric tortilla maker to make the bread YOU need quickly and easily.

Revised Edition: ISBN 1-887624-11-2 or 978-1-887624-11-4  . . $19.95

Original Edition: ISBN 1-887624-02-3 . . . . . . . . . . . . . . . . . . $14.95

*Allergy Cooking With Ease* (Revised Edition). This classic all-purpose allergy cookbook was out of print and now is making a comeback in a revised edition. It includes all the old favorite recipes of the first edition plus many new recipes and new foods. Contains over 300 recipes for baked goods, main dishes, soups, salads, vegetables, ethnic dishes, desserts, and more. Informational sections of the book are also totally updated, including the extensive "Sources" section.

ISBN 1-887624-10-4 or 978-1-887624-10-7 . . . . . . . . . . . . . . $19.95

*The Ultimate Food Allergy Cookbook and Survival Guide: How to Cook with Ease for Food Allergies and Recover Good Health* gives you everything you need to survive and recover from food allergies. It contains medical infor-mation about the diagnosis of food allergies, health problems that can be caused by food allergies, and your options for treatment. The book includes a rotation diet that is free from common food allergens such as wheat, milk, eggs, corn, soy, yeast, beef, legumes, citrus fruits, potatoes, tomatoes, and more. Instructions are given on how to personalize the stan-dard rotation diet to meet your individual needs and fit your food prefer-ences. Contains 500 recipes that can be used with (or without) the diet. Extensive reference sections include a listing of commercially prepared foods for allergy diets and sources for special foods, services, and products.

ISBN 1-887624-08-2 or 978-1-887624-08-4 . . . . . . . . . . . . . . . $24.95

*The Low Dose Immunotherapy Handbook: Recipes and Lifestyle Tips for Patients on LDA and EPD Treatment* gives 80 recipes for patients on low dose immunotherapy treatment for their food allergies. It also includes organizational information to help you get ready for your shots.

ISBN: 1-887624-07-4 or 978-1-887624-07-7 . . . . . . . . . . . . . . . .$9.95

*How to Cope With Food Allergies When You're Short on Time* is a booklet of time saving tips and recipes to help you stick to your allergy diet with the least amount of time and effort.

$4.95 or FREE with the order of two other books on these pages

# You can order these books by mail using the order form on the next page or by going to www.food-allergy.org.

# Online credit card orders can be placed with Amazon.com at www.amazon.com.

# *Order Form*

| ITEM | QUANTITY | PRICE | TOTAL |
|---|---|---|---|
| *Easy Cooking for Special Diets** | | $24.95 | |
| *The Ultimate Food Allergy Cookbook and Survival Guide** | | $24.95 | |
| *Easy Breadmaking for Special Diets** | | $14.95 | |
| *Allergy Cooking with Ease** | | $19.95 | |
| *The Low Dose Immunotherapy Handbook* | | $ 9.95 | |
| *How to Cope With Food Allergies When You're Short on Time* | | $ 4.95 or FREE | |

| | | |
|---|---|---|
| Order any 2 of the first four books above and get *How to Cope with Food Allergies when You're Short on Time* **FREE!** | SUBTOTAL | |
| | SHIPPING (see table below) | |
| | Colorado residents add 4.1% sales tax | |
| | TOTAL | |

Ship to:

_____

NAME:

_____

STREET ADDRESS:

_____

CITY, STATE, ZIP

_____

PHONE NUMBER (in case of questions about order):

Please make check payable to:
Allergy Adapt, Inc. and send it and this order to:
Allergy Adapt, Inc., 1877 Polk Ave., Louisville, CO 80027

## SHIPPING TABLE

**IF YOU ARE ORDERING JUST ONE BOOK, FOR SHIPPING ADD:**

*Easy Cooking for Special Diets**.....................................add $4.00

*The Ultimate Food Allergy Cookbook and Survival Guide**...............add $4.00

*Easy Breadmaking for Special Diets** ...............................add $3.50

*Allergy Cooking With Ease** .......................................add $4.00

*The Low Dose Immunotherapy Handbook* ...........................add $2.00

*How to Cope With Food Allergies When You're Short on Time* ............add $1.50

**TO ORDER MORE THAN ONE BOOK, FOR SHIPPING ADD:**

*Up to 3 starred* books and 2 non-starred books* .......................add $6.00

*4 starred* books and up to 2 non-starred books* ........................add $9.00

Call 303-666-8253 or e-mail foodalle@food-allergy.org if you have questions about shipping calculations or questions on large order discounts.

Printed in the United States
66062LVS00003B/52-72